Case Conceptualization and Effective Interventions

SAGE was founded in 1965 by Sara Miller McCune to support the dissemination of usable knowledge by publishing innovative and high-quality research and teaching content. Today, we publish more than 750 journals, including those of more than 300 learned societies, more than 800 new books per year, and a growing range of library products including archives, data, case studies, reports, conference highlights, and video. SAGE remains majority-owned by our founder, and after Sara's lifetime will become owned by a charitable trust that secures our continued independence.

Los Angeles | London | Washington DC | New Delhi | Singapore | Boston

Case Conceptualization and Effective Interventions

Assessing and Treating Mental, Emotional, and Behavioral Disorders

Lynn Zubernis
West Chester University of Pennsylvania

Matthew Snyder
West Chester University of Pennsylvania

Los Angeles | London | New Delhi
Singapore | Washington DC | Boston

Los Angeles | London | New Delhi
Singapore | Washington DC | Boston

FOR INFORMATION:

SAGE Publications, Inc.
2455 Teller Road
Thousand Oaks, California 91320
E-mail: order@sagepub.com

SAGE Publications Ltd.
1 Oliver's Yard
55 City Road
London EC1Y 1SP
United Kingdom

SAGE Publications India Pvt. Ltd.
B 1/I 1 Mohan Cooperative Industrial Area
Mathura Road, New Delhi 110 044
India

SAGE Publications Asia-Pacific Pte. Ltd.
3 Church Street
#10-04 Samsung Hub
Singapore 049483

Cataloging-in-publication data is available from the Library of Congress.

ISBN 978-1-4833-4008-1

Acquisitions Editor: Kassie Graves
Editorial Assistant: Carrie Montoya
Production Editor: Olivia Weber-Stenis
Copy Editor: Janet Ford
Typesetter: C&M Digitals (P) Ltd.
Proofreader: Alison Syring
Indexer: Diggs Publication Services
Cover Designer: Candice Harman

15 16 17 18 19 10 9 8 7 6 5 4 3 2 1

BRIEF CONTENTS

DETAILED CONTENTS

ACKNOWLEDGMENTS

The authors wish to thank Dr. Rick Parsons and Dr. Naijian Zhang for their support and encouragement, and for allowing us to be part of the Sage Counseling and Professional Identity Series. We are grateful for their insightful comments and recommendations, as well as the input of our reviewers who contributed their expertise in order to help us find the right balance of depth and breadth in this book.

Special thanks to our intrepid graduate assistant, Emma Harrison, who will be a fabulous counselor herself someday soon. And to Kassie Graves from SAGE who shepherded us through the publication process with efficiency and good humor.

Finally, we would like to thank our families (Emily, Jeffrey, and Kevlin, and Carrie and Adam) for allowing us the time and space to tackle an ambitious project—and for understanding our passion for counseling.

SAGE wishes to acknowledge the contributions of the following reviewers: Wanda P. Briggs, Winthrop University; Mary J. Didelot, Purdue University Calumet; Franco Dispenza, Georgia State University; Carolyn F. Hester, Grambling State University; Lisa Hollingsworth, Purdue University Calumet; Jo Anne Jankowski, Pennsylvania State University Eberly; Karen Sue Linstrum, Northwestern Oklahoma State University Alva; Christine Sacco-Bene, Barry University; Anthony T. Strange, Winthrop University; Cory Viehl, Georgia State University; and Joshua C. Watson, Mississippi State University Meridian.

SERIES EDITORS' FOREWORD:
INTRODUCTION TO THE SERIES

Counseling and Professional Identity in the 21st Century

As members of the Counseling Profession, we are committed to the promotion of wellness. Rather than curing disease, our Profession distinguishes itself among other helping professions by retaining a focus on development, prevention, client-environment interaction, and empowerment. The wellness and preventive perspective on assessment and treatment of mental health issues has made mental health counselors fully understand and highly value the need for engagement in remedial services.

As counselors we are required to engage in a process of case conceptualization while providing professional services. The case conceptualization that includes data collection, data organization, and finding meaning, can either target remediation or prevention. This process not only becomes the foundation for the formulation and implementation of our interventions and treatment plans, but also establishes a clear

and valid conceptualization. However, it is quite challenging to connect this conceptualization to a well-established and empirically supported intervention. This challenge is not only addressed, but also made easier to overcome, by the text you hold in your hands—*Case Conceptualization and Effective Interventions*.

Case Conceptualization and Effective Interventions not only provides current research on mental, emotional and behavioral disorders found in the Diagnostic and Statistical Manual of Mental Disorders -5 (DSM-5) but also frames these disorders within a unique model for case conceptualization. The Temporal/Contextual (T/C) Model of case conceptualization created by Zubernis and Snyder is a comprehensive, practical, easy-to-apply framework for interacting with and understanding clients. Their extensive use of case illustrations and guided exercises helps counselors not only comprehend, but apply the model within their own practice. As noted within each chapter of the book, the T/C model of case conceptualization provides the counselor with the insight needed to formulate intervention and treatment plans, which reflects the evidence based on the most recent research valuing the uniqueness of the human condition in its diversity and individual variation. We believe *Case Conceptualization and Effective Interventions* is an essential tool for all counselors seeking informed, ethical and effective decisions in practice.

As is obvious, one text or one learning experience will be neither sufficient for mastery of the process of case conceptualization, nor possible for the successful formation of your Professional Identity and Practice. The formation of both your Professional Identity and Practice will be a lifelong process – a process that we hope to facilitate through the presentation of this text and the creation of our series: *Counseling and Professional Identity in the 21st Century.*

Counseling and Professional Identity in the 21st Century is a new, fresh, and pedagogically sound series of texts targeting counselors in training. This series is NOT simply a compilation of isolated books matching those which are already on the market. Rather, each book with its targeted knowledge and skills will be presented as part of a larger whole. The focus and content of each text serves as a single lens through which a counselor can view his/her clients, engage in his/her practice and articulate his/her own professional identity.

Counseling and Professional Identity in the 21st Century is unique not just in the fact that it 'packaged' a series of traditional texts, but that it provides an *integrated* curriculum targeting the formation of the counselor's professional identity and efficient, ethical practice. Each book within the series is structured to facilitate the ongoing professional formation of the counselor. The materials found within each text are organized in order to move the counselor to higher levels of cognitive, affective and psychomotor functioning, resulting in his/her assimilation of the material into both his/her professional identity and approach to professional practice. As essential to the practice of counseling, each book in the series will emphasize the following:

a. the assimilation of concepts and constructs provided across the texts found within the series, thus fostering the counselor's ongoing development as a competent professional;

b. the blending of contemporary theory with current research and empirical support;

c. a focus on the development of procedural knowledge, with each text employing case illustrations and guided practice exercises to facilitate the counselor's ability to translate the theory and research discussed into professional decision making and application;

d. the emphasis on the need for and means of demonstrating accountability, and;

e. the fostering of the counselor's Professional Identity and with it the assimilation of the ethics and standards of practice guiding the counseling profession.

We are proud to have served as co-editors of this series, feeling sure that each text book, just like *Case Conceptualization and Effective Interventions,* will serve as a significant resource to you and your development as a professional counselor.

Richard Parsons, Ph.D.
Naijian Zhang, Ph.D.

PREFACE

As the profession of counseling continues to grow, counselors provide services in a wide range of settings, from community mental health centers to schools and hospitals. As a mental health counselor, you work with diverse populations of clients and help them deal with a wide variety of challenges. In order to do so effectively, an understanding of the process of case conceptualization is critical; to help your clients, you must be able to figure out what is standing in the way of their optimal development, help them set goals for how to achieve that optimal development, and identify the strengths and supports that allow them to get there.

Case Conceptualization and Effective Interventions provides the tools for you to accomplish your goal of becoming an effective counselor. We introduce an innovative new model for case conceptualization called the Temporal/Contextual (T/C) Model, which gives you a comprehensive, practical, easy-to-apply framework for interacting with and understanding your clients. Using case examples, you learn to use the T/C Model to gather information and generate hypotheses about a wide variety of clients. We also include a summary of the current information on mental, emotional, and behavioral disorders found in the Diagnostic and Statistical Manual of Mental Disorders (DSM). A complete reiteration of all the DSM criteria is beyond the scope of this text, and would be both overwhelming and redundant. Instead, we focus on presenting problems most often found in counseling settings and then summarize the information in an accessible, easy-to-understand format.

In addition, we address the competencies identified by the Council for the Accreditation of Counseling and Related Educational Programs in their latest standards as essential to competent counseling practice in a multicultural society (CACREP, 2009). The current standards include an increased emphasis on the applied aspects of counseling, especially those that are evidence based. As you work your way through this book, each chapter brings the counseling experience to life by blending current theory and research with case illustrations that anchor the material in real-world experience.

The first section of the book describes the process of counseling within the historical context of the profession and the unique professional identity of a counselor. Counseling is a complex process. Before we can effectively help our clients, we must have an understanding of who we are as counselors. What is our history, what are our goals, and what is our identity as counselors? In this section, we review the literature on counseling effectiveness, including skills, attributes, and theoretical orientation. Although these concepts are covered in introductory courses in most counseling programs, we apply them here to illustrate their use in the process of case conceptualization. Rather than including an exhaustive variety of theoretical approaches, the text briefly discusses the theories most often employed by counselors, emphasizing application in case conceptualization and treatment planning.

An understanding of professional identity, history, skills, and theory provides the lens through which we encounter our clients, and the template which we use to make sense of clients' challenges and strengths. In this section, you also learn and practice applying the T/C Model, which provides a framework to understand and help our clients. The T/C Model helps you become a reflective counselor, continually assessing the counseling process, and an intentional counselor, asking the questions and utilizing the tools which help you to help your clients.

The second section includes chapters on the most common presenting problems in counseling settings, and includes empirically supported interventions to address these problems, which are both culturally and situationally responsive. *Case Conceptualization and Effective Interventions* provides a pathway for treatment of mental, emotional, and behavioral disorders based on the most recent evidence-based research, while at the same time recognizing that diagnosis and treatment are part of a dynamic and evolving field that embraces human diversity and individuality. Thus, the text is not designed to present a rigid formula for assessment, prevention, and intervention, but rather to help counselors make informed, ethical, and effective decisions to benefit their clients. The American Counseling Association's code of ethics stresses the need to employ interventions with the greatest chance of success; therefore, the text focuses on research-based treatment strategies most often used for the disorders included.

An in-depth discussion of specific interventions is beyond the scope of this text; rather, the most commonly employed empirically supported treatments are described, with links to more extensive training materials provided in the "Go Further" section at the end of each chapter. In addition, this book is not intended to teach general counseling skills. We assume that you already have the fundamental knowledge and skills to work effectively with clients; this book shows how to employ those skills more effectively with the application of the case conceptualization model presented here.

Finally, the third section emphasizes the importance of integrating the information, principles, and practices of counseling within an evolving professional identity. As you go forward, the T/C Model that you learn in this book enriches your counseling practice by ensuring that the case conceptualization is carried out in context and that the process is an intentional one. In addition, this final section ties case conceptualization to the next steps with a focus on effective interventions that truly help clients.

The Case of Katy

Katy is a 23-year-old Korean American female. She sought counseling because of family and relationship issues. She graduated in May from college with a bachelor's degree in English Literature and a grade point average (GPA) of 3.92, but has yet to find a job and lives at home with her mother, stepfather, and two younger half-brothers. She states that she is self-referred; however, she also says that she is seeking counseling because her on again/off again boyfriend made it a condition for getting back together. Prior to this visit, Katy sought counseling for a few sessions in college at the university counseling center when her main issue was feeling caught in the middle between her mother and stepfather's frequent arguments.

Katy reports high levels of depression and anxiety. She has trouble falling asleep because "my mind just won't turn off." When she does fall asleep, she often wakes up at 4:00 or 5:00 am and cannot go back to sleep. She often feels queasy, and says she "just isn't hungry" a lot of the time. Katy hasn't been to see a medical doctor, but admits that she's gone down a few jean sizes and appears slightly underweight.

In her first session with the counselor, Katy appears nervous. She speaks very rapidly, as though she just wants to get the words out. Her eye contact is sporadic; sometimes she glances at the counselor as if to gauge the counselor's reaction, but then quickly looks away. At other times, she looks down at her hands, which she clasps and unclasps in her lap. Katy shifts position on the chair often, and generally appears uncomfortable.

Katy describes her situation as "hopeless," says that she is "a failure" who will "never find a job." Her rocky relationship with her boyfriend has also made her doubt herself, and she fears she'll be "alone all my life." She is confused by what her next steps should be in life and feels "adrift," now that she has graduated. Because she doesn't have a job, she moved back in with her mother and stepfather three months ago. While they were fine with that decision, it's clear they consider the arrangement to be temporary, and they expect Katy to find employment. Katy has been on several job interviews, but none were in her field, and she has received no job offers. She is beginning to feel hopeless about the prospect of getting a job, and is envious of her two best friends who are employed and living independently. Katy is certain that her parents and her stepparents are all looking at her with disapproval and consider her a failure.

While Katy was never in trouble in high school or college, since she has graduated she mentions several instances of participating in risky sexual behaviors (one-night stands, unprotected sex, promiscuity), and says her friends would describe her as "crazy," and "out of control." She described a recent incident on a bus where she "just lost it." She felt like she couldn't breathe and that her heart was pounding out of her chest, and she started to feel dizzy. It got so bad that she had to have the bus driver stop to let her out before he reached the next bus stop. Since then, she has been avoiding public transportation. Unfortunately, she does not own a car, so she often feels "stuck" in the house during the day when her mother and stepfather are at work. On several other occasions, Katy

(Continued)

(Continued)

experienced the same feelings when she was in an unfamiliar place, and ended up leaving. The list of places she wants to avoid is growing, and the avoidance is starting to limit her daily life, especially when she booked a job interview for next week that she requires taking the bus.

Katy's parents divorced when she was six. Her mother and father have both remarried. Katy's father is the owner of several neighborhood grocery stores. Her father grew up in Korea and immigrated to the United States as a young man. He opened his first store when he was 20 and now has four very successful stores. He was and still is very demanding and does not understand why Katy does not have a job yet. While Katy visited her father every weekend when she was younger, recently she has been avoiding going to see him because she expects a lecture.

Katy's mother and stepfather are currently separated, but still live together "for the sake of the children." Katy's stepfather, a tax accountant, is the parent she talks to the most and from whom she feels she receives unconditional love. When she was younger, Katy and her stepfather were quite close. Her stepfather is not home as much anymore, however, and Katy believes he may have a girlfriend. She misses their time together, but doesn't want to rock the boat and risk him moving out completely.

Katy reports having different "roles" depending on which parent she is with. Katy's mother is a financial analyst. She has always expected A's from her daughter, and held strict expectations for Katy about school and socializing. Katy describes her mother as "a worrier," who didn't let Katy go to sleepovers or to amusement parks because "bad things might happen." Her mother tends to have a few drinks every night after dinner "to help me relax." Katy remembers several periods of time during her childhood when her mother went out constantly, and she overheard arguments with her stepfather accusing Katy's mother of cheating and "spending all their money." During these times, Katy says she avoided her mother because "I never knew what would set her off and start her screaming and throwing things. She was crazy; it was horrible." More than once, Katy says that she was hit by a thrown object, and her younger brothers have been as well. Other times, her mother just seemed withdrawn, and rarely smiled. Katy's mother has never been affectionate, and Katy sometimes feels she needs to do negative things in order to get any attention from her mother.

While Katy reports also being "a worrier" all her life, especially about her grades, she is usually quite social and enjoyed the new freedom to go out and socialize when she went to college. She was a member of a sorority as an undergraduate, and she enjoys going out with friends. She drank in college, but not to excess. Recently, however, when she does go out she frequently drinks to the point of blacking out. Her friends are worried about her, and Katy is concerned that they might stop inviting her to go out with them.

PART I

THINKING AND ACTING AS A PROFESSIONAL COUNSELOR

1

A JOURNEY INTO THE PROFESSION

INTRODUCTION

Counselors tend to be "doers." Most of us who enter the field do so in hopes of providing assistance to people to help them live fuller and more productive lives (e.g., Katy, whose case we presented in the Preface). But, what does it mean to help someone as a counselor? How is the process of helping different for counselors than for the many other people who also value making a difference in people's lives, such as physicians, attorneys, social workers, psychologists, nurses, volunteers, and clergy? What is the nature of the profession, and what is our role as professional counselors?

To be effective in the profession of counseling, we need to understand not only the issues that face our clients, but also the theory and research that support the processes that facilitate change. Further, we need to understand these change agents and how to effectively implement them within the broader context of the profession. Thus, we begin this text by setting the stage. To know what makes counseling unique among the helping professions, and to craft your role within the profession, is essential if we are to become more than simply people who want to help—people who are professional counselors.

We begin this chapter and your introduction to the process of case conceptualization by taking a trip back through history. Understanding our roots as counselors and how the profession developed allows you to develop your own professional identity. Only with a clear understanding of your role as a counselor can you begin the process of understanding your client. Throughout the first section of this book, we revisit the case of Katy and apply the information learned in each chapter to develop a conceptualization and goals to help her grow and change.

A BRIEF HISTORY OF COUNSELING

The American Counseling Association (ACA) defines counseling as "a professional relationship that empowers diverse individuals, families, and groups to accomplish mental health, wellness, education, and career goals" (ACA, 2010). Professional counseling is part of a wide range of mental health and human services professions, including psychiatrists, psychologists, social workers, marriage and family therapists, and pastoral counselors. Counseling was an interdisciplinary field from the start, interlinked with, but distinct from these related fields, and influenced by both psychology and education. An awareness of the historical underpinnings of the field enables a deeper understanding of the current norms, traditions, philosophy, and challenges of professional counseling today. In this chapter, we examine both the common influences among mental health professions and the ways that each profession is distinct from the others. Only with an understanding of the profession's history and evolution can we as counselors develop a professional identity and way of practicing that allows us to effectively understand and help our clients. Counselors conceptualize and intervene in ways which are distinct from other mental health professions, and hold an identity and ethical imperatives that set us apart from our fellow practitioners.

While there have always been people who are motivated to help their fellow humans, helping as a profession can trace its beginnings to the nineteenth century.

Late 1800s

The profession of psychiatry traces its beginnings to medical professionals who organized to seek humanitarian reforms in the treatment of the mentally ill in the mid-1800s. These practitioners formed the Association of Medical Superintendents of American Institutions for the Insane (AMSAII) in 1844, even before the American Medical Association was established (Fancher, 1995). During this time period, biological causes for some of the most serious forms of mental illness were discovered, including the cure for syphilis, inspiring the "medical model" of treatment for mental disorders that continues to be the basis for psychiatric treatment today. The medical model is based on the idea that there is a scientific basis and biological roots for psychological problems. This model has influenced all subsequent helping professions and continues to shape the mental health field today. While counseling as a field diverges from the medical model in some ways, counselors also recognize and consider the impact of biological factors on human emotional and mental health. By the late

1800s, the medical specialty of neurology emerged. Although this specialty focused more on scientific inquiry than humanitarian reforms, neurologist Sigmund Freud began to use "talking therapies" with his clients who were suffering from neuroses, and the Institute of Psychoanalysis was established in Vienna leading to the emergence of psychiatry.

The field of psychology was also developing; psychology draws its roots from philosophy and evolved to emphasize the application of scientific principles to understand the mind and human behavior. Wilhelm Wundt, a philosopher and physiologist, opened the first psychological laboratory in 1879, defining psychology as the study of immediate experience (Resnick, 1997). In 1892, the American Psychological Association was established, diverging from philosophy. The new field of psychology, with the establishment of its own professional organization, focused on psychophysics, behavior, and assessment. The first psychological clinic opened in 1896 in Philadelphia to treat physical and mental problems in children (Witmer, 1896).

At the same time, the discipline of professional social work grew out of the settlement house movement and the Charity Organization Society (COS), which attempted to empower clients to help themselves. Social workers focused on helping families who were underprivileged and disenfranchised through what they termed "friendly visiting" (Haynes & White, 1999).

All three related professions—psychiatry, psychology, and social work—sought to help people live fuller and more functional lives, but each profession focused on the different internal and external forces impacting individuals, and thus differed in their views of how to help. For example, a psychiatrist working from the medical model might focus on Katy's physiological symptoms—difficulty sleeping, rapid heartbeat and dizziness in certain situations, changes in appetite—or might want to gather more information about her mother's history of mood swings, impulsive behavior, and alcohol use. A psychologist might want to know more about Katy's feelings of hopelessness, and her belief that she's a failure. A social worker might concentrate on the family dynamics in Katy's household with her mother and stepfather and how those dynamics impact Katy and her two younger brothers, or her relationship with her father.

As we see in the next two chapters, the field of counseling shares aspects of all three related fields. The model of case conceptualization and treatment planning presented in this text incorporates elements that are emphasized by psychiatry, psychology, and social work by using a comprehensive lens to investigate and understand clients.

1900s

Counseling as a profession began in the early 1900s, diverging from the other three fields to chart its own course and find unique ways of conceptualizing people's challenges and ways to help them. During this time, the rapid urbanization of the United States caused high levels of unemployment, especially among young people. The first counselors were also social reformers who were concerned about the adverse effects of the Industrial Revolution on employment. Reformers felt that people could develop more fully when they had some kind of guidance or direction. This conviction spurred Frank Parsons to found the Vocational Guidance Bureau in Boston in 1908, which paved the way for the first formalized approach to counseling. Parsons believed that people would benefit from guidance in selecting careers that would be rewarding, so he attempted to match individuals' skills and abilities with appropriate work settings. Parsons' approach included several key ideas that would define the new field; he focused on normal development during stressful transitions, emphasized the importance of prevention and early intervention by targeting an at-risk population, and gathered information from multiple sources, taking a contextual approach (Smith, 2012). At the same time, Jesse B. Davis set up a systematized guidance program in public schools with a similar focus on prevention and teaching children how to deal with life

transitions, which was also an influence on the new field of counseling (Aubrey, 1977).

Several important developments during this time impacted all the mental health professions. Clifford W. Beers published an autobiographical account of his experience as an inpatient in mental institutions in *A Mind That Found Itself* (Beers, 1908). Beers' account created a public outcry for more humane mental health care that led to the establishment of the mental health movement and the National Mental Health Association. During this period, Sigmund Freud's psychoanalytic theory was also influential in how people with mental illness were treated and opinions about what sort of treatment was believed to be most effective.

As we explore the process of case conceptualization in detail in Chapter 3, the influence of these early emphases on behavior, family and social networks, normal developmental processes, coping with transition, and prevention becomes clear. The humanitarian reforms that Beers advocated were in line with the beliefs of the young profession of counseling; these beliefs are reflected today in counselors' emphasis on wellness instead of pathology, and their view of mental health as a continuum instead of a strict line between "sick" and "well."

1910s

Just as psychiatry, psychology, and social work established themselves as professions by forming professional associations, counseling soon followed suit. The first national professional association for the counseling field, the National Vocational Guidance Association, was founded in 1913 (Hershenson, Power & Waldo, 1996). Because of the need for screening tests for the U.S. Army during World War II, there was interest in developing effective testing, and the vocational guidance field began to use psychometric tests for civilian populations as well. The Association published a bulletin that eventually became the *Journal of Counseling and Development*, which is still in publication today.

1920s

During this decade, the focus of the counseling field began to expand. In New York City, the first marriage and family counseling center was established by Abraham and Hannah Stone, expanding the field of counseling from vocational issues. Several new psychometric assessments were published in the 1920s, including the Strong Vocational Interest Inventory in 1927 (Strong, 1943), which gave counselors a tool to help people make career decisions.

The 1920s and 30s also brought an increased concern about the mental health of children across the helping professions, which led to the establishment of Child Guidance clinics. These clinics used a team approach with psychiatrists in leadership roles, psychologists providing assessment and therapy, and social workers responsible for casework and serving as liaisons with the community (Nichols, 2010).

During the same time, higher education professionals were also realizing that mental health issues were a growing concern on campuses across the nation. At the American Student Health Association meeting in 1920, "mental hygiene" was acknowledged as a significant roadblock for many college students. This led to a discussion of what mental health resources should be made available to students as part of the services provided by colleges (Kraft, 2011).

By the end of this decade, the augmented focus on children and college students as well as adults, and a concern with the healthy functioning of marriages and families in addition to individuals, led all the helping professions to expand the range of potential clients.

1930s

The Great Depression brought a higher demand for job counseling, which was mostly the domain of counselors. This led to the development of the first articulated theory of counseling. E. G. Williamson's trait-factor counseling, also called the Minnesota point of view, stressed the counselor's teaching,

mentoring, and influencing skills and took a scientific empirical approach to problem solving (Williamson & Biggs, 1979). Williamson's approach came to be known as directive counseling, based on an extension of Parsons' ideas. According to Williamson, the goal of counseling was to help clients stop thinking and behaving in ways which were not productive, allowing them to make more effective decisions (Lynch & Maki, 1981). The development of a coherent theory about the purpose of counseling helped set the growing field apart from the other helping fields.

There was also an increased need for vocational rehabilitation counseling during this time. In response to this need, the Social Security Act was passed in 1935, providing educational and counseling resources for persons with disabilities. The influx of financial support helped the field continue to grow.

1940s

By the 1940s, the scope of counseling began to broaden further from occupational concerns. Carl Rogers, who had become disillusioned with the type of treatment conducted at child guidance clinics, published *Counseling and Psychotherapy* in 1942 (Rogers, 1942). In this book, Rogers challenged the trait and factor approach of Parsons and Williamson, as well as Freud's psychoanalysis, and focused instead on individuals' ability to make their own life choices and on their intrinsic motivation toward health and wellness. Rogers emphasized the counselor-client relationship over testing and vocational issues (Rogers, 1961). His belief that counselors could help clients through a nondirective and accepting approach influenced both counseling and psychology. Rogers' emphasis on wellness continues to be reflected in the counseling field.

Professional organizations for the mental health fields were established as the fields expanded. The American Association of Marriage and Family Counselors (AAMFC—later renamed

American Association of Marriage and Family Therapists or AAMFT) was founded in 1942, and established training standards for marriage counseling programs. The National Association of Guidance Supervisors and Counselor Trainers (NAGSCT) was established in 1940, with a focus on training and research (now known as the Association for Counselor Education and Supervision, or ACES).

World War II impacted the vocational landscape during this time, with traditional occupational sex roles expanding as women moved into the workplace and families sought counseling to help with the role transitions. Counselors also worked with military personnel who suffered trauma and emotional breakdowns, prompting the Veteran's Administration to fund training of counselors and psychologists to meet this need (Smith, 2012), again contributing to the growth of both fields.

1950s

Professional associations have played a pivotal role in defining each mental health field. Prior to the 1950s, counselors and psychologists overlapped in many of their views of mental health and wellness and treatment goals. In 1949, The American Psychological Association refined its definition of "psychologist", specifying that clinical psychologists were scientist-practitioners, trained in PhD programs in psychology or a closely related field (Cummings, 1990). This created a clear dividing line between psychologists—including counseling psychologists—and counselors. Counselors with master's degrees could no longer be members of the APA, and the Veterans Administration funded only doctoral-level internships, leaving masters-level counselors ineligible. In 1950, psychology was the first mental health profession other than psychiatry to legislate state licensing laws, further setting that profession apart from counseling.

In 1952, Division 17 of the American Psychological Association was renamed from the Division of Counseling and Guidance to the Division of Counseling Psychology as counseling psychologists broadened their focus from their historical common roots with vocational guidance (Dawis, 1992). Division 17 was created with a focus on mental health instead of mental illness, as a result of some psychologists' desire to work with a more "normal" population than clinical psychologists often did. The distinction between the work that psychologists in Division 17 were doing and the work that counselors were doing was blurry at best.

In response to the APA's changes, in 1952 the American Personnel and Guidance Association (APGA) was created to provide a professional home for counselors (Kaplan, 2002). The APGA's goal was to work with clients with normal, developmental concerns instead of the psychopathology focus of the psychiatrists and clinical psychologists. Historically, counselors focused on multicultural competence and a more positive prevention approach and the field continues to emphasize these important areas.

The APGA combined the National Vocational Guidance Association (NVGA), the American College Personnel Association (ACPA), and the Student Personnel Association for Teacher Education (SPATE) into one professional organization. Shortly after these changes, the fifth division of the American Personnel and Guidance Association (currently the American Counseling Association) was formed in 1953. This division, now known as the American School Counselors Association, continues to have a large influence on the school counseling profession and the roles that school counseling professionals play within school systems.

Pulling from the related fields of public health, nursing, social work, and school counseling, the field of rehabilitation counseling also came into its own in the 1950s, with the availability of federal funding for rehabilitation counseling programs. Historically, rehabilitation counselors primarily worked with adults with disabilities, but today there is a need for these services for individuals of all ages who have disabilities. Therefore, rehabilitation counselors work in both public human service agencies and in private practice settings as well as in a variety of areas, including as Vocational Counselors in state rehabilitation programs, as Disability Counselors at colleges and universities, and in various administrative positions at social service agencies.

Rehabilitation counseling programs stress the importance of community service to a culturally and ethnically diverse population, emphasizing the systemic barriers and harmful societal attitudes that adversely impact the health and welfare of persons with disabilities. The assistance provided by rehabilitation counselors extends beyond workplace issues, as they often serve as advocates for their clients and work as community activists.

In some states, these counselors are licensed as Licensed Rehabilitation Counselors, while in other states, rehabilitation counselors are Licensed Professional Counselors (LPCs). The Commission on Rehabilitation Counselor Certification grants certification to counselors who meet educational requirements and have passed an examination indicating that they possess the competency and skill to become a Certified Rehabilitation Counselor.

National and international events also impacted the growing field of counseling in the 1950s. Motivated by the Space Race and Sputnik launch, The 1958 National Defense Education Act (NDEA) provided grants for school counselor training with the hope of placing more counselors in schools to steer students toward math and science careers. The number of school counselors increased significantly as a direct result of the NDEA (Gladding & Newsome, 2010). Also during this time, vocational counselors recognized the need for more support for individuals with physical and mental disabilities.

The evolution of related mental health professions continued to impact the field of counseling as well. The American Psychiatric Association published the first Diagnostic and Statistical Manual of Mental Disorders (DSM) in 1952, a diagnostic and classification system still used today. In the United States, as described in Part II of this text, the current version of the DSM continues to be the diagnostic standard for mental health treatment.

1960s

The 1960s brought sweeping social changes to the United States. With the advent of effective antipsychotic medications and the influence of social reform efforts, patients were released from inpatient hospitals and sought treatment in their local communities instead. Pharmacological treatment spurred the development of counseling theories and techniques that could be employed outside of inpatient settings and the idea of community-based treatment took off. The Community Mental Health Centers Act of 1963 funded the delivery of preventive mental health services, counseling, and outreach in the community (Guindon, 2011), and masters- and doctoral-level counselors filled the many open positions in outpatient centers and substance abuse treatment facilities.

Several influential new theories emerged from the related field of psychology during this time, including the behavioral theories of Joseph Wolpe (1958), the rational-emotive theory of Albert Ellis (1961), and the cognitive theories of Aaron Beck (1967). For the first time ever, effectiveness of counseling and therapy for mental health disorders was demonstrated in empirically based outcome studies. Counselors and psychologists worked alongside psychiatrists in outpatient facilities and community mental health centers, and counselor education programs began to expand their focus to prepare counselors to work in community settings. At the same time, the counseling field also responded to the growth of the humanistic movement, and to increased recognition of the power of helping people in groups (Gladding, 2008). During this time, clinical social workers followed the lead of psychology associations and successfully lobbied for state licensing laws.

1970s

In the 1970s, the division between psychology and counseling further solidified. The case of *Weldon v. Virginia State Board of Psychologists*

Examiners in 1974 established that counseling was a profession distinct from psychology. Two years later, counselors were first licensed to practice in Virginia in 1976 as LPCs (Licensed Professional Counselors), due in part to the state boards of examiners for psychology barring graduates of counseling programs in education departments from taking the psychology licensing exam (Gladding, 1997; Ohlsen, 1983).

At the same time, the need for mental health counselors in community centers shifted the focus of counselors from schools to communities, and counselors began to deliver a wide variety of services similar to the established mental health professions of psychiatry, psychology, and social work. Counselors were increasingly recognized as professionals who provided personal counseling to clients, as well as vocational and educational assistance. Since counselors who worked in community and agency settings instead of schools felt they lacked representation within APGA, the American Mental Health Counselors Association (AMCHA) was formed in 1976 as a division of APGA. It quickly became the largest division with an often contentious relationship with the APGA (Colangelo, 2009).

During the 1970s, the Rehabilitation Act of 1973 also expanded opportunities for rehabilitation counselors who worked with persons with disabilities. In the same year, the Association for Counselor Education and Supervision (ACES) developed standards for master's and doctoral degrees in counseling (Stripling, 1978). The counseling field began to develop its own training standards with researchers, such as Egan (1970, 1975), Carkhuff and Anthony (1979), and Ivey (1971) articulating fundamental counseling skills that are still taught today.

1980s

The 1980s saw a further move toward training standards and certification that helped to establish a professional identity for counseling. The Council for Accreditation of Counseling and Related Educational Programs (CACREP) was created in 1981 as an independent legally incorporated accreditation body by APGA, responsible for accrediting counselor education programs and creating training standards (Colangelo, 2009). CACREP began to accredit programs in school, community/agency, mental health, marriage and family counseling, and personnel services for college students.

The National Board for Certified Counselors (NBCC) was also created in 1982 to certify counselors at the national level. Counselors had to pass a standardized test and meet character qualifications to become a National Certified Counselor (NCC) (Herr, 1985). Chi Sigma Iota, an international counseling honor society, was formed in 1985.

Counseling as a field continued to evolve. APGA changed its name to the American Association for Counseling and Development (AACD) in 1983, as a result of leadership realizing that "personnel" and "guidance" no longer described the scope of many counselors' practices (Herr, 1985). Counselors began to emphasize the challenges of working with individual differences, including gender, ethnicity, culture, and sexual orientation (Gladding & Newsome, 2010). Carol Gilligan's (1982) research infused feminist theory into the counseling field. Multicultural counseling themes, including the challenges of working with diverse ethnic and cultural groups, were also emphasized. In addition, there was an increased emphasis on human development across the lifespan, inspired by the research of Erik Erikson (Hamacheck, 1988).

At this point, the counseling profession had grown large enough to encompass a number of specialty areas that began to fragment the field. There were now many counselors who were not school counselors or vocational counselors, but worked in a variety of community and agency settings. In 1988, CACREP recognized mental health counseling as a specialty area, but debate continued for decades about the distinction between community counselors and mental health counselors. Community counselors historically viewed their specialty as set apart from other types of counseling by their focus on taking into account the effects of the community environment on individuals and their focus on empowering clients through advocacy. Rather than being defined by the setting where they work, community counselors saw themselves as providing preventive and rehabilitative services to a wide variety of clients in diverse settings (Hershenson & Berger, 2001). Mental health counselors also viewed their specialty as distinct from community counselors, vocational counselors, and school counselors.

1990s

The advent of managed care in the 1990s resulted in a sweeping decrease in mental health funding and counselors began to fight for equitable reimbursement for services. Progress continued for the young profession, however. For the first time, the statistics published by the National Institute of Mental Health included counselors, putting the profession on a par with psychiatry, psychology, and social work (Gladding & Newsome, 2010).

In 1992, the AACD became the American Counseling Association (ACA). The counseling field continued to broaden its focus with continuing fragmentation among specialty areas. Divisions now included the American College Counseling Association, the Association for Gay, Lesbian, and Bisexual Issues in Counseling, and Counselors for Social Justice. Multicultural competencies for counselors were published in 1992 (Sue, Arredondo, & McDavis, 1992). When the American College Personnel Association (ACPA) established itself as a separate entity, the ACA created the American College Counseling Association as a new division (Spurgeon, 2012).

2000s

While fragmentation still continues, today there is more and more overlap in the practice of counselors in diverse settings. Mental health counselors may work in the local school systems, dealing with clinical problems that school counselors cannot address due to other responsibilities within the system. Conversely, school counselors may work with students who have serious clinical mental health issues, as the only qualified practitioners in the school. CACREP requires trainees to prepare for one specialty area of counseling, but the reality of many practice settings requires a broader base of training.

There has been progress toward unity in the field, however. A common definition of counseling was reached at the ACA's 20/20 Initiative: A Vision for the Future of Counseling convention in 2010. CACREP was recognized as the accrediting agency for counselor education programs, with Standards reviewed and revised every seven years (American Counseling Association, 2010). The 2009 Standards combined the specialty areas of community counseling and mental health counseling programs into a new program called Clinical Mental Health Counseling, which resulted in increased unity to the profession.

Rehabilitation counseling and working with clients with disability issues is also an important realm of counseling practice. Rehabilitation counselors focus on the mental health, well-being, development, and care of all persons living with any form of disability. The Council on Rehabilitation Education, or CORE, is the accrediting body for rehabilitation counselors. The CORE accreditation process promotes effective delivery of rehabilitation services to individuals with disabilities. In July of 2013, CACREP and CORE entered into a historic affiliation agreement which further unified the counseling field. CACREP became the accrediting body for Clinical Rehabilitation Programs, with the review process conducted jointly by CACREP and CORE.

The various mental health professions continue to impact each other as well. Martin Seligman's (2002, 2011) research on positive psychology had an influence on both counseling and psychology, distinguishing between mental health and mental illness and advocating a strengths-based approach which both fields embraced.

PROFESSIONAL IDENTITY

You now have an understanding of the history and the evolution of the field. The next important question to consider is: *Who* are we now, and how can we best help our clients? The concept we now discuss is known as professional identity.

Why is it important?

Parsons and Zhang (2014) note that the main difference between professional counselors and any sort of helper is that professional counselors view themselves as members of a unique profession and embrace an identity as a professional. Professional identity is defined as the philosophy, training model, and scope of practice that characterize a profession (MacCluskie & Ingersoll, 2001). As is clear from the often inter-twined histories of the various mental health professions, developing a unique professional identity can be a challenge. Yet, there is a consensus among researchers that a strong sense of professional identity is critical to the continued growth and health of a profession, as well as to individual practitioners. The ACA identifies finding a shared professional identity as critical to the future of the profession (American Counseling Association, 2009).

Professional identity is thus important to the profession as a whole, but embracing a professional identity is just as critical to each individual counselor. Without a clear and articulated model of who a counselor is and what a counselor does, it is impossible to develop a road map of how to help clients. Understanding one's professional identity provides the starting point for becoming that "doer" that we discussed. From identity flows norms for behavior, values for practice, ethics for intervening, and a sense of professional pride. These, in turn, are essential for helping others change, from case conceptualization through intervention. Let's look more closely now at the concept of professional identity and its importance to counselors.

What is it?

Remley and Herlihy (2005) describe counselors' professional identity as the ability to describe the process of the profession, including the services provided, the training required, and the philosophical foundation, without referring to other mental health professions. At the same time, counselors should be able to describe both what sets their profession apart, and what the profession has in common with related professions. When a counselor's view of "self as professional" is combined with a sense of competence as a professional, there is congruence between personal worldview and professional view (Reisetter et al., 2004). A strong professional identity has both external and internal benefits. A sense of pride and security in one's profession is related to identity (Myers, Sweeney, & White, 2002) and can help counselors clearly define their roles and make decisions accordingly (Brott & Myers, 1999). When a profession is conceptualized as unique, a collective identity of shared values, beliefs, and assumptions develops, contributing to pride and security (Daniels, 2002).

Professional identity is facilitated by both legal recognition, such as licensure law, and certification. To practice a profession in a certain state, one must be licensed; to use the title of the profession, one must be certified. Membership in professional organizations and standards of behavior defined in a code of ethics also contribute to professional identity.

A coherent professional identity remains a struggle for the counseling profession. The multidisciplinary nature of counseling and the considerable overlap in the types of clients served and services provided by other mental health professionals has contributed to some of the identity confusion that both the profession and the public experience. From a practical standpoint, this identity confusion has consequences. In order to develop a case conceptualization for a client, the counselor must have a clear understanding of which aspects of human emotional, behavioral, and mental health fall under his or her purview. Which problems can the counselor help and which are better served by other helping professionals? Which aspects of the client's life are relevant for the counselor to investigate and understand in order to effectively assist the client? What spheres of influence do counselors believe are integral to human development and functioning? What do counselors value, and what ethical norms do we uphold? The answers to these important questions are the foundations on which the profession of counseling is based. Helping the client rests on a thorough and accurate case conceptualization; the case conceptualization itself depends on the counselor's clear understanding of their role in the helping process. Thus, we as counselors must articulate our role and values clearly, with an understanding of both our similarities to other helping professions and our differences.

To distinguish itself as a profession, counseling needs a common definition a common training curriculum, national and regional professional associations, and federal recognition. ACA articulated a common definition of counseling as "a professional relationship that empowers diverse individuals, families, and groups to accomplish mental health, wellness, education, and career goals" (American Counseling Association, 2010). CACREP standards now define a common training curriculum. There are both national and regional professional associations (see Box 1.3), and federal recognition has been granted through professional licensure, the most powerful form of regulation of professional practice (Remley & Herlihy, 2010; Spurgeon, 2012). The Department of Veterans Affairs recognized Licensed Professional Counselors as approved service providers in 2010.

The counseling profession also has an established Code of Ethics (American Counseling Association, 2014). The recently revised code made some significant changes from the 2005 version, an indication of the constantly evolving profession and the constantly changing world of both the counselors and clients. Some of the most important changes in the new code are a clarification of the values of the counseling profession,

which are now explicitly spelled out in the preamble as enhancement of human development, promoting social justice, honoring diversity and multiculturalism, the integrity of the therapeutic relationship, and practicing with competence (Kaplan, 2014).

The 2014 Code specifically addresses the confusion regarding when it is and is not appropriate and ethical to make referrals. The 2005 Code did not make it clear that referring a client because of the counselor's personal values, essentially imposing those values on the client, was unethical for a profession whose primary value is recognizing the worth and dignity of all people. Referrals should be made because of lack of skills and competency and not because of clashing values. Understanding a client's values and beliefs is an integral part of case conceptualization using the T/C Model, and respecting those values and beliefs is equally important.

Another major change in the 2014 Code was the recognition of distance counseling as an increasingly common and viable method of service and social media as a part of most of our daily lives. The code reminds counselors that they are subject to the rules and regulations of the state in which they practice, as well as the state where their client is residing. Issues such as data security (for example, Skype is not HIPAA [Health Insurance Portability and Accountability Act] compliant), encryption, informed consent, and disclosure are also covered in the new code. Distance counselors must have a crisis plan in place in case technology fails, and must make sure that clients have local resources if needed. Maintaining a professional image on social media is also included; for example, maintaining clients' privacy by not reading their Facebook posts without consent, having separate personal and professional accounts, and not "friending" clients online. On the other hand, it is crucial for counselors to have a thorough understanding of social media. In particular, school counselors and college counselors will have many clients who have experienced cyberbullying and should understand the ways that it occurs and its impact on young people.

The 2014 Ethics Code also incorporates more of a social justice perspective, both in its clarification of values and its recognition that *pro bono* work is in keeping with the social justice focus of the field, while acknowledging that not all counselors are financially able to provide services at no cost. The revised code allows for other ways that counselors can contribute, including free public speaking engagements and volunteering during disasters.

Now that there is a common definition of counseling, recognized training standards, and a professional Code of Ethics in place, the 20/20 Initiative (Kaplan & Gladding, 2011) identified the development of a clear professional identity as a priority for counselors, while also advocating partnership with the sister professions of mental health care providers. In order to strengthen professional identity, the 20/20 Initiative recommends identifying the core commonalities of the profession, a core body of knowledge and skills shared by all counselors, and a view of counseling as a single profession composed of counselors with specialized areas of training.

WHO ARE WE NOW?
COUNSELING AND RELATED PROFESSIONS

The ability to distinguish counseling from closely related fields is an important contributor to professional identity (Pistole & Roberts, 2002). Collaboration among various types of mental health professionals is facilitated by each profession having a strong professional identity and an understanding of the professional identity of their colleagues. While it is important to understand those aspects of counseling which are distinct from other related professions, it is also important to recognize the commonalities so that collaboration can build on each profession's strengths and expertise. In many agencies, hospitals, and schools, counselors are part of a multidisciplinary team of mental health professionals, each contributing their unique skills and perspectives to best serve their clients.

Some professionals attempt to distinguish between mental health professions on the basis of the severity of client problems treated, but this distinction is problematic. Although as we have seen, the counseling profession traditionally focused on prevention and wellness using a developmental model, many counselors work with clients experiencing more serious mental health concerns. In addition, other mental health professionals are increasingly recognizing the value of a developmental and strengths-based approach. Thus, a distinction based on similarities and differences in philosophy and training requirements may be more helpful.

Psychiatry

Psychiatry is based on a medical model of treatment, and practitioners hold medical degrees (MacCluskie & Ingersoll, 2001). Until recently, psychiatrists were the only mental health providers who could prescribe medications (some states now grant limited prescription privileges to psychologists). There is a focus on pathology, but the most recent version of the Diagnostic and Statistical Manual of Mental Disorders (DSM-5) takes a more contextual, bioecological approach to diagnosis and treatment (American Psychiatric Association, 2013). A psychiatrist, for example, might consider prescribing a medication for Katy's depression and/or her anxiety symptoms.

Social Work

Social work's mission is to improve quality of life for individuals, promote social values, and encourage self-advocacy and self-realization (Gilbert, 1977). Practitioners usually earn a Master's Degree in Social Work (MSW). The unique emphasis of the profession is the prominence placed on social welfare, which helps define the professional identity of social workers (LaFleur, 2007). A social worker, for example, might be concerned with the stability of Katy's family system, particularly since she has younger brothers living at home. A social work perspective might also encompass consideration of cultural factors, taking into account traditional Korean vocational, gender, and family norms. However, other mental health professionals also recognize the impact of social and cultural influences on their clients.

Psychology

Psychology emphasizes the scientist-practitioner basis of the field as a unique characteristic, as well as psychologists' expertise in testing and assessment. As distinguishing features of their professional identity, clinical psychologists identify the breadth of problems addressed and populations served, and the focus on individual differences (American Psychological Association, 2013). A psychologist might want to do a thorough developmental history by examining Katy's childhood educational, relational, and emotional functioning, or utilize some standardized assessment instruments. However, both counselors and psychologists focus on developmental issues and healthy functioning, training and supervision, and multicultural concerns (Goodyear, 2000).

Counseling

Counseling differs from other mental health professions in several ways. First, its wellness focus, which builds on a client's strengths and resources to help them reach levels of optimal well-being (Witmer & Granello, 2005). Second, its emphasis on prevention, which goes beyond addressing issues of pathology. Third, its application of human development principles to a wide range of client issues, and its holistic framework. Counselors of all specialties retain this framework as they work with clients during normal developmental transitions as well as working with those facing serious emotional and mental disorders.

Counselors also work from a biopsychosocial perspective, as opposed to a medical model of mental disorders, which takes into account the various contextual influences on human development—biological, social, emotional, and psychological.

The bioecological model of Urie Bronfenbrenner (1979) provides a theoretical foundation for counseling and case conceptualization which we incorporated in the T/C Model. Similar to social work's systemic perspective, counselors take into account the reciprocal relationships that exist at all levels of a client's environment, both immediate and distal. This traditional emphasis puts the field of counseling on the forefront of multicultural competence, and allows counselors to work effectively within complex systems.

At the same time, there is an emphasis on the importance of the client-counselor relationship and the use of developmental principles to understand client functioning (LaFleur, 2007) as well as a core belief in humanistic values. Counselors use a developmental perspective in their work with clients, interpreting challenges as a natural response to transitions and as a part of normal development. Humanistic philosophy laid the groundwork for the counseling profession, with a view of the person as a whole and the therapeutic relationship as crucial for change (Hansen, 2000). Nevertheless, counselors in many settings are expected to diagnose and develop interventions using the medical model of the DSM, resulting in a sometimes complex integration of opposing theories.

Thus, as a counselor, from the start of your work with Katy, you would likely assess her strengths as well as her current challenges. For example, Katy is clearly intelligent, and able to navigate the transition to college and become academically and socially successful there. Taking a biopsychosocial approach includes considering both Katy's physiological symptoms and the possibility of a family history of depression and anxiety, as well as contextual influences, such as her parents' and stepparents' difficulties. Cultural considerations include the impact of Katy's Korean background and the norms and values she learned from her family, the acculturation challenges her parents may have faced, and Katy's own negotiation of American and Korean beliefs. From a developmental perspective, how did Katy adapt to the demands of college, and how is the transition from college impacting her? The traditional counseling focus on vocational aspirations is also relevant as Katy struggles to decide what she wants to do next and how to integrate her interests with her parents' wishes. As a counselor working from a biopsychosocial perspective, an understanding of the various internal and external factors impacting Katy is the starting point for developing the sort of client-counselor relationship that can empower Katy to make positive changes in her own life. The T/C Model enables the counselor to conduct a comprehensive assessment and to organize the data in a way that makes sense, to both counselor and client.

Box 1.1 summarizes the differences in training, licensing, and philosophy for various mental health professions, including social workers, psychiatrists, psychologists, and counselors. Box 1.2 summarizes the various counseling specialties.

WHERE ARE WE NOW?

Professional counseling today retains a focus on development, prevention, client-environment interaction, and empowerment rather than a focus on curing disease. Counselors view mental health as a continuum, with the goal to help an individual move toward wellness and to empower clients to solve their own problems as they develop better coping skills and insight. Counselors understand that mental and emotional issues can be understood through a developmental perspective, and emphasize prevention and early intervention for at-risk populations (Remley & Herlihy, 2010).

Counselors possess unique skills and knowledge for promoting wellness, and view the assessment and treatment of mental health issues from a wellness perspective. At the same time, counselors understand that promoting mental health goes hand in hand with remediating psychopathology (Guerney, 1977; Van Hesteren & Ivey, 1990). Counselors, like professionals in the closely related mental health fields, need basic knowledge and skills in diagnosis and treatment of mental disorders, while retaining the preventive, developmental,

multidisciplinary approach that characterizes the field. In addition to their expertise in normal development and prevention, counselors need to be competent in diagnosing and treating mental health challenges, including DSM diagnosis, case conceptualization, psychopathology, and substance abuse (Smith, 2012).

All the mental health professions are increasingly recognizing the commonalities as well as the unique strengths of each profession. In the *Great Psychotherapy Debate: Models, Methods and Findings*, Wampold (2001) conducted a meta-analysis of outcome research and concluded that the "common factors" of counseling are the ingredients of change, not the specific ingredients of a particular treatment model. In subsequent chapters, we further explore the research on the elements of change. However, there remains concern about the feasibility of asking counselors to learn the entire spectrum of mental health and illness, while at the same time continuing to focus on prevention and gaining the expertise to use a developmental lens. Many researchers believe that a better and more thorough understanding of the DSM and diagnosis will strengthen the identity of professional counselors (Eriksen & Kress, 2006; Hansen, 2003; Spurgeon, 2012), and this text reflects that belief. Counselors help clients not just with issues amenable to short-term intervention, but those with more serious problems as well, which requires an understanding of evidence-based treatment protocol. Dealing effectively with pathology does not preclude the developmental focus for which counseling is known; in fact, an understanding of normal development and the impact of life transitions can enhance the effectiveness of treatment of many disorders. Counselors must be trained to understand pathology and mental illness, but utilize treatment strategies which incorporate a developmental and wellness perspective.

Counselors today help clients with a wide range of developmental and mental health issues, including career challenges, relationship issues, stress, trauma, addictions, grief and loss, and mental health disorders. Thus, there is a need to select evidence-based treatments in

BOX 1.1   Mental Health–Related Professions

Profession	Degree	Professional Association & License	Emphasis & Expertise	Work Environment
Social Work	Master's in Social Work (MSW) Internship	National Association of Social Work (NASW) Licensed in all 50 States	Enhance Social Functioning, Advocate for Social Change, Systems and Contextual Focus	Schools, Public Health Agencies, Community Agencies, and Substance Abuse Treatment Facilities
Psychiatry	Medical Degree (MD, DO) Residency	American Psychiatric Association Licensed in all 50 States	Biomedical Model or Biopsychosocial Model Specialization in Diagnosis, Treatment, and Prevention of Mental Illness Prescribes Medication	Private Practice, Health Agencies, Outpatient Treatment Centers, and Hospitals
Psychology	Doctoral Degree (PhD, EdD, PsyD) Internship	American Psychological Association (APA) Licensed in all 50 States	Assess, Diagnose, and Treat Mental and Emotional Distress May Specialize in Testing and Assessment	Private Practice, Hospitals, Health Agencies, Educational institutions, and Substance Abuse Treatment Facilities
Counseling	Master's or Doctorate Internship	American Counseling Association (ACA) Licensed in all 50 States	Wellness Model, Focus on Prevention, Developmental Focus, Biopsychosocial Perspective	Private Practice, Hospitals, Health Agencies, Educational Institutions, and Substance Abuse Treatment Facilities
Marriage and Family Therapist	Master's or Doctorate Internship	American Association of Marriage and Family Therapists (AAMFT)	Diagnose and Treat Parent-Child, Couple, and Individual Problems with a Systems Focus	Private Practice or Agencies

| BOX 1.2 | Counseling Specialties |

Specialty	Traditional Philosophy, Expertise, and Settings
Community counselor or more recently clinical mental health counselor	Effects of the community environment on individuals Empowerment of individuals as advocates Preventive and rehabilitative services Bioecological model (Bronfenbrenner) Agency settings
Mental health counselor or more recently clinical mental health counselor	Prevention, intervention, consultation, diagnosis, and treatment of mental disorders Agencies, inpatient, outpatient, and substance abuse facilities Employee assistance programs
School counselor (Certified by each state)	Prevention, intervention, consultation At-risk and special needs populations Advocacy Developmental focus Elementary, middle, high school
Addiction counselor	Diagnosis and treatment of substance abuse and addictions (gambling, internet, eating disorders) Substance abuse programs Employee assistance programs
Career counselor	Diagnosis and treatment of personal issues that influence career decisions Schools Higher education settings
College counselor	Counseling, advising, program development College and university settings
Gerontological counselor	Facilitate wellness and empower older individuals Substance abuse, bereavement, advocacy Community agencies, nursing homes
Marriage and family counselor	Family systems assessment and intervention Developmental perspective, working with life transitions Private practice, community agencies
Rehabilitation counselor	Assist and empower clients with disabilities Systems focus Advocacy rehabilitation centers, employee assistance programs, hospitals

order to determine what techniques work best for each individual client and counselor, taking into account both the presenting problem and the setting where treatment takes place. Counselors now use interventions developed by other mental health professions, and other professions have incorporated counseling's focus on normal development, prevention, and wellness.

WHERE ARE WE GOING? LOOKING TO THE FUTURE

In today's health care climate, counselors work in a variety of settings, and treat a range of emotional and behavioral issues. Mental health counselors, as defined by the United States Department of Labor, are a varied group of professionals that provide services to individuals, families, couples, and groups (Bureau of Labor Statistics, 2013). Many work with specific populations (the elderly, college students, children, etc.) or in specialized settings (drug and alcohol rehabilitation, inpatient facilities, community agencies, etc.). Mental health counselors treat a variety of clinical issues, such as anxiety, depression, grief, low self-esteem, stress, and drug abuse. Moreover, they help with mental and emotional health issues, and relationship problems. Counselors also work in employee assistance programs (EAPs), which are programs that some employers provide to help employees deal with personal or mental health problems. Licensed professional counselors can also work in private practice and collect third party reimbursements (Bureau of Labor Statistics, 2013). Mental health counselors comprised about 120,000 jobs in 2010 and in the next ten years, this number is expected to grow by 37% much faster than the average for all occupations (Bureau of Labor Statistics, 2013).

Insurance companies increasingly provide for reimbursement of counselors and marriage and family therapists as a less costly alternative to psychiatrists and psychologists. People seeking mental health treatment are more likely to see a mental health counselor or a marriage and family therapist over other providers. In addition, it is expected that the number of people seeking mental health services will continue to rise. This trend will cause an increase in the demand for professionally trained and licensed counselors in various settings (Bureau of Labor Statistics, 2013).

We can anticipate from our exploration of the history of the profession that the role of the professional counselor will continue to evolve and grow. As we look toward the future, counselors need to collaborate with other mental health professionals and rebuild relationships that may have been strained in the past as counselors fought to establish a distinct place for the profession among the established mental health providers. Debates have taken place over who is qualified to deliver and be reimbursed for testing and diagnostic services and who is not. In most states, counselors have been successful in establishing their competence in these areas, but the debate has left some bad feelings on all sides. In order to effectively help clients, a model of integrated service delivery is optimal. Counselors benefit from the expertise of related mental health professions, and treatment teams benefit from counselors' knowledge of development, prevention, wellness, and personal growth.

The distinctive way that counselors work within communities by using a strength-based approach and an expertise in human development becomes even more important in our increasingly interconnected world. The impact of managed care, the advent of technology, climate change, and natural disasters, the increase in man-made violence and conflict, from school shootings to terrorist attacks, all create a need for increased mental health services. In addition, growing populations of the elderly, military veterans, and families contribute to this need. Professional counselors are well positioned to meet the changing needs of society and promote healthy response to ongoing transitions.

BOX 1.3	Professional Organizations and Websites

American Counseling Association	www.counseling.org/
American Psychological Association	www.apa.org/
American Psychiatric Association	www.psych.org/
American School Counselor Association	www.schoolcounselor.org/
American Mental Health Counselors Association	www.amhca.org/
National Association of Social Workers	www.socialworkers.org/
American Association for Marriage and Family Therapy	www.aamft.org/
American College Counseling Association	www.collegecounseling.org/
American Rehabilitation Counseling Association	www.arcaweb.org/

BOX 1.4	Typical Duties for a Mental Health Counselor from the U.S. Department of Labor *Occupational Outlook Handbook (2013)*

- Diagnose and treat mental and emotional disorders, such as anxiety and depression
- Encourage clients to discuss their emotions and experiences
- Help clients process their reactions and adjust to changes in their lives, such as divorce or job layoffs
- Guide clients through the process of making decisions about their future
- Help clients develop strategies and skills to change their behavior or cope with difficult situations
- Coordinate treatment with other professionals, such as psychiatrists and social workers
- Refer clients to other resources or services in the community, such as support groups or inpatient treatment facilities

BOX 1.5	Industries With the Highest Percentage of Mental Health Counselors In 2010

Individual and family services	18%
Outpatient mental health and substance abuse centers	16%
Hospitals; state, local, and private	12%
State and local government, excluding education and hospitals	11%
Residential mental health and substance abuse facilities	10%

COUNSELING KEYSTONES

- Professional counseling is part of a wide range of mental health and human services professions, including psychiatrists, psychologists, social workers, marriage and family therapists, and pastoral counselors.
- While many people are "helpers," professional counselors are distinguished by viewing themselves as members of a unique profession, and embracing an identity as a professional.
- Professional identity encompasses membership in professional organizations, accreditation of training programs, adherence to ethical standards, and a common definition of the profession.
- Counseling differs from other mental health professions in its wellness focus, its emphasis on prevention, its holistic framework, and its application of human development principles to a wide range of client issues.
- Professional counseling today retains a focus on empowerment rather than curing disease, with the goal of helping individuals move toward wellness and solving their own problems as they develop better coping skills and insight.
- As we look toward the future, counselors need to collaborate with other mental health professionals, building strong relationships with other established mental health professions.

EXERCISES

EXERCISE 1.1 Where Do Problems Come From?

Mental health professionals all have beliefs about the basis of a client's problem and who is responsible for its resolution. How counselors view this attribution gives us insight into the professional beliefs they hold. Brickman and his colleagues came up with a theory of helping and coping that describes both the attribution of responsibility for the problem as well as the attribution of responsibility for the solution (Brickman et al., 1982):

Moral Model: Clients are responsible for their problems as well as their solutions.

Compensatory Model: Clients are not blamed for their problems, but are responsible for finding and implementing a solution.

Medical Model: Clients are responsible neither for the origin of their problems nor for finding solutions.

Enlightenment Model: Clients are not blamed for their problems, but they do have the ultimate responsibility for finding and implementing a solution.

CLASS EXERCISE: Students answer questions individually followed by large group discussion.

Question 1: Which modality do you feel best fits your beliefs? Why?

Question 2: Below is a list of value statements. First, decide what you personally feel about the statement, and then decide which of the above modalities it most closely reflects.

- People are responsible for their own problems.
- Clients are the experts in their own lives.
- Many difficulties are out of our control.
- The causes of most people's problems are external in nature.
- I believe in the saying "physician heal thyself."
- Everyone has internal resources and strengths that they can pull from.
- You can't direct the wind, but you can adjust your sails.
- Fools think their own way is right, but the wise listen to the advice of others.
- Success takes time. Success takes desire. Success takes action. Success takes commitment.

EXERCISE 1.2 What Sets Counseling Apart?

Below is a list of counseling philosophy statements.

The counseling philosophy

- takes a holistic approach;
- is concerned with the integration of the mind, body, and spirit;
- comes from a developmental approach;
- believes in client empowerment;
- is grounded in advocacy for clients;

- believes that the client has to be active in their own treatment; and
- focuses on strengths, not just problems.

CLASS EXERCISE: In small groups, discuss each of the statements and how a counselor's viewpoint might be different from that of a psychiatrist, psychologist, or a social worker. Using the case of Katy, identify examples of differences in focus and emphasis that a counselor would use to help, compared to the other three professions.

EXERCISE 1.3 How Do We Compare to Other Mental Health Professionals?

Below are definitions of counseling, clinical psychology, and clinical social work developed by some of the primary professional organizations.

Definition of Counseling

The ACA agreed on a unified definition of counseling at their annual conference in 2010. It states that "Counseling is a professional relationship that empowers diverse individuals, families, and groups to accomplish mental health, wellness, education, and career goals." The delegates made it clear that the definition was a basic framework and that each participating organization (or division) was welcome to add a statement that fleshes out the particular specialty or area of focus (ACA, 2010).

Definition of Clinical Psychology

Clinical Psychology is both a general practice and a health service provider specialty in professional psychology. Clinical Psychologists provide professional services relating to the diagnosis, assessment, evaluation, treatment, and prevention of psychological, emotional, psychophysiological, and behavioral disorders in individuals across the lifespan. These services include procedures for understanding, predicting, and alleviating intellectual, emotional, physical, psychological, social, and behavioral maladjustment, and mental illness, as well as other forms of discomfort. In addition, it includes services for the enhancement of functioning in all of these areas (American Psychological Association, 2013).

Definition of Social Work

Graduates of schools of social work (in the United States, hold either a bachelor's, master's, or doctoral degree) who use their knowledge and skills to provide social services for clients (who may be individuals, families, groups, communities, organizations, or society in general). Social workers help people increase their capacities for problem solving and coping, and obtain needed resources, facilitate interactions between individuals and between people and their environments, make organizations responsible to people, and influence social policies. Social workers may work directly with clients addressing individual, family, and community issues, or they may work at a systems level on regulations and policy development, or as administrators and planners of large social service systems (Barker, 2003).

CLASS EXERCISE: Large group discussion.

Question 1: What are some of the differences between the professions? Similarities?

Question 2: Which definition do you feel best fits how you would like to practice as a professional?

EXERCISE 1.4 What Would You Choose?

Box 1.3 shows the websites of some of the largest professional organizations in the helping professions.

CLASS EXERCISE: Students take a few minutes to navigate each website. Followed by small group discussions.

Question: What do you think each organization views as important?

EXERCISE 1.5 Back to the Case of Katy

Practicing as a professional counselor is both different from and similar to the ways in which other helping professionals seek to assist clients. Now that you have a clear understanding of our common roots, as well as the ways in which the various professions have diverged over time, let's return to the case of Katy. In subsequent chapters, we apply the T/C Model in order to develop a case conceptualization for Katy. For now, let's think about where you might want to begin.

CLASS EXERCISE: Small group discussion followed by large group discussion.

Question 1: As a counselor, where would you want to start in order help her?

Question 2: What aspects of her history and current issues would you focus on?

GO FURTHER

Diagnostic and Statistical Manual of Mental Disorders (5th ed.) by American Psychiatric Association (2013) American Psychiatric

ACA Code of Ethics at counseling.org/ethics

2

WHAT MAKES COUNSELING WORK?

INTRODUCTION

In Chapter 1, we explored the history of counseling and the state of the profession today. Over the past decades, counseling has developed as a profession and established a unique professional identity. As counselors, we understand our common roots with the other helping professions as well as those attributes which make counselors unique. Counselors share with related professions the goal of facilitating healthy development and helping those with mental or emotional health challenges.

In this chapter, we examine some of the attributes which allow counselors to be competent and effective helpers, highlighting relevant research in this area. Some of these skills and dispositions should be familiar to you from a Counseling Fundamentals course. We review the attributes of effective counselors because each attribute is essential to the process of case conceptualization, as well as to the treatment decisions carried out through the counseling relationship. It is the intentional application of these skills and dispositions which enable effective counseling and facilitate change.

Counseling has been called both an art and a craft, incorporating components of each. There is consensus among researchers that a competent counselor needs to possess certain skills, including the ability to establish relationships, effective interpersonal communication, and the capacity for self-awareness. Such skills can be learned and practiced, but it is the counselor's self-awareness, intentionality, and commitment to understanding the client which ultimately determines his or her effectiveness (Inskipp, 2006). In this chapter, we break down the components of effective counseling: we examine personal characteristics of effective counselors; the ingredients of a healthy helping relationship; and client variables which impact counseling progress. To help you explore your own strengths and areas for improvement, practical exercises are provided to increase your self-awareness and ability to develop those attributes which will allow you to be a successful counselor.

There has been a great deal of research over the past forty years in an effort to identify the specific factors that contribute to positive outcomes for clients. For the past two decades, much of that research has been on "empirically supported treatments" in an attempt to identify which interventions work best for which specific mental health issues. Yet, a consistent finding is that there are universal aspects of the counseling process that are related to client outcome, no matter what the specific modalities, treatments, and client populations. Certain attributes, attitudes, and skills of the counselor play a major role; for example, effective counselors have a positive, accepting view of their clients (Young, 2005) and are committed to their own growth, development, and self-awareness. At the same time, knowledge about counseling theory and proficiency with basic counseling strategies also contribute to successful outcomes. Counselors are most effective when they purposefully and ethically integrate certain personal attributes that are discussed below with knowledge and professional competencies.

There is evidence that a variety of treatment approaches are of approximately equal effectiveness for a number of disorders, including depression (Wampold, Minami, Baskin, & Tierney, 2002), posttraumatic stress disorder or PTSD (Powers, Halpern, Ferenschak, Gillihan, & Foa, 2010), and substance abuse (Imel, Wampold, Miller, & Fleming, 2008). It should be noted that some studies interpret the evidence differently, suggesting that some treatment approaches are more effective than others (Clark, Fairburn, & Wessely, 2007; Ehlers et al., 2010). However, the majority of researchers believe that if there are differences, these differences are quite small (Wampold, 2010).

One of the most robust research findings is the importance of the therapeutic relationship itself (Lutz, Leon, Martinovich, Lyons, & Stiles, 2007; Wampold, 2006). In fact, research suggests that empirically validated treatments may not be effective unless they are carried out within the context of a healthy helping relationship. Virtually all treatment approaches to counseling hold that therapist variables, such as warmth, empathy, genuineness, and positive regard, are necessary for client growth and change (Lambert & Ogles, 2004).

Unlike many professions, the counselor as a person is an important variable in determining successful treatment outcomes. This is both an opportunity and a significant pressure, particularly for beginning counselors—YOU are an integral part of the equation.

PERSONAL CHARACTERISTICS OF THE EFFECTIVE COUNSELOR

Certain individual qualities of the counselor have been identified in research studies as important components to a positive counseling outcome (Duncan, Miller, Hubble, & Wampold, 2010; McAuliffe & Lovell, 2006; Norcross, 2011; Wampold, 2007). These include curiosity and inquisitiveness and some degree of comfort with emotional intimacy. The capacity for spontaneity and a sense of timing are also helpful (Wilcox-Matthew, Ottens, & Minor, 1997), and a sense of humor goes a long way.

Effective counselors possess the ability to listen and the capacity for empathy, which allows the client to feel understood and believe that the counselor can be helpful to them. The therapeutic alliance is critical to clients' ability to change and requires both the establishment of trust and a collaborative agreement about the goals of counseling. The counselor's purposefulness, stability, and constancy facilitate the bond between counselor and client (Patterson & Welfel, 2005).

Clients who are in distress are looking for an explanation for their suffering, so the counselor's ability to provide an explanation that the client can hear and accept is also important (Wampold, 2007). When counselors achieve a balance of interpersonal and technical competence (including an openness to their own experience, the capacity for emotional insight, and intellectual competence), they are able to help clients achieve better outcomes (Cormier & Cormier, 1998).

While working collaboratively, effective counselors are also comfortable with power (Gladding, 2009) and have the ability to be persuasive, which facilitates client enactment of beneficial change. At the same time, counselors must also have the ability to be flexible, adjusting the goals and course of counseling to take into account client readiness for change, resistance, and external barriers to change. Counselors who are not overly concerned about being "wrong" and thus willing to rethink hypotheses and strategies are more likely to be effective in helping their clients. Effective counselors are constantly looking for ways to improve their own skills, and comfortable with asking for client feedback.

The counselor's willingness and ability to gain insight from his or her own struggles (that is, to be a reflective counselor) and apply that insight to understanding clients are also related to effectiveness. For instance, a counselor who has experienced their own struggles with becoming independent from parents and has learned from that experience might apply that understanding to Katy's situation, with greater empathy and insight.

Working effectively with each client calls forth different counselor characteristics. For example, in the first session with Katy, she presents as agitated, speaking quickly and jumping from topic to topic. She insists her situation is hopeless, and wrings her hands as she talks, barely giving you time to ask questions or provide reassurance. In this type of first session, a counselor with the ability to listen is more effective than one who interrupts or cuts the client off. Similarly, if the counselor sets aside his or her own needs (perhaps to be in control of the session or with a strong need to rescue or "cheer a client up") and instead pays attention to Katy's need to be heard, the therapeutic relationship has a better start.

Such an extensive list of qualities can seem daunting, and no individual possesses every attribute. On the other hand, the research data provides the basis for goals in counselor education and training programs, and gives individual counselors a focus for aspiration. Self-awareness is a component of all accredited training programs, and counselors strive for greater awareness throughout their careers through continuing education, consultation, and peer supervision. It may be helpful at this time of your training to assess both your strengths and weaknesses in regard to the above attributes.

THE THERAPEUTIC ALLIANCE

Who the counselor is as a person is important to the success of the process, because the counselor is one side of the therapeutic relationship and the quality of the helping relationship is the foundation underlying effective counseling practice. Across diverse treatment modalities, the strength of the helping relationship has been found to be the strongest and most consistent predictor of client outcome (Castonguay, Constantino, McAleavey, & Goldfried, 2010; Friedlander, Escudero, Heatherington, & Diamond, 2011; Horvath & Bedi, 2002; Horvath, Del Re, Fluckiger, & Symonds, 2011; Orlinsky, Rønnestad, & Willutzki, 2004). Meta-analyses of empirical studies in both child and adult populations have shown a consistent association between therapeutic alliance and client outcome (Martin, Garske, & Davis, 2000; Shirk & Karver, 2003). Research also shows the consistency of the impact of the alliance across different treatment modalities (Krupnick et al., 1996). In fact, differences in counselor effectiveness may be largely due to their ability to form a strong therapeutic alliance with their clients (Crits-Christoph et al., 2009; Elvins & Green, 2008).

The power of the relationship itself may lie in its potential for healing. Virtually all cultures identify "healers" who help restore individuals to a state of being whole (Comas-Diaz, 2006). Clients move toward wholeness and integration by interacting with the counselor and experience a sense of healing through that relationship. When the counselor interacts with the client with warmth and genuineness, and works to understand the meaning of the client's life through the client's own eyes, then the relationship creates the conditions for change (Yalom, 1980).

There is a significant body of research devoted to the importance of the helping relationship. A large-scale study from the Division 29 Task Force on Empirically Supported Therapy Relationships of the American Psychological Association investigated which relationship variables are evidence based (Norcross, 2002a, 2011). The dual aims of the Task Force were to identify what works in a therapeutic relationship, and to identify what works for particular clients and problems. This large-scale study was the logical follow-up to a 1999 Task Force which identified empirically supported treatments. The Task Force found that counselor empathy is crucial to client outcome. Positive regard, congruence, quality of the working alliance, goal consensus and collaboration, and the counselor's ability to manage therapy ruptures and countertransference also had empirical support (Norcross & Lambert, 2011a). A meta-analytic study of the importance of the therapeutic relationship in counseling children and adolescents also found that the best predictors of outcome were relationship-based, including the interpersonal skills of the client and the counselor's direct influencing skills (Karver, Handelsman, Fields, & Bickman, 2006). Because children and adolescents are less likely to be self-referred, a strong helping relationship can be crucial in managing resistance when working with these age groups (Shirk & Karver, 2003). Extratherapeutic variables, such as child and parent willingness to participate in treatment, were also related to outcome; while child and parent motivation for change are ideal, inevitably all counselors will encounter resistance. Cultivating strong interpersonal skills in order to establish a healthy working relationship increases the client's trust in the counselor and engagement in the process.

A healthy working alliance is a collaborative relationship. An affective bond has been established between client and counselor, characterized by negotiation in working toward mutually agreed on goals (Martin et al., 2000). All theories and modalities of counseling recognize the importance of the working alliance in counseling effectiveness, regardless of discipline, type of intervention, or diagnosis. An effective working alliance is created early in treatment, through the counselor's warmth, sense of collaboration, and lack of judgment (Horvath & Bedi, 2002).

In order to form a healthy working alliance with Katy, a counselor needs to spend some time listening to her story. Katy has not had many people in her life want to listen, so a counselor conveying that he or she wants to hear her story—the way she herself sees it—can be a powerful foundation for their relationship. The basic skills of listening, reflecting, and encouraging Katy can be ways of both gaining helpful information and

of helping Katy to see herself as someone whose perspective is important.

Katy's counselor, for example, might listen to her for a while without interrupting, nodding to show that they are following along, or providing brief prompts or questions to encourage her to keep going from time to time. The counselor's reflection might be: "It sounds like you've had to navigate some difficult transitions in your life, starting from the time you were quite little. Tell me more about how you've managed to do that and be so successful in college." With only a few sentences, this counselor conveys warmth, lack of judgment, and an appreciation for Katy's resilience and strength.

It's important to note that it is the *client's* view of the helping relationship which is a significant predictor of outcome (Harmon, Hawkins, Lambert, Slade, & Whipple, 2005). Thus, it is important throughout the course of treatment to ask the client for input on the relationship and progress in general. Several studies highlight the importance of evaluating the working alliance periodically throughout the course of counseling. A strong working alliance is established when clients feel understood, validated, optimistic about change, and trust the counselor. The alliance varies in strength and intensity as counseling progresses. There will be times when the counselor fails to understand the client, as well as times when the client experiences resistance to insight, both of which impact the alliance. When counselors get regular feedback from clients, outcomes tend to be significantly better (Miller, Duncan, Sorrell, & Brown, 2005).

FACILITATIVE CONDITIONS WHICH SUPPORT THE HELPING RELATIONSHIP

The therapeutic bond is supported by identified facilitative conditions that allow a strong and effective helping relationship. Decades of research identify several components of the helping relationship that are consistently related to positive client outcomes. The groundbreaking research of Carl Rogers (1957, 1995) identified conditions for therapeutic change; conditions which Stiles (2006) described as, (a) be yourself; (b) trust the client; and (c) listen. Counselors need to be open to their own experience and the client's in order to create an environment of trust where the client feels supported toward change.

When the counselor can display qualities such as empathy, genuineness, and positive regard, and can communicate these qualities to their clients, counseling is more effective. Rogers stressed that it is not enough that these conditions are present; they must also be communicated to and perceived by the client (Rogers, 1951, 1957). Paulson, Truscott, and Stuart (1999) found that clients report these facilitative conditions to be the most helpful components of counseling.

Empathy

Empathy is the most studied facilitative condition, which is defined as the ability to understand another person's point of view from their perspective rather than our own—to stand in someone else's shoes. Rogers (1957) described empathy as being able to sense the client's private world as if it were your own, but without ever losing the "as if" quality. There is empirical support for empathy as an effective element of the helping relationship (Elliott, Bohart, Watson, & Greenberg, 2011; Norcross, 2002b, 2011).

The capacity for empathy begins in childhood and is facilitated by neurological underpinnings, including the existence of mirror neurons in the brain that allow us to mirror the emotions and physiological responses of another person (Siegel, 2006). We experience the bodily sensations and emotional reactions of the other person, allowing us to resonate with their life experience. In a counseling relationship, this allows the counselor to "get it," or to understand where the client is coming from. As a result, the client feels understood and validated, which lays the groundwork for change. The various theoretical models have somewhat different definitions of empathy. Rogers viewed empathy as laying the groundwork for the client to actualize and express their real self, which had been damaged

or repressed by the client's life experience. In contrast, Kohut's self-psychology views empathy as the foundation for corrective emotional experience that allows a client to begin the process of building a coherent self; a developmental process that in some clients has been cut off by trauma (Kohut, 1971). When caregivers do not meet a young child's needs for validation and mirroring, children grow up without a coherent, genuine sense of self; instead, the child creates a false self to please the caregivers, splitting off the true self and authentic emotions that allow people to relate to others in a genuine way (Teyber, 2006). When counselors work with these clients, empathy provides a "corrective emotional experience," where the counselor validates the client's genuine feelings and gradual expression of the true self. The counselor creates a "holding environment" (Winnicott, 1958) with appropriate boundaries and limits, conveying a genuine understanding and acceptance of the client's felt emotional experience. This allows the client to begin to experience their own emotions in a safe environment.

Genuineness

Also called congruence, the facilitative condition of genuineness refers to the counselor's ability to express their own real self or to "be real." The counselor is somewhat transparent, interacting with the client without playing a role or taking refuge in a facade. There is a close match between what the counselor experiences as a gut feeling (i.e., what the counselor is consciously aware of), and what the counselor communicates to the client. Counselors who take the time to explore their own values and beliefs are more likely to demonstrate consistency between their words and actions, and less likely to impose their beliefs on their clients. Congruence has also been found to be an important ingredient of an effective helping relationship (Kolden, Klein, Wang, & Austin, 2011).

Again, it is not enough for the counselor to feel a sense of genuineness; that sense must also be communicated to the client. Effective counselors express congruence with nonverbal behaviors, such as eye contact, leaning toward the client, or mirroring the client's physical position and expression. Being genuine involves a sense of comfort with oneself, which allows the counselor to avoid emphasizing the hierarchical relationship inherent in counseling. There are cultural differences in clients' response to counselors as authority figures, but in general too much emphasis on the counselor's position of power can intimidate clients. Being genuine requires the self-awareness to recognize when one's emotions and behaviors are inconsistent, and to acknowledge and explore this incongruence. Genuineness also includes the capacity for spontaneous and unrehearsed expression with the caveat that not everything a counselor thinks or feels should be communicated to the client.

Genuineness can be conveyed by the counselor's verbal or nonverbal encouragers. For example, remember when the counselor working with Katy mentioned the difficult transitions that she has navigated in her life and asked how she managed to do that? This language would only be effective if the counselor was convinced of Katy's resilience. Otherwise, the words would be hollow, a quality easily recognized by clients.

Positive Regard

The ability to value and respect the client as a person with worth and dignity is referred to as positive regard (Rogers, 1957). Holding the client in positive regard is another facilitating factor that establishes and maintains the helping relationship, according to recent research (Farber & Doolin, 2011; Farber & Lane, 2002). Rogers referred to this as "prizing" the client: allowing the client to feel whatever emotion is happening for them and to be in the moment with that emotion—confusion, resentment, fear, love, anger, pride (Rogers, 1957). According to Egan (2007), counselors convey respect for their

clients through various affective and behavioral strategies, including a sense of commitment (ensuring confidentiality, keeping appointments, preserving the client's time for their exclusive use) and ensuring their own competence (through supervision, consultation, and continuing education). Clients feel respected when counselors work hard to understand them, asking appropriate questions and communicating their understanding.

Positive regard can be compromised by counselors who have judgmental attitudes toward their clients. Conversely, expressing warmth with verbal affirmations, eye contact, welcoming gestures or touch, and soft tone of voice allows the client to feel respected and to connect interpersonally with the counselor (Johnson, 2006). Without warmth and positive regard, counselors can use the best empirically supported treatments yet still not have successful outcomes (Goldstein & Higginbotham, 1991).

For example, a different counselor working with Katy began the initial session by interrupting Katy after she had blurted out a few sentences. "Before you tell me about that, let me ask you about symptoms. Are you experiencing headaches?" The interruption and lack of validation for what Katy just shared does not convey warmth or positive regard. Similarly, a raised eyebrow or skeptical expression after a client divulges something painful also conveys a judgmental attitude without the use of words.

As counselors go through the process of case conceptualization, the underlying expression of empathy, genuineness, and positive regard facilitate trust and establish the working alliance which are crucial to understanding and helping clients.

Trust

Trust is also considered a "core trait" in an effective helping relationship (Levitt, Butler, & Hill, 2006). The process of establishing trust takes time for clients, and takes effort for counselors. Clients begin to trust counselors through respectful, nonjudgmental interactions; each time the client takes a risk and divulges something previously split off or suppressed and the counselor reacts with acceptance and validation, the client comes to trust the counselor a bit more. While trust takes time to establish, unfortunately it can be destroyed much faster if counselors impose their own agendas on clients, are critical, or fail to work at understanding the client's worldview. Clients who have experienced trauma are understandably slow to trust, and need evidence that they can be vulnerable and self-disclosing in counseling without being exploited (Johnson, 2006). Often clients 'test' the counselor to determine whether the counselor is trustworthy; negotiating these tests can either facilitate a stronger working alliance, or interfere with the development of trust (Fong & Cox, 1983).

As Katy's counselor, listening to her story with acceptance would facilitate trust. On the other hand, failing to consider and ask about the impact of Katy's cultural background and family expectations could jeopardize a trusting relationship. If Katy believes her counselor does not care enough to understand her, and thus does not "get" her, she will be less likely to trust that the counselor can help her solve her problems.

TRANSFERENCE AND COUNTERTRANSFERENCE

Both the counselor and the client experience challenges to emotional intensity and objectivity during the course of treatment, often related to unfinished business with significant relationships in the past. In addition to establishing facilitative conditions for counseling and a strong working alliance, negotiating these challenges competently is related to positive client outcome (Horvath & Bedi, 2002). Transference and countertransference are derived from psychoanalytic theory, but most theoretical models recognize the impact our past relationships have on our present. Relational models describe these ideas as "dysfunctional relational schemas" (Ornstein & Ganzer, 2005).

Transference refers to the impact of the client's past relationships on the client's emotions, fantasies, and reactions in the present. Ornstein and Ganzer (2005) describe this as the "here and now experience of the client with the therapist who has a role in eliciting and shaping the transference" (p. 567). The client reacts to the counselor unconsciously as if they are reacting to a significant person from their past, whether parents, caregivers, siblings, friends, or anyone who might have significantly impacted the individual. In other words, the client reenacts their past relationships through their relationship with the counselor. Unmet needs, longstanding wishes, and old hurts are projected onto the counselor (Kohut, 1984). By helping the client to develop insight about patterns of relating and the influence of past relationships, and by validating the client's wishes and needs (without necessarily fulfilling them), counselors can make use of transference.

Countertransference refers to the counselor's unconscious reactions to the client, which may be realistic or related to the counselor's past, and can be either useful or damaging (Kahn, 1991). If the counselor is aware of their countertransference reactions, the information can be helpful in understanding the client better. However, if the counselor is unaware, their own emotions and issues can get in the way of focusing on the client, can allow the counselor's needs to take precedence, or can result in the counselor playing out the role projected onto them by the client. Negative countertransference reactions, such as the counselor feeling disappointed by the client or irritated by the client are associated with client deterioration (Mohr, 1995).

Gelso and Hayes (2002) recommend that counselors pay attention to their emotional responses that are unexpected or out of proportion to what the client discloses. Counselors should keep an ongoing focus on what is occurring here and now in the counseling session. Setting appropriate boundaries allows the counselor to empathically respond to the client without becoming overwhelmed by their own affect.

Case example: In their fourth week of working together, Katy pauses as she's opening the door to leave her session with her 45-year-old female counselor. "Oh, I forgot to mention, I slept with a guy at that party too. Don't remember his name—I had a few drinks. Well, I guess more than a few." The counselor who is able to step back and think about her own reaction to this unexpected remark can hypothesize that this might be an instance of transference. Perhaps Katy is playing out her customary way of getting attention from her mother, who is about the same age as the counselor. This insight can be helpful in understanding the client better, and eventually helping Katy develop insight as well.

Later in their work together, the counselor finds herself urging Katy to enroll in a graduate program instead of taking a job with her stepfather's company. However, the counselor notices that her reaction is unexpectedly strong. She subsequently realizes that she is reacting to Katy as though Katy were her own daughter (who is currently depressed and stuck in a job she hates). Recognizing this as countertransference, the counselor can again step back and help Katy make her own choices.

RELATIONSHIP RUPTURES

While establishing an effective helping relationship is important, inevitably ruptures in that relationship occur. Disagreement about goal setting, cross-cultural misunderstandings, and enactment of transference and countertransference themes can all contribute to ruptures (Safran & Muran, 2006; Safran, Muran, Wallner Samstag, & Stevens, 2002). Counselors can be pulled into clients' transference themes if they are not aware of their own susceptibility, resulting in a rupture. The strength of the working alliance fluctuates when counselors have difficulty understanding their clients, make mistakes, or when clients experience resistance to insight, or previously hidden negative emotions begin to emerge during the course of treatment (Stiles, 2006). Subtle or overt rejections by the counselor are particularly damaging to the helping relationship (Safran, Muran, Samstang & Winston, 2005).

The relationship can be repaired, once the counselor is aware and hopefully with greater understanding on the part of both the counselor and client. Safran and Muran (2006) emphasize that the counselor's acknowledgment of the part they played in the rupture can go a long way toward making the experience of repair a healing one.

COUNSELOR SELF-AWARENESS

It should be clear from our discussion so far that self-awareness is a critical skill for counselors. Self-awareness refers to the counselor's openness to their own emotions, attitudes, and values and the impact these have on their clients. Counseling effectiveness depends not only on the counselor being able to communicate understanding to the client, but on how aware the counselor is of what's going on inside of them, what they imagine is going on inside the client, and whether they can reflect on their own internal processes. Such "inside skills" are often not specifically taught, but are critical to the counseling outcome (Inskipp, 2006). Rogers (1957) emphasized the importance of making "psychological contact" with clients, which requires awareness of the counselor's own feelings, sensations, and perceptions while interacting with a client.

Counselors are only able to use themselves as vehicles of change if they continually engage in the process of self-understanding, including being aware of their human vulnerability to being hurt and their own resulting defenses. Self-awareness allows counselors to view their own needs and emotions as separate from those of their clients by continually questioning their own responses during counseling. Asking "why am I feeling like this?" or "what's really going on here?" can help counselors avoid over-identification, or projecting their own feelings and perceptions onto the client.

In order to be effective, counselors need to remain attuned to their own emotions and true to themselves, aware of both what is occurring in the present and the impact of what has happened in the past. Such an attunement helps counselors avoid projecting their own unresolved emotions, fears, and inadequacies on their clients. Self-awareness also contributes to a counselor's ability to be open-minded, and to approach their own lives as well as their clients' lives with curiosity and flexibility.

MULTICULTURAL COMPETENCE

An important component of self-awareness is an understanding of the counselor's own cultural values, perceptions, and beliefs and the ways in which they differ from those of their clients. Multicultural counseling emphasizes the counselor's awareness of their own assumptions, values, and biases and the necessity of developing culturally relevant case conceptualizations and treatment plans. Recognizing differences of gender, race, sexual orientation, class, ethnicity, and ability is critical to understanding clients. Counselors who have examined their own values and beliefs are more comfortable with clients who hold different beliefs, and thus better able to help clients from diverse backgrounds.

Sue and colleagues developed a framework for multicultural competence for counselors in 1982 (Sue, Bernier, Durran, Feinberg, Pedersen, Smith, & Vasquez-Nuttall, 1982). Since that time, the counseling field has recognized that clients live within and are continually impacted by multiple environmental systems and contextual influences. There is evidence that multicultural competence is at the core of effective counseling. Coleman (1998) found that culturally neutral counseling does not exist, and that the essence of all effective counseling was the counselor's ability to respond to cultural nuances in the therapeutic relationship, concluding that an understanding of the context in which the client's problems developed is a crucial component of effective counseling.

Further, counselors must demonstrate this understanding and appreciation to the client in order for the client to feel that their entire experience is validated. Sociopolitical factors, cultural oppression, and issues of social justice around race, gender, sexual orientation, and disability have an impact on all of us, and each individual client is affected in a unique way. A recognition of the importance of understanding the context of a client's life is a basic underpinning of counseling with a multicultural focus.

In some way, virtually all counseling relationships are "cross-cultural" and what makes for effective counseling varies from culture to culture. Clients from Eastern cultures may benefit more from a counselor who is an authority figure, and less from the nondirective approach that may be expected by clients from Western cultures. Clients from collectivist societies are proficient at nonverbal communication and subtle contextual cues, and may benefit less from a direct and explicit counseling style (Comas-Diaz, 2006). Traditional Western models of counseling tend to focus on client's self-actualization and modifying current behaviors, newer models of multicultural counseling emphasize the client's awareness of sociopolitical influences and aim to foster the client's empowerment and "psychological liberation" (Duran, Firehammer, & Gonzalez, 2008). Research by Sue and colleagues (2007) found that counselors may inadvertently commit subtle verbal and nonverbal derogatory comments and slights that are often based on differences in race, sexual orientation, disability, or gender. These "microaggressions" can damage the helping relationship, particularly if counselors are unaware that they have exhibited racism or prejudice. Some microaggressions result from counselor misunderstanding of the many subtle and nuanced differences in language, style, customs, and values between cultures. In some cultures, for example, eye contact is considered disrespectful instead of viewed as evidence of warmth and connection (Sue & Sue, 2003).

Counselors should be knowledgeable about various cultures, aware of their own cultural heritage, and develop the capacity to value diversity. It is impossible for a counselor to experience every event in the lives of their clients, but being able to understand and respect the client's world is necessary. There is increasing recognition within the counseling field that traditional counseling theories were developed based on White, male, middle-class Euro-centric values and perspectives, which limit their usefulness. Awareness of what is appropriate within a client's particular culture is crucial. There are many kinds of family structures and child-rearing practices, and counselors must be careful to distinguish between what is cultural custom and what is problematic, especially when the counselor is coming from a Euro-American background (Helms & Cook, 1999).

Even when counselors work to understand these differences, their understanding is sometimes limited to the cognitive level, which can adversely impact effective empathy (Ridley & Lingle, 1996). When working with clients from different cultural backgrounds, the counselor must recognize and validate the very real sociopolitical factors impacting the client's life experience (Comas-Diaz, 2006). Non-dominant groups may have vastly different life experiences than a counselor from the dominant culture.

Effective counseling also requires understanding of the impact of oppression, discrimination, stigma, marginalizing, and other forms of injustice (Arredondo & Perez, 2003). Counselor education programs increasingly recognize the need to help students develop a more comprehensive perspective on the external factors that contribute to clients seeking help. The T/C Model (discussed in detail in Chapter 3) facilitates such a comprehensive perspective by prompting students to assess for sociocultural factors as well as intrapsychic and relational contributors to client issues.

Predictably, clients have difficulty trusting a counselor who invalidates their experience, conveys subtle insults, or simply misunderstands their culture. Sue and colleagues believe that a counselor's willingness to discuss differences like race is critical to establishing a strong working alliance. Ivey, Gluckstern, and Ivey (1993) expand the concept of empathy to "cultural empathy." Counselors must not only understand the individual worldview of their client, but the cultural worldview as well. The sociopolitical,

cultural, and ethnic background of a client informs the way they see the world. Clients with a history of oppression, prejudice, and discrimination do not expect the counselor to understand them; consequently, empathy, and validation are especially important when working with these clients (Teyber, 2006).

Some clients from non-dominant racial backgrounds have been found to have an overly positive reaction to counselors from the dominant culture, simply because the client has not had any positive cross-racial interactions prior to entering counseling (Helms & Cook, 1999). Conversely, clients from minority groups may begin from a standpoint of mistrust, since their previous life experiences may have provided many reasons for that mistrust. The counselor must earn the client's trust over time, providing alternative experiences of risk taking, disclosure, and validation. As noted by Helms and Cook (1999), transference also is not solely tied to a client's past relationships, but also to their racial and cultural history. Racial-cultural transference occurs when the client reacts to the counselor as they reacted to members of the counselor's racial-ethnic group in the past. Counselors must also examine their own reactions, being aware of countertransference issues.

When working with clients from marginalized groups, an emphasis on empowerment and egalitarian decision making is important. Counselors who make unilateral decisions for the client can be particularly damaging to a client's ability to trust when the client comes from a disempowered or oppressed group. Clients with diverse backgrounds may tend to be self-protective and reticent to trust and may engage in more tests of trust in order to feel safe in what is an inherently unequal relationship (Sue & Sue, 2003). When counselors do not give weight to the client's sociopolitical context and history of oppression, trust is difficult to establish. For example, a counselor working with Katy who is unfamiliar with Korean culture may hold stereotypes, both positive and negative, about what it means to be Korean-American. Counselors who are aware of their own cultural backgrounds and the limitations of their own cultural lenses, and who retain curiosity about the client's culture, are more successful in developing a case conceptualization which takes cultural influences into account. Assuming either similarities or differences can be problematic, as every client and every client's family is unique.

Multicultural counseling and lesbian, gay, and bisexual (LGB) counseling developed in parallel, but have recently been considered as complementary in recognition of the intersection of LGB and multicultural concerns. Counselors should be aware that racial and ethnic minorities and sexual minorities may share experiences of discrimination, stereotyping, and oppression, as well as unique processes of identity development (Cass, 1979; Zubernis, Snyder, & McCoy, 2011). In addition, the importance of examining one's own biases and stereotypes is equally important when working with LGB individuals.

Research suggests some additional competencies and knowledge in order to work effectively with sexual minority clients. For example, counselors working with LGB clients must have an even greater knowledge of community support resources, since these clients (unlike ethnic minority clients) have usually not been raised in families which share their sexual minority status (Garnets, Hancock, Cochran, Goodchilds, & Peplau, 1991). Researchers also encourage counselors to challenge binary ideas of gender and sexual orientation in order to understand the fluidity and multiple dimensions of these concepts (Dworkin, 2000; Fox, 2000). When working with clients from any minority group, counselors should be vigilant regarding bias in test instruments as the bias may be quite subtle for sexual minority clients—heterosexist language is contained in many assessment instruments. Since sexual minorities are an "invisible minority," counselors should pay attention to their own language to avoid heterosexist bias, as well as be attentive to the messages in books and materials in the office (Buhrke & Douce, 1991).

A multicultural counseling perspective also encompasses an understanding of the impact of disability, which has been a focus of rehabilitation counselors for decades. Physical, mental, developmental, emotional, and cognitive disabilities impact clients' careers, relationships, and identity development. Just as clients from racial, ethnic, cultural, and sexual minorities face issues of discrimination, stigma, prejudice, and oppression, clients with disabilities also are impacted by these and other psychological and sociopolitical forces. Empowerment is a crucial component when working with clients with disabilities, since a medical model of treatment and mobility issues may have restricted clients' agency and independence. Counselors should keep in mind that some disabilities are "invisible" as well, and there may be a significant amount of shame associated with disclosing disability status. Self-awareness for counselors includes the need to view clients with disabilities as individuals, instead of seeing only the disability (Shallcross, 2011).

Finally, a competent counselor does not lose sight of the fact that what constitutes "normal" is defined by societal and cultural contexts. Different cultures problematize different symptoms, and a specific disorder may look quite different (or may not exist at all) outside the society where we live. Identical symptoms may be perceived differently depending on gender and cultural expectations. Thinking critically about the societal and cultural factors which might influence the development of a disorder or our perception of that disorder is an important component of cultural competence.

ACCOUNTABILITY

As noted above, self-awareness is a continuous process. When counselors are confronted with divergent attitudes, beliefs, values, and experiences, they gain greater understanding of their own beliefs. The process of self-assessment is an important component of counselor accountability. Counselors can ask themselves questions such as, "What's really going on here? Why am I feeling this way? How well am I listening to what my client is saying?" (Okun & Cantrowitz, 2008). By being self-aware, counselors are able to monitor their own effectiveness. Counselors need to ask themselves if they are uncomfortable with certain clients or certain situations, and then examine why. Do they need to be liked? Perfect? In control? Do they need the client to "get better"? Counselors must be aware of their own avoidance strategies, and of the fears that get in the way of relating to clients.

One of the best ways to improve the effectiveness of counseling is to ask for client feedback (Duncan, Miller, & Sparks, 2004; Hubble, Duncan, Miller, & Wampold, 2010). Outcome-informed therapy makes clients collaborators in their own treatment, and allows the therapist to continually adjust the counseling to the needs of the individual client based on client feedback. While counselors are at times fearful that outcomes assessment will point to deficiencies, outcomes research can confirm the effectiveness of counseling interventions and improve counselors' ability to diagnose and provide treatment to clients (Erford, 2011). Research suggests that counselors often do not recognize when clients are getting worse. Thus, they overlook negative changes, and make inaccurate predictions of client improvement, leading to continuing deterioration (Lambert, 2013).

In the managed care environment, accountability is essential for all mental health providers. In the spirit of evidence-based therapy, counselors must be able to demonstrate the effectiveness of the services they provide. This requires practicing counselors to conduct outcome assessment themselves to monitor their own effectiveness, as well as to keep abreast of the research on outcomes and empirically supported treatments. Studies that explore the outcomes related to the common factors and core conditions of counseling are as important to understand as those studies which examine the research data on treatment protocols and techniques (Erford, 2011).

Counselors can have clients complete standardized rating scales (periodically or before each session), which assess their current functioning and allow the counselor to monitor client progress and prevent treatment failure as early as possible (Lambert, 2013).

THEORETICAL ORIENTATION

The research we reference here distinguishes the therapeutic relationship from theoretical approaches to counseling and specific techniques. However in reality, the theory, intervention, and relationship are intertwined and constantly informing each other (Lambert, 2013). The effectiveness of evidence-based methods depends on their context, which includes the helping relationship (Lambert, 2011). Further, all three (theory, intervention, and relationship) inform the moment-by-moment decisions that counselors make when working with a client—conceptualizing, establishing rapport, planning treatment, conducting intervention, and assessment. Now, we turn to the contribution of theory, and a discussion of how every counselor develops a primary theoretical orientation that becomes part of one's professional identity and informs one's conceptualization, relationship building, and practice.

One of the core professional competencies for counselors is knowledge of the various theoretical approaches to counseling, including similarities and differences between these, and the value of using various approaches with different clients. Approaches differ in focus and emphasis, strategies and interventions, and approaches to case conceptualization. A consistent research finding is that the type of therapy offered does not generally matter, as long as the intervention is theory-driven (Lambert, 2013). Many common factors are shared by diverse treatment approaches, and these contribute more to outcomes than specific intervention strategies (Cuijpers et al., 2012).

As we explore in more detail in the next chapter, different theories emphasize different influences and offer different treatment approaches. Psychodynamic theories emphasize the integration of conscious and unconscious processes and the value of interpretation and insight, with a focus on past as well as present. Cognitive behavioral theories and reality-based therapies aim to help clients change self-defeating behaviors and restructure distorted perceptions, with a focus on the present and a more directive and psychoeducational context. Gestalt theory contributes strategies, such as visual imagery and body work, while client-centered theory emphasizes the helping relationship, establishment of warmth, and positive regard, and takes a non-directive approach. The Bioecological Model developed by Uri Bronfenbrenner emphasizes the reciprocal relationships that exist in the client's environment and impact development (Bronfenbrenner, 1979). Postmodern approaches emphasize multicultural counseling, client empowerment, and the importance of sociopolitical forces that impact all of us.

While counselors should be knowledgeable about the diverse theoretical approaches, in reality many counselors do not adopt a single theoretical orientation. While the field was for many years mired in debate about which theoretical approach was most effective, more recently, practitioners have begun to look for commonalities among theoretical approaches (Norcross & Beutler, 2011). Eclectic counselors use techniques and strategies from various theories, selecting which strategies fit the problem, the client, and the context. However, critics of an eclectic approach to counseling assert that it consists of selecting strategies haphazardly, without a sound theoretical rationale for doing so, resulting in confusion and decreasing effectiveness.

The eclectic approach to counseling involves a technical integration of treatment techniques, without the necessity to subscribe to a specific theoretical orientation. In contrast, theoretical integration attempts to create a conceptual synthesis of different theoretical approaches, constructing an overarching conceptual framework that blends aspects of two or more theoretical approaches. The underlying theories are integrated, not just the specific strategies. An integrative view of counseling aims to combine the best components of different modalities in order to articulate a complete theoretical model that leads to effective treatment (Goldfried, Pachankis, & Bell, 2005).

Counselors follow an integrative approach when they develop their own understanding of human growth, development, and change and draw from theories that fit this understanding.

There is some criticism of theoretical integration as limited in application because it attempts to integrate many theories, while in reality only succeeding in integrating a few, resulting in a focus on only specific disorders. Critics point out that only some aspects of diverse theories are compatible, further limiting the usefulness of theoretical integration (Messer, 2007).

Another integrative approach to counseling which holds promise is the assimilative integration approach, introduced by Messer in 1992. Assimilative integration is conceptualized as a sort of theoretical eclecticism that is a bridge between theoretical integration and technical eclecticism. The counselor practices mostly from a particular theoretical modality, but selectively incorporates strategies and techniques from other compatible approaches as well. There is increasing recognition that no single theoretical approach can account for the wide range of human behavior or the diverse types of client populations and presenting problems. Many researchers stress the need for a flexible and integrative practice, tailored to the needs of each unique client and situation (Norcross & Wampold, 2011). In Chapter 3, we discuss specific theoretical approaches to counseling in more detail.

WHAT ABOUT THE CLIENT?

As we suggest, much of the variance related to treatment outcome lies not with the counselor or the technique, but with the client. In fact, the client's contribution to outcome is greater than that of either the specific modality or the strength of the helping relationship. There is recognition in the field today that counseling is carried out with one individual person, influenced by that unique individual's perceptions of the process and the counseling relationship.

In order to empathize with another person, we must understand them. One of the strengths of the T/C Model of case conceptualization is that it reminds counselors of the importance of taking into account client characteristics and context—culture, ethnicity, spiritual beliefs, age, gender, support systems, sexuality, socioeconomic status, family dynamics, and a plethora of other contextual domains are all crucial to understanding an individual client. The counselor's ability to generate and sustain hope in working with the client is dependent on a recognition of the client's support systems and strengths, and the counselor's ability to mobilize these.

Many client factors impact the outcome of counseling. The severity of the client's issues, including number of symptoms, level of motivation, and the client's ability to establish a working alliance with the counselor, are related to outcome (Lambert & Anderson, 1996). Recent outcome studies show that about two-thirds of clients who are treated improve or recover (Lambert, 2013). Unfortunately, some clients do get worse during counseling. Client variables like severe pathology are associated with client deterioration in treatment, especially with interventions that break down existing coping strategies (Lambert & Cattani-Thompson, 1996). Therefore, it is important to understand and accurately assess the impact of client variables in order to create and deliver effective interventions. This component of counseling effectiveness is discussed further in Chapter 3, and in more detail in Part II of this text, which focuses on specific diagnoses and treatments.

PULLING IT ALL TOGETHER

While there have been a number of large-scale studies which demonstrate the effectiveness of psychotherapy (Prochaska & Norcross, 2010), the data also show that diverse treatment approaches achieve similar levels of success. The similarity in outcomes across many different counseling methods appears to be explained by "common factors" that are part of all counseling modalities. Counseling effectiveness is more strongly influenced by these pantheoretical factors than by specific techniques of the different counseling modalities. Research shows that common factors account for 30% of the variance in treatment outcome, above and beyond the

15% accounted for by specific therapeutic modalities (Lambert & Barley, 2002).

The facilitating conditions discussed in this chapter make up those critical common factors. Research identified empathy, support, warmth, the working alliance, opportunity for catharsis, hope, working through conflicts, self-reflection, and practicing new behaviors as related to positive client outcome (Lambert, 2011; Norcross & Beutler, 2011; Prochaska & Norcross, 2010). The helping relationship itself is one of the strongest predictors of client outcome for both children and adults (Horvath & Bedi, 2002; Shirk & Karver, 2003). When these common factors are present, a more cooperative working relationship is created. The client experiences an environment of trust and security, which allows for growth and change (Lambert & Cattani-Thompson, 1996).

Hubble, Duncan, Miller, and Wampold (2010) conducted a summary of research studies and found that client change is attributable to extra-therapeutic client factors (40%), the therapeutic alliance (30%), hope and expectancy factors (15%), and theoretical models and techniques (15%). These percentages reflect the data first delineated by Lambert in a groundbreaking outcomes research study in 1992. There is little evidence for the efficacy of specific theoretical approaches or techniques (Lambert & Cattani-Thompson, 1996). Diverse approaches work equally well because much of the explanation for change is due to the client; in other words, no one modality of treatment is more effective than the others (Luborsky, Singer & Luborsky, 1975). The therapeutic relationship is emphasized across approaches.

These nonspecific variables, which are common to all theoretical approaches, can form the basis of integrative approaches to counseling (Lambert, 2011). Most modalities of treatment accept the importance of the therapeutic relationship as critical to counseling effectiveness and client change (Lambert, 2011). Theoretical models of helping have integrated Rogers' ideas with empirically supported interventions with the counselor establishing the facilitative conditions and then implementing specific interventions while maintaining the holding environment (Tursi & Cochran, 2006). The helping relationship and specific techniques and strategies are employed in concert, each informing and facilitating the other (Norcross, 2002a).

New modalities of treatment are being developed that will shape the counseling field in the next decades. These include distance counseling in addition to the traditional face-to-face model. Counseling by phone has existed since the 1950s when the Samaritans instituted a suicide prevention hotline in London (Centore & Milacci, 2008), and continues to be used for counseling, assessment, crisis intervention, and supervision. Recently, web-based counseling has become more common, including sessions by text, e-mail or teleconferencing using Skype, FaceTime, or other online portals. Some studies have found distance counseling to be effective (Reese, Conoley & Brossart, 2002), while others have found it less effective than face-to-face counseling (Hian, Chuan, Trevor, & Detenber, 2004).

Some advantages of distance counseling have been identified, including the client's sense of safety and anonymity that may encourage openness (Worona, 2003), and increased accessibility in areas that are underserved by counseling professionals or when clients are unable to leave the house for physical or mental health reasons. However, ethical concerns remain about distance counseling, including concerns about confidentiality and working with clients in crisis (Kraus, 2004). A 2008 study by Centore and Milacci surveyed clinicians and found that the participants perceived their "ability to fulfill ethical duties" was decreased with distance counseling. More research is needed to determine the efficacy of these alternative forms of service delivery, but with the ease and familiarity of online communication today, distance counseling may become more common in the future.

As you move through your training as a counselor and adopt a therapeutic orientation, developing the skills and facilitative conditions discussed in this chapter will form the basis of your effectiveness as a counselor. The T/C Model can be used as the basis of case conceptualization with whatever theoretical orientation you adopt. Depending on the needs of the individual client, the theoretical lens and specific techniques you use may vary; however, the T/C Model will continue to provide a consistent organizing framework for your work.

COUNSELING KEYSTONES

- There is consensus among researchers that a competent counselor needs to possess certain skills, including the ability to establish relationships, effective interpersonal communication, and the capacity for self-awareness.
- Research findings emphasize the importance of the therapeutic relationship itself as critical to client progress and change.
- Individual characteristics of effective counselors include curiosity, listening skills, emotional insight, ability for introspection, a sense of humor, enjoyment of conversation, and comfort with emotional intimacy.
- Purposefulness, stability, spontaneity, sense of timing, and the ability to gain insight from one's own struggles and apply that insight to understanding clients are beneficial qualities for effective counselors.
- Empathy is the most studied facilitative condition, defined as the ability to understand another person from their perspective, instead of one's own—to stand in someone else's shoes.
- Also called congruence, the facilitative condition of genuineness refers to the counselor's ability to express their own real self or to "be real."
- Another facilitative condition for client change is the counselor's ability to value the client as a person with worth and dignity, and to respect the client, which is referred to as positive regard.
- Clients begin to trust counselors through respectful, nonjudgmental interactions; each time the client takes a risk and divulges something previously split off or suppressed, and the counselor reacts with acceptance and validation, the client's trust increases.
- Transference (the impact of the client's past relationships on the client's emotions, fantasies, and reactions in the present) and countertransference (the counselor's unconscious reactions

to the client, which may be realistic or related to the counselor's past) can be either useful or damaging to the counseling process.

- Counseling effectiveness depends not only on the counselor's ability to communicate understanding to the client, but also on how aware the counselor is of what's going on inside of them, what they imagine is going on inside the client, and whether they can reflect on their own internal processes.
- An important component of self-awareness is an understanding of the counselor's own cultural values, perceptions, and beliefs, and the ways in which they differ from those of their clients.
- One of the core professional competencies for counselors is knowledge of the various theoretical approaches to counseling and the value of using various approaches with different clients.

- The client's contribution to outcome is greater than that of either the specific modality or the strength of the helping relationship—the severity of the client's issues, level of motivation, and the client's ability to establish a working alliance with the counselor are all strongly related to outcome.

EXERCISES

EXERCISE 2.1 How Do You Measure Up?

In this chapter we discussed the personal characteristics identified in research as important components of a positive counseling outcome. Below is a list of these attributes accompanied by

Attribute	Rating 1–Poor, 2–Fair, 3–Average, 4–Above average, 5–Superior
Comfort with emotional intimacy	
Sense of humor	
Capacity to set aside personal needs to pay attention to the needs of others	
Ability for introspection	
Emotional insightfulness	
Capacity for empathy	
Curiosity and inquisitiveness	
Ability to listen	
Ability to gain insight from one's own struggles	
Comfort with being in a position of power	
Energy and capacity for support	
Spontaneity and sense of timing	
Openness and lack of defensiveness	
Interpersonal competence	
Comfort and enjoyment with conversation	

a rating scale. First, rate yourself on each item, and then answer the questions below.

CLASS EXERCISE: Students complete the exercise individually and then discuss with a dyad partner.

> **Question 1:** In your opinion, which are the most important?
>
> **Question 2:** Which are the most difficult to improve?
>
> **Question 3:** Pick one attribute that was one of your lower scores. What are a few things you could do that might increase your abilities in this area?

EXERCISE 2.2 What Is the Power of the Relationship?

Empirical studies in both child and adult populations show a consistent association between therapeutic alliance and client outcome. Many experts believe that the power of the relationship itself may be the key to the counseling relationship's potential for healing.

CLASS EXERCISE: Students answer questions individually, followed by large group discussion.

> **Question 1:** To what extent do you believe this is true?
>
> **Question 2:** How can the attributes described in Exercise 2.1 help counselors create effective counselor/client relationships?
>
> **Question 3:** What elements might get in the way of developing a positive therapeutic relationship?

EXERCISE 2.3 What Is Your Definition of Empathy?

The text describes the many ways in which different theoretical orientations define empathy.

CLASS EXERCISE: In small groups, students compare their definitions of empathy. Are there marked differences? Similarities? Common themes? Do the same exercise for the attributes of genuineness and positive regard.

> **Question 1:** Take a few minutes and write down your personal definition of empathy.
>
> **Question 2:** Which theory or theorist is it more consistent with?

EXERCISE 2.4 Making It Happen

Counseling is more effective when counselors can display empathy, genuineness, and positive regard, and can communicate these qualities to their clients.

CLASS EXERCISE: After a large group discussion, students break into small groups to role-play client and counselor interaction that demonstrates empathy, genuineness, and positive regard.

> **Question 1:** How will you know that your client perceives these qualities (e.g., consider verbal and nonverbal cues)?
>
> **Question 2:** Are these abilities innate personality characteristics or can they be learned? If so, how?

EXERCISE 2.5 What About Trust?

Trust is an important component of an effective therapeutic relationship. There are many definitions of trust in the literature.

CLASS EXERCISE: Large group discussion.

> **Question 1:** Discuss the following definition of trust:
>
> Trust is defined by our ability to predict what is going to happen in the future.
>
> **Question 2:** Is trust always something positive, or just the ability to predict a future occurrence from our past experience (even if that's a negative prediction)?
>
> **Question 3:** How can counselors build trust with clients as a positive part of the helping relationship?

EXERCISE 2.6 What Do You Think?

Counselors struggle with objectivity, open mindedness, and detachment with many clients.

Below is a list of issues and subjects that may provoke strong feelings in clients and counselors alike. Take a few minutes to reflect on your beliefs and attitudes regarding each of these.

CLASS EXERCISE: Students reflect on issues individually. Followed by large group discussion focused on this prompt: How would you work effectively with a client around these issues?

Religion	Abortion
Cultural diversity	Infidelity
Political views	Child abuse
Prejudice	Criminal activity
Racism	Pornography
Homophobia	Drugs and alcohol
Misogyny	Conflicting values

EXERCISE 2.7 Getting in the Client's Headspace

Clients approach counseling and the initial session with predetermined views on what counseling is and what the counselor is going to be like.

CLASS EXERCISE: Students discuss in dyads, followed by large group discussion. Follow up with large group discussion using this prompt: How can counselors respond to clients' fears and misperceptions?

Question 1: What are some common misconceptions that clients may hold regarding the counseling relationship?

Question 2: Where do you think they get these ideas?

Question 3: Think of how a popular movie or TV show has portrayed a counselor or therapist. Was it accurate? Flattering? Insulting? Misleading?

GO FURTHER

Becoming a Therapist: On the Path to Mastery by Thomas M. Skovholt (2012) Wiley
On Being a Therapist by Jeffrey A. Kottler (2010) Jossey-Bass
On Becoming a Person: A Therapist's View of Psychotherapy by Carl Rogers (1995) Mariner Books
Introduction to Professional Counseling (Counseling and Professional Identity) by Varunee F. Sangganjanavanich and Cynthia A. Reynolds (2014) SAGE

3

CASE CONCEPTUALIZATION
THAT WORKS

INTRODUCTION

As the prior chapters make clear, counseling is a complex process, requiring an understanding of professional identity and history, knowledge of theory and research, and certain skills and attributes. In turn, this understanding provides the lens we use to encounter our clients, and the template used to conceptualize clients' challenges and strengths. Counseling is also an intentional and purposeful process, as the counselor helps a client move toward growth and change. Before a treatment plan can be developed and in order to guide the counseling process, the counselor must come to a deeper understanding of the client by gathering information and weaving all that they know about a client's life and history together.

Case conceptualization is the process counselors use to understand the client's symptoms, thoughts, emotions, behaviors, and personality constructs and to make sense of a client's presenting problems. Effective case conceptualization entails thinking integratively, developing and testing hypotheses, and planning treatment based on those hypotheses. The model presented in this book (the Temporal/Contextual Model of

case conceptualization, or T/C Model) is atheoretical, allowing students to incorporate constructs from various theoretical paradigms into their case conceptualizations. The model provides a framework or template for counselors to focus their observations and generate inferences about meaning.

In this chapter, we look at three components of the counseling process and how these components are integrated: diagnosis, where the counselor identifies and describes the client's presenting problem and needs; case conceptualization, where the counselor comes to an understanding of the client's needs and situation; and treatment planning, where the counselor develops strategies and interventions to address the client's needs and move the client toward change. While we often think of diagnosis and case conceptualization as preceding treatment planning, in reality the three components may occur simultaneously as the counselor listens to the client and develops a deeper understanding of the client's issues. Assessment and evaluation also occur throughout the process of counseling, and effective counselors are continuously hypothesizing and revising their understanding based on additional information.

DIAGNOSIS AND PROBLEM IDENTIFICATION

In order to help a client, the counselor and client together need to define the problem that's getting in the client's way. While some clients come to counseling with an idea of the issue, others do not. Clients may feel down or have a vague sense that "something's wrong" without a clear understanding of just what that signifies. The process of defining this problem is referred to as "diagnosis" in the medical and psychiatric professions. Depending on the setting where they practice, counselors may call this process diagnosis or problem identification. Because this text identifies problems based on the *Diagnostic and Statistical Manual* (DSM-5), we use the terms interchangeably. Even if a counselor is not practicing in a setting which requires a formal diagnosis, an understanding of the DSM codes is essential in order to collaborate with other helping professions and provide the best care.

The process of diagnosis is based on the client's presenting problem—the reason the client provides for why he or she was referred or is seeking counseling from the viewpoint of the client. Problem identification addresses the basic question, "How does the client describe their problem?" The initial session with a client also includes a brief history of the problem and a description of attempted solutions and their outcomes. Sometimes a written or computer generated intake form is used to collect this information, or a symptom checklist is filled out by the client or counselor. A client interview then helps clients identify specific problems, as well as explore the onset, severity, and frequency of symptoms and whether the client has previously experienced similar symptoms.

For mental health professionals in the United States, diagnosis most often refers to the identification of symptoms using the *Diagnostic and Statistical Manual of Mental Disorders* (DSM-5) (American Psychiatric Association, 2013). The DSM uses observable features to identify criteria for a wide variety of mental and emotional disorders, categorizing these based on symptom patterns. The DSM-5 is the most widely accepted diagnostic standard, although the World Health Organization's International Classification of Diseases (ICD10) is also commonly used. The DSM-5 and ICD10 codes are often used together in practice. In this text, we concentrate on the DSM-5 system to categorize client issues.

The diagnostic formulation also allows the counselor to identify the most appropriate means of service delivery for the client. A client in crisis or who is suicidal may need to be hospitalized; a client with substance abuse issues may benefit from a drug and alcohol treatment facility; outpatient treatment may be most appropriate for other clients.

Based on the medical model which ties symptoms to an underlying physiological or biological problem, the DSM takes a categorical approach to understanding and treating mental health issues, as opposed to the more dimensional approach which counselors often use in understanding client problems. There remains some controversy about using a categorical approach which forces a dichotomy between health and pathology. Many counselors, reflecting the history and values of the profession, view wellness as a continuum with clients' issues not fitting into rigid categories. The newest version of the DSM, published in 2013, moves in a more dimensional direction, attempting to build in some flexibility to the diagnostic categories.

While acknowledging the limitations of a categorical approach, nevertheless a diagnosis is crucial in order to communicate effectively with other mental health professionals, and provides a method for objectively describing a client's presenting problems. Furthermore, integrating the categorical and dimensional approaches can help the counselor fully understand the nature of the client's issues as well as the context within which the problems develop and are maintained, as we see in the next task, case conceptualization.

Clients may already have a diagnosis when they present for treatment; however, there may be other issues impacting the client and different clinicians may disagree about appropriate diagnoses. In later chapters, we discuss in more depth the diagnostic criteria for some of the issues most commonly encountered by counselors.

CASE CONCEPTUALIZATION

As the counselor engages in a collaborative exploration with the client and identifies a diagnosis, the counselor begins to develop a framework to explain the etiology of the problem. How did the problem begin and what situational contexts contributed to its development? What is sustaining the problem? Conversely, what strengths and resources does the client have which can be mined to create hope and produce change? There are multiple lenses through which to conceptualize a case, and each individual counselor will use a different lens which emphasizes different aspects of the client's life and history. Case conceptualization, therefore, is not an exact science nor is there one way to conceptualize a case. After all, counseling is an ongoing and continuously unfolding relationship with both the counselor and the client bringing to the table their own unique strengths and attributes. The effective counselor continually assesses their own effectiveness, and reviews the research on case conceptualization and intervention on a regular basis.

Seligman (2004) describes the case conceptualization process as allowing the counselor to more fully understand the client's needs and situation and providing a "blueprint" for how to interact with, listen to, and help. An articulated model of case conceptualization is particularly important in today's health care climate, which values efficient, cost effective, evidence-based treatment (Wampold, 2001). Case conceptualization has been identified as integral to quality and effective counseling (Sperry, 2010) and is considered a core competency for counselors (Betan & Binder, 2010). As we have seen, forming a therapeutic alliance with the client is a crucial skill; the alliance then informs and is part of the case conceptualization process. The trust and rapport established between counselor and client allows the client to be open to sharing critical information. The counselor then bases the conceptualization on this information, as we illustrate with the case of Katy in Chapter 1 and Chapter 2.

The way that a counselor conceptualizes a case influences the entire process of counseling—what questions to ask, how to interpret the answers, what hypotheses to develop, and how to test them. The case conceptualization tells the counselor where the client has been, and provides an understanding of where the client might be able to go. Neukrug and Schwitzer (2006) define case conceptualization as a tool for observing, understanding, and integrating a client's thoughts, feelings, actions, and physiological status. They define three related processes: evaluation, organization, and orientation.

Evaluation

As the counselor begins to develop a case conceptualization, the counselor assesses and measures observable behaviors. These include the symptoms associated with the presenting problem. For example, a client experiencing anxiety may have difficulty sleeping, irrational fears associated with certain situations, or physiological symptoms, such as gastrointestinal problems or rapid heartbeat. Evaluation goes beyond the diagnosis of presenting symptoms to assess the client's situational context. What is the client's family context, work or school situation, interpersonal relationship status?

Specifically, the counselor working with Katy in the initial session observes her rapid speech and that she appears nervous, twisting her hands in her lap. Katy makes some eye contact with the counselor, but only sustains it for a moment before glancing away or down at her hands. The counselor takes note of her difficulties with sleeping, changes in appetite, anxiety attacks, depressed mood, and her risk-taking behavior. However, evaluation goes further. The counselor also takes into account the stress that Katy is currently experiencing, the reality of her conflicted relationships with her family and her boyfriend, the fact that she is in a time of developmental transition, and her confusion about selecting a career.

Sometimes evaluation is by informal interview; in other cases, formal measures and assessment instruments supplement the counselor-client conversation. Katy's counselor might ask her to fill out a depression symptoms inventory, such as the Beck Depression Inventory, or might use a structured assessment of drug and alcohol use.

Background information gathered includes sex, race, ethnicity, age, socioeconomic status, medical history, prior mental health treatment, religious background and spirituality, sexual orientation, gender identity, family background, relationship history, marital status, educational background, employment data, substance use, peer relationships, trauma and abuse history, and physical appearance. Katy's counselor already knows that she is the child of Korean immigrants, but will need to find out more about her cultural background, acculturation status, and family roles and values. As you can see from the description of background variables, there is a great deal of information that Katy's counselor does not yet have about her client.

In addition, precipitating events that preceded the development of the client's presenting problem, such as life transitions, recent losses, romantic breakups, job transitions, or developmental challenges, should be assessed. It is also important to assess suicidal ideation or experiences. Katy mentioned her boyfriend's condition for staying in the relationship as dependent on Katy seeking counseling; her counselor will want to find out more about that relationship, as well as past romantic breakups. Katy's parents' divorce and her mother and stepfather's conflict are possible past and current stressors that should be evaluated as well. An effective counselor will also take into account the client's developmental stage and any recent transitions. As a young adult just out of college, Katy has just weathered a major transition and is facing another: finding a job. Developmental theory can be helpful in understanding the impact of such a transition on a 22-year-old young woman (Chickering & Reiser, 1969; Erikson, 1994).

The evaluation phase of case conceptualization also includes determining the client's readiness for change. Has the client come in on his or her own, or is someone else in their life more motivated than they are to change? Has the client already spent time thinking about what changes might be beneficial, or even started to take small steps in that direction? Or is there still a great deal of ambivalence around the possibility of change,

perhaps because the task seems overwhelming or the payoff is not yet clear? In Katy's case, how much was counseling her idea, and how much was it to appease her boyfriend?

A variety of tests and assessment instruments can be used to amass client data. Behavioral and self-report questionnaires; intellectual, achievement, psychological, and personality tests; and medical, educational, and legal records are all sources of information. In addition, artwork, journals, poetry, songs, videos, and other creative works that clients produce can provide insight.

Box 3.1 provides an overview of a biopsychosocial assessment with some examples of areas to be assessed in particular domains.

While the evaluation process seems like merely a collection of facts, the way that counselors process and record the information has an impact on the subsequent phases of counseling (Anderson, 1997; O'Hanlon & Weiner-Davis, 1989). The counselor's choice of words and the order of recording facts result in differences in meaning which then become part of the counselor's conceptualization of the client. Since we know that hope and expectancy are related to client outcome (Lambert, 1992), it seems clear that when the counselor develops a positive conceptualization of the client from the start, the client is more likely as well to be hopeful about change. Therefore in this early phase of counseling, assessing and documenting the client's strengths and resources should be a significant part of the evaluation; some researchers suggest that these should be at the top of the record, not near the end, because this creates a sense of optimism in the counselor. Describing the client's abilities, successes, positive personal qualities, social and community supports, and spiritual resources can be a source of hope for both client and counselor.

As we saw in Chapter 1, Katy's counselor has already begun to point out her strength and resilience, and to communicate that positive regard to Katy. As the evaluation process continues, the counselor's evaluation of Katy's challenges will be balanced against her strengths, providing a clearer and more hopeful picture of Katy the individual.

| BOX 3.1 | Biopsychosocial Assessment |

Domains	Possible Areas of Assessment
Biological/ Physical	Medical history; hospitalizations, chronic illness, genetics/risk factors; current medications; general health; sexual development, substance use/abuse
Psychological	Cognitive style, suicidal ideation, coping strategies (includes risk taking, self-injury, eating disorders), attitudes, values, beliefs, spirituality, attachment style, intelligence, self-efficacy, self-esteem, identity, psychological strengths
Social	Interpersonal functioning, family dynamics, peer relationships, romantic and sexual relationships, communication skills, support systems
Cultural	Cultural identity, religious or spiritual resources and beliefs, cultural and societal norms, acculturation

Organization

The organization stage is the inferential phase of the case conceptualization process where the counselor organizes observations, measures, and assessments from the evaluation phase with the goal of making inferences and identifying themes or patterns. A case conceptualization provides an understanding of etiology as well as maintenance. How did the client's problem develop, and how is the problem being sustained? The conceptualization provides a framework for how the counselor will engage the client throughout the counseling process, allowing the counselor to develop a theory of problem formation and resolution.

As we saw with the case of Katy, clients often arrive at their first counseling session with a great deal to say. They may have waited a long time to be heard, and thus may convey a lot of information in a short period of time. This can lead to a feeling of catharsis for the client, but the amount of information can also be overwhelming to both client and counselor. During this phase of conceptualization, the counselor begins to discriminate central information from peripheral information, and to focus the session on those areas which are connected to the client's

core issues. Clinical hypotheses are drawn from observations and assessments, and working models are generated of how the client's problems developed and the mechanisms sustaining them (Stevens & Morris, 1995).

Case conceptualization calls for the counselor to identify themes in the client's story, and to begin to make sense of the problematic patterns which the client is experiencing. The counselor develops hypotheses about what the client's core issues might be, and then uses intentional questions and reflections to explore and clarify. These underlying concerns are often connected to multiple concerns and problem situations; the counselor gains leverage in focusing on core issues, more effectively helping the client. These patterns and themes then inform the client's goals for change.

For example, as the counselor listens to Katy's story in the initial session, she develops hypotheses about why Katy is currently feeling depressed and anxious. At first, the counselor might attribute Katy's problems to the conflict in her relationship with her boyfriend. As she continues to listen, however, the counselor modifies that hypothesis as additional information is added to the conceptualization. Perhaps Katy's depression is related to feelings of loss around her parents' divorce. What role have her mother's outbursts and disapproval played in Katy's symptoms? How do her mother's and father's choice of career impact Katy's current struggle to find her own profession?

In this phase of case conceptualization, the counselor pulls together the diverse threads of information obtained from the client and from assessment instruments and other sources into a coherent understanding of the client's core issues, patterns, and life themes. For example, the counselor may ask questions about the first time and any subsequent times that a client noticed a particular symptom, and when (if ever) the symptom lessens. The counselor develops an explanation of when the client's problem started, how it developed, what's keeping it in place, and how the client is attempting to cope with the problem. Once all the information is integrated, a map of the client's life story is created, which then guides action plans and goal setting. Having an articulated case conceptualization also helps the counselor anticipate and prepare the client for possible challenges and roadblocks to change (Sperry, 2010).

Concurrently, the counselor develops a cultural formulation of the client's problem in order to understand how the client's culture and broader sociological context impact the issues. An assessment of the client's cultural context includes such diverse factors as gender, ethnicity, socioeconomic status, geographic region, sexual orientation, and many other elements that influence how a client views themselves and others. For example, poverty can be as influential in sustaining depression as irrational ways of thinking or a serotonin imbalance. Diversity often brings both challenges and resources that are necessarily reflected in the case conceptualization process. Marginalized groups can experience trauma and abuse; they may also develop strong and supportive social networks.

The counselor working with Katy will want to explore her family's Korean heritage, including the impact of immigration on her parents, her relationship with extended family, and the norms and values that her family holds. For example, what are her family's and her culture's beliefs about gender roles or about adult children living with their parents? Because norms vary between cultures, they are important to understand as the counselor develops a case conceptualization.

In addition to the verbal content of the client's story, counselors pay attention to tone of voice, changes in modulation and volume, rate of speech, and syntactic complexity (Stevens & Morris, 1995). Observation of nonverbal behavior also helps the counselor decide what is important and what is not—eye contact, body posture, facial expressions, gestures, and proxemics all convey information that add meaning to the client's story.

Katy's counselor will take note of how rapidly she's speaking, her sporadic eye contact, and the way she clasps and unclasps her hands, as well as the way she constantly shifts position. During the case conceptualization process, the counselor makes meaning from all her observations. Perhaps she concludes that Katy is anxious, and that she may have a difficult time trusting the counselor. On the other hand, she seems eager to share her story, possibly because she doesn't feel heard by the important people in her life. Would you agree with the counselor's assessment? What are some other explanations for Katy's presentation?

As the counselor considers observations and integrates information, insight into the client's emotional experience emerges, further contributing to an understanding of problem areas. Specifically for clients who are cut off from their own emotional experience by trauma or ineffective coping strategies, and thus are less able to talk about their experience than Katy, counselors can use emotion checklists to help clients uncover and label their own emotions. However, even with a checklist the relationship between the client and the counselor allows the client to begin to share. As the counselor listens and validates what the client is expressing, trust builds, and the client becomes more comfortable sharing what he or she really feels.

As you will discover, the T/C Model facilitates the process of evaluation and organization, providing a clearly articulated framework to begin to understand the client's context. The Model is also a reminder to the counselor of those domains which are important to assess, as some information may be left out of the client's initial description or may get lost in the outpouring of information.

Another important source of information to include in the evaluation is the counselor's own reactions to the client, which can be used to generate hypotheses about how others in the client's life may react to them. The counselor's emotional experience of the client may give support to particular hypotheses. For example, a counselor in a community mental health center met with a new client, a young man who is having trouble making friends at a community college. The client repeatedly stresses to the counselor that he is "too smart to be in a community college" and "doesn't belong there." The counselor finds himself thinking that the client isn't very likable, and doesn't seem all that intelligent either. A reflective counselor recognizes his own emotional reaction as information to include in the case conceptualization. If the counselor's initial reaction was negative, perhaps that has been the reaction of the client's new classmates too.

Awareness of this "parallel process," where the experience of counselor and client in session mirror the client's experience with others outside the session, is an important source of information (Ronnestad & Skovholt, 1993). Some training programs encourage students to characterize the nature of the counselor-client relationship in a metaphor (friend, parent, mentor, protector, etc.) in order to understand the relationship in a more useful way.

Orientation

Embedded within the case conceptualization process is the counselor's understanding of how problems develop, how they are sustained over time, and what causes them to change. Counselors tend to develop a theoretical orientation over time, a collection of beliefs about what is needed to create change. Counselors use these assumptions as a frame for mapping problems and for interpreting what happens during a client session.

During the process of case conceptualization, the counselor uses a theoretical orientation to interpret and analyze the information gathered about the client, integrating their own observations with assumptions drawn from formal theories of counseling. While counselors' intuition is a valuable asset in making inferences and generating hypotheses, nevertheless intuition must be grounded in empirically tested patterns of understanding (Hoshmand, 1991). Applying a theoretical framework allows the counselor to make sense of the factors that contributed to the development and maintenance of the client's problem. The information which is most important to consider depends on the theoretical perspective selected.

In the previous chapter we briefly reviewed various theoretical approaches; counselors are expected to match the appropriate theory (or theories, in the case of integrative or eclectic approaches) to client needs (Corey, 2009; Dattilo & Norcross, 2006; deShazer & Dolan, 2007; Wampold, 2001). The techniques used by the counselor vary according to the theory, and are connected to how the counselor engages the client and develops the case conceptualization. While empirical research has not demonstrated the superiority of any particular model, nevertheless, having a theoretical orientation allows the counselor to organize the counseling process and guide the sessions. Counselors need to find the theoretical orientation which is the best fit for them, as well as to decide whether an integrative or eclectic approach is compatible with their personal view of human development and change.

As we discuss, case conceptualization is not an exact science, nor is one theoretical model prescribed by research. After thirty years of studies comparing the efficacy of different types of counseling and therapy, there is still controversy about the so-called "dodo bird effect." This is the colorful name for the idea that different types of psychotherapy are similarly effective. The alternative view is that there are specific therapies that are more effective for a particular diagnosis. Some researchers contend that the meta-analyses supporting the dodo bird verdict rely on methodology which makes it difficult to uncover significant differences (Budd & Hughes, 2009).

In this text, we already presented the idea that all therapeutic models act as vehicles through which the common factors of therapeutic change operate (Sprenkle & Blow, 2004). Recall that research shows that all theoretical models are impacted by the extratherapeutic factors which occur outside the counseling relationship, and account for 40% of client change, and all models value the therapeutic alliance, which accounts for approximately 30% of client improvement (Lambert, 1992). When the counselor is confident and hopeful about the outcome of treatment, client expectancy and hope are also raised, accounting for another 15% of client outcome, with the remaining 15% explained by the use of a theoretical model (Lambert, 1992).

At the same time, there is a great deal of research exploring the effectiveness of a particular counseling intervention for a specific diagnosis ("empirically supported treatments"). In Part II of this text, we look at some of this research as we examine the presenting issues commonly encountered in counseling settings, and discuss treatment options. Counselors are most effective when they keep in mind the research on common factors and how these are incorporated into case conceptualization, while also using the literature on empirically supported treatments. Equally important, counselors must continually assess the effectiveness of the counseling process, from case conceptualization to intervention to follow-up.

Notably, the counselor's theoretical orientation does have an impact on the way the counselor evaluates and understands the client, and on the strategies chosen to help the client change; the questions asked during the evaluation and organization process vary depending on theoretical orientation. In the next section, we briefly review the theoretical approaches most commonly used by counselors, and examine the focus, questions, assessments, and strategies a counselor with that orientation might employ. This chapter is not intended to be a comprehensive review of counseling theory, but we do include an overview of theoretical orientations as they relate to case conceptualization.

Solution Focused Brief Therapy (SFBT)

Based on the principles of exploring what happened in the client's life before the problem situation developed, solution focused counselors look at the client's past successes and clarify the strengths and resources that clients are already employing (deShazer & Dolan, 2007, deShazer, 1991). A solution focused counselor might ask questions that help the client identify and own their strengths and successes as the case conceptualization process unfolds, encouraging "self-complimenting" (Delong & Berg, 2008). The therapeutic alliance is built around the counselor's "cheerleading" and supporting of the client's new awareness of their strengths and successes, and the focus on positives increases the client's sense of hope and expectancy and helps move them from a focus on problems to a focus on solutions.

For example, Katy's counselor might give her some feedback after listening to Katy tell her story:

Counselor: *"It sounds like you were dealing with a lot of family stress while you were at college, and yet you managed to graduate Summa Cum Laude! How did you manage to do that?"*

Reminding Katy of her intelligence, perseverance, and resilience will help her use those strengths as she works through her current challenges.

Cognitive Behavioral Therapy (CBT)

Cognitive Behavioral Therapy (CBT) was first described by Aaron Beck (Beck, 1976). A CBT case conceptualization looks at the client's cognitions and how they impact behavioral decisions, physiology, and emotions. Counselors come up with hypotheses about the cognitive mechanisms that are causing the client's problems, how these came about from the client's life experience, and the environmental triggers producing and maintaining them (Beck, 1995; Persons, 1989, 2012). Such mechanisms include cognitive distortions, negative thoughts, or schemas that are maladaptive. According to researcher Judith Beck (1995), the cognitive model of case conceptualization proposes that distorted or dysfunctional thinking is common to all psychological disturbances.

Recall from your theories class that one of the earliest and most basic cognitive models is Ellis' ABC model of Rational Emotive Therapy (Ellis, 1961). According to the ABC model, the client experiences an **A**ctivating Event (**A**) that acts like a stimulus to interpret or think about what is happening. Our understanding and interpretation of this event leads to specific **B**elief(s) about the event, ourselves, and our environment. Once we develop this belief, we experience emotional **C**onsequences. These consequences, in turn, impact the ways in which a client responds. Subsequently, the goal of counseling is for clients to understand their cognitive processes so that distortions and misconceptions are identified in a more realistic manner. We eventually develop core beliefs and assumptions about ourselves, others, and the world which shape how we experience day to day events and trigger what Beck referred to as automatic thoughts. These automatic thoughts, especially when negative, can have a significant impact on our emotional state and our behavioral choices.

A counselor working with Katy from a CBT perspective would try to identify any dysfunctional thoughts and beliefs that are impacting her current situation.

Counselor:	*"You said that your situation was hopeless, and that you would never find a job. Can you tell me more about that?"*
Katy:	*"Nothing ever works out for me. Why should this be any different?"*
Counselor:	*"That's a really painful way to feel. But, I remember a few minutes ago, you told me that when you went to college, you were dealing with the stress of being stuck in the middle between your parents, and yet you were still able to succeed academically. It sounds like maybe one thing worked out for you—and a pretty big thing too!"*

During the case conceptualization process, the counselor listens for any automatic thoughts and beliefs that are getting in Katy's way. At the same time, she searches out any evidence that challenges Katy's thinking so that Katy can begin to see herself and her future more realistically. These conceptualizations are done in collaboration with the client and can then lead to goal formulation based on the information and insight provided.

Psychodynamic Approaches

Psychodynamic case formulation revolves around the inherent motivation for people to search for and maintain meaningful relationships. The counselor looks for commonalities and themes across relationships, places, and perceptions. Clients' problems are conceptualized as maladaptive patterns of thinking and acting that stem from early childhood experiences and are maintained in the present. The early experiences and perceptions can turn into schemas through which the client views their lives, and can negatively impact the interpersonal relationships that clients have in the present (a process referred to as circular causality). These same patterns are acted out within the counseling relationship, so the counselor can use the dynamics which play out during the sessions to formulate hypotheses about the rest of the client's experience and self-perceptions. The "here and now" interactions between client and counselor, and the transference and counter-transference reactions each have to the other, inform the conceptualization process.

A counselor conceptualizing the case of Katy from a psychodynamic perspective would want to know more about her early life experience. For example, Katy's parents divorced when she was quite young, and she may have been unable at the time to make sense of a traumatic event for her. Now in young adulthood, she may be trying to make meaning of that trauma and struggling to do so in order to establish romantic relationships herself. A psychodynamic case conceptualization might focus on that early loss experience, and how a sense of being abandoned may be influencing Katy's relationship with her partner.

Humanistic Approaches

Humanistic counseling emphasizes liberating clients from negative assumptions and attitudes that are incapacitating. A counselor working from a humanistic perspective views human nature as basically good and believes that clients have an innate potential to create healthy, meaningful relationships. The focus is on present processes and responsible self-actualization rather than past experiences or cognitive distortion. Carl Rogers (1951) believed that formal diagnosis was not necessary, and in fact might sometimes be unwise. As we have seen, Rogers greatly influenced the counseling field, and many counselors emphasize the importance of the relationship over diagnosis. When conceptualizing with a humanistic focus, counselors emphasize "unconditional positive regard" and respect for the client, and prioritize helping clients make their own choices. A humanistic counselor tries to empower the client toward self-actualization and positive growth.

For example, a counselor working with Katy from this perspective would listen without judgment, and convey valuing of the client.

Counselor: (warm tone of voice): "You've been through a lot, Katy. And yet here you are, a college degree under your belt, having the courage to start figuring out where you go from here."

Existential Approaches

The existential formulation is focused on clients finding philosophical meaning by thinking and acting authentically. According to this perspective, some of the principal difficulties clients face revolve around existential concepts, such as despair, loneliness, and lack of meaning. Problems stem from not exercising choice and judgment well enough to build meaningful and fulfilling lives. In the face of this anxiety and suffering, clients work with counselors toward leading more meaningful lives through creativity, love, authenticity, and conscious choice. The focus of counseling then becomes helping the client create meaning in life and making choices in agreement with their values and beliefs. In addition, there is an exploration of environmental factors that are limiting the client's ability to exercise this choice and live a meaningful life.

Katy seems to be facing an existential crisis as she comes to counseling. She is at a transition point in her life, no longer moving forward with the structure of a college curriculum and college residence hall. Without that structure or a clear plan for the future, Katy seems to be drifting, searching for meaning in both her career goals and her relationships. A counselor working from an existential perspective would focus on this crisis of meaning, and help Katy clarify her values and beliefs in order to make informed choices for her future.

Family Systems

As you might expect, a counselor working from a family systems perspective would focus on the client's family and other systems in their lives. The counselor might, for example, use a genogram to gain a deeper understanding of the client's family dynamics and interpersonal relationships. Genograms are structural diagrams that chart family relationships across three or four generations, explicating roles, norms, communication patterns, and significant life events that impacted the client. Some counselors use genograms to gather and chart detailed information about the client's life and history, while others select a few important types of information to chart. Making patterns and themes visual can help clients talk about and understand their family history and its impact on the present—both strengths and challenges can be made tangible, helping the client understand both. Genograms fit well into a bioecological model of client assessment (such as the T/C Model), as they encourage both client and counselor to take into account multiple spheres of influence across time (Carlfred & Broderick, 1993; Kaslow, Broth, Smith, & Collins, 2012; Lewis, Beavers, Gossett, & Phillips, 1976; Nichols & Schwartz, 2004).

A counselor working from this perspective would explore Katy's family background in more detail. Her parents' relationship and breakup, her mother's dating and marriage to her stepfather, her grandparents' and great-grandparents' history, and Katy's relationship with her half-brothers would all provide important information for the case conceptualization. An understanding of who Katy is closest to in the family helps identify sources of support, while patterns of conflict help the counselor develop hypotheses about how anger and conflict are handled in the family. Intergenerational patterns and ways of coping, such as alcohol or drug use, divorce, and vocational values, can also be identified, and might be useful in working with Katy.

Postmodern Approaches

Postmodern theories of counseling include narrative, feminist, and social justice approaches as well as the multicultural focus discussed in Chapter 2. Narrative counseling is a postmodern approach based on a view of the self which is changeable and fluid and that opens up the possibility for change—as Carl Rogers said, we are all engaged in the process of "becoming" (Rogers, 1961). Developed by Michael White and David Epston (1990), counselors working within a narrative paradigm help the client focus on times when their dominant (problem) life story was not their primary narrative (White, 2007). Narrative theories of change assume that we all construct personal stories that organize and give meaning to our experience. We are all the narrators of our life stories, and they script the way we relate to others and form identities (Stewart & Neimeyer, 2001). When clients' narratives are limited by sociocultural ideas related to power and gender, or influenced by past traumatic experiences, counselors help the client revise and re-author their life story (Meekums, 2005).

Similar to the solution focused idea of identifying exceptions, helping the client uncover and value an alternate narrative can help the client see themselves in a more positive way. The therapeutic alliance is built through what White (2007) called a "conversational partnership" as the client and the counselor together explore and discover meaning in the client's alternative life story. The counselor practicing narrative therapy does not take the position of expert, but rather is a collaborator discovering the alternate narrative along with the client. The alternative life story is more hopeful and less problematic, thus helping the client view themselves and their future more positively.

In her first session with her counselor, Katy tells her life story as one of repeated loss and challenge, ignoring instances of her own success and instead including only stories of failure. A counselor working within a narrative perspective would begin to question this version of her life story, helping her to explore those more positive chapters and eventually to rewrite a more realistic, and more hopeful, narrative.

Feminist, multicultural, and social justice approaches also fall under the category of postmodern theories of counseling. There is increasing recognition that the traditional counseling theories are limited due to their basis on Eurocentric White male perspectives and values, and some researchers believe that these traditional theories may be inappropriate for minority clients (Ivey, D'Andrea, Ivey, & Simek-Morgan, 2007).

Multicultural, social justice, and feminist approaches emphasize that working to reduce social injustice, oppression, discrimination, marginalization, and economic inequality are critical to client mental health (Crethar, Torres Rivera, & Nash, 2008). Counselor education programs are beginning to address issues of privilege and social injustice which impact the lives of all clients, and there is increasing recognition of the impact of context on client mental health. Counselors who work from these perspectives are committed to fostering positive change for their individual clients while at the same time advocating for positive changes in their clients' sociopolitical contexts (Arredondo & Perez, 2003; Arredondo & Toporek, 2004).

Feminist counseling, which grew out of the women's moment in the 1960s and 1970s, focuses on the importance of interconnectedness for women, an idea that is often de-emphasized or even pathologized in more traditional theories. Feminist theories also question the acceptance of traditional social roles for women and aim to help women rediscover their authentic selves (Wastell, 1996). Empowerment is a primary goal of feminist counseling. Feminist counselors believe that clients know what is best for them, and view individual problems as embedded within sociopolitical and cultural contexts, often impacted by gender-based discrimination and violence. The feminist counselor works to educate clients about social activism, emphasizing that individual change occurs through social change (Remer, 2008). Similarly, social justice and multicultural counselors also promote social, political, and cultural change instead of focusing solely on intrapsychic issues. Individual symptoms are seen as a result of larger sociocultural forces. The relationship between client and counselor in these approaches is egalitarian, with issues of power discussed openly. Counselors work collaboratively with clients to expand clients' awareness of the effect of sociopolitical factors on their lives.

A counselor working with Katy from a feminist, multicultural, or social justice perspective would want to explore the gender role messages that Katy has absorbed both from her family and from the broader culture. Where does her fear of being alone come from, and how does that impact her relationship with her on-again-off-again boyfriend, and her fear of being alone? What experiences has Katy had as a Korean American? Have Katy or her family experienced instances of discrimination, prejudice, or stereotyping? An understanding of the various sociocultural factors impacting Katy's view of herself and her world will be helpful as she moves forward and figures out who she wants to be and where she wants to go.

Biopsychosocial Approaches

A biopsychosocial perspective can be useful in considering the diverse contextual influences that impact all of us. Bronfenbrenner's (1979) model of contextual development describes the reciprocal relationships which contribute to development, including the individual, the proximal (immediate

and face-to-face interactions), and distal (more removed, but nevertheless having an impact) environments, and the interactions that occur within those environments. At the most proximal level, interactions with family, peers, school, and work take place in each of these domains, which Bronfenbrenner called "microsystems." The interrelationships between those microsystem spheres make up the "mesosystem," which also impacts the individual. Finally, the more distal systems comprise the "exosystem," influencing the client in a less direct way. In modern society, "macrosystem" influences are more influential than ever, with technology conveying cultural norms and messages in a more immediate and continuous manner. Bronfenbrenner acknowledged these influences as part of the individual's "chronosystem," the evolution of the client's context over time, through developmental transitions and the changing world we live in.

A biopsychosocial perspective is particularly helpful when looking at the client as embedded in multiple systems of influence, and encourages counselors to conduct comprehensive assessments that take into account cultural and social factors. The T/C Model of Case Conceptualization we introduce in this text incorporates a biopsychosocial perspective. In the next section of this book, we apply the T/C Model to various clients, and scaffold you to begin the process of case conceptualization yourself.

Readiness for Change

As mentioned previously, an important aspect of the case conceptualization process is a client's level of motivation and readiness for change. The most well-known and researched theory of the change process is Prochaska's *Transtheoretical Model of Change* (Prochaska & DiClemente, 1986; Prochaska, DiClemente, & Norcross, 1992). The theory centers around four core constructs: the processes of change, decisional balance, self-efficacy, and temptation. The model describes change readiness progressing through six stages (precontemplation, contemplation, preparation, action, maintenance, and termination) and recommends that interventions should be tailored to the current stage of the client.

A client's advancement through these stages is facilitated by what Prochaska called processes of change. These *processes of change* can be overt behaviors or covert cognitive shifts that help the client gain insight into their problems and find motivation to modify their behaviors toward more positive outcomes. *Decisional balance* refers to the client weighing the pros and cons of any specific behavioral change. *Self-efficacy* is the client's confidence that they can sustain the change and that it will result in the desired outcome. *Temptation* represents the client's urge to go back to their previous behaviors, and is the counterpart to self-efficacy.

As you develop a case conceptualization, it is important to not only gather information about a client's presenting problem, but also get an idea of their motivation toward change. It is also valuable to gain an understanding of what the client has tried already—what has worked and what hasn't. You also need to know what internal and external resources the client can employ to help them with the difficult process of change; to gain a full understanding of our client we have to gather information about resources and positives as well as deficits. This helps the counselor not only develop a conceptualization, but can be crucial for choosing goals and selecting the most effective intervention techniques.

See Figures 3.1 and 3.2 for more information on the stages of change.

THE T/C MODEL: AN INTEGRATIVE APPROACH TO CASE CONCEPTUALIZATION

As is evident from our discussion so far, developing a case conceptualization is a multi-faceted process. Counselors need to establish the relationship; listen attentively; gather relevant information; reflect and provide feedback, validation, and encouragement; assess readiness for change; and start to engage in hypothesis testing and problem solving. Not only do counselors need to be experts in process, they need to be able to formulate a working hypothesis of the presenting problem, think thematically, and help the client set appropriate goals for change. Conceptualizing skills enable the construction of a model that represents the client's world and experiences. It is only from this understanding that counselors can be truly effective in helping clients establish goals and select appropriate intervention strategies.

Figure 3.1   Transtheoretical Model Stages of Change

1. Precontemplation: Clients do not intend to change behavior in the near future and may in fact be unaware of the need to change or fully cognizant of their problems and their impact.

2. Contemplation: Clients may intend to change behavior in the near future and may be more aware of the pros of changing. However, there is still ambivalence about change, the price of change, or the ability to change, which could cause them to put off taking action.

3. Preparation: Clients are motivated toward change, feel that there are more pros to the change than cons, and are contemplating options.

4. Action: Clients are goal driven and are actively changing their behaviors.

5. Maintenance: Clients have made behavioral changes and are trying to maintain the changes and integrate them into normal daily functioning.

Figure 3.2 Transtheoretical Model Processes of Change

- Processes of change are the covert and overt activities that people use to progress through the stages of change.
- As explained by Prochaska and colleagues (1992), there are ten such processes:

  1. Consciousness Raising (Increasing awareness)

  2. Dramatic Relief (Emotional arousal)

  3. Environmental Reevaluation (Social reappraisal)

  4. Social Liberation (Environmental opportunities)

  5. Self-Reevaluation (Self-reappraisal)

  6. Stimulus Control (Re-engineering)

  7. Helping Relationship (Supporting)

  8. Counter Conditioning (Substituting)

  9. Reinforcement Management (Rewarding)

  10. Self-Liberation (Committing)

- The first five are classified as *Experiential Processes* and are used primarily for the early stage transitions.
- The last five are labeled *Behavioral Processes* and are used primarily for later stage transitions.

The T/C Model introduced here acts as a road map for gathering client information and exploring client problems and strengths. The model draws from various theoretical approaches commonly used in counseling, including the theories we reviewed above. In formulating this model, we specifically incorporate aspects of Padesky's Five Aspect Model (Greenburg & Padesky, 1995), Bronfenbrenner's bioecological model (Bronfenbrenner, 1979), and Prochaska's stages of change (Prochaska, DiClemente, & Norcross, 1992). The T/C Model expands on these existing theories, however, taking a holistic approach and not only encompassing the internal mechanisms of personality, but also taking into account external influences both past and present. The model, while drawing from diverse theoretical approaches, is itself atheoretical. This allows counselors who practice from multiple theoretical perspectives to use the model effectively. In addition, the T/C Model is practical in its implementation, designed

to facilitate goal setting and intervention, as well as conceptualization. The model's developmental approach reflects the complexity of the client's experience while at the same time allowing the counselor to focus on targets for change. An additional characteristic which sets the T/C Model apart is its ability to be applied both situationally (to describe a specific event in the client's life) and globally (reflecting the entirety of the client's experience in a holistic manner). The various constructs depicted in the Model are interrelated and interdependent, and are not intended to be exclusive categories.

Importantly, the T/C Model itself is both flexible and comprehensive. Not only does the model assist counselors in gathering information about client problems, but the breadth of the model encourages counselors to focus on clients' strengths, resources, and past successes beginning in the first session. This creates a mindset in both client and counselor that focuses on the future

Figure 3.3 Temporal/Contextual Model of Case Conceptualization

Developed from:
- Padesky's 5 Aspects Model
- Bronfenbrenner's Ecological Systems Theory
- DiClemente and Prochaska's Stages of Change Model

Developed from case conceptualization literature:
- Psychodynamic
- CBT
- Solution Focused
- Humanistic
- Narrative

TEMPORAL CONTEXTUAL (T/C) MODEL OF CASE CONCEPTUALIZATION

Client's Outside World / Environment:
- Culture
- Relationships
- Societal Influences
- Counseling Relationship

AFFECT

Coping skills and strengths

Readiness for change

Symptomology

IPCs
Biology
Physiology

Life roles

BEHAVIOR

COGNITION

Internal Personality Characteristics
- Attitudes
- Values
- Beliefs
- Self-Esteem
- Self-Efficacy
- Attachment Style

Client's internal world

Client's interaction with the outside world

Past   Present   Future

55

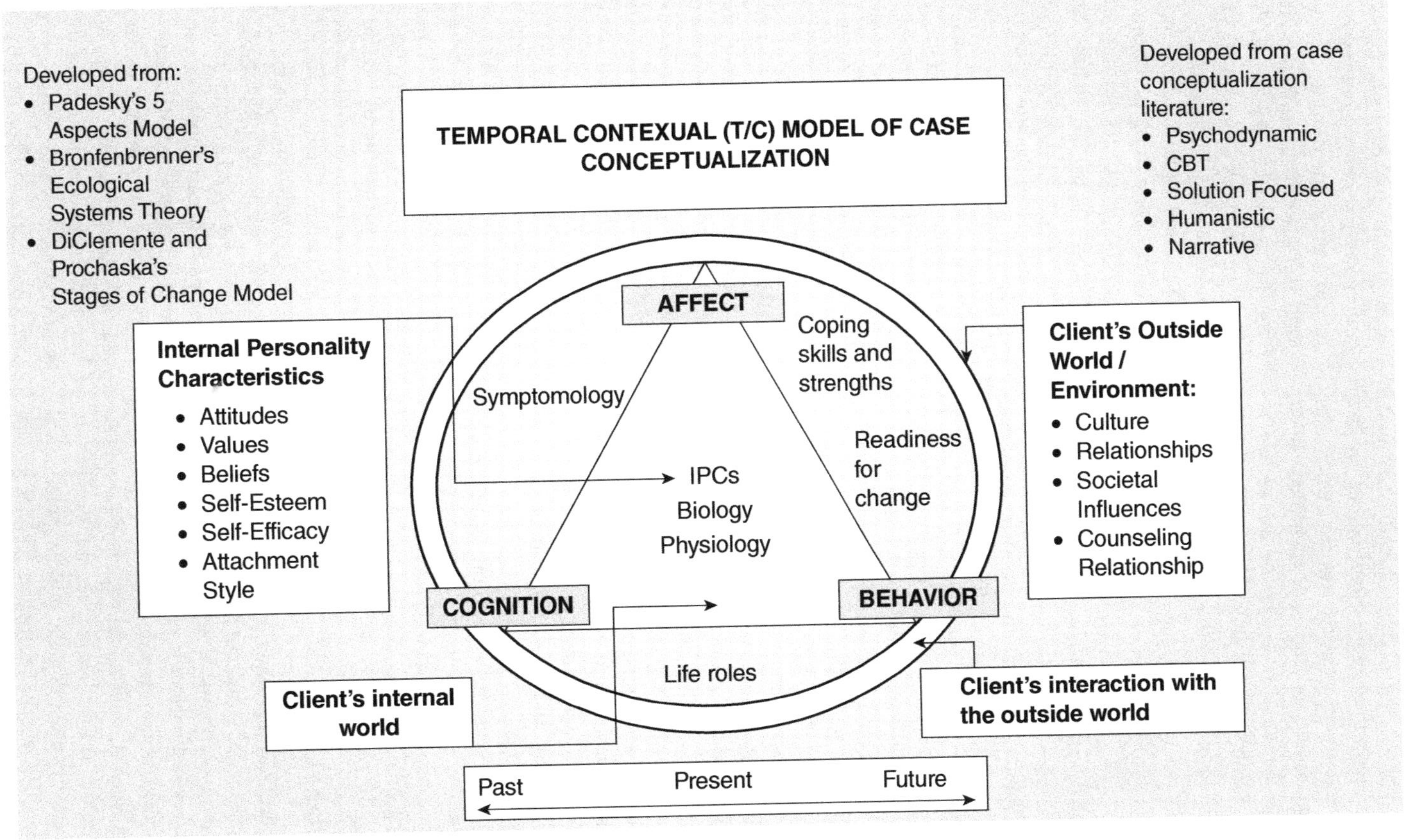

and incorporates hope. Consequently, the model provides a path to change. Interventions are then selected based on existing research, the information gathered, and the path identified. In the following chapters, we apply the model to various case studies, identifying pathways, selecting interventions, and employing these in order to best help clients.

OVERVIEW OF THE MODEL

All counselors recognize the importance of case conceptualization; however, there are few models of case conceptualization which provide an articulated framework of the process. The T/C Model is visually rendered in such a way as to facilitate the counselor's understanding of the client. Highlighted within the model are the client's internal world, including attitudes, values, and belief systems; the client's external world, including environment, relationships, and culture; and the important processes of interaction between the internal and external worlds (behaviors, symptoms, readiness for change, coping skills, and life roles). In addition, the model uses the timeline concept, which allows a focus on past experiences and future goals, as well as the here and now of the present counseling experience.

In the next section, we explore each component of the T/C Model. Finally, we revisit the case of Katy and use the T/C Model to develop a conceptualization of Katy's strengths and challenges.

The Triangle

In Figure 3.3, the triangle represents the three major elements of human experience and expression: behavior, cognition, and affect (emotion). In other words, the triangle represents the client's internal world, both psychological and physiological. Represented within, and expressed by these three elements, is the client's personality. The client's personality embodies the internal personality constructs ("IPCs") that form the client's values

and beliefs, self-concept, and worldview. These internal personality constructs also include the client's attachment style, sense of self-efficacy, and self-esteem. In turn, the internal personality constructs impact the way that the client perceives their environment, how well they cope, and the client's readiness for change.

Cognition includes how the client perceives and interprets information from the environment. Interpretation occurs through the filters of the client's interpersonal schemas and internal working models, as well as through their beliefs about self, others, and the world (both rational and irrational). These beliefs are influenced by attachment and relationship style, and by the norms and values that the client absorbed, from gender roles to cultural beliefs to spirituality (Sperry, 2001). The client's internal world is developed through interaction with the environment, and colored by past experience (at times creating mistaken beliefs and misperceptions).

Behavior encompasses what clients "do"—eating, sleeping, activity level, and withdrawal, as well as the counselor's observations of the client in session, in the here and now. Is the client fidgeting? Sweating? Avoiding eye contact? Keep in mind that the client's behavior and all the constructs in the model interact, reflecting reciprocal relationships between constructs. The client's choices, beliefs, and feelings all impact behavior. It's important for counselors to understand WHY clients do what they do, and not just interpret behaviors at face value.

Affect includes the client's ability for emotional regulation, as well as awareness and expression of emotions. Again, affect does not exist in a vacuum—emotions are tied to thoughts and experience. Clients vary in their capacity for emotional regulation, which is influenced by parenting and attachment history. Counselors can be most effective by keeping in mind the interrelationships between constructs, in order to understand and empathize with clients.

The client's biological experience is also an internal construct. Physiology and biology takes into account clients' individual differences as well as strengths and vulnerabilities in physical health and constitution. This construct also includes an understanding of genetic predispositions and temperament, reaction to stress, biochemical differences in neurotransmitter function, and other brain chemistry factors. These important factors are sometimes neglected in counseling models of case conceptualization.

These genetic and physiological factors influence the client's thoughts, emotions, and behavior, the points of the triangle. For example, the client's beliefs, developed from the interaction of personality, biology, and experience (environment) create "hot thoughts" which are directly connected to affect. For example, Katy's belief that her situation is hopeless is tied to her anxiety and depression. The link between cognition and behavior is also important—for example, without the belief that she can succeed (self-efficacy), Katy is unlikely to change her behavior.

The Inner Circle

The inner circle represents the boundary between the client's internal and external worlds, the space where the client interacts with the environment and the environment is in turn impacted by the client. Symptomology is the first and perhaps most obvious construct on the inner circle. Both somatic symptoms and psychological symptoms must be assessed and understood before moving forward to a diagnosis or goal setting. Once again, the interrelationships between symptoms and internal and external constructs is important to understand. For example, somatic symptoms may be associated with emotional response; in Katy's case, her anxiety and depression are expressed behaviorally as difficulty sleeping and eating. Katy's symptoms are a reflection of her internal conflicts and discord, which are in turn impacted by her current circumstances and her way of thinking about those circumstances.

Also included in the inner circle are the client's coping skills and strengths. As we've seen, assessment of the client's strengths is as important as a thorough understanding of the client's challenges. Uncovering the client's strengths

and supports that often are initially outside the client's awareness is vital so that these can be applied as the client moves forward into the process of change. In addition, the client's current readiness for change impacts the counselor's conceptualization and how to proceed with goal setting and planning. These coping strategies, client strengths, and motivation for change are located on the inner circle, since they can impact the development of either symptoms or healthy adjustment.

The final construct in the inner circle is an understanding of the client's life roles. We all play multiple roles in life—mother, daughter, sister, coworker, accountant, friend—and each role influences both what we do and how we view ourselves. Life roles are depicted along the inner circle, since these impact the way the client responds to stressful environmental events. Accordingly, life roles are influenced by the norms, values, attitudes, and beliefs that the client has absorbed as well as the individual's attachment style, once again emphasizing the interconnectedness of the T/C Model and the client's real-life experience. The client's negotiation of multiple and sometimes conflicting roles has an influence on identity development, and can impact the client's self-esteem and stress levels that are all relevant issues in counseling.

The Outer Circle

The outer circle represents the multiple environmental and relational influences that impact the client (and are in turn impacted by the client). These include the client's interpersonal relationships (family, peer, and romantic), culture, socioeconomic status, community, social structures, and societal norms that influence identity and experience. An important relationship which impacts the client going forward is the counselor-client relationship. As we have seen, the therapeutic relationship is closely related to client outcome.

Again, keep in mind that the interrelationships between constructs are reciprocal. Environment, for example, plays a critical role in how the client's IPCs are constructed, and various environmental conditions have differential impact depending on the client's developmental stage. Within the environment reside the precipitating stressors which may have brought the client to counseling. Symptoms occur when the person's risk factors and vulnerabilities overwhelm their strengths and coping strategies, and are depicted in the diagram as located in the intersection between person and environment.

The counseling relationship is also a unique and influential part of the client's environment. Through our interactions with the client, we can help the client explore how the environmental influences of their past continue to impact their present and future. The therapeutic relationship plays out in the here and now allowing a comprehensive assessment and interpretation of the impact of all the components in the model. The relationship itself is a powerful means of gaining understanding and insight.

Timeline

The line at the bottom of the model represents time: past, present, and future. The timeline implies both context and setting, and reminds both counselor and client that events which happened in the past can be interpreted differently in the light of the present. The T/C Model is contextual in nature, and can be implemented with a focus on the past, present, or future depending on the counselor's theoretical orientation and the needs of the client.

Environmental factors from the client's past may have shaped the cognitions and self-concept the client has in the present. Thus, it may be important to explore the client's early family experiences in order to gain insight into whether certain cognitions are distorted or behaviors are maladaptive. All of us learn some irrational beliefs as part of the socialization process of childhood (Corey, 2009). The incorporation of the timeline allows counselors to be flexible in assessing a client's current circumstances by examining a client's identity

across time, and focusing on the future. The client's understanding of the past can be used to imagine a future self, with fewer problems and a healthy, positive identity. This imagined future is the source of both future goals and motivation to move toward those goals. The client's past and current experience impact readiness for change. Finally, counselors need to take into account the client's behaviors, thoughts, and feelings in the present by using a here and now focus to clarify and correct whatever is getting in the client's way.

Applying the T/C Model

Depending on the theoretical approach taken, different aspects of the T/C Model are expanded on and emphasized. Once a thorough case conceptualization is developed, a deeper understanding of the client's problems and strengths emerges, which leads to the trust and rapport that allows an effective counseling relationship and serves as a bridge to goal setting and treatment planning.

Let's take a moment to apply the T/C Model of Case Conceptualization to Katy's situation. What do we know about the various domains represented in the model, and what do we still need to find out? Using the T/C Model as a framework allows you to fill in the blanks, while also making clear the gaps in your knowledge. In subsequent chapters, we will again apply the model to cases. While the cases are necessarily brief, in actual practice you will have more information to create a detailed case conceptualization using the model.

THE CASE OF KATY

Example of T/C Case Conceptualization Model Outline

(* Areas that the counselor believes require more information)

Presenting Problem: family and relationship conflict, high levels of depression and anxiety

**Internal Personality
Constructs and Behavior:**

Self-efficacy: low, dismisses past history of academic success in the midst of challenge; dismisses past social success at sorority and at college; details of academic history*

Self-esteem: low

Attitudes/Values/Beliefs: beliefs about success and what is important in life*; gender roles and beliefs*; religious or spiritual beliefs*; sexual attitudes and relationship values*; sexual orientation

Attachment Style: possible insecure anxious ambivalent attachment with mother*, separation from father*

Biology/Physiology/Heredity: 23-year-old young adult; female; sexually active; medical history*; details of parental history of anxiety and alcohol use (mother)*

Affect: depression, anxiety

Cognition: confusion, feeling adrift, "mind won't turn off"

Hot Thoughts: "It's hopeless." "I'm a failure." "I'll never find a job." "My parents think I'm a failure."

Behavior: weight loss, job search, sporadic eye contact, wringing hands, restless, alcohol use, risk taking; details of alcohol use and risk taking*

Symptomology: difficulty sleeping, lack of appetite, panic attacks

Coping Skills and Strengths: intelligent, has friends, mother and stepfather are financial supports, stepfather is emotional support

Readiness for Change: contemplation (aware of need for change, but ambivalent)

Life Roles: negotiating transition from student to prospective employee with difficulty; daughter; friend; girlfriend

Environment:

Relationships: recent breakup with boyfriend, conflict with mother; past relationship history*; relationship with father not well understood*; relationship with stepfather possible strength*; relationship with friends*; relationship with siblings*

Culture: Korean family background; specific cultural information*; acculturation status*

Family Norms and Values: parental expectations for career; parental expectations for academic success; gender roles and beliefs*; family values*; religious or spiritual beliefs*

Societal Influences: socioeconomic expectations*; societal norms around alcohol use*

Timeline:

Past Influences: Parents' immigration*; parents' divorce*; partner breakup*; mother and stepfather conflict*; parents' remarriages*; mother's anxiety; mother's drinking; mother's possible infidelity*; academic and social success at college; sorority membership

Present Influences: conflict with boyfriend; graduation; transition to living at home; conflict with mother; separation from father, and less involved with stepfather

Future Goals: job interview*; career goals unexamined*; relationship goals unexamined*

<u>**Question:**</u> What else would you want to ask, to complete this case conceptualization?

TREATMENT PLANNING

In the course of the case conceptualization process, the counselor begins to understand and develop hypotheses about the etiology of the client's problem, the larger systems impacting the client, and how the symptoms are being sustained. Once you have an understanding of what caused the problem, figuring out what to do about it is much simpler. Thus, the treatment planning process is based on the case conceptualization.

In this phase, the information collected and the analysis of that information is integrated into specific interventions. The treatment plan is a map for how the client can make changes and achieve their goals based on the information gathered, the patterns identified, and the theoretical approach applied to that understanding

(Seligman, 1993). Interventions selected and techniques chosen should be compatible with the inferences and assumptions arrived at in case conceptualization, since treatment plans flow from the conceptualization.

Treatment planning for most counseling approaches includes a behavioral definition of the presenting problem; identification of specific achievable goals; selection of intervention strategies; and outcome measures to examine progress. During each stage of treatment planning, the client's readiness for change, available resources and support, level of dysfunction, and cultural and family context are considered. Goals are set with these factors in mind, to optimize the client's chance of success and allow the restoration of hope and self-efficacy. The counselor's knowledge of common factors, best practices, and evidence-based treatment options, as well as the counselor's ability to select an appropriate theoretical orientation for the client, inform the intervention strategies in the treatment planning stage.

As we've reviewed, assessment of effectiveness is useful not just at the termination of counseling, but throughout the process. There is an emphasis on accountability in the mental health field today, so the development and application of outcome measures is crucial to demonstrate effectiveness (Seligman, 1996). The phases of counseling are not static; rather, effective counselors are constantly reassessing, testing, and modifying conceptualizations, and revising and updating treatment plans as needed.

COUNSELING KEYSTONES

- Case conceptualization is the process by which counselors make sense of a client's presenting problems and come to understand the client's symptoms, thoughts, emotions, behaviors, and personality constructs.
- Three integrated processes of counseling can be identified: diagnosis, where the counselor identifies and describes the client's presenting problem and needs; case conceptualization, where the counselor comes to an understanding of the

client's needs and situation; and treatment planning, where the counselor develops strategies and interventions to address the client's needs and move the client toward change.
- The *Diagnostic and Statistical Manual* (DSM-5) is widely used for diagnosis, using observable features to identify criteria for a wide variety of mental and emotional disorders, categorizing these based on symptom patterns.
- During case conceptualization, the counselor begins to develop a framework to explain the etiology of the client's problem.
- An articulated model of case conceptualization gives counselors a lens through which to understand their clients, which provides a blueprint for how to interact with, listen to, and help.
- The case conceptualization process includes: evaluation, in which the counselor assesses and measures observable behaviors and catalogs symptoms; organization, during which the counselor organizes observations and assessments to make inferences, identify themes and patterns, and develop hypotheses; and orientation, in which counselors employ a particular view of how problems develop and how people behave (a theoretical orientation).
- Another important aspect of the case conceptualization process is a client's level of motivation and readiness for change, as described by Prochaska's *Transtheoretical Model of Change.*
- The Temporal/Contextual Model of case conceptualization (T/C Model) is an atheoretical model that provides a framework or template that counselors can use to focus their observations and generate inferences about the meaning of client presenting problems.
- The T/C Model is flexible and comprehensive, takes a holistic approach, encourages an early focus on client strengths, and not only encompasses the internal mechanisms of personality, but also takes into account external influences both past and present.
- The treatment planning process is based on the case conceptualization, during which the information and analysis is integrated into specific interventions.
- There is an emphasis on accountability in the mental health field today, so the development and application of outcome measures are crucial

to demonstrate effectiveness, with counselors constantly reassessing, testing, and modifying conceptualizations, and revising and updating treatment plans as needed.

EXERCISES

EXERCISE 3.1
Writing Your Job Description

Having a job description is crucial for any profession; the job description defines the scope of responsibilities and the expectations for the position, detailing both what roles are appropriate and (equally important) what roles are inappropriate.

CLASS EXERCISE: Small group discussion, followed by large group discussion.

> **Question 1:** If you were asked to write a job description for a professional counselor, what would it say?

> **Question 2:** What are the main components of the job?

EXERCISE 3.2
Where Do You Begin?

The first session with a new client sets the stage for the way that the therapeutic relationship develops.

CLASS EXERCISE: Large group discussion.

> **Question:** When starting a counseling relationship, what are some opening questions you might ask?

EXERCISE 3.3 What's the Focus?

The way in which counselors process and record information can have an impact on the subsequent phases of counseling. The counselor's choice of words and the order in which questions are asked can result in differences in meaning which then become part of the counselor's conceptualization of the client.

CLASS EXERCISE: Students work individually to brainstorm information needed, followed by large group discussion.

> **Question 1:** Brainstorm the information you want to know about a client during your information gathering process?

> **Question 2:** What elements are you focusing on and why?

EXERCISE 3.4
Asking the Right Questions

There is certain specific information you need to gather in order to make a diagnosis and formulate a case conceptualization.

CLASS EXERCISE: Discuss in small groups, followed by large group discussion. Write down five questions you might ask under each of the following areas:

- Past experiences
- Present behaviors
- Thoughts
- Environmental stressors
- Resources or areas of strength
- Physical symptoms
- Emotions
- Values and beliefs

EXERCISE 3.5 The
Pros and Cons of Diagnosis

The DSM-5 is widely used across the helping professions to provide a diagnosis for clients, which then guides treatment and reimbursement from insurers.

CLASS EXERCISE: Students discuss in small groups, followed by large group discussion.

> **Question 1:** When you think of being given a diagnosis yourself, what thoughts come to your mind?

> **Question 2:** How might your client view his or her diagnosis?

EXERCISE 3.6
What Lens Best Fits You?

You read about the different theoretical lenses used in case conceptualization.

CLASS EXERCISE: Large group discussion.

Question 1: Which theoretical lens do you feel best fits you? Why?

EXERCISE 3.7 Stages of Change

Determining a client's stage of readiness for change can help you decide where to start to help you and the client set appropriate and achievable goals.

CLASS EXERCISE: Students discuss in small groups, working with the Stages of Change

Model presented earlier in the chapter, followed by each group presenting their assessment and a discussion of the basis for that assessment.

Question 1: Think about the case of Katy. What stage of readiness for change do you think Katy is in? Why?

GO FURTHER

Mind Over Mood: Change How You Feel by Changing the Way You Think by Dennis Greenberger and Christine Padesky (1995) Guilford Press

Systems of Psychotherapy: A Transtheoretical Analysis by James O. Prochaska and John C. Norcross (2009) Cengage Learning

Making Human Beings Human: Bioecological Perspectives on Human Development (The SAGE Program on Applied Developmental Science) by Urie Bronfenbrenner (2004) SAGE

PART II

Case Conceptualization and Evidence-Based Treatments for DSM-5 Diagnoses

4

DEPRESSIVE DISORDERS

The Case of James

James, a 30-year-old man dressed in jeans and a rumpled shirt buttoned wrong, sat slumped in his chair at the counselor's office, wringing his hands in his lap and looking down.

"Can you tell me how you're feeling?" the counselor urged, and James finally looked up. His eyes were red-rimmed, and he struggled to blink back tears as he met the counselor's gaze.

"It's just getting worse," he said, his voice so soft that the counselor could hardly hear him. "I can't bring myself to even answer the phone when my friends call. They don't really want to hang out with me anyway, they just feel obligated. I've been missing work too."

"What's making it hard to go to work?" the counselor asked, keeping eye contact with James.

James shook his head sadly. "I get these terrible headaches, and I'm just so tired all the time, I can't think straight—so why bother trying to work? I'm failing at that—failing at everything."

"You're having trouble concentrating—anything else?"

James nodded, looking down again. "Sleeping, eating, thinking . . .you name it. I wake up at 4 a.m. and can't get back to sleep, thinking about how hopeless it all is."

The counselor leaned forward in his chair, speaking softly as well. "How long have you been feeling this way?"

James paused, then went on, even more softly.

"A long time—six months, maybe a year. Why do I even bother? Everyone would be better off if I wasn't even alive."

INTRODUCTION

We all experience feelings of sadness in our daily lives, especially when we are confronted with stressful life events, loss, or conflict, but these feelings tend to be fleeting. We occasionally feel "down" or "blue," but those feelings tend to pass quickly. Depression, in contrast, lasts longer and interferes with daily living—work, school, concentration, eating, or sleeping. Depressive disorders are characterized by a sad, empty, or irritable mood as well as cognitive and physiological

65

changes. These symptoms have a significant impact on the person's ability to function, as we can see from the case of James.

In the United States, approximately 9.5% of the adult population in a given year are diagnosed with a mood disorder, which translates to over twenty million people (Kessler, Chiu, Demler, & Walters, 2005). Depression can be chronic (Spijker et al. 2002), and major depressive disorder is the second largest healthcare problem in terms of disability caused by illness, according to the World Health Organization (Levav & Rutz, 2002). Depression can cause physical suffering, such as headaches, stomach upset, or chronic pain, as well as emotional pain. Feelings of hopelessness, helplessness, and self-blame are common, and individuals suffering from depression may lose interest in daily activities, hobbies, and relationships. Depression can be overwhelming, keeping people from interacting with others and participating actively in their own lives. They may withdraw from family and friends, and this isolation can actually make the depression worse. Some depressed individuals may consider or attempt suicide.

Unfortunately, there is still some stigma associated with seeking help for depression, especially when viewed as a sign of weakness. Advice to "snap out of it" can lead to feelings of self-blame when depressive symptoms persist, but people with depression often cannot just "feel better"—if they could, they most likely would! When depressed individuals do not seek treatment, over time symptoms can worsen. Fortunately, depression is highly treatable, even when the symptoms are severe.

The DSM section on depressive disorders underwent some of the most controversial changes from DSM-IV to DSM-5, with several new disorders added and some removed. In addition, "Bipolar and Related Disorders" is now a separate chapter. In the sections below, we summarize the symptoms and characteristics of the depressive disorders that counselors most often encounter and treat.

DISRUPTIVE MOOD DYSREGULATION DISORDER (DMDD)

Disruptive mood dysregulation disorder (DMDD) was added in the newest edition of the

---

The Case of Jesse

A counselor is meeting with the parents of Jesse, a 9-year-old who is struggling both in school and at home.

Mom: "I just don't know what to do anymore. He's out of control so often, and he's getting too big for me to pick up and put in time out."

Dad: "He won't stay there anyway, not when he's in one of his 'moods.' He doesn't even seem to hear us when he gets like that."

Counselor: "So Jesse has outbursts of temper and you can't get through to him during those times? When do these outbursts happen?"

Dad: "When he doesn't get his way. It can be anything—we can tell him it's time for bed . . ."

Mom: (interrupts) "Oh God, bedtime, it's become a nightmare. He just won't go!"

Dad: "He just lies down on the floor and pounds his fists and kicks his feet and screams—it's like he's a 2-year-old again."

Mom: (nodding) "It's terrible. And even when he's not having a tantrum, every little thing sets him off."

Counselor: "Jesse is easily irritated, would you say?"

Parents: (nodding)

Mom: "He's just so angry all the time. What are we doing wrong? Why isn't he happy?"

Diagnostic and Statistical Manual of Mental Disorders (DSM-5). This disorder typically presents in children; as a result it appears first in the Depressive Disorders section, and applies to children up to the age of 12. The addition of this disorder is in part a response to the increase in diagnosis of bipolar disorder in children and adolescents from 1994 to the present. However, standard treatments for bipolar disorder, such as lithium, were not effective for these young people, and many went on to develop depression or anxiety instead of bipolar disorder. This suggested a diagnostic gap for children with mood dysregulation and angry outbursts.

The core feature of DMDD is chronic severe persistent irritability, marked by temper outbursts (usually in response to frustration) that must occur on average three or more times per week for at least one year and in two settings (i.e., home and school). The episodes of behavioral dyscontrol must be developmentally inappropriate. Another manifestation of the severe irritability in DMDD is chronic, persistently irritable or angry mood present between the severe temper outbursts, which must be present most of the day nearly every day and noticeable by others. When a child has DMDD, family and peer relationships are significantly disrupted.

DMDD must be diagnosed during childhood—before age 10, but after age 6. DMDD peaks during the elementary school years. Some children with Oppositional Defiant Disorder (ODD) may meet the criteria for DMDD; however, there is no requirement of severe anger outbursts three times a week or underlying irritable mood present in ODD, and not as many of the acting out externalizing behaviors. (In other words, DMDD is the severe end of the ODD spectrum.)

PREMENSTRUAL DYSPHORIC DISORDER (PMDD)

The Case of Genevieve

Genevieve, a 25-year-old woman, sought counseling at a community behavioral health center. She is an attractive woman who holds a responsible position as assistant manager of a boutique clothing store in the city and is engaged to be married. However, despite Genevieve's many successes, she is having bouts of severe depression that are starting to adversely impact both her job and her relationship.

Genevieve: *"I don't get it. Most of the time, I can deal with things just fine. But, sometimes it's like everything is horrible. I find myself crying for no reason one minute, and then I'm snapping at the customers the next. I'm starting to be afraid for my job!"*

Counselor: *"Are there any other symptoms you can remember that happen during these times?"*

Genevieve: *"I fight more with my boyfriend—it's like everything he does is wrong, and yet I know he's a great guy. I know he's not going to leave me, but suddenly I'm convinced that he's about to. Am I going crazy?"*

Counselor: *"Can you tell me if these symptoms worsen at the same time every month, perhaps around the time of your monthly menstrual cycle?"*

Genevieve: *"My . . . I never thought about that. I don't know—wait, actually, I think that might be true. It definitely happened this past month a few days before."*

Counselor: *"And when did you start to feel better again, more like yourself?"*

Genevieve: *"A few days after, I guess. Actually yes, I remember that by Thursday I was sleeping better again, and my fiancé and I went out to dinner and I could just enjoy myself."*

premenstrual dysphoric disorder (PMDD) was also added in DSM-5, formerly appearing only in the Appendix of DSM-IV. In general, the DSM-5 reflects the accumulation of research which indicates that medical issues affect mental health.

PMDD disorder requires significant affective symptoms in the week prior to the menstrual cycle that quickly disappear after the cycle, and that symptoms appear in all menstrual cycles over the past year. These include affective lability (mood swings, sensitivity to rejection), irritability and increased interpersonal conflicts, depressed mood (including hopeless and self-deprecating thoughts), and anxiety, as well as one or more additional symptoms. Some individuals report decreased interest in their usual activities, difficulty concentrating, lack of energy, change in appetite, sleep problems, feeling overwhelmed or out of control, or physical symptoms, such as breast or joint tenderness or feeling bloated. PMDD can occur any time after menarche. Symptoms may worsen near menopause and cease afterwards.

While PMDD is not a culture-bound syndrome and has been observed worldwide, nevertheless the ways in which the symptoms are expressed and interpreted is related to the client's social and cultural background, family and religious beliefs, and the culture's norms about gender, sexuality, and help seeking. In Genevieve's case, she was open to the diagnosis of PMDD once the counselor brought it up, and even appeared relieved to have an explanation for her confusing mood swings. Other clients may not be so open to a PMDD diagnosis, or may not want to pathologize what they view as normal biological functioning. PMDD is distinguished from Premenstrual Syndrome (PMS) by severity of symptoms and significant impairment or distress, but counselors are cautioned not to pathologize normal functioning.

MAJOR DEPRESSIVE DISORDER (MDD), INCLUDING MAJOR DEPRESSIVE EPISODE (MDE)

James, the client we met at the beginning of this chapter, is experiencing a major depressive episode (MDE), which is defined in DSM-5 by a depressed mood or a loss of interest or pleasure, plus four other symptoms. These include middle insomnia (waking in the middle of the night) or terminal insomnia (waking in the very early morning), psychomotor retardation or agitation, fatigue or loss of energy, difficulty with concentration, or suicidal ideation. It's important to note that a client can meet criteria for a MDE without depressed mood, but instead with irritability or loss of interest or pleasure in life, especially for children or the elderly, for whom loss of interest and somatic symptoms are common. Clients must exhibit these symptoms for at least two weeks, and there must be clinically significant distress or impairment in social, occupational, or other important life roles. Risk of recurrence is greater the longer the depressive episode is sustained. If even mild symptoms of depression remain during remission, the risk of recurrence is increased.

The DSM-5 requires clear-cut changes in mood, thinking, and neurovegetative functions for a diagnosis of major depressive disorder (MDD), and these symptoms must remit between major depressive episodes. A client can be diagnosed after a single episode, but major depressive disorder is often recurrent.

Symptoms include depressed mood most of the day nearly every day, which can be described as "feeling flat" or without feelings, or can manifest as irritability in children. A lack of interest or pleasure in activities that the person used to enjoy is also a symptom of depression, which clients sometimes describe as "I just don't care anymore." Unintentional weight loss or change in appetite, sleeping too much or difficulty sleeping, and changes in level of activity (unable to sit still, or fatigue and low energy) are symptoms of depression as well. Clients may report feelings of guilt or worthlessness, have difficulty concentrating, or report thoughts of suicide.

Depressive symptoms can appear at any age, although the incidence of MDD appears to peak in the twenties. The course of MDD varies across individuals. Some people have isolated depressive episodes that are separated by several years throughout which mood is normal, while others suffer clusters of major depressive episodes that occur tightly together. Still others with Major Depression experience increasingly frequent episodes as they grow older.

It's important to rule out a bipolar disorder diagnosis whenever a client presents with depression symptoms. Asking the client if they have ever had a period of time where they felt the opposite of how they feel now is helpful; for example, when they felt really good, didn't need as much sleep, and other people noticed their mood was different. When working with an adolescent, keep in mind that the individual may not have had a manic episode yet, but could develop one in the future. The "with mixed features" specifier is used to indicate the presence of coexisting manic or hypomanic symptoms, such as rapid speech or reduced sleep, when there are not enough of such symptoms to satisfy criteria for a manic episode. The use of this specifier allows for the existence of manic features in clients with a diagnosis of major depressive disorder. These symptoms may indicate the need for different or a combination of medications, or may suggest a risk of bipolar disorder in the future.

A significant change to the DSM-5 was the removal of the "bereavement exclusion," which applied if depression symptoms began within two months of the death of a loved one. The change removes the implication that bereavement tends to last only several months, and recognizes it as a serious stressor that can precipitate a major depression episode. While most people experience bereavement without developing depression, individuals who have a history of past depressive episodes are at greater risk of becoming depressed after the death of a loved one. Symptoms similar to depression are common in the months following any sort of significant loss, whether from death, divorce, retirement, loss of functioning, or a serious health diagnosis. Instead of broadening the exclusion, the DSM-5 simply removed it, along with the two-month restriction. However, it is important to consider recent losses when diagnosing depression, since symptoms of grief may resemble a MDE. When MDD occurs with bereavement,

there can be even greater pain. If a client had recurrent depressive episodes over their life span, they may be more likely to develop a MDE after a loss event. With grief, the predominant feelings are of emptiness and loss; with a MDE, the persistent depressed mood and little expectation of happiness or pleasure are predominant. In addition, the depressed mood of MDE is more persistent, whereas grief often "comes in waves." It's up to the clinician to make the judgment as to whether depression post loss is normal or not.

In addition to the elimination of the bereavement exclusion, new specifiers were added to the DSM-5, including "with anxious distress" (tension, restlessness, frequent worry). When depression is combined with anxious distress, prognosis is worsened and risk of suicide increases, complicating treatment. Other specifiers include "with melancholic features" (profound loss of interest or pleasure), psychotic features (thought insertion, depersonalization), catatonia (motionless for hours), and atypical features (sleeping more and eating more instead of less). Peripartum Onset is also a specifier, which is a new addition to the DSM-5 and reflects the problem of depression during pregnancy. Most postpartum depression is believed to begin during pregnancy, with CBT (cognitive behavioral therapy) and IPT (interpersonal therapy) found to be effective for the 3 to 5% of women who develop this problem. "With seasonal pattern" is also a specifier for MDD, replacing seasonal affective disorder. Finally, the "recurrent" specifier takes into account the increased risk of developing a future MDE once a client has experienced one in the past, allowing counselors to more effectively prevent future episodes.

We'll return to the case of James at the end of this chapter, and listen in as the counselor develops a case conceptualization using the T/C Model.

PERSISTENT DEPRESSIVE DISORDER (PDD)

Persistent depressive disorder (PDD) is a chronic depressive spectrum disorder that replaces the

The Case of Tom

Tom, a man in his fifties, comes to see a counselor at the insistence of his wife.

Tom: "I think my wife has just had it with me. I just don't want to do anything anymore. I don't have the energy. Sometimes I don't even want to get out of bed."

Counselor: "How long have you felt his way?"

Tom: (sighing) "A long time, I guess. I've felt depressed on and off since college, and sometimes it got pretty bad . . ."

Counselor: "How bad? Bad enough to feel hopeless and think of killing yourself?"

Tom: (nodding) "A few times, yeah. But, it usually got a little better after a while and I sort of tried to just keep living with it."

Counselor: "And this time, it isn't?"

Tom: (shakes his head) "It's just starting to feel like this is the way things are—this is how I am. I don't think it's going to change. My dad was the same way, he went out on disability when he wasn't quite sixty, and he basically just drunk himself to death after that."

Counselor: "I'm so sorry, that must have been very difficult for you."

Tom: "It was, I guess. My mom kept trying to get him to eat something, to stop drinking, to get up off the couch. He just never did."

Counselor: "Tom, are there any times during the day that you don't feel depressed?"

Tom: (shakes his head again) "Not really. It's all day, every day."

Counselor: "And how long have you felt this way?"

Tom: "It's hard to say, I think it sort of snuck up on me. My wife says it's been at least two years, maybe three. I don't think there's much hope of changing anything now. I don't blame her for thinking about leaving me."

---

dysthymia category from the DSM-IV, and expands the symptom constellation to include the older diagnoses of both dysthymia and chronic major depression. The DSM-5 conceptualizes chronic depression differently, with both chronic major depressive disorder and the previous category of dysthymic disorder incorporated in this new category. The DSM-5 task force found no clinically meaningful differences between the two disorders; specifiers are now used to identify different pathways to the diagnosis. Symptoms must be present for two years, but the new disorder also

includes more severe symptoms that are chronic and may include major depressive episodes. Specifiers distinguish between the less severe symptoms that were typical of dysthymia, persistent MDEs (formerly referred to as "double depression"), and intermittent MDEs with or without current MDEs.

This disorder can be diagnosed when the mood disturbance continues for at least two years in adults or one year in children. Adults who are diagnosed with PDD have not been symptom free for more than a two-month period during those two years. The essential feature of PDD is depressed mood for most of the day for most days, with two or more other symptoms, including poor appetite or overeating, sleeping too much or too little, low energy or feeling fatigued, low self-esteem, difficulty concentrating or making decisions, and feelings of hopelessness. As with MDD, there has never been a manic or hypomanic episode. There is often an early and insidious onset of PDD.

SUBSTANCE/MEDICATION INDUCED DEPRESSION

Substance/Medication Induced Depression is also included in DSM-5. Medications, such as blood pressure and hypothyroidism treatments, and use of alcohol or drugs, can be associated with depression. Diagnosis of this disorder requires sufficient time for the counselor to disentangle the medication or substance use from the depression. For example, if the depression emerged prior to the client's alcohol use, a more appropriate diagnosis might be major depressive episode. If the client stops using alcohol and the depression symptoms disappear, again, this diagnosis would not be appropriate. This type of depression sometimes includes atypical symptoms, such as lack of feelings, worthlessness, or low self-esteem.

OTHER SPECIFIED AND UNSPECIFIED DEPRESSIVE DISORDERS

Finally, the Depressive Disorders chapter of DSM-5 includes other specified and unspecified, which replaces the DSM-IV category of not otherwise specified (NOS), which was overused according to the DSM task force. If a client does not meet criteria for a MDE, for example, but is experiencing symptoms which are significant and serious, an OSDD (other specified depressive disorder) diagnosis can be used with the severe symptoms described.

COMORBIDITY

When there are co-occurring disorders, treatment of depression can be more complicated. Other mental and physical disorders can be precipitating factors in developing depression, can be more likely because of depression, or can simply occur simultaneously. Anxiety disorders are the most common co-occurring problems, including posttraumatic stress disorder (PTSD), panic disorder, social phobia, generalized anxiety disorder, and obsessive-compulsive disorder (OCD) (Devane, Chiao, Franklin, & Kruep, 2005; Regier, Rae, Narrow, Kaebler, & Schatzberg, 1998). As previously mentioned, experiencing a traumatic event can be a risk factor for developing depression; individuals can also develop PTSD after experiencing a trauma. A National Institute of Mental Health (NIMH) study of people who had experienced a traumatic event found that over 40% who developed PTSD also suffered from depression four months post trauma (Shalev et al., 1998). Individuals with depression also commonly have issues with substance abuse (Conway, Comptom, Stinson, & Grant, 2006). The pain of depression is difficult to bear, and those who do not get appropriate treatment may self-medicate with alcohol or other drugs.

Co-occurring medical conditions that are chronic or disabling also complicate the course of depression. Chronic illness, such as heart disease, diabetes, cancer, multiple sclerosis, fibromyalgia, human immunodeficiency virus (HIV), and Parkinson's disease are also risk factors for depression. The hopelessness that can come with a chronic diagnosis creates a predisposition for depression, and both diagnoses tend to worsen when they occur together (Cassano & Fava, 2002).

Substance abuse, panic disorder, obsessive compulsive disorder, anorexia, and bulimia nervosa also may be comorbid with MDD. In addition to mood and anxiety disorders, DMDD has high rates of comorbidity with autism spectrum disorders, and PMDD can co-occur with medical diagnoses, such as allergies, asthma, and migraines. Pathological gambling co-occurs with substance/medication-induced disorder. In addition, certain personality disorders may be comorbid, including paranoid, histrionic, and antisocial personality disorder. Comorbid disorders common with PDD include anxiety disorders and substance use disorder. When the disorder is diagnosed before age 20, there is a higher risk of comorbid personality disorder or substance use disorder.

CULTURAL CONSIDERATIONS AND POPULATION FACTORS

Depression touches all groups of people, regardless of age, gender, ethnicity, or socioeconomic status. There are, however, differences in prevalence and symptom constellation in various groups of people.

Major depressive disorder is more prevalent in women than men. Females are 1.5 to 3 times more likely to be diagnosed with MDD than males, beginning in early adolescence (Cyranowski, Frank, Young, & Shear, 2000). Contributing factors include hormonal shifts with the menstrual cycle, ovulation, childbirth, and menopause, as well as cultural norms which may call for women to take on both work and home responsibilities, leading to role confusion and stress (Rubinow, Schmidt, & Roca, 1998). There is no specific diagnosis of what is commonly referred to as "Postpartum Depression"; however, a specifier of "with peripartum onset" can be used if the depressive episode occurs during pregnancy or after childbirth (Cuijpers, Brannmark, & Van Straten, 2008).

Women and men also experience different symptoms with depression. Women report more sadness, guilt, and feelings of worthlessness, while men have trouble sleeping, and experience fatigue, anger, and irritability (Cochran & Rabinowitz, 1998).

In contrast, DMDD is more common in males and school-age children, less in females and adolescents. Clients diagnosed with Substance/Medication Induced Depression are also more likely to be male than female, and more likely to be Black.

There are also age-related differences in the symptoms and prevalence of depression.

Children with depression may exhibit anxiety or irritability more than feelings of sadness. These can manifest as school refusal, clinginess, or behavioral difficulties (Walker & Roberts, 2001). By adolescence, depression can be connected to issues of identity, including sexual orientation, ethnic affiliation, and gender identity. Substance abuse and eating disorders commonly occur with adolescent depression, and suicide is a significant risk (Shaffer et al., 1996; Weissman et al., 1999).

Among older adults, depression can be caused or exacerbated by certain medical conditions or medications. For example, vascular depression occurs when blood vessels harden with age and become constricted. Loss is more frequent for the elderly, which can lead to either normal grieving or depression. The elderly may be unwilling to talk about being depressed, leading to misdiagnosis and lack of treatment. White men over the age of 85 have the highest suicide rate in the United States (Luoma, Martin, & Pearson, 2002).

The effectiveness of counseling for individuals diagnosed with a mood disorder has been demonstrated across a wide range of ages and diverse populations, including older adults, children and adolescents, low income clients, and individuals with disabilities (Kazdin, 2008; Kazdin et al., 2010). It is important to keep in mind, however, that certain underserved populations can benefit from specific adaptations to evidence-based treatments. For example, research suggests that racial/ethnic minorities, people with disabilities, those living in poverty, and members of the LGBT community may face specific challenges not addressed by current evidence-based treatment. Counselors should be sensitive to these challenges and pursue appropriate adaptations (Glickman, 2009; Livneh & Sherwood, 2001; Radnitz, 2000; Smith, 2005; Sue & Lam, 2002).

ETIOLOGY AND RISK FACTORS

Like most mental disorders, depression is not caused by a single precipitating factor. Rather, depression is multiply determined with various genetic, biological, chemical, social, psychological, and environmental factors impacting the development of the disorder. A combination of risk factors and environmental stressors can bring about an episode. The causes of depression are not always immediately apparent, so the case conceptualization process is crucial.

The Role of Experience

Sometimes the stressors which contribute to depression are acute and current; other times, there is a history of abuse or trauma that contribute to negative thought patterns and difficulties with identity and self-esteem. Significant transitions and major life stressors, such as the death of a loved one, the loss of a job, or relationship fractures like divorce or separation, can help bring about depression. Other more subtle factors that lead to a loss of self-identity or self-esteem may also contribute, like persistent bullying.

Normal developmental milestones, such as puberty, marriage, launching adult children, or retirement, may also serve to trigger depression when a particular event is personally distressing. Thoughts or situations that trigger a depressive episode may be new or reoccurring, or they may be past events that are re-traumatizing. Individuals who have experienced a traumatic event, such as a military battle, sexual assault, severe accident, or natural disaster, are more likely to experience a major depressive episode than people who have not experienced such trauma.

There are additional risk factors associated with specific depressive disorders. Seasonal changes and cultural norms for sexual behavior and gender roles can be risk factors for PMDD; a history of chronic irritability is a risk factor for DMDD; low income can be a risk factor for Substance/Medication Induced Depression; and parental loss or separation is a risk factor for PDD.

Biological and Genetic Factors

Certain mood disorders tend to run in families, suggesting a genetic component (Tsuang & Faraone, 1990). Close family members of clients with MDD have a risk two to four times higher than the general population of developing MDD, especially for early onset of depression symptoms. An imbalance in brain chemicals (neurotransmitters) has been found to be implicated in the development of depression, and there are differences in brain scans in people with depression on MRI scans (magnetic resonance imaging). Temperament risk factors associated with risk for developing a depressive disorder include neuroticism (negative affect).

TREATMENT INTERVENTIONS

Left untreated, depression may last for months or years, and can worsen over time. However, depression is a treatable disorder; those who seek treatment often see significant improvement in symptoms. Individuals with depression who do not seek help suffer needlessly. When feelings and worries are not expressed, the isolation experienced can lead to worsening depression, which can last for long periods of time. Even individuals with severe depression can benefit from treatment.

Many research studies have demonstrated that counseling is effective for treating depression and relieving symptoms experienced by individuals who suffer from depression. Early treatment is beneficial—psychological treatments may prevent a person with milder depression from becoming more severely depressed. Further, although a past history of depression increases the risk of future episodes, there is evidence that ongoing counseling may lessen the chance of recurrence.

Several different approaches to counseling can help people recover from depression, specifically by identifying the behavioral, interpersonal, psychological, and situational factors that contribute to their symptoms and helping them deal more effectively with these influences.

Counseling Interventions

There have been numerous empirical studies which have established that psychotherapy is effective in treating depressive disorders (Cuijpers, Brannmark, & Van Straten, 2008; Cuijpers, van Straten, Warmerdam, & Smits, 2008; Elkin et al., 1989). Research demonstrates the efficacy of various modalities of treatment for mood disorders. Counseling approaches include cognitive behavioral treatment, reality therapy, client-centered counseling, and interpersonal therapy. Studies comparing the relative effectiveness of various types of psychotherapy show no significant differences in effectiveness (Castonguay & Beutler, 2006; Norcross, 2011). Compared to no treatment, the efficacy of counseling approaches across diverse conditions, including depression, are well established (Lambert & Archer, 2006; Shedler, 2010; Wampold, 2007). According to the research, most clients experiencing depression are able to return to normal functioning after a relatively brief course of counseling (Baldwin, Berkeljon, Atkins, Olsen, & Nielsen, 2009; Stiles, Barkham, Connell, & Mellor-Clark, 2008; Wampold & Brown, 2005).

Counseling is effective for adults, as well as in special populations, such as older adults (Cuijpers, van Straten, & Smit, 2006) and women with postpartum depression (Lumley, Austin, & Mitchell, 2004). Psychotherapy is also an effective treatment for children and adolescents with depression (Kazdin et al., 2010; Weisz, McCarty, & Valeri, 2006). Older adults with depression can benefit from problem solving and supportive therapy (Alexopoulos et al., 2011; Areán et al., 2010) as well as from reminiscence and life review (Bohlmeijer, Smit, & Cuijpers, 2003).

Psychological and pharmacological treatments for depression show comparable effects (Robinson, Berman, & Neimeyer, 1990), and combined treatment is more effective than treatment with medication alone (Arnow & Constantino, 2003; Friedman et al., 2004; Pampanolla, Bollini, Tibaldi, Kupelnick, & Munizza, 2004).

Cognitive Behavioral Interventions

Cognitive behavioral therapy (CBT) has been shown to be effective for the treatment of depression (Churchill et al., 2001; Gloaguen, Cottraux, Cucherat, & Blackburn, 1998; Pace & Dixon, 1993; Wampold, Minami, Baskin, & Tierney, 2002).

Based on the work of Aaron Beck and colleagues (Beck, Rush, Shaw & Emery, 1979), cognitive models of depression emphasize our cognitive schemas, or core beliefs. These underlying assumptions about self and others develop out of early experiences. Depressed individuals often develop negative beliefs about themselves and others, which lead people to interpret life events through a negative filter, distorting reality to fit their schemas. Cognitive treatment is based on the idea that when people experience stressful life events, negative ways of thinking which they have developed over the life course can be activated, along with negative automatic thoughts. The self-defeating thoughts create a negative filter which the person uses to view themselves and others, which leads to depression, which in turn reinforces the negative ways of thinking, producing a vicious cycle. Cognitive therapy challenges these negative automatic thoughts and beliefs, teaching the client to engage in reality testing and eventually replacing the dysfunctional and irrational thoughts with more functional and rational ones. The client can then challenge these negative beliefs in the future, reducing symptoms of depression.

Counselors working from a cognitive or cognitive behavioral orientation help clients become aware of negative and distorted patterns of thinking and behavior that contribute to feelings of hopelessness, helplessness, and self-blame. When clients revise their habitual ways of thinking, a more realistic view of self and others develops, resulting in more positive interactions and relationships. A counselor working from a CBT perspective helps the client identify the life problems that contribute to their depression, and helps them understand which aspects of those problems they may be able to solve or improve. Perhaps the client was depressed in the past and found some coping strategies that worked, at least partially. Identifying past successes and the parts of contributing factors which are solvable creates a sense of hope, allowing clients to set realistic goals for the future and move toward them. As treatment progresses, the client may also develop new skills for preventing future depressive episodes, strengthening support networks, and crafting new routines for physical and emotional self-care.

Let's revisit the counselor we introduced at the beginning of this chapter as work with James continues using a CBT approach.

Counselor: *"You said before that you don't bother answering the phone when your friends call."*

James: *"Right."*

Counselor: *"It seems like you usually assume that they're only calling because they're obligated, not because they want to spend time with you."*

James: *(nods)*

Counselor: *"I'm a little confused about that, because I remember you saying that a few of your close friends planned a surprise party for your birthday several months ago. That takes a lot of effort—do you think it was only out of obligation?"*

James: *"I don't know, maybe."*

Counselor: *"So they didn't have fun at the party, or seem like they wanted to be there."*

James: *(shrugs) "No, they . . . I guess they did have fun that night."*

Counselor: *"So, it seems as if you have a negative filter on when you think about your friends, and assume that they don't like you when it seems like they probably do."*

James: *"I never thought about it like that. I don't know."*

Counselor: *"We all develop habitual ways of thinking about ourselves and about other people, out of our past experiences. Can you think of some reasons you might assume the worst about your friends?"*

James: *"Well, I haven't had a lot of close friends—we moved around a lot when I*

was a kid, and I was always the new kid, you know? It was hard to make friends, and I got teased a lot. Bullied, I guess."

Counselor: *"That must have been really hard. How did you deal with it?"*

James: *"I just kinda gave up on having friends, kept to myself."*

Counselor: *"Do you think that's contributing to your depression?"*

James: *"Yeah. I feel worse when I stay in my room and don't talk to anyone, but at least I'm not getting hurt."*

Counselor: *"It's understandable that you might worry about the friends you have now, but it seems like that negative filter isn't realistic for you now. Your friends do seem to care."*

James: *"I guess I could give them the benefit of the doubt more often."*

Counselor: *"What would that change, do you think?"*

James: *(with a slight smile) "Well, I might answer the phone more often when they called."*

Counselor: *"And then you might end up not being on your own so much. I wonder if that might make life seem a little less hopeless."*

James: *"And make it a little easier to get out of bed in the morning."*

Meta-analyses have indicated the effectiveness of cognitive therapy as compared to pharmacotherapy or wait-list (no treatment) control conditions for depressive disorders (Dobson, 1989; Elkin et al., 1989; Gloaguen, Cottraux, Cucherat, & Blackburn, 1998; Miller & Berman, 1983; Pace & Dixon, 1993; Robinson, Berman, & Neimeyer, 1990). Cognitive therapy has been shown to prevent recurrent episodes of depression more effectively than antidepressant medication alone (Vittengl, Clark, Dunn, & Jarrett, 2007). While there were no differences in effectiveness for CBT compared to other counseling treatments, or compared to medication alone, recent studies did find that combined CBT and pharmacotherapy was significantly more effective than medication alone (Cuijpers et al., 2013; Cuijpers, Dekker,

Hollon, & Andersson, 2009). There were also long term effects of CBT for depression, with lower relapse rates at one-year and two-year follow-ups compared to individuals who received medication alone (Vittengl, Clark, Dunn, & Jarrett, 2007; Dobson et al., 2008).

Interpersonal Therapy

Interpersonal Therapy (IPT) is also an empirically supported treatment for depression. IPT focuses on the relationship between the client and counselor, reworking past problematic relationships and crafting a more positive healthy identity. Problematic relationships contribute to depression; as relationships improve with IPT, depression symptoms lessen.

Family Systems

Family systems counseling explores the ways that family history and family relationships sustain the client's depression, and aims to discover ways in which family members can support client progress. Family systems approaches to treating depression focus on families as interconnected and interdependent networks; therefore, in order to help the individual, it is necessary to work with the family system.

Developed by Murray Bowen, Family Systems holds that individuals cannot be understood or treated in isolation, since in a family system each member must adapt to the others (Bowen, 1978). For example, if one family member struggles with alcoholism, the rest of the system adapts. One person may cope with denial, another may act out, and a third may become depressed or avoid the problem by withdrawing or leaving the family. Treatment explores roles within the family, as well as the rules adopted for interaction and the boundaries set between members. When these are problematic, each individual in the family is adversely impacted. Family therapy breaks down the system's inherent resistance to change and helps family members develop healthier roles, rules, and boundaries.

The counselor working with James from a family systems perspective would focus on James' past and current relationship with his parents and family to examine what impact the family system has on his depression.

Counselor: *"Can you tell me more about your family? Is there a history of depression in your family?"*

James: *"I guess maybe there is. My dad was always sort of up and down. Maybe more down than up. And my mom, she was definitely depressed after my dad left. Hardly came out of her room at all for a long time, years maybe."*

Counselor: *"It must have felt like losing both your parents then . . . "*

James: (tearful) *"It did, it really did."*

Counselor: *"You said your parents divorced when you were a child—how old were you?"*

James: *"I was ten. I still remember the yelling and screaming; and then my dad left."*

Counselor: *"That must have been devastating for a 10-year-old."*

James: *"It was. My dad promised to stay in touch, said we'd have all kinds of adventures on the weekends—fishing and going to the races and stuff. But, he pretty much disappeared after they got divorced."*

Counselor: *"You never saw him much after he left?"*

James: *"Every now and then. Sometimes he'd make plans and then never show up. I think he just felt obligated to see me sometimes, but he didn't want to—he wanted to move on, start a new life; and he did."*

Counselor: *"That's a really difficult loss for a child, and hard to understand."*

James: *"Well, I had to pull myself together. My mom needed me."*

Counselor: *"She needed you?"*

James: *"She fell apart. I had to be the man of the house, you know? She always said,*

men are supposed to be there, to take
care of women. I tried to take care of my
little brother—and to take care of her,
too. But, she never did get better, started
drinking. I guess I failed at that too."

Counselor: "You were just a kid. Do you think your
mother blames you for her drinking?"

James: "I think she blames me for everything.
Maybe she's right, maybe I was such a
rotten kid that my father had to go. No
wonder he didn't come back."

The counselor working with James from a
family systems perspective will want to explore
further James' experience of his parents' divorce
and his troubled relationship with both of them
today, and how these experiences are contributing to his depression.

Brief Treatments

Brief counseling approaches, including brief
versions of CBT and Problem Solving Therapy
have also been effective in remediating depression, although a recent meta-analysis found
larger effect sizes for treatment of longer duration (Cape, Whittington, Buszewicz, Wallace, &
Underwood, 2010).

Other Counseling Approaches

As discussed previously, counselors incorporate many different theories of counseling into
their work with clients. While CBT and IPT are
empirically supported treatments, counselors also
use other theoretical approaches to help clients
experiencing depression. Person centered counseling also helps clients understand their issues and
relationships through the therapeutic relationship.
Reality therapy helps clients identify which problems are in their control and which are not, and
then set realistic goals for the future and change.
Psychoanalytic approaches examine the ways that
the client's past is impacting their present symptoms and helps clients develop insight into these
influences, with the goal of moving forward.

Some of the newer DSM-5 diagnoses do not
yet have empirically supported treatments identified. For example, in the case of DMDD there is
no identified empirically supported treatment rec-
ommendation as yet, but CBT is suggested along
with parent training and parent support workshops.
Suggested treatments for PMDD also include dietary changes (increased carbohydrates in the week
before), as well as CBT and medications.

Most counseling approaches also help the client identify and strengthen support networks,
promote physical health, and improve coping
skills. These changes are effective in remediating the current episode of depression, as well as
preventing future episodes (Daley, 2008).

Medications

Several classes of medication have also been
found to be effective in treating mood disorders,
either alone or (ideally) in combination with
counseling. An NIMH funded study of adolescents found that a combination of medication
and psychotherapy was most effective in remediating depression (March et al., 2004).

Pharmacologic treatment of depression
impacts certain chemicals in the brain. When
brain chemicals are out of balance, depression
may result. Some of the earliest medications used
to treat depression were the monoamine oxidase
inhibitors (MAOIs), which are particularly effective with some of the less common symptoms of
depression, such as a greater need for sleep or
food, sometimes known as "atypical depression."
MAOIs can also help with co-occurring anxiety. However, a life threatening interaction with
food and drink containing tyramine and medications, such as birth control pills, aspirin, herbal
supplements, and cold and allergy medications
can occur with MAOIs, which necessitates close
monitoring.

Tricyclics (including Imipramine and Nortrip-
tyline) are also an older treatment for depression.
These medications were effective, but had serious
side effects in some clients, including heart problems, dizziness, dry mouth, and weight gain, and
overdoses of Tricyclics can be life threatening.

More recently, selective serotonin reuptake inhibitors (SSRIs) and serotonin and norepinephrine reuptake inhibitors (SNRIs) have shown effectiveness in treating depression. These medications (including the brand names Prozac, Zoloft, Lexapro, Paxil, Celexa, and Effexor) regulate the amount of specific neurotransmitters available in the brain, such as serotonin, dopamine, and norepinephrine with fewer side effects than earlier generations of medication. Buproprion (brand name Wellbutrin) is a newer medication which impacts the neurotransmitter dopamine, also with fewer side effects. Nevertheless, most medications for depression do have some side effects, including headaches, stomach upset, sleep problems, agitation, and sexual difficulties. The tricyclics can cause dry mouth, constipation, blurred vision, and problems emptying the bladder. SSRIs interact with MAOIs to cause problems with blood pressure, heart function, and seizures, so these two medications should not be taken simultaneously. See Figure 4.1 for a list of common medications used for depression as well as common side effects.

In addition, the herbal remedy St. John's wort is also used for mild to moderate depression, both in the United States and Europe. However, some studies found that St. John's wort is not effective for treatment of major depression (Hypericum Depression Trial Study Group, 2002) and can lessen the effectiveness of birth control pills and certain heart and seizure medications.

While it is not commonly used today, electroconvulsive therapy (ECT) is also used for severe depression which does not respond to medication or counseling. Clients who receive ECT are under mild anesthesia and the treatment is brief. However, side effects can include memory loss, confusion, and disorientation, most of which are short-term (Lisanby, 2007).

When clients are prescribed medication, counselors work closely with the prescribing practitioner to monitor side effects and to help clients cope with their uncertainties about taking medication. Counselors can emphasize to clients the need to take an antidepressant for 4 to 6 weeks before the full effect will be experienced, preventing clients from feeling hopeless or giving up on treatment too quickly. In addition, counselors are instrumental in helping clients continue their medication regimen even after they start to feel better, making relapse less likely. Discontinuing an antidepressant suddenly can result in withdrawal symptoms or worsening depression or anxiety. Counselors also support clients as they work with a physician to find the medication that's best for them; some clients have to try several medications before this is accomplished, which can be a frustrating and frightening experience.

While research shows that the benefits of medication for depression outweigh the risks, nevertheless counselors should be aware that there is an increased risk of suicidal ideation or suicide attempts in some children and adolescents who are prescribed antidepressants (Bridge et al., 2007). In the United States, the Food and Drug Administration includes a "black box" warning on antidepressants for children and young adults up to age 24. The risk is greatest when clients begin a medication, so counselors should monitor clients during this time and work closely with the prescribing physician.

Now that we've examined the research and diagnostic categories for depressive disorders, let's return to the case of James and follow along as the counselor develops a case conceptualization.

CASE CONCEPTUALIZATION FOR DEPRESSION USING THE T/C MODEL

Like most disorders, depression has biological, psychological, and environmental risk factors which contribute to the etiology of the disorder. It is important to pay attention to all these domains when developing a case conceptualization.

In the physiological/biological domain, the client's description of any issues with eating, sleeping, or level of activity are relevant. Both lack of appetite or wanting to eat all the time can be associated with depression; similarly, feeling

Figure 4.1 Antidepressant Medications and Side Effects

Antidepressants	Brand Medications	Common Side Effects
SSRIs—work by increasing the amount of serotonin, a neurotransmitter found in the brain	Prozac®, Zoloft®, Lexapro®, Paxil®, Celexa®, Luvox®, Sarafem®	Dizziness, headaches, nausea right after ingestion, insomnia, jitteriness, sexual problems, including low sex drive or inability to have an orgasm are common, but reversible
Tricyclics—work by increasing the available amount of serotonin and/or norepinephrine in the brain	Tofranil®, Anafranil®, Adapin®, Aventyl®, Elavil®, Endep®, Pamelor®, Sinequan®, Zonalon®	Dry mouth, blurred vision, increased fatigue, weight gain, muscle twitching, constipation, bladder problems, dizziness, increased heart rate, sexual problems
MAOIs—increase the amount of norepinephrine and serotonin in the brain	Emsam®, Eldepryl®, Nardil®, Marplan®, Parnate®, Zelapar®	Must avoid certain foods and medications to avoid dangerous interactions. Side effects may include headaches, heart racing, chest pain, neck stiffness, nausea and vomiting
Bupropion—may increase the amounts of the neurotransmitters norepinephrine and dopamine in the brain	Aplenzin®, Budeprion®, Buproban®, Forfivo®, Wellbutrin®	Weight loss, decreased appetite, restlessness, insomnia, anxiety, constipation, dry mouth, diarrhea, dizziness, seizures
SNRIs—increase the levels of the neurotransmitters serotonin and norepinephrine in the brain	Cymbalta®, Effexor®, Fetzima®, Khedezla®, Pristiq®	Drowsiness, blurred vision, lightheadedness, strange dreams, constipation, fever/chills, headaches, increased or decreased appetite, tremors, dry mouth, nausea

too tired and discouraged to get out of bed, or having difficulty falling asleep or staying asleep may be indicators of depression. Other behaviors which may be of concern are social isolation and difficulty concentrating. Clients may describe their lives as without pleasure, and may be unable to enjoy much of anything. In addition, keep in mind that depression can manifest in somatic symptoms, such as chronic pain, headaches, or stomach pain.

There are also psychological and cognitive factors that play a role in developing or sustaining depression. What is the client's explanatory style? How do they view the world and others (safe and trustworthy, or dangerous and unpredictable)? Do they tend to see themselves and others through a negative filter, increasing vulnerability to depression? Because the explanatory styles of clients with depression tend to be unrealistically negative, it is essential to thoroughly assess the client's existing strengths and abilities so that their automatic thoughts can be challenged. In addition, having an understanding of the resources and supports the client has in place or can cultivate will help the client recover from depression and maintain that recovery.

Excessive guilt and low self-esteem also put a client at risk for depression. These may have been learned in childhood and never questioned. Clients with depression may be hopeless, or think about suicide to end the pain they're experiencing. Asking about suicidal thoughts and intent is a critical part of the case conceptualization process when working with a client who is depressed.

Environmental factors to assess include experiences of loss, both recently or in the past, current stressors, and relationship conflict. In addition, consider whether the client's episodes of depression occur at a particular time of year, or whether depression for female clients is tied to the menstrual cycle or childbirth.

Let's see how a case conceptualization using the T/C Model is developed for the client we met at the beginning of this chapter: James.

The Case of James

Example of T/C Case Conceptualization Model Outline

(* Areas that require more information)

Presenting Problem: Depression, isolation, problems with eating, sleeping, and concentration

Internal Personality Constructs and Behavior:

Self-efficacy: feels hopeless, doubts efficacy in relationships and at work

Self-esteem: low, feels paralyzed by depression and hopelessness

Attitudes/Values/Beliefs: sense of responsibility, belief that men are supposed to take care of women

Attachment Style:

Biology/Physiology/Heredity: male, 30, headaches, medical history*, family history of depression*, mother's history of alcohol use*, temperament (negative affect)

Affect: depressed, hopeless

Cognition: belief that people only spend time with him because they're obligated; belief that he is responsible for parents' divorce

Hot Thoughts: "My friends don't really want to hang out with me anyway, they just feel obligated. Everyone would be better off if I wasn't even alive."

Behavior: isolating, missing work, visibly distraught in session, can't even answer the phone

Symptomology: headaches, fatigue, difficulty sleeping, trouble concentrating, appetite changes

Coping Skills and Strengths

Readiness for Change: contemplation stage—ambivalent about change, but willing to consider, hopeless

Life Roles: career*, family*

Environment:

Relationships: conflicted relationship with both parents*, past negative experiences with friends, was bullied*, difficult to trust

Culture: family background*

Family Norms and Values: Belief that men are supposed to take care of women

Societal Influences:

Timeline:

Past Influences: bullied, parents' divorce, father's abandonment, mother's drinking

Present Influences: work stress, depressed mood, difficulty sleeping, eating, and concentrating, conflicted relationship with mother,* relationship with father*

Future Goals: closer friendships, able to go to work, increased confidence at work

Question: What else would you want to ask, to complete this case conceptualization?

Counseling Keystones

- Depressive disorders are characterized by a sad, empty, or irritable mood, as well as cognitive and physiological changes.

- Depression can cause physical suffering, such as headaches, stomach upset, or chronic pain, as well as emotional pain, and some depressed individuals may consider or attempt suicide.
- Disruptive mood dysregulation disorder was added in DSM-5 as a disorder which must be diagnosed in childhood. The core feature is chronic severe persistent irritability, marked by temper outbursts (usually in response to frustration).
- Premenstrual dysphoric disorder was also added in DSM-5, and is characterized by significant affective symptoms (mood swings, irritability, depression, anxiety) in the week prior to the menstrual cycle, which quickly disappear after the cycle.
- Major depressive disorder is defined in DSM-5 by a depressed mood or a loss of interest or pleasure, with four other symptoms, including sleep difficulties, fatigue, difficulty concentrating, and thoughts of suicide.
- Persistent depressive disorder is a chronic depressive spectrum disorder (with symptoms lasting two years) which replaces the dysthymia category in DSM IV, and expands the symptom constellation to include the older diagnoses of both dysthymia and chronic major depression.
- Anxiety disorders are the most common co-occurring problems, including posttraumatic stress disorder (PTSD), panic disorder, social phobia, generalized anxiety disorder, and obsessive-compulsive disorder (OCD).
- Depression is not caused by a single precipitating factor. Rather, depression is multiply determined with various genetic, biological, chemical, social, psychological, and environmental factors impacting the development of the disorder.
- Certain mood disorders tend to run in families, suggesting a genetic component.
- Many research studies have demonstrated that counseling approaches (including cognitive behavioral and interpersonal therapies) are effective for treating depression and relieving symptoms experienced by individuals who suffer from depression.
- Several classes of medication have also been found to be effective in treating mood disorders, either alone or (ideally) in combination with counseling. An NIMH funded study of adolescents found that a combination of medication and psychotherapy was most effective in remediating depression.

EXERCISES

EXERCISE 4.1 What Words Do People Use to Describe Depression?

CLASS EXERCISE: Small group work followed by large group discussion.

Question 1: What are some typical words or phrases that clients might use to describe their depression?

Question 2: Are there certain words or phrases that seem to point to more severity? Which ones?

Question 3: What follow-up questions can counselors ask to get at the underlying thoughts that are associated with these descriptions?

EXERCISE 4.2 How Do You Classify Your Experience of Sadness?

CLASS EXERCISE: Individual work followed by large group discussion.

Question 1: How would you describe your experience when you are having a bad day?

Question 2: Categorize your symptoms using the T/C Model, with specific focus on environment, cognition, and behaviors.

Question 3: What do you typically do to "feel better"?

EXERCISE 4.3 Dig Deeper Using the Case of Genevieve Described at the Start of This Chapter

CLASS EXERCISE: Small group discussion followed by large group discussion.

Question 1: What questions would you ask next following this dialogue?

Question 2: What else would you want to know?

Question 3: How would you help Genevieve gain a better understanding of her depression?

EXERCISE 4.4 Case Conceptualization Practice Using the Case of Tom Described Earlier

CLASS EXERCISE: Small group discussion followed by large group discussion.

> **Question 1:** What is your case conceptualization of this case so far?
>
> **Question 2:** What else would you want to know?
>
> **Question 3:** What would be three possible goals for Tom in counseling?

GO FURTHER

Depression: Causes and Treatment by Aaron T. Beck and Brad A. Alford (2009) University of Pennsylvania Press

Mind Over Mood: Change How You Feel by Changing the Way You Think by Dennis Greenberger and Christine Padesky (1995) Guilford Press

Mindfulness-Based Cognitive Therapy for Depression by Zindel V. Sega, J. Mark G. Williams, John D. Teasdale, and Jon Kabat-Zinn (2012) The Guilford Press

Treatment Plans and Interventions for Depression and Anxiety Disorders by Robert L. Leahy, Stephen J. F. Holland, and Lata K. McGinn (2011) The Guilford Press

5

Bipolar Disorders

The Case of Betsy

Betsy, a 27-year-old attorney, comes to a crisis center to see a counselor with her husband, John. John made the initial phone call, and is very concerned about his wife. Betsy agreed to come, but insists her husband is being overly protective and "just doesn't understand."

Betsy recently won her first important case, and she and John celebrated with a trip to Jamaica. Everything seemed to be fine, with Betsy in a very good mood until a week ago when Betsy began staying up very late, sometimes until 3 am or 4 am, saying she was working on her next project. Since Betsy had followed this pattern before when working on an important case, John didn't worry until some time had passed and Betsy was sleeping less and less. John realized there was something wrong when she started waking him up in the middle of the night to tell him excitedly about a conspiracy that she had uncovered that her firm and hundreds of others all over the world were involved in. Yesterday, John got a phone call from the senior partner at Betsy's firm asking if she was okay and sharing that Betsy has been telling her colleagues about the conspiracy theory and creating quite a bit of chaos at the firm. Her colleagues were complaining that they can't get any work done, because Betsy keeps coming into their offices to "discuss her theory." When John confronted Betsy, she became very angry and accused him of being "in on it."

John was able to calm her down enough to have her agree to an evaluation, but Betsy is clearly still angry. In the session, she at first folds her arms and glares, but when the counselor asks her what's been going on, Betsy launches into a detailed explanation of the conspiracy. She speaks rapidly and excitedly, waving her arms and jumping quickly from topic to topic, making it hard to follow her train of thought. Betsy says that since she's the one who discovered the conspiracy, she's going to be the one to expose it and fix it, and that will inevitably result in her being promoted to senior partner at the firm (she's presently a junior associate). When the counselor questions the likelihood of that conviction, Betsy becomes angry at her as well.

The Case of Dorothy

Dorothy is a 19-year-old college sophomore. She comes to the counseling center complaining of trouble sleeping and problems with anxiety. Dorothy wrings her hands as she talks, and her knee bounces up and down almost constantly.

Dorothy: "I don't know what's going on with me, I just . . . it's getting harder and harder to get to sleep at night. I find myself staying up later and later, and it's like my brain just won't shut off. I can't calm down."

Counselor: "What kind of thoughts are going through your mind at night?"

Dorothy: "It's not usually anything specific. I've just had so much energy, I feel like I can write ten papers in a night, but I have so many ideas it's hard to get them all typed out!"

Counselor: "Can you remember a time when this has happened before?"

Dorothy: "Not really. I've had some bad times, mostly when I'm really down, but never this sort of extra energetic feeling."

Counselor: "How bad did the bad times get? Have you ever felt so bad that you thought about killing yourself?"

Dorothy: (looking down) "A few times, yeah. I never planned it out or anything, but yeah, it got pretty bad a few times. I don't feel like that now though—I mean, I feel kinda good, but I also feel like I'm just not . . . myself, and I'm just so jittery all the time, everything bugs me. It makes me snap at my friends, and I don't like that."

Counselor: "Have you found that anything helps the jittery feeling?"

Dorothy: "The only thing I've tried is drinking. I don't usually drink that much, but it seems to help a little. I know it's probably not a good thing though. I've got a bottle in my dorm room all the time now, in case I need it."

Counselor: "How is this impacting your relationships?"

Dorothy: "My roommates are annoyed with me, and worried I guess; and I . . . I guess I've been hooking up with guys more often when we're at parties, especially if I drink. It's not . . . not really like me."

The Case of Chuck

Chuck comes in for treatment after taking half a bottle of painkillers in a suicide attempt. At 56, Chuck has been married twice, and was recently divorced again. He is currently unemployed, and has an employment history that includes multiple job losses. Sometimes these were the result of Chuck being laid off or let go; other times, Chuck quit impulsively and then struggled to find another job. The counselor has assessed Chuck's depressive symptoms and suicide risk. Let's pick up in the middle of the interview:

Counselor:	"It seems as if you've had these very difficult times for most of your adult life, when you feel hopeless and overwhelmed with sadness."
Chuck:	"All my life. I just couldn't take it anymore."
Counselor:	"Has there ever been a time in your life when you felt quite differently? When you were bursting with energy and felt like you could do anything?"
Chuck:	(looking surprised) "Actually, yes. There have been a couple times when that's happened."
Counselor:	"Tell me about those times. Was your sleep affected?"
Chuck:	(nodding) "Definitely. In fact, I felt like I didn't need sleep at all, like I could just stay up all night and do just about anything. One of those times ruined my first marriage. I guess I thought I could have a mistress and my wife would never know—I just felt invincible."
Counselor:	"Anything else happen during that time?"
Chuck:	"I also spent a lot of our money. There was this new product, something that took dents out of cars or something, and I thought we could make a fortune. I guess I invested most of our savings and it just didn't pan out. Quit my job and everything. My wife was furious. But, at the time I just thought she was being an idiot, getting in my way."

INTRODUCTION

Betsy, Dorothy, and Chuck are all suffering from a bipolar disorder. Bipolar disorder is not only one of the most difficult mental health issues to treat, but also one of the most stigmatized and misunderstood. Formerly included with the other Depressive Disorders, the DSM-5 created a separate category for Bipolar and Related Disorders in order to facilitate correct diagnosis and understanding. Unlike the depressive disorders, bipolar disorders include episodes of both depression and the opposite "pole," mania or hypomania.

Most of us know what depression is. In some ways, mania is considered the opposite—a state of intense elation or irritability. The disorders are referred to as "bipolar" because most people who experience a manic episode also experience a depressive episode. When in a manic state, individuals do not think or behave in the same way as they usually do. Often they speak more loudly and more quickly, jumping from subject to subject, known as "pressured speech." It is difficult to interrupt their stream of conversation, which has been described as a "flight of ideas." Social judgment may also be impaired, with people missing the social cues that ordinarily tell us when another person doesn't welcome a particular interaction. Some individuals engage in sexual relationships that they otherwise would not, or in other reckless behavior, such as spending large amounts of money or driving too fast. During a manic episode, people tend to sleep less, but feel more energetic and there may be increased motor activity. There may be grandiose thinking and heightened self-esteem, with individuals convinced they can accomplish great things, but there is also often the tendency toward angry outbursts and episodes of rage. Manic episodes tend to begin abruptly over a one or two day time period.

Bipolar disorders are differentiated by the duration and severity of the manic symptoms.

Bipolar I disorder is diagnosed if there is at least one manic episode during the individual's lifetime. Bipolar II is diagnosed if the individual meets criteria for hypomania (but not mania) for at least four days and a major depressive episode. Hypomania is similar to mania, but less extreme. The individual in a hypomanic state is more grounded in reality and thinking more clearly, although there is a change in normal functioning. People may be more sociable, may engage in flirtatious behavior, and may feel energetic and productive. The client may feel euphoric, but behavior does not have the driven quality of a manic episode. These changes must be observable to others, but unlike a manic episode, these changes in behavior are less likely to cause significant disruption to everyday activities. Consider the three clients we met in the beginning of this chapter. Dorothy is experiencing a hypomanic episode, while Betsy is in the midst of a manic episode, and Chuck is experiencing a depressive episode after having been through several manic episodes.

To improve the accuracy of diagnosis and to help detect the disorder earlier, the criteria for manic and hypomanic episodes in DSM-5 now includes changes in activity and energy level, in addition to mood changes. A diagnosis of bipolar I used to require that the person meet criteria for both a major depressive episode and a manic episode; in DSM-5, this requirement is removed. Instead, a new specifier, "with mixed features," can be applied to episodes of mania or hypomania when depressive features are also present, and to depressive episodes when manic or hypomanic symptoms are present. In addition, specifiers like "with anxious distress," "with mixed features," and "with rapid cycling" can also be added.

Most clients diagnosed with bipolar disorder have recurring depression or manic episodes after their initial diagnosis. After even one episode, the percentage of lifetime recurrence is 95% (Goodwin & Jamison, 2007). Most will experience at least one depressive episode over the course of their lifetime, and on average will spend a third of their time in a depressive phase

compared to 11% in a manic or hypomanic phase (Kupka et al., 2007; Post, Baldassano, Perlis, & Ginsberg, 2003).

The first symptoms of bipolar disorder often appear in the mid- to late teens, usually with an episode of depression. Depressive symptoms occur three to four times more often than manic symptoms (Judd, Schettler, & Akiskal, 2002; Post et al., 2003). The depressive phase is associated with a high risk of disability, and a significant level of suffering. Compared to manic episodes, bipolar depression is related to more impairment in relationships, family, employment, and social life, and a greater risk of suicide (Calabrese, Hirschfeld, Frye, & Reed, 2004; Goldberg & Harrow, 2011). The lifetime risk for suicide attempts and completed suicide is one of the highest among all psychiatric diagnoses; some studies estimate that risk of suicide is fifteen times higher than in the general population, especially during a depressive phase (Goodwin & Jamison, 2007). Assessment and treatment during this phase is critical.

The DSM-5 also includes the category of "other specified bipolar and related disorder" for people with a history of major depressive disorder and who also meet the criteria for a hypomanic episode except the duration criterion of at least four consecutive days, or if the duration criterion is met, but the person doesn't meet full criteria for hypomania.

As you can see from the case of Betsy, a diagnosis of bipolar I disorder is a serious one. Bipolar disorder is associated with an increased suicide rate, a strong risk of recurrence, and high personal and social costs. The disorder is a major cause of impaired quality of life, reduced productivity, and increased mortality (IsHak et al., 2012). Individuals diagnosed with bipolar disorders have a wide range of social problems, including dealing with the social stigma of having the disorder, relationship difficulties, and unemployment. People who have been hospitalized for a manic episode often struggle to get back on their feet, with a third unable to return to work within one year (Harrow, Goldberg, Grossman, & Meltzer, 1990). The disorder interferes with work or schooling in approximately a quarter of the individuals who are diagnosed (Kessler et al., 2006), and suicide rates are high with 25% of people with bipolar I and 20% of people with bipolar II making a suicide attempt (Merikangas et al., 2011).

Bipolar disorder is an episodic, potentially lifelong, disabling disorder with a higher rate of recurrence than major depressive disorder. Over half of the people with bipolar I disorder will have four or more episodes during their lifetime (Goodwin & Jamison, 2007). However, most clients can see significant improvement with ongoing treatment. Long-term preventive treatment is recommended, with a treatment protocol that combines medication and psychological treatment to manage the disorder.

Bipolar disorder is less common than major depressive disorder. Internationally, approximately 6 out of every 1,000 people meet the criteria for bipolar I (Merikangas et al., 2011). Within the United States, the rates are higher with about 1% of the population diagnosed with bipolar I over the course of a lifetime (Merikangas et al., 2007). Prevalence estimates for bipolar II disorder vary, in part because diagnostic instruments are not as reliable for the milder forms of this disorder, with estimates ranging from 0.4% to 2% (Merikangas et al., 2007, 2011). Bipolar disorder has a mean age of onset before 25 in about half of the people with the diagnosis, and has been diagnosed at younger ages recently (Merikangas et al., 2011).

COMORBIDITY

Certain factors can increase the severity or worsen the course of bipolar disorder, including untreated medical issues, other psychiatric disorders, and psychosocial stressors. The majority of clients with bipolar disorder have at least one comorbid psychiatric or medical disorder; thus, treatment should take into consideration the interrelationships between these conditions and life stressors.

Epidemiological, clinical, and familial studies indicate that anxiety disorders are the most commonly co-occurring disorder, with two-thirds of the people diagnosed with bipolar disorder also diagnosed with an anxiety disorder. Comorbid anxiety disorder is associated with more intense symptoms, lower recovery rates, substance use, and suicidal thoughts (McIntyre et al., 2006).

More than a third of people with bipolar disorder report substance abuse or a history of substance abuse. Substance abuse may precede a manic or depressive episode, or clients may use in order to reduce their symptoms during an episode. Comorbid substance use is associated with slower remission, lower rates of remission, higher risk of suicide, a more severe clinical course, and poorer outcomes in general. In addition, substance abuse can complicate both assessment and treatment (Bolton, Robinson, & Sareen, 2009; DSM-5).

There is a high rate of comorbidity among children and adolescents with bipolar disorder as well, with more than 40% of clinical samples and 10% of community samples having comorbid attention deficit hyperactivity disorder (ADHD) (Tramontina, Schmitz, Polackzyk, & Rohde, 2003). When ADHD and bipolar disorder co-occur, outcome and response to treatment is worsened (Consoli, Bouzamondo, Guile, Lechat, & Cohen, 2007).

Medical conditions that co-occur with bipolar disorder can adversely impact recovery, increase mortality, reduce quality of life, and lead to a more severe course of the disorder (McIntyre et al., 2007). People with comorbid bipolar disorder and chronic medical disorders experience more psychosocial stressors in terms of employment and disability, and have a higher use of health services (McIntyre et al., 2007). The chronic medical condition itself can cause mood disturbances, in addition to complicating the course of treatment. Medical conditions, such as cardiovascular problems, diabetes, obesity, thyroid disease, neurological, infectious, and endocrine disorders can worsen the course of bipolar disorder (Kupfer, 2005).

CULTURAL CONSIDERATIONS AND POPULATION FACTORS

Women experience more depressive episodes than men, but gender differences have not been reported for the prevalence of bipolar I disorder (Altschuler et al., 2010). Some studies suggest that bipolar II disorder is more common in women (Leibenluft, 1996). Further, the course of bipolar disorder in women may be influenced by the menstrual cycle, pregnancy, the postpartum period, and menopause. Older individuals with bipolar disorder have a higher rate of comorbid psychiatric disorders, including substance abuse, posttraumatic stress disorder, anxiety disorders, and dementia (Sajatovic, Blow, & Ignacio, 2006). When the diagnosis of Bipolar disorder occurs later in life, some studies have found that episodes are longer and more debilitating (Young & Klerman, 1992).

Bipolar disorder manifests differently in children than in adults with symptoms sometimes overlapping with other psychiatric disorders, such as ADHD, depression, obsessive compulsive disorder, or anxiety disorders. If an incorrect diagnosis is made, children may be treated with medications that can worsen their bipolar disorder, such as stimulant medications or antidepressants. Children and adolescents with bipolar disorder are more likely to show symptoms of depression than mania or hypomania, but are at risk for developing manic symptoms if treated with SSRIs (selective serotonin reuptake inhibitors). Evidence-based treatments for children and adolescents with bipolar disorder include interpersonal and social rhythm therapy for adolescents, cognitive behavior therapy, dialectical behavior therapy (DBT) for adolescents, and family focused therapy for adolescents (Cosgrove, Roybal, & Chang, 2013).

As previously mentioned, rates of bipolar I disorder are higher in the United States. Cultural beliefs shape interpretation of symptoms, and some studies suggest that researchers from the United States tend to view symptoms as more severe, leading to higher rates of diagnosis (Mackin et al., 2006). Variations in cultural norms for diet also appear to impact prevalence. In countries with more fish in the normal diet (such as Japan and Iceland), rates of both bipolar and other depressive disorders tend to be lower (Hibbeln, Nieminen, Blasbalg, Riggs, & Lands, 2006).

ETIOLOGY AND RISK FACTORS

Biological and Genetic Factors

Both genetic and biological factors appear to be important in the etiology of bipolar disorder. In addition, environmental factors and psychosocial stressors influence course and severity. Twin studies show that bipolar disorder has a strong heritability component, with some studies estimating a heritability of 93% (Kieseppa, Partonen, Hauldea, Kaprio, & Lonnqvist, 2004). As with other depressive disorders, research on isolating a genetic component of bipolar disorder has been difficult to replicate. However, studies suggest that certain regions of the brain which are involved in MDD are also involved with bipolar disorder, including the amygdala, the anterior cingulate, the hippocampus, and the prefrontal cortex (Houenou et al., 2011; Phillips, Ladouceur, & Drevets, 2008).

Neuroimaging studies indicate that both depressive and biopolar disorders are associated with differences in the regions of the brain which are involved in emotion and emotional regulation. In functional MRIs, bipolar I disorder is associated with elevated amygdala response, increased anterior cingulate activity when regulating emotion, and reduced hippocampus and prefrontal cortex activity (Houenou et al., 2011; Phillips, Ladouceur, & Drevets, 2008). Reduced activity of the dorsolateral prefrontal cortex and the hippocampus, and greater activity of the subgenual anterior cingulate, lead to problems with emotional regulation. An overactive amygdala leads to heightened emotional reactivity. Problems with regulation of cortisol levels are also seen in people with bipolar disorder and other depressive disorders after cortisol challenge tests (Vieta et al., 1999; Watson, Thompson, Ritchie, Ferrier, & Young, 2006).

Certain brain regions appear to be affected in people with bipolar disorder, but not individuals diagnosed with MDD. Changes in the striatum, a region of the brain which responds to reward, are seen with bipolar disorder, but not with major depressive disorder. During a manic episode, but not during a depressive episode, the striatum is overly active (Marchand & Yurgelun-Todd, 2010). Another difference unique to bipolar disorder is change in the cellular membranes that impact the activation of neurons. People with bipolar disorders, but not those with MDD, have deficits in these membranes (Thiruvengadam & Chandrasekaran, 2007).

Neurotransmitter models of bipolar disorder focus on serotonin, dopamine, and norepinephrine, particularly on differences in receptor sensitivity. Dopamine receptors may be overly sensitive in bipolar disorder (Anand et al., 2000). Also, bipolar disorder may be related to reduced sensitivity of serotonin receptors (Sobczak, Honig, Nicolson, & Riedel, 2002).

The Role of Experience

Since bipolar disorders often include both manic and depressive episodes, research examined the triggers for both. Similar to people diagnosed with MDD, stressful environmental events can instigate depressive episodes in bipolar disorder as well. Other triggers are also similar to those of depressive disorders, including neuroticism, a negative cognitive style, and lack of social support (Reilly-Harrington, Alloy, Fresco, & Whitehouse, 1999; Yan, Hammen, Cohen, Daley, & Henry, 2004).

Research identified two models which predict an increase in manic symptoms over time: reward sensitivity and sleep deprivation. Both of these models take into account psychological and biological vulnerability to manic symptoms. A reward sensitivity model suggests that mania reflects a problem with the brain's reward system. On self-report assessments, individuals with bipolar disorder describe themselves as highly responsive to rewards. This factor predicts the onset of bipolar disorder as well as a more severe course of manic symptoms (Alloy et al., 2008; Meyer, Johnson, & Winters, 2001). Certain types of life events have been found to predict increased manic symptoms among individuals with Bipolar disorder, particularly those that involve attaining important goals or achieving some sort of success; getting married, having a baby, graduation, or being accepted to law school could be potential predictors of mania (Johnson et al., 2008). Researchers hypothesize that success experiences produce greater confidence, which may trigger cognitive changes. These changes are reinforcing, and may lead to excessive pursuit of goals, triggering manic symptoms.

Another model which explains increase in manic symptoms involves sleep disruption. Mania is intricately tied to problems with sleep and circadian rhythm, and sleep deprivation often precedes an increase in manic symptoms. In one sleep study, 10% of individuals who were forced to stay awake all night experienced at least mild symptoms of mania by the following morning (Colombo, Benedetti, Barbini, Campori, & Smeraldi, 1999), and many people report a sleep disruption before the onset of manic episodes (Malkoff-Schwartz et al., 2000). In contrast, ensuring sufficient and undisrupted sleep can reduce manic symptoms.

In addition to the role of stressors in disrupting sleep, several studies have found that stress mediates the relationship between biological vulnerability and relapse in clients with bipolar disorder, with negative life events associated with slower recovery from depressive episodes (Johnson & Miller, 1997) and success events associated with an increase in manic symptoms (Johnson et al., 2000).

TREATMENT INTERVENTIONS

Although diagnosis and treatment of bipolar disorder is complex, effective treatment can lead to good outcomes for many patients. A correct diagnosis is critical, particularly since clients often present initially in a depressive episode. Bipolar disorder is often misdiagnosed, and can take years to diagnose correctly. Symptoms can fluctuate seasonally, and children are sometimes misdiagnosed with ADHD.

In addition to a thorough clinical interview, which can be facilitated with the T/C Model, there are various diagnostic instruments available. These include the Bipolar Inventory of Symptoms Scale (BISS), the Young Mania Rating Scale (YMRS) for manic symptoms, and the Bipolar Depression Rating Scale (BDRS) for bipolar depressive symptoms. Family history should also be assessed for history of Bipolar disorder and depressive disorders (Seligman & Reichenberg, 2012).

Treatment for Bipolar disorders takes into account the various phases of the disorder—acute treatment of mania or hypomania; acute treatment of depression; maintenance treatment; and treatment of comorbid disorders. Medication is a necessary evidence-based treatment for Bipolar disorders, but psychological treatment is an important supplement to medication. Adjunctive counseling is often needed because outcomes remain less than optimal for many clients with Bipolar disorder. A significant portion of clients do not take medication consistently or discontinue medication over time. Counseling offers an effective way of encouraging recovery, and the frequent contact with clients that allows an awareness of early warning signs of relapse and encourages greater medication adherence.

Counseling Interventions

Counseling benefits bipolar clients by improving psychosocial functioning, and reducing the substantial social and psychological problems that often accompany the disorder. There is increasing recognition of the contribution of psychological therapies to symptom relief, relapse prevention, and optimal functioning. Research shows that there is a significant need for adjunctive counseling to supplement and optimize the benefits of medication and to improve quality of life (Miklowitz & Scott, 2009). Counseling can improve clients' insight and knowledge about the disorder, which can be particularly difficult to manage because of its cyclical nature.

In addition, counseling focuses on independent contributors to poor outcomes, including life stressors, comorbid physical and psychiatric disorders, and social and relationship difficulties. A large scale treatment study (Miklowitz et al., 2007) found that counseling, in combination with medication, helped relieve depression more than a collaborative care control treatment. Cognitive approaches, family-focused therapy, and interpersonal therapy were found to be equally effective.

Empirically supported treatments for Bipolar disorder include psychoeducation, cognitive behavior therapy, family focused therapies, interpersonal counseling, and collaborative care approaches (Lolich, Vazquez, Alvarez, & Tamayo, 2012). These approaches are particularly helpful after an acute manic or depressive phase, combined with medication maintenance treatment. Research studies have explicated the role of stress in precipitating manic and depressive episodes in clients with Bipolar disorder. Counseling can help clients develop the skills and strategies to cope more effectively with life stressors, improving their quality of life and outcomes.

Psychoeducation

Psychoeducation is an important part of treatment for many disorders, including Bipolar disorder; it is crucial to educate individuals about the development of symptoms and the environmental and biological factors that can lead to a more serious course of the disorder and a greater risk of recurrence.

In addition, having an understanding of specific biological and psychological triggers for depressive and manic episodes is particularly useful for individuals with Bipolar disorder. Medication adherence and consistency are a challenge for many clients with Bipolar disorder, since many medications not only relieve the "lows" (depressive episodes), but also reduce the "highs" (manic or hypomanic episodes). A better understanding of symptoms, treatment, and coping strategies have been found to improve medication adherence in clients prescribed lithium, for example (Colom et al., 2003).

Psychoeducational groups for clients with Bipolar disorder that take a chronic care management approach are increasingly employed for these individuals. Psychoeducational counseling that is client focused, but includes family members and other significant persons in the client's life, also have been found to be effective (Sajatovic, Davies, & Hrouda, 2004).

Whether individual or group modalities are employed, psychoeducation approaches aim to make the client an active partner in treatment. Education on the symptoms and course of the disorder, the risks and benefits of various medications, encouragement of medication adherence, techniques that allow clients to monitor mood states, and an awareness of triggers and warning signals of relapse are included in most psychoeducational approaches (Scott & Gutierrez, 2004). Behavioral interventions to ensure regular and sufficient sleep and to prevent substance abuse can also be taught. Several studies have found that psychoeducation is effective in reducing levels of manic symptoms, and length of manic episodes, and in preventing relapse (American Psychiatric Association (APA), 2002; Colom et al., 2003).

Psychoeducation can also help with treatment adherence, which is a problem for many clients with Bipolar disorder. Some studies have estimated that nonadherence is as high as 30% (Colom et al., 2003; Sajatovic et al., 2004). If clients are experiencing significant side effects, such as fatigue or weight gain, feeling depressed, or experiencing some psychotic symptoms, adherence is impacted. Conversely, when clients start to feel better after a depressive episode, they may be less likely to continue medication. The psychological stress of accepting long-term treatment, especially with potential side effects, is significant. Clients are often ambivalent about undergoing treatment (APA, 2002).

Cognitive Behavioral Interventions

A significant number of clients with Bipolar disorder experience persistent cognitive problems, including difficulties with memory, planning, and attention even during periods of remission (Demant, Almer, Vinberg, Kessing, & Miskowiak, 2013). Additionally, deficits in verbal memory, sustained attention, executive functioning, and social cognition were found (Bozikas, Tonia, Fokas, Karavatos, & Kosmidis, 2006; Goldberg & Chengappa, 2009). These deficits have a detrimental impact on social, relational, and occupational functioning for clients already struggling with Bipolar disorder (Arts, Jabben, Krabbendam & Van, 2011; Torrent et al., 2012).

Cognitive remediation (CR) is a relatively new psychological intervention that targets the improvement of cognitive functioning, helping the client develop coping skills which improve psychosocial adjustment. CR includes a psychoeducational component, teaching of adaptive and compensatory strategies to improve attention and concentration (some using computer assisted techniques), mindfulness meditation, and homework which builds in practice of new skills and further improves executive functioning. There is also an emphasis on establishing routines and structure in daily life, and using a calendar to schedule exercise and sleep. While CR has been shown to be effective with clients diagnosed with schizophrenia, trials are ongoing to determine efficacy with clients with Bipolar disorder (Demant et al., 2013).

Cognitive therapies for Bipolar disorder include many of the components previously described for individuals with MDD, with the addition of building skills to recognize and deal with the early signs of manic symptoms. CBT is considered an evidence-based treatment as an adjunct to medication for clients with Bipolar disorder who are not currently in an acute manic episode. Both CBT and Psychoeducation approaches teach clients self-monitoring—how to recognize early symptoms—and better coping strategies. CBT also adds cognitive and behavioral techniques, such as identifying dysfunctional thoughts, learning to challenge and replace these thoughts, behavioral activation, and cognitive restructuring. In addition, clients learn the early warning signs of relapse and ways to change behavior to increase quality of life and positive experiences.

Studies have found lower rates of relapse and less time spent in manic or depressive episodes with adjunctive CBT (Lam et al., 2003; Lam, Hayward, Watkins, Wright, & Sham, 2005). Research suggests that CBT is most appropriate for patients in the early stages of the disorder who have had fewer than twelve prior episodes and may be most effective in treating depressive symptoms (Scott et al., 2006).

Both CBT and psychoeducational interventions have been found to have similar impact on clients' ability to cope with the development of manic symptoms. CBT seems to be more effective in reducing ineffective coping strategies, such as denial and blame to explain manic symptoms (Parikh et al., 2013).

Interpersonal and
Social Rhythm Therapy (IPSRT)

Interpersonal and social rhythm therapy focuses on stabilizing moods by improving medication adherence, building coping skills and relationship satisfaction, and shoring up the regularity of daily rhythms or social routines to stabilize sleep and waking patterns. In addition, IPSRT focuses on the interpersonal context of manic and depressive episodes, aiming to lessen interpersonal problems by improving communication and problem-solving skills. By keeping a log of daily routines, such as sleep and wake times, exercise and work, clients can lessen the impact of life events that disrupt stability and impact mood. As with CBT, the client is an active partner in treatment and IPSRT is an adjunctive treatment along with medication. IPSRT is recommended for clients who are not in an acute manic or depressive phase. Several studies have found that clients who were able to regulate their social routines and sleep-wake cycles had lower rates of relapse and longer times between recurrences, although IPSRT was less effective if there was a comorbid medical disorder (Frank et al., 2005).

Family Focused Therapy

Family counseling approaches have been used for many years for clients with Bipolar disorder.

Family Focused Therapy (FFT) educates both the client and the client's family about the disorder, and aims to improve communication and problem-solving skills within the family. This form of counseling introduces practical procedures for helping families understand the nature of bipolar disorder, strengthens their communication skills, solves day-to-day problems, and reduces the risk and severity of relapse. Several studies in the 1990s demonstrated empirical support for the effectiveness of FFT for clients who recently experienced an acute episode, including delaying relapse when used with medication (Clarkin et al., 1990; Miklowitz & Goldstein, 1990). Clients receiving FFT also had less severe depressive and manic symptoms over the course of a two-year study (Simoneau, Miklowitz, Richards, Saleem, & George, 1999).

FFT includes psychoeducation about the symptoms and course of the disorder, warning signs of relapse and prevention skills, and emphasizes medication adherence. In addition, clients and their families learn positive communication strategies, such as active listening and expression of feelings. Families high in expressed emotion have responded differently to FFT compared to families low in expressed emotion; improvements in the emotional tone of clients' interactions with their families was related to less severe symptoms (Miklowitz, George, Richards, Simoneau, & Suddath, 2003).

Consider Chuck, the client we met in the beginning of this chapter. The counselor working from an FFT perspective would work with Chuck, his current wife, and adult children by making certain that all family members had an understanding of the symptoms of Bipolar disorder and the warning signs of both depressive and manic episodes. In addition, the counselor provides psychoeducation on the importance of medication in treatment of Bipolar disorder. The counselor stresses, both to the family and the client, that it is critical to take medication consistently on a daily basis and to continue the medication even when the client begins to feel better. It is important that both the client and family understand the gradual nature of improvement that medication brings, and how to recognize potential side effects. The client and the family should also be educated about the potential risk that some medications carry of being able to switch a client's mood from depressed to a hypomanic or manic episode.

Once the family and Chuck are on the same page and openly able to discuss the challenges of the disorder and the importance of medication, the counselor could begin by choosing one problem for the client and family to address. In Chuck's case, that might be developing a plan to keep Chuck safe from acting on his suicidal impulses. With the counselor's help, Chuck and his family members work together to define the problem and the context, and identify specific situations that put Chuck at increased risk for suicidal thoughts and actions. Situations which trigger suicidal impulses for Chuck, and for many clients, often involve loss or humiliation. For example, Chuck's recent suicide attempt came after he once again lost a job, this time due to company-wide layoffs.

Once Chuck and his family discuss and identify triggers, they brainstorm ways to keep Chuck safe and agree on a plan, with all family members buying into the solution. The counselor also works collaboratively with Chuck to develop strategies for closely monitoring his moods, to identify the triggers and warning signs of mood shifts, and to find ways to cope with those triggers.

In addition, as part of the FFT intervention, the counselor facilitates the development of better communication within the family. Family members can role-play beneficial skills like active listening; teaching the family to listen closely to what other members say; asking questions to clarify anything they don't understand; and then reflecting and paraphrasing each other's statements.

There are numerous studies comparing the relative effectiveness of the various counseling modalities employed to treat clients with Bipolar disorder. Clients in FFT had fewer recurrences and hospitalizations than clients in individual counseling, perhaps because their family members knew what to look for in terms of early warning signs of relapse (Rea et al., 2003). Miklowitz (2008) found that CBT was better than psychoeducation in reducing symptoms, but not as effective as FFT. Another study by Miklowitz and colleagues (2003) found beneficial effects of a combined IPSRT and FFT treatment protocol, with longer time periods between recurrence and less severe depressive symptoms. Other studies have found that intensive psychosocial treatment regardless of modality is more effective than brief psychoeducational treatment in stabilizing clients after a depressive episode (Miklowitz et al., 2007).

Chronic Care Model Interventions

Chronic care models (CCMs) are multimodal interventions that include both counseling and assistance with access to and continuity of care for clients with mental health issues, including Bipolar disorder (Wagner, Austin, & Van Korff, 1996). CCMs emphasize client self-management, and aim to link clients to a variety of community resources. Chronic care models address psychosocial stressors in the client's life, build networks of support, encourage a healthy lifestyle, and monitor social and occupational functioning.

Research shows that CCMs for Bipolar disorder improve quality of life and overall functioning, and reduce emotional distress when used in conjunction with a counseling modality (Kilbourne et al., 2008). In a study conducted with veterans, psychoeducation plus CCM resulted in fewer weeks of depressive and manic episodes, and improved overall functioning and quality of life (Bauer et al., 2006a,b). A meta-analysis comparing counseling approaches found that group psychoeducation combined with CCM reduced manic episodes, while CBT, IPT, and FFT approaches were more effective in reducing depressive episodes (Miklowitz, 2008).

Dialectical Behavior Therapy (DBT)

While not an empirically supported treatment, DBT is also used to treat Bipolar disorder. Clients learn mindfulness skills, distress tolerance, emotional regulation, and skills for interpersonal communication. The goal of DBT is to manage the emotional mood shifts and minimize the frequency and intensity of manic episodes and episodes of depression. Clients learn to calm themselves at times of extreme emotion, recognize and respond to triggers, and develop a plan for dealing with crisis. Like most other forms of counseling, DBT for bipolar disorder emphasizes the development of healthier coping skills and relationships.

Medications

Medication is the primary treatment for Bipolar disorder. As previously indicated, the combination of medication and psychological counseling is particularly effective.

Medications that reduce manic symptoms are called mood stabilizers. Lithium, a naturally occurring chemical element, is the most well-researched mood stabilizer and has been used the longest. Although a majority of individuals improved at least somewhat when taking lithium (and experienced milder symptoms), many clients continue to experience some manic and depressive symptoms while taking lithium; some studies have found relapse rates of up to 40% (Geddes, Burgess, Hawton, Jamison, & Goodwin, 2004). Lithium also has serious potential side effects which require careful monitoring. Regular blood tests are needed to ensure that lithium levels are not too high, since high levels can be toxic.

Mood stabilizers, such as lithium and valproate are important in the treatment of bipolar disorder, but because they are not always well tolerated or completely effective, other medications are often added (Culver, Arnow, & Ketter, 2007) Atypical antipsychotic medications have been found to be effective for manic and depressive episodes, either alone or as an adjunct to lithium or valproate. However, antipsychotic medications are associated with side effects, such as weight gain, obesity, and problems with metabolism that can lead to long-term complications (Bowden et al., 2005; Lyseng-Williamson, 2013). These side effects also reduce medication compliance.

The Food and Drug Administration (FDA) has approved several anticonvulsants (antiseizure medications), including divalproex sodium (Depakote), and antipsychotics like olanzapine (Zyprexa) for the treatment of acute mania. These medications also have potential side effects. Anticonvulsants are associated with a small increase in suicidal ideation in a study comparing a placebo control group (FDA, 2008).

Clients with bipolar disorder are often prescribed lithium in combination with these other medications. A significant number of clients do not respond to a single medication, particularly for manic episodes. In addition, the medications used to treat bipolar disorder are not usually started at a full therapeutic dose, because of the risk of side effects. Medication is often adjusted over time. Lithium takes effect over an extended period of time, so an antipsychotic medication is often started in conjunction and takes effect immediately. This is particularly critical when the client is having an acute manic episode, since the antipsychotic has a calming effect that may prevent serious risk-taking behavior (Scherk, Pajonk, & Leucht, 2007).

Research shows greater improvement in manic symptoms, depressive symptoms, and quality of life for clients on combined treatment regimens of lithium or valproate with olanzapine (Namjoshi, Risser, Shi, Tohen, & Breier, 2004; Tohen et al., 2002). Lithium or valproate combined with quetiapine also has been shown to decrease manic symptoms (Sachs et al., 2004; Yatham, Paulsson, Mullen, & Vagero, 2004). Risperidone and aripiprazole were also found to be helpful in combination with mood stabilizers (Sachs et al., 2006; Yatham, Grossman, Augustyns, Vieta, & Ravindran, 2003). However, there are potential side effects for many of these medications.

Mood stabilizers (lithium and anticonvulsants), atypical antipsychotics, and antidepressants are the most recommended treatments for Bipolar depression. Some clients continue to feel depressed while taking a mood stabilizer to treat manic symptoms, although these medications may also relieve depressive symptoms in other individuals. If depressive symptoms persist, an antidepressant may be added to the regimen. However, certain antidepressants may increase the risk of recurrence, trigger manic symptoms, or increase suicide risk (Bottlender, Rudolf, Strauss, & Moller, 2001; Tondo, Vazquez, & Baldessarini 2010; Vieta & Valenti, 2013).

A number of clinical studies examined the efficacy of various medications for children and adolescents with Bipolar disorder. Lithium and Aripiprazole are approved by the Federal Drug Administration as maintenance treatments for children and adolescents with bipolar disorder (Welge & DelBello, 2013), and aripiprazole was found to be effective and relatively well tolerated as monotherapy in a pediatric sample (Findling et al., 2013). Recent meta-analyses suggest that second generation antipsychotics (including risperidone, aripiprazole, quetiapine, and olanzapine) are effective in reducing manic symptoms among children and adolescents, but there is a significant risk of side effects, especially when these medications are used in combination (Peruzzolo, Tramontina, Rohde & Zeni, 2013). Risperidone was found to be more effective than lithium or valproate for manic symptoms in children, but there are concerns about long-term effects (Vitiello, 2013).

The neurobiological underpinnings of bipolar disorder may also involve receptor sensitivity. Research investigating how medication influences receptor sensitivity during both manic and depressive episodes found that high levels of G-proteins (guanine nucleotide-binding proteins) play a role in modulating cell activity during manic episodes. Lithium may work because of its ability to regulate these G-proteins (Manji et al., 1995). Atypical antipsychotics are thought to work because of their impact on neurotransmitters, especially dopamine and serotonin receptors (McCormack & Wiseman, 2004; Post & Calabrese, 2004).

CASE CONCEPTUALIZATION FOR BIPOLAR DISORDERS USING THE T/C MODEL

Much like the depressive disorders discussed in the previous chapter, clients with bipolar disorders have physiological/biological vulnerabilities, cognitive risk factors, and environmental stressors that exacerbate these vulnerabilities. Since there is a heritability factor, exploration of the client's family history is important. Because heightened reward sensitivity and sleep deprivation are known triggers for manic episodes, the case conceptualization should include an assessment of recent successes as well as stressors. How many hours the client sleeps a night and what their sleep patterns are like is also critical.

Careful assessment of the common symptoms of manic episodes can help diagnose bipolar disorders. Reckless spending, risk taking (fast driving, increased sexual activity), grandiose thinking, high energy levels and high self-esteem, and reduced need for sleep can be associated with manic episodes. Some people experience angry outbursts or have paranoid thoughts during a manic phase. As part of your assessment, take note of speech patterns; clients who are in a manic episode often have pressured speech that is quite rapid and very difficult to interrupt. Clients in hypomanic episodes tend to be more social and flirtatious.

Individuals with bipolar disorder may attempt to self-medicate, so assessment of substance use is helpful. Comorbid diagnoses such as anxiety disorders complicate treatment; therefore, symptoms of anxiety should be assessed as well. Clients with bipolar disorder are at risk for suicide, which makes this an important part of the case conceptualization.

As with other Depressive disorders, individuals with bipolar disorders often have irrational beliefs and negative automatic thoughts, which can be identified and later challenged. A thorough assessment of the client's strengths and accomplishments can be a source of challenge, and identifying the client's support system is crucial for successfully managing and treating bipolar disorders.

Finally, the social and cultural beliefs about bipolar disorder are relevant, as there is still a great deal of misinformation and stigma around the disorder, which is often misrepresented in film and television.

With these treatment considerations in mind, let's consider another client who enters counseling with symptoms that might be consistent with a bipolar disorder.

The Case of Jason

Jason is a 42-year-old salesman. He has been married for fifteen years to Judy, and they have two teenage children. Jason has struggled with depression on and off ever since his early teens. He says his childhood was "difficult" because his older brother was often depressed. His mother was a functional alcoholic who had multiple affairs. He grew up in an Irish Catholic family and as the family was very religious, his mother's affairs were painful for Jason's father and for Jason and his brother. His mother was hospitalized several times. Later in life, she was diagnosed with bipolar disorder, but passed away before treatment could be effective.

Jason came to counseling at the insistence of his wife, after he woke up one morning a few weeks ago and announced that he hated his job and was wasting his considerable talents. He quit his job without having any prospects for another, withdrew $20,000 from the family bank account, and purchased several custom guitars, announcing his plan to become a professional musician. He is cheerful when he comes to see you, but he also looks frazzled as if he got dressed too quickly and wasn't paying attention.

"I was wasting my life, I just wasn't meant to be some lowly sales person, day in day out dealing with all these idiots who've never had a creative thought in their life, and why should I? They don't know that I can run circles around them—think circles around them—so why shouldn't I? I should have done this long ago."

The counselor tries to interrupt, but Jason keeps talking.

"Do you know what I did last week? I put an ad on Craig's List, right? Looking for a drummer and a lead singer, because I want it to be a band, not just me, I don't wanna be Justin Bieber, you know? And I got so many calls, just these incredible people—musicians, real artists, like me—and they understand me. I spend most of my time just talking with them, planning. We're gonna take off, I can tell, it's obvious really . . . inevitable . . . I'm the next Elvis!"

"Have you always felt you should be a musician?" the counselor interjects.

Jason bursts into excited laughter. "No! Isn't that the damnedest thing? It must have been latent in me all this time, just waiting to get out! I think my success at the store was what made me realize I had it in me, because I made so much money last month, I was just on fire, everything I touched I could sell, and then I realized, I should do more than this!"

"Have you been sleeping?" the counselor asks when there's a slight pause.

Jason shakes his head. "Not really—but I don't really need to! Creative people, we don't need sleep like the rest of the world, we're different. But, I'll tell you what I have been doing—I've been seeing a girl. Don't tell my wife! She just won't understand, but Kathleen, she understands, she's amazing, I never thought I'd do this, but I can't resist her, she's amazing. I met her at the bar I've been stopping at on the way home, and we're just—I think we're meant to be. Life is wonderful!"

THE CASE OF JASON

Case Conceptualization Example Using the T/C Model

(* Areas that require more information)

Presenting Problem: manic episode, racing thoughts, sleep disruption, irrational beliefs

Internal Personality Constructs and Behavior:

Self-efficacy: grandiose thinking

Self-esteem: inflated, "wasting considerable talents"

Attitudes/Values/Beliefs: previously believed affairs were hurtful, change in belief recently

*Attachment Style:**

Biology/Physiology/Heredity: married 42-year-old with 2 teenage children, family history of depression (brother), bipolar disorder (mother), alcoholism (mother), reduced need for sleep

Affect: manic episode, elation

Cognition: delusions, grandiose thinking

Hot Thoughts: "I was wasting my life"; "I'm the next Elvis"

Behavior: not sleeping, quit job, over-spending, having an affair, pressured speech

Symptomology: not sleeping, irritable

Coping Skills and Strengths; stable relationship, intelligent, successful

Readiness for Change: precontemplation stage

Life Roles: husband; quit job

Environment:

Relationships: conflict with wife, current affair

Culture: Irish Catholic background*

Family Norms and Values: strong religious background,* influence of parents' beliefs*

Societal Influences: beliefs about what it means to be successful*

Timeline:

Past Influences: mother's history of alcoholism, extramarital affairs, and bipolar disorder, brother's history of depression, possible history of depression, difficult childhood

Present Influences: recent job success as possible trigger, manic symptoms, current affair, and economic risk-taking

Future Goals: wants to be famous musician, relationship/family goals*

Question: What else would you want to ask to complete this case conceptualization?

COUNSELING KEYSTONES

- Bipolar disorders include episodes of both depression, and the opposite "pole," mania or hypomania.
- Manic episodes are characterized by "flight of ideas," impaired social judgment, reckless behavior and risk taking, reduced need for sleep, high energy level, and grandiose thinking.
- Hypomania is similar to mania, but less extreme and less disruptive—the individual is grounded in reality and thinking more clearly, but there is a change in normal functioning, including increased sociability, increased energy, and productivity.
- Bipolar I disorder includes a manic episode, while bipolar II disorder requires a hypomanic episode.
- Most clients diagnosed with bipolar disorder have recurring depression or manic episodes after their initial diagnosis.
- A diagnosis of bipolar I disorder is associated with an increased suicide rate, a strong risk of recurrence, and high personal and social cost.
- Most clients can see significant improvement with ongoing treatment. Long-term preventive treatment is recommended, with a treatment protocol that combines medication and psychological treatment to manage the disorder.
- Bipolar disorder is less common than major depressive disorder, with approximately 6 out of 1,000 people internationally meeting the criteria for bipolar I.
- Anxiety disorders are the most commonly co-occurring disorder, with substance abuse and certain medical conditions also comorbid with bipolar disorders.

- Both genetic and biological factors appear to be important in the etiology of bipolar disorder. In addition, environmental factors and psychosocial stressors influence course and severity.
- Reward sensitivity, sleep deprivation, and environmental stressful life events impact the development of manic and depressive symptoms.
- Empirically supported counseling treatments include psychoeducation, cognitive behavioral therapy (CBT), interpersonal and social rhythm therapy (IPSRT), family focused treatment (FFT), and chronic care models of treatment.

- Medication is the primary treatment for bipolar disorder, with the combination of medication and psychological counseling particularly effective.
- Medications that reduce manic symptoms are called mood stabilizers. Lithium, a naturally occurring chemical element, is the most well-researched mood stabilizer and has been used the longest.
- Medication adherence is a significant problem in the treatment of bipolar disorder, and treatment with a combination of medications is often recommended.
- Antipsychotic medications and several anticonvulsants have also been found to be effective, but carry significant risk of side effects.

The Case of Jerome

Jerome is a 28-year-old Cuban American male who came to the crisis clinic with his parents. The parents are worried and frustrated, since Jerome, who was always a "good boy" and a good student, just quit his job as a financial analyst and broke up with his boyfriend of four years. The parents were very proud of Jerome's success and felt that his relationship with George was a good one, and they're confused and devastated by the sudden changes in Jerome. The family highly values academic and professional success and they are concerned that Jerome has now moved back in with them and is refusing to look for another job, saying that there are too many people "out to get me out there."

The family also says that Jerome is sleeping on the couch, but he is not actually sleeping at all. Instead, he stays up most of the night, sometimes pacing and talking to himself. George has called several times to try to talk to Jerome, who refuses to speak to him. George tells the parents that Jerome has been going to clubs and engaging in risky sexual behavior, and often drinks too much when he is out. Jerome's parents are dumbfounded, since Jerome has never been in trouble and has always shared his parents' values about alcohol and promiscuity.

When the counselor asks Jerome how he's doing, Jerome jumps up and angrily accuses both the counselor and his parents of persecuting him. He speaks so rapidly that the counselor can't understand him, and soon realizes that some of what Jerome is saying does not make sense. He insists that the room is bugged and that "they're listening" and appears agitated as he looks around the room for evidence.

Jerome's parents say that he has never behaved like this before. They do state that Jerome had episodes of depression when he was a teenager, but they attributed that to the social stigma of coming out and hoped that it had passed. Jerome's paternal grandfather was an alcoholic, and Jerome's dad recalls times when "my dad sounded just like Jerome does now."

EXERCISES

EXERCISE 5.1 Treatment Options

This chapter begins with a description of three clients, all of whom would be diagnosed with a Bipolar disorder. Consider what you now know about medication and counseling treatments for Bipolar disorder.

CLASS EXERCISE: Small group discussion followed by large group discussion.

> **Question:** What treatment (or combination of treatments) might be beneficial for Betsy, Dorothy, and Chuck? Why?

EXERCISE 5.2 Case Conceptualization Practice

Now that you have listened in on several counselors working with clients who have various types of bipolar disorders, it's time to see what you can do. How would you conceptualize the case of Jerome, in order to most effectively develop a diagnosis and collaborate on a treatment plan?

CLASS EXERCISE: Small group discussion followed by large group discussion

> **Question 1:** What is your case conceptualization of this case?

Question 2: What else do you want to know?

Question 3: What are three possible goals for Jerome in counseling?

Question 4: What interventions can you employ given the answers to your first two questions?

GO FURTHER

An Unquiet Mind: A Memoir of Moods and Madness by Kay Redfield Jamison (1997) Random House

Clinician's Guide to Bipolar Disorder: Integrating Pharmacology and Psychotherapy by David J. Miklowitz, PhD and Michael J. Gitlin, MD (2014) Guilford Press

The Bipolar II Disorder Workbook: Managing Recurring Depression, Hypomania, and Anxiety by Stephanie McMurrich Roberts, PhD, Louisa Grandin Sylvia, PhD, Noreen A. Reilly-Harrington, PhD, and David J. Miklowitz, PhD (2014) New Harbinger

The Dialectical Behavioral Therapy Skills Workbook for Bipolar Disorder: Using DBT to Regain Control of your Emotions and Your Life by Sheri Van Dijk and Zindel V. Segal, PhD (2009) New Harbinger

Bipolar Disorder: A Family-Focused Treatment Approach by David J. Miklowitz, PhD (2010) The Guilford Press

Handbook of Diagnosis and Treatment of Bipolar Disorders by Terence A. Ketter (2009) American Psychiatric Publishing

Bipolar Disorder: A Cognitive Therapy Approach by Cory F. Newman, Robert L. Leahy, Arron T. Beck, Noreen Reilly-Harrington, and Laszlo Gyulai (2013) American Psychological Association

6

ANXIETY DISORDERS

INTRODUCTION

The words *anxiety* and *anxious* are part of our everyday conversation. Perhaps you, like most others, have noted that you were anxious about an upcoming test or doctor's appointment; or perhaps, you experienced a feeling of anxiety before going to a social event or while driving to a job interview. You may even have noted that you were simply feeling "anxious" without a clear understanding of why. Anxiety is part of the human condition and can be useful when it helps us anticipate and appropriately respond to possible danger. When we experience a stressful event, whether real or imagined, the body reacts by activating the sympathetic nervous system, which leads to a fight-or-flight response.

Not all stress is harmful. In fact, normal stress, or eustress, is part of everyone's daily life. The term eustress was first used by Richard Lazarus (1966) to describe the healthy response to stress that leads to a positive behavioral response and feelings of achievement and fulfillment. Lazarus believed that people had to perceive a situation as anxiety provoking in order to trigger this stress response—the thoughts that an individual associates with an event determine if it is perceived as threatening, and if a positive outcome is viewed as achievable (Lazarus, 1966). If a positive outcome is viewed as possible, then, we face the stressor, do what we have to do, and feel good

about it afterward. In fact, there is a great deal of research that shows that some stress or anxiety (however, not too much) actually increases performance (Davies, Matthews, Stammers, & Westerman, 2013).

Children experience normal fears and anxiety as they develop, though the most common fears change as children grow older. Fears of loud noises, strangers, and separation from caregivers are normative in infancy, while school-age children are afraid of being evaluated, of social situations, or of bodily injury. These normal fears are only problematic when they become severe enough to interfere with daily life and impair academic, family, and relationship functioning.

Unfortunately, for some, the normal level of anxiety can become extreme and excessive, and the ways of responding to it can then become dysfunctional. Typically, when clients talk about stress and anxiety, they are describing an event and an emotional state that negatively impact their mental and physical well-being (Wagner, 1990). In this chapter, we discuss anxiety disorders, a cluster of mental health disorders marked by feelings of excessive worry, physical distress, and apprehension about the future. This severe anxiety occurs during situations where most people would not experience such a significant level of concern or worry, and these reactions are markedly different from normal reactions to stress. Unlike the comparatively mild and transitory anxiety caused

101

by a stressful event, such as a minor car accident or a presentation at work, anxiety disorders last much longer and get progressively worse if not treated. Anxiety disorders have various symptoms, but normally center around excessive irrational fear and dread.

Anxiety disorders as a group are among the most common mental health issues in the United States. A National Institute of Mental Health report in 2009 reveals that anxiety disorders impact roughly 12% to 20% of the adult (over 18) population at any given time, translating into 40 million individuals (Kessler, Berglund, Demler, Jin, & Walters, 2005). Numbers are similar if not larger for children and adolescents (Beesdo, Knappe, & Pine, 2009). Anxiety disorders commonly occur along with other mental or physical illnesses, including alcohol or substance abuse, which may start as a form of self-medication. In some cases, these co-occurring disorders need to be treated before or simultaneously in order for the client to respond to treatment for the anxiety disorder (Kessler, Chiu, Demler, & Walters, 2005).

A variety of therapeutic interventions for anxiety disorders are available, and there are new treatments that can help individuals lead satisfying and productive lives. Many individuals, however, do not seek treatment because they are ashamed to seek help or feel that they are coping the best they can under difficult circumstances. When not treated, anxiety disorders can become debilitating, impacting personal relationships, career, or school, and can even make such common activities as shopping, driving, or making a

phone call extremely difficult. Anxiety disorders have been shown to affect morbidity and mortality rates, work productivity, and alcohol and other drug use (Hoffman, Dukes, & Wittchen, 2008; Leon, Portera, & Weissman, 1995; Wittchen & Fehm, 2001).

In this chapter, we focus on the anxiety disorders which counselors most often encounter in their practice settings: generalized anxiety disorder (GAD), panic disorder, specific phobias, social anxiety disorder (SAD), and agoraphobia. As we introduce clients who are struggling with each disorder, we look at the specific elements of the case on which a counselor would focus by using the T/C Model.

GENERALIZED ANXIETY DISORDER (GAD)

People with generalized anxiety disorder (GAD) suffer from extreme amounts of worry accompanied by physical distress and behavioral disturbances. This excessive worry has no specific trigger and lasts for several hours to most of the day. As the name applies, the anxiety is generalized to almost all aspects of the client's life, unlike other anxiety disorders like specific phobias or social phobia. GAD regularly includes thoughts of impending disaster which focus on family, financial, career, social interaction, or health (American Psychiatric Association, 2013). For clients with GAD, just getting out of bed and thinking about the upcoming day can lead to severe anxiety.

The Case of Glenn

Glenn is a 32-year-old math teacher with a wife and two young children. He came to counseling at the request of his wife. She says she cannot take it anymore, that Glenn always has to be in control, and says that his excessive worry about "everything" is driving them apart. The last straw for her was when Glenn started calling her at work numerous times a day to make sure that she was safe. He is worried about his marriage and is motivated to do whatever it takes to keep his family intact.

People diagnosed with GAD commonly believe they have no control over their thoughts, even though they realize that much of their anxiety is irrational or unjustified. They have trouble sleeping or staying asleep and often describe themselves as being in a heightened state of arousal. This excessive worry is associated with specific physical symptoms that are typical with anxiety disorders and include: muscle tension, easily fatigued, difficulty concentrating or mind going blank, irritability, sleep disturbance, and feeling keyed up, restless, or on edge.

GAD affects about 3% of the population which translates into 6.8 million American adults (Kessler et al., 2005; Kessler, Chiu, Demler, & Walters, 2005). GAD can begin at any age, but usually develops gradually between childhood and middle age. Although a specific cause is not known, there is evidence that heredity and environment may play a role (Hettema, Neale, & Kendler, 2001). Many suffering from GAD report that they have had these thoughts and feelings for as long as they can remember (APA, 2013). The GAD sufferer may feel better or worse at times, often getting worse during times of stress, but the anxiety always comes back. GAD tends to be chronic and can come and go across the lifespan; unfortunately, rates of full remission are very low (APA, 2013). What differentiates GAD from other anxiety related disorders is an excessive amount of worry about some future event or occurrence. This apprehensive expectation happens in multiple situations (i.e., school, work, driving); happens more days that not; and lasts for at least 6 months (APA, 2013). Individuals with GAD find it difficult to control their thoughts, which often spin out of control. They become preoccupied with thoughts of imminent disaster, making it difficult to concentrate or focus on specific tasks, and have trouble controlling their emotions, even when they realize that their responses are extreme given the situation. They may even express the belief that this worry somehow helps them prepare for what is coming or that their hypervigilance is somehow productive, as you can see from the counselor's discussion with Glenn. Listen in as the counselor meets with Glenn for the first time and begins the process of case conceptualization.

Counselor:	*"Tell me more about what that means, to worry about 'everything.'"*
Glenn:	*"I don't know, I mean—there's just so much that could go wrong on a daily basis. Money, my job, my parents—they're getting up there—or something could happen to the kids, or to my wife. I don't know what I'd do if that happened, I just couldn't . . ."*
Counselor:	*"Can you remember a time when you weren't so worried, and could relax more?"*
Glenn:	*(frowning) "Not really. I can't remember not worrying. My mother always used to yell at me for being a 'worrywart,' and now my wife says the same thing. I did really well in school—got straight A's actually, and graduated with a 4.0."*
Counselor:	*"Wow, that's impressive."*
Glenn:	*(wry smile) "Well, that's what you have to do to get ahead, isn't it? You have to stay one step ahead of everyone else. That's what I did—it's what I have to keep doing."*
Counselor:	*"That sounds like a lot of pressure. How is all this worrying affecting you?"*
Glenn:	*(frowning again) "I guess it's taking a toll. I can't really fall asleep, I just lie there thinking about what could go wrong the next day. Or if I do fall asleep, I wake up at 5 am and start worrying all over again. It's making it hard to concentrate at work, and now . . . God, I don't know what we'll do if I lose my job! I worry every day that my principal will come in and observe my class, and things won't go well. And what if my students don't do well on the standardized tests coming up?"*
Counselor:	*"That's a lot to worry about, and I can understand that it's hard to sleep when you're so worried. Anything else?"*

Glenn:	"Headaches . . . I've always had migraines. My stomach bothers me a lot too. And I've started to think maybe I need to go to a chiropractor, I'm constantly sore, my neck, my back."
Counselor:	"Anxiety causes a lot of tension, which might be causing the soreness in your neck and back. That's a lot to deal with."
Glenn:	"It is. I know my wife is angry that I keep calling her at work, but I get so worried that something bad has happened to her, I just have to call and check."
Counselor:	"So it sounds like the worrying is really taking a toll on you."
Glenn:	"I guess . . . but it's what gives me an edge, you know? If you don't worry about bad things happening, that's when bad things happen!"
Counselor:	"If you think that, it must make it hard not to worry."
Glenn:	(sighing) "I know that's kind of crazy, I mean, I know it's not really true, but I just can't seem to stop believing it. Can you help me?"

PANIC DISORDER

Panic disorder's primary feature is recurring severe panic attacks that come out of nowhere—sudden and repeated bouts of fear that usually last for several minutes, but can last longer. Attacks usually happen in situations that are not normally considered threatening or dangerous, and revolve around thoughts of disaster, death, or losing control. These thoughts are accompanied

The Case of Doug

Doug is a 50-year-old married businessman who travels frequently for work. He has sought counseling because he has recently developed severe anxiety while flying. Doug started to become fearful and anxious during a recent trip to California when the plane ran into severe turbulence. He began to believe that the plane was in trouble and could possibly crash. His heart started to race and he felt like he could not catch his breath. He also felt very trapped, knowing he could do nothing about what was taking place. The woman sitting next to him became upset when Doug began sweating profusely until he eventually took off his seat belt and retreated to the bathroom. Doug was so concerned that he went to the ER to get checked out after he landed, certain he was having a heart attack. The hospital assured him, however, that he was fine.

On the return trip, Doug tried having three drinks before getting on the plane, but experienced another panic attack which started shortly after the plane took off. Although that flight did not have any turbulence, Doug experienced the same rapid heartbeat, sweating, and dizziness that he had experienced on the previous flight. He barely managed to remain in his seat that time. This was three months ago and he has not been able to get on a plane since coming back from this business trip. Worse, Doug experienced the same symptoms and trapped feeling recently when he was in a busy department store waiting in line to check out. He ended up tossing the items on a table and leaving the store, and is now nervous about returning. Doug has already made an appointment with his general practitioner and intends to request more medical tests to "figure out what's wrong with me."

by strong physical symptoms, the most common of which are sweating, heart palpitations, trembling, chest pain, dizziness, nausea, and numbness or tingling. Because the physical symptoms of a panic attack can be quite severe, many are mistaken for life-threatening physical issues like heart attacks. The association that a sufferer feels between the panic attack and the belief that they are in the middle of a medical emergency can lead to future attacks, called anticipatory attacks. Those experiencing a panic attack frequently visit emergency rooms, and tests may be performed to rule out other medical conditions that can create further anxiety.

Panic attacks can be differentiated from normal reactions to stress, even severe ones. Normal reactions to environmental stressors build over time or have a specific trigger that starts the fight-or-flight response. Panic attacks are acute sudden events that feel like they come out of the blue. The duration of these attacks are shorter in comparison and symptoms feel more intense and out of control.

Panic attacks can occur at any time, which makes them very anxiety provoking. Their severity and frequency can vary widely, and seem to have no trigger, which leads to a persistent and intense worry about when the next attack will happen. People often significantly change their behaviors in order to avoid having another episode. This leads to avoiding places and people associated with previous attacks, eventually developing into agoraphobic behaviors.

The age of onset is usually during early adulthood with about 50% of cases developing before the age of 24 (Kessler et al., 2005; Kessler, Chiu, Demler, & Walters, 2005), with a lifetime prevalence of about 3% to 4% of the U.S. population.

Panic disorders can be very debilitating, and clients may be ashamed because of their inability to carry out normal routines, such as flying, grocery shopping, or driving. If left untreated, panic disorder can lead to job loss or relationship issues. On the other hand, panic disorder is often amenable to treatment. Research identifies a variety of contributing factors, including past stressful events, temperament that is more susceptible to anxiety, biological, and genetic factors. A counselor working with Doug could focus on these possible contributing factors as he constructs a case conceptualization.

Counselor:	*"You described a flight that was very stressful. Was this the first time you've experienced this kind of physical reaction?" (looking for past stressful events)*
Doug:	*"I think . . . well, looking back, there were some times in the past too, where I had a strong reaction."*
Counselor:	*"Can you describe one of those times?"*
Doug:	*"I remember being a kid, maybe nine or ten, and my little sister and I got stuck on an elevator in Atlantic City in one of those big high rises. She was freaking out and I couldn't get it going, and I just—I remember I thought I was gonna faint or something. I had nightmares about that for years."*
Counselor:	*"Were you a pretty laid back kid?" (exploring temperament)*
Doug:	*(laughs) "I don't think anyone would say that, no. I guess I've always been a little anxious—normal stuff, you know, giving talks in front of the class. Or crowds, I've never liked crowds."*
Counselor:	*"How about your parents and your sister? Are they more or less laid back than you?" (exploring family history of anxiety)*
Doug:	*"Oh, my mom is less laid back—a lot less! She's always worried about something, and constantly thinks there's something wrong with her. You know, cancer or something."*

As you can see from this brief segment of the counselor's session with Doug, the case conceptualization model helps the counselor focus on those elements that are most relevant to figuring out the problem and then helping Doug find a path to change.

> ### The Case of Amy
>
> *Amy is an 8-year-old who lives with both her parents in a suburban town. A few weeks ago, Amy was playing in the yard with her best friend Jill, when a man who lived two streets over came by walking his large dog. The dog began barking at the girls and then pulled its leash out of its owner's hand and raced into the yard. Both girls screamed and ran, and were extremely frightened by the event. Her parents brought her to see a counselor concerned that she's still very anxious.*

SPECIFIC PHOBIAS

Specific phobias, previously called simple phobias, refer to enduring irrational fear and anxiety caused by a specific object or situation that has little or no associated danger (APA, 2013). People with phobias work hard to avoid things, environments, and circumstances that they irrationally or exceedingly associate with danger. In most cases, they are aware that their fear makes no sense, but they believe that they are unable to control it. These phobias can interrupt daily routines, affect work productivity, decrease self-efficacy and self-worth, and negatively impact interpersonal relationships. In severe cases, people will do whatever they can to avoid the severe anxiety and dread they are experiencing, which can in turn also lead to agoraphobic behaviors.

Specific phobias have a lifetime prevalence of about 9% of the adult U.S. population, but only about one-third of these individuals seek treatment (Kessler et al., 2005; Kessler, Chiu, Demler, Walters, 2005). The causes of specific phobias are not known, but they are believed to be learned or associated with traumatic experiences. Children may learn them from observing other's phobic reactions; for example, a fear of dogs or snakes. Fears about animals, the natural environment, and blood or injections tend to begin in childhood, whereas situational fears tend to appear later (Lewis-Fernandez et al., 2009).

A specific object or situation elicits the fear (see Figure 6.1 for a list of common triggers),

the trigger produces a severe response almost every time, and is excessive and out of the ordinary. The person suffering from a phobia almost always avoids the object or situation, and can become anxious just thinking about it. If they are exposed to the trigger, symptoms are similar to those of a panic attack; rapid heart rate, sweating, depersonalization, difficulty breathing, dizziness, and nausea (in children symptoms can include all of the above plus a feeling of choking, freezing, trembling, and tantrums). Symptoms rapidly subside once the trigger is no longer present.

The counselor working with Amy should ask the parents more about the frightening event, the impact that Amy's fears are having on her, and why they believe her fear is not subsiding. These and other questions can help the counselor determine whether a diagnosis of specific phobia is appropriate. When working with a child, speaking with the parent or guardian is a helpful part of the case conceptualization.

Counselor: *"Can you tell me what's going on now? You mentioned that Amy still seems anxious."*

Amy's mother: *"She is—I don't think it's getting any better. In fact, it's getting worse?"*

Counselor: *"What exactly is getting worse?"*

Amy's mother: *"She's nervous all the time. She doesn't want to walk to school anymore, because she's afraid a dog will be nearby and might bite her. She doesn't even want to go outside for*

Figure 6.1   The Most Common Specific Phobias

Animal: These are the most common. Examples include the fear of dogs, snakes, bees, or rats.

Situational: These include flying, driving, public transportation, bridges or tunnels, or being in closed-in places like elevators or a packed train.

Environmental: Fear of storms, lightning, heights, or water.

Injury Related: These involve a fear of being injured, seeing blood, or medical procedures, such as injections with a needle

Figure 6.2   Anxiety or Phobia?

Everyday Anxiety	Phobia
Feeling uneasy while climbing a tall tree	Not being able to attend a business meeting because it requires travel
Worrying about travelling in a snow storm	Turning down a great job because it involves getting on a highway to go to work
Feeling anxious around your neighbor's big dog	Not visiting your neighbor because of his small friendly dog

recess; her teacher says she's been finding excuses to stay in, and that's not like her at all. I'm afraid she's going to lose friends over this."

Counselor: "Has Amy always been an anxious child?"

Amy's father: "A little bit, yes. She takes after my mother, her grandmother, I think. In fact, my mom has always been nervous around our own dog, Maisie. She's a 10-year-old Bassett hound, but my mother always insists we lock her in her crate when she visits. She's harmless!"

Counselor: "How has Amy been around Maisie?"

Amy's mother: "Actually that's worrying me too. Amy is even nervous around her own dog now. She moves away when Maisie tries to come sit near her and even cried the other day when Maisie barked when the doorbell rang. She's never done that before!"

Amy's father: "I didn't want to say anything" (looks at his wife) "but she put her hands over her ears the other night when a dog on television barked, and then she asked me to change the channel."

Amy's mother: "This is getting out of hand! She's been asking to sleep in our room at night too, saying she has nightmares and is afraid a dog might come in her room while she's sleeping. What's going on?"

The counselor also speaks to Amy to gather information about her fears (cognitions, beliefs, and "hot thoughts") and her avoidance behaviors. Once a clearer picture of Amy's fears and how her avoidance is impacting her, then a treatment plan can be developed.

The Case of Anna

Anna was referred to you, her school counselor, by her homeroom teacher. She is a 16-year-old high school junior with two older sisters who went to the school as well and were very popular. Anna is constantly anxious and seems preoccupied with the way she looks and what other students think about her. She is generally a good student and has a few close friends, but has not had any romantic relationships. Her teachers are all concerned about Anna's inability to speak in front of the class. She either calls in sick on the day she's supposed to give a presentation, or gives up halfway through and runs to the rest room, saying she's ill.

SOCIAL ANXIETY DISORDER (SAD)

Social situations or circumstances where we have to perform in some way cause nervousness for most of us. Who among us has not felt anxious before going on a first date, taking scholastic aptitude tests (SATs), or giving a presentation to the class? Everyone has experienced knots in their stomach, or felt tongue tied while trying to make conversation with a stranger. However, with social anxiety disorder everyday social situations cause extreme feelings of anxiety, humiliation, and shame.

Social anxiety disorder (SAD) is perhaps the most common anxiety disorder with roughly 12% of Americans reporting it during their lifetimes (Kessler et al., 2005; Kessler, Chiu, Demler, & Walters 2005). About 7%, roughly 15 million American adults, have social phobia in any given year (Kessler, Chiu, Demler, & Walters, 2005). SAD often appears at an early age; the average onset age is 13, and 50% of those who have this disorder develop it by the age of 11, and 80% develop it by age 20 (Kessler et al., 2005).

With symptoms similar to a panic attack, SAD is triggered by social or performance situations, with the anxiety brought on by perceived or actual scrutiny from others. Fear of negative evaluation by others is the hallmark of SAD. The disorder affects emotions, thoughts, and behavior and can cause significant physical symptoms. Cognitive symptoms include intense fear of interacting with strangers, worry about being judged, embarrassment or humiliation, and fear that others will notice the individual's distress or that they will have a panic attack.

The triggers for social anxiety are based on the social standards and expectations of the individual's culture; the same social behavior may be considered normal in one culture and excessive in another. Individuals with SAD fear violating whatever they perceive to be the social norms of their particular group, as defined by culture, ethnicity, gender, social status and sexual orientation. Thus, there is cultural variation in both symptoms and prevalence. For example, in certain cultures like in an orthodox Jewish society, value is placed on women being modest; thus there is no expectation for women to participate in public events, and the rates of social anxiety disorder among females are low (Greenberg, Stravynski, & Bilu, 2004). Research also suggests that a mismatch between an individual's personal orientation and social values and those that are normative in the person's culture is related to social anxiety symptoms. When considering a diagnosis of SAD, the counselor should take into account the client's social and cultural background and beliefs.

Physical responses are typical of anxiety disorders, including shaky voice, blushing, trembling, stomach upset, and rapid heart rate. The symptoms cause significant distress and impair functioning in some aspects of daily life. The sufferer may be aware that their reactions are excessive, but feel as though they have no control over their reactions. As we have seen with other anxiety disorders, individuals with SAD avoid situations that cause these unpleasant responses, which can disrupt day to day activities. Avoidance creates a vicious cycle which eventually makes symptoms worse, as the avoidance is reinforcing—the person escapes from the situation and quickly feels better, leading to more avoidance in the future. Clients usually realize that their anxiety or fear is out of proportion to the situation, but feel powerless to change it.

Counselor: "Anna, can you tell me what happens when you have to speak in front of the class?"

Anna: (wringing her hands in her lap and visibly blushing. When she speaks, her voice trembles) "I just can't do it, I don't know why. I feel like I'm having a heart attack just thinking about having to stand up there in front of everyone."

Counselor: "That sounds really difficult—can you tell me what that feels like, when it feels like a heart attack?"

Anna: "My heart starts beating way too fast, like it's gonna jump right through my chest, and I feel dizzy too. I can feel myself turning red, and I know everyone can see it!"

Counselor: "Anything else?"

Anna: "I get sick to my stomach. That's why I have to leave and go to the rest room; I know I'm gonna be sick. I can't help it!"

Counselor: "Can you tell me what you're afraid of? What are you concerned might happen?"

Anna: "I don't know—I guess, that I'll sound dumb? That people will all be sitting there thinking 'OMG, she's so stupid' or 'OMG she's so ugly, what a loser.'"

Counselor: "No wonder it's hard to stand up there, if you believe that's what everyone is thinking!"

Anna: (making better eye contact) "It is pretty awful. And I know it's stupid, I mean, I'm not sitting there thinking that when other people are up there . . ."

Counselor: "Are there any other times you feel these kind of symptoms?"

Anna: (nodding) "Yeah, lots of times actually."

Counselor: "Can you give me some examples? It will really help us figure this out."

Anna: "Sure, okay. Well, I sort of feel this way every time I have to go to a party or something where there are people I don't know—or any group of people really. I'm fine just hanging out with my best friend, but as soon as there are a few people, I clam up. And I start to feel queasy and get all red and just want to get out of there."

Counselor: "How about romantic relationships? Are you seeing anyone?"

Anna: (blushing again) "No, no. I wish, but no. There have been a couple guys who said they were interested, but I can't help believing they just asked me to make fun of me. Besides, I got so nervous I couldn't even answer them. I'd rather just avoid the whole thing."

Counselor: "And yet, you said 'I wish.'"

Anna: "Yeah . . . I guess I do. But, I don't think I'll ever be able to. I just can't change how I feel."

The information the counselor gathered here is a good start toward a case conceptualization of Anna's problem, suggesting a diagnosis of social anxiety disorder. The irrational thoughts that are associated with Anna's behavior become part of the treatment plan as well.

AGORAPHOBIA

Agoraphobia can be defined as the fear of being outside, in public, or in a place from which escape is difficult or embarrassing (APA, 2013). The client will avoid these situations if at all possible, which leads to becoming isolated and unable to complete even the simplest tasks. A little less than 2% of adults and adolescents

The Case of Tanya

Tanya's first panic attack happened in a grocery store. She started to feel her heart race and she couldn't catch her breath. It got so bad she felt like her heart would come right out of her chest. Her hands felt numb and her legs just gave out underneath her. It was so bad the store manager called an ambulance, but at the ER they found nothing wrong. Tanya was extremely embarrassed and could not believe what a fool she was. She eventually recovered and drove home. She chalked the incident up to not feeling well or being dehydrated.

About a week later Tanya was sitting in the waiting room in her dentist's office when she had another attack. She felt trapped and was totally embarrassed. Not wanting to have to call an ambulance again, she quickly left the dentist without saying a word. About five minutes later, the feeling subsided as she was sitting in her car. This time, however, she had to call her boyfriend to drive her home because she was afraid to drive for fear of having another attack. Since then, her attacks have increased in number and severity, and she has started to avoid many social situations or being in public.

receive this diagnosis every year, with two-thirds diagnosed before the age of 35 (APA, 2013). About twice as many women are diagnosed than men with this condition.

Individuals with agoraphobia have extreme difficulty with such things as taking public transportation, walking across a parking lot, being in a crowded area, or standing in a line. Distorted thoughts, such as "I can't get out of here," "no one will help me," or "I'll make a fool out of myself and they will all laugh" contribute to the sense of panic. These thoughts are accompanied by fear and anxiety that is way out of proportion to the actual situation. Because of these thoughts and feeling, clients with agoraphobia react by curtailing normal daily activities to avoid these situations. For example, they may get food delivered to their house instead of eating out or going to the grocery store. Eventually, many clients become homebound in an attempt to shield themselves from this anxiety.

The counselor working with Tanya will want to know more about the "hot thoughts" that are influencing Tanya's behavior, as well as the impact that her avoidance of many situations is having on her life and happiness.

COMORBIDITY

Those suffering from an anxiety disorder are likely to fit the diagnostic criteria for one or more of the other anxiety disorders discussed in this chapter as well (Brown & Barlow, 1992; Brown, Campbell, Lehman, Grisham, & Mancill, 2001). For example, many clients diagnosed with panic disorder also suffer from agoraphobia. Clients with GAD are especially susceptible to having another anxiety disorder (Yonkers, Dyck, Warshaw, & Keller, 2000).

Clients with anxiety disorders are also likely to fit diagnostic criteria for another mental health disorder; these include depressive, eating, or substance abuse disorders. One study found roughly 60% of clients receiving treatment for an anxiety disorder meet criteria for major depression as well (Brown et al., 2001). Studies show that many clients seeking treatment for an eating disorder also fit the criteria for one or more of the anxiety disorders (Godart, Flament, Perdereau, & Jeammet, 2002; Kaye, Bulik, Thornton, Barbarich, & Masters, 2004). There is also a high comorbidity with substance abuse, with studies suggesting that as many as 54% of clients with an anxiety disorder also have a co-occurring substance disorder (Jané-Llopis & Matytsina, 2006; Kessler, Chiu, Demler, & Walters, 2005). Differential diagnosis is also essential to make certain that the symptoms are not due to substance use/abuse or a medical condition.

CULTURAL CONSIDERATIONS AND POPULATION FACTORS

Both gender and culture are linked to prevalence and symptom variation of anxiety disorders. Different cultures vary in norms for how anxiety and worry are expressed. In some cultures, physical symptoms may predominate in the expression of anxiety, while in other cultures cognitive symptoms are more prevalent (APA, 2013). Therefore, it's important to take background and culture into consideration when making an evaluation. For example, the prevalence of social anxiety disorder and the way that the disorder is expressed varies between cultures. Asian cultures show the lowest rates of SAD, while Russia and the United States reveal the highest rates (Hoffmann, Asnaani, & Hinton, 2010). Within the United States, risk for SAD increases if you are younger, have a low income, or are female or American Indian (Lewis-Fernandez et al., 2009). A large-scale epidemiologic survey found that Whites had a higher risk for generalized anxiety disorder and social anxiety disorder; however, the lower rate for Hispanic subjects was only found in younger age groups (i.e., under the age of 43) (Hoffmann et al., 2010). Studies also suggest that Whites have a higher rate of panic disorder (Lewis-Fernandez et al., 2009).

In Japan, a common anxiety disorder is similar to social anxiety disorder, but instead of focusing on fear of embarrassing oneself, the fear is more about displeasing or embarrassing others, which may be related to the culture's emphasis on concern about other people's feelings (McNally, 1997). In Latin American cultures, fright illness (i.e., *susto,* which means fright in Spanish) focuses on the fear that the soul might leave the body after the person is scared. The objects of anxiety in a particular culture tend to relate to environmental challenges and belief systems that are specific to that culture (Kirmayer, 2001).

Cultural variation in symptoms may also be impacted by variation in common fears and thought patterns. For example, Latin American and Asian individuals are more likely to report ringing in the ears, sore neck, or headaches with panic attacks. African American clients are more likely to report physical symptoms of paresthesias associated with panic attacks. This may be because among this cultural group there is a greater fear of diabetes and related complications like amputation. When there is a pervasive cultural fear, clients may be hypervigilant for those specific symptoms, and may overreact to any indication of those symptoms with escalating panic. The content of specific phobias varies as well—Nigerian and Chinese young people had fears about physical safety (electricity, animal attacks), while Americans and Australians had fears about personal safety (getting lost, burglary) (Lewis-Fernandez et al., 2009).

Some cultural groups tend to experience symptoms that are not included in the Diagnostic and Statistical Manual of Mental Disorders (APA, 2013) criteria at all, making diagnosis complicated. For example, uncontrollable screaming or crying, or feelings of heat in the head, neck, and chest are common among Latin American and Caribbean cultures with panic attacks (Lewis-Fernandez et al., 2009). The counselor's own cultural beliefs about the meaning of anxiety symptoms can influence the diagnosis as well.

Until recently, anxiety in children was viewed as less serious than anxiety in adults, with more children referred for behavioral problems, acting out, substance use, or suicidal thoughts than for anxiety. Yet, anxiety disorders are the most common type of mental disorder in children as well as in adults and can have a significant impact on child development. Anxiety interferes with children's ability to make friends, with their academic success, with career options, with self-esteem, and with family relationships. Children who suffer with anxiety have fewer friends on average (Rapee & Melville, 1997), which may then delay the development of their socialization and relationship skills. Since they struggle with assertiveness, these children may be more likely to be bullied and may avoid group experiences, such as dances or class trips. Anxious children who do not receive treatment may also be likely to grow up to be anxious adults, putting them at risk for substance abuse, depression, and relationship problems.

While many of the symptoms of anxiety are similar to those of adults, some symptoms of anxiety disorders vary with age. Both children and adults may be overly focused on negative outcomes, experience somatic symptoms, and avoid frightening situations. Young children may also exhibit symptoms such as bedwetting, selective mutism, acting out, or may be unusually dependent on a parent or caregiver. Because of their developmental stage, children usually have less cognitive insight into what is causing the anxiety, and parents often experience great distress when children have panic attacks, further complicating the child's reaction. Parents, teachers, and clinicians sometimes misinterpret children's symptoms as due to oppositional behavior instead of anxiety. For example, an anxious child may refuse to go to school because of fear and due to avoidance, whereas an oppositional child may refuse to go to school in order to be able to remain at home playing video games. The behavior is the same, but the motivation is different.

In general, anxiety disorders are more prevalent in women than in men, with women twice as likely to be diagnosed with an anxiety disorder (APA, 2013; de Graaf, Bijl, Ravelli, Smit, & Vollenbergh, 2002; Wittchen, 2002). The difference may be related to gender roles, with men more pressured to "face their fears," which can be more effective than avoidance in reducing the cycle of anxiety. The same gender differences in referrals are found for children. Parents may be less willing to accept and recognize anxiety symptoms in boys, and thus less likely to seek

treatment for them. Women are also more likely to have experienced some sort of trauma, including higher rates of sexual assault, which can lead to an increased sense of vulnerability and the perception of danger (Tolin & Foa, 2006). Males, however, tend to have more comorbid diagnoses of substance disorders.

ETIOLOGY AND RISK FACTORS

Biological and Genetic Factors

Studies suggest that anxiety disorders can be caused by biological, genetic, and environmental factors. Practitioners and researchers are continually striving for a more comprehensive model of the roles that stress, biology, and genetics play in anxiety (Bystritsky, Khalsa, Cameron, & Schiffman, 2013). Some of the current research focuses on genetics, brain chemistry, and neuroimaging, including chemical imbalances (norepinephrine and serotonin) in the brain (Charney, 2003; Dell'Osso, Buoli, Baldwin, & Altamura, 2010; LeDoux, 2000). Regions of the brain which control the fear response seem to play a large part in some anxiety disorders.

Temperament factors may play a role in genetic predisposition toward anxiety. Individuals who are highly reactive to changes in their environment may experience an elevated stress response when faced with life stressors and transitions. There are several individual characteristics associated with eventually receiving an anxiety disorder diagnosis, including behavioral inhibition (Hirshfeld-Becker et al., 2008), negative affectivity or neuroticism (Carthy, Horesh, Apter, & Gross, 2009), heightened physiological response (Weems, Zakem, Costa, Cannon, & Watts, 2005), emotional dysregulation (Carthy et al., 2009; Suveg & Zeman, 2004), and harm avoidance (APA, 2013).

Anxiety disorders also tend to run in families, suggesting that a combination of genes and environmental stresses can produce the disorders, with risk factors associated both with a genetic predisposition and the ways that heredity interacts with environment. Twin and family studies of anxiety disorders estimate heritability across the anxiety spectrum in the range of 30% to 50%, which is notably a lower percentage than for other disorders, such as schizophrenia and bipolar disorder. These estimates allow for the largest amount of the variance to be explained by individual and environmental factors (Hettema, Neale, & Kendler, 2001).

The Role of Experience

Research on environmental factors linked to anxiety disorders suggest that while some individuals' anxious tendencies may be inherited, anxiety and worry can also be learned from significant others who regularly exhibit anxiety around them. For example, a child with a parent who is afraid of clowns may learn to fear clowns.

Environmental factors linked to anxiety disorders include parental anxiety and overprotection (van Brakel, Muris, Bogels, & Thomassen, 2006), mothers with depressive disorders (Field, Henandez-Reif, & Diego, 2006; Pelaez, Field, Pickens, & Hart, 2008), and exposure to traumatic events (Briggs-Gowan et al., 2010; Litrownik, Newton, Hunter, English, & Everson, 2003). A traumatic experience may also trigger excessive anxiety in a person who had previously been coping in an adaptive way with stressors (APA, 2013). Parental overprotection and childhood trauma have been linked with anxiety disorders in general, but not to specific disorders.

TREATMENT INTERVENTIONS

Anxiety disorders can be effectively treated with specific types of counseling interventions, medications, or a combination of both. Research shows the effectiveness of cognitive and behavioral interventions, pharmacological treatments, or combinations of these approaches (Antony & Stein, 2009). There is also research suggesting the effectiveness of newer interventions, such as motivational interviewing and mindfulness-based strategies (Antony, 2011).

In this section, we discuss the current evidence-based treatments that are used for Anxiety Disorders, focusing on interventions commonly used in counseling settings. In general, the treatment options discussed are shown to be effective over the spectrum of anxiety disorders. A thorough description of the various counseling interventions is beyond the scope of this text; we include recommendations for comprehensive texts covering counseling interventions for anxiety disorders in the "Go Further" section at the end of this chapter.

Counseling Interventions

Cognitive and Behavioral Interventions

Various forms of Cognitive Therapy, Behavioral Therapy, and Cognitive Behavioral Therapy (CBT) have been shown to be effective in the treatment of anxiety disorders (Antony & Stein, 2009; Hanrahan, Field, Jones, & Davey, 2013; Hoffmann & Smits, 2008; Joesch et al., 2013; National Institute of Health, 2009, 2010a, 2010b). Cognitive interventions focus on recognizing irrational and maladaptive thoughts and subsequently help the client change these thoughts (Beck, 1976; Beck, 2011). Behavioral interventions focus on problematic behaviors and help clients change these into more productive behaviors. Critical to all of these approaches are the concepts of core beliefs, emotional regulation, and coping strategies. Most often, cognitive and behavioral concepts and strategies are combined in cognitive-behavioral treatment.

CBT interventions are usually shorter in duration than other psychotherapies, and last on average twelve weeks or less. They can be implemented individually or in group settings and often include "homework" assignments to complete between sessions. In order for a client to have a successful outcome, clients need to be motivated toward change, able to gain insight into how their thoughts and feelings of anxiety are connected, and have enough self-efficacy to engage in the process. Side effects are minimal, especially compared to medications, although there may be some discomfort associated with the temporarily increased anxiety during an intervention like exposure therapy.

In general, CBT interventions for anxiety can be broken down into five main areas; psychoeducation, self-awareness, cognitive restructuring, exposure to stimulus, and relaxation training.

The psychoeducational component usually comes first and helps the client understand the connections between thoughts, feelings, and actions. You will recall from Theories coursework that CBT is a collaborative approach to counseling. The case conceptualization that the counselor generates is shared with the client, as well as the proposed treatment and how it works. Irrational thoughts, behavioral responses, and physical reactions are all explained and linked together for the client.

For example, the counselor working with Doug might begin treatment by providing some information about panic disorder. Clients often feel like they're "dying" because of associated rapid heartbeat and dizziness. Once the client understands that these symptoms are very uncomfortable, but are not life threatening (confirmed by a physician), the client can then begin to gain some mastery over the symptoms. In addition, psychoeducation about the disorder normalizes the experience and helps the client feel less alone in this process and less "crazy."

Once there is a greater understanding of how the stress response starts, the client is taught how to be more aware of their physical reactions to stress and the thoughts and situations that cause them. This self-awareness is important in helping the client recognize the antecedents and consequences of their thoughts and actions.

Psychoeducation and greater self-awareness can set the stage for the client to start changing their anxiety provoking thoughts and associated maladaptive behaviors. Cognitive restructuring refers to the process of identifying negative thoughts and evaluating their truthfulness, accuracy, and likelihood of occurrence. The counselor and client work on replacing these negative thoughts with more adaptive ones that do not elicit anxiety.

For example, the counselor working with Anna might focus on her "hot thoughts" about being under constant negative evaluation when she's giving a presentation in class or meeting a potential romantic partner. Once the irrational thoughts are identified (*People are all sitting there thinking "OMG, she's so stupid" or "OMG, she's so ugly, what a loser."*) then these thoughts can be challenged. What evidence does Anna have that this is true? Is there any evidence that something else might be going on? This evidence could be something that disputes her negative mind reading (e.g., several classmates told her that they wanted to hear more of her paper the last time she gave up in the middle); or it could be something that disputes her belief that she is everyone's focus of attention (i.e., most of her classmates weren't even paying attention to any of the presentations, instead checking their phones or looking out the window). Once the accuracy of Anna's dysfunctional thoughts is challenged, the counselor and Anna work on replacing the negative thoughts with more realistic ones.

Similarly, a counselor could help Glenn challenge his irrational belief that something bad is happening to his family, or Amy's insistence that her own family dog has become dangerous.

Clients can also be taught relaxation techniques that, if employed correctly, reduce the physical symptoms of anxiety. Common interventions include progressive muscle relaxation, breathing techniques, and guided imagery. All the clients we've met in this chapter could benefit from relaxation techniques that are used in conjunction with the other techniques as part of CBT treatment. The counselor works collaboratively with the client to figure out which techniques work best—a child of Amy's age might not have the cognitive development to benefit from guided imagery, but breathing exercises might help. Glenn might find progressive muscle relaxation helpful, with its focus on physical symptoms.

Cognitive restructuring is a cognitively based approach; on the other hand, exposure therapy has its roots in behavioral theory. Remember that behaviorism emphasizes that behavior, both adaptive and maladaptive, is learned—and therefore can be unlearned. Exposure is the slow and systematic presentation of anxiety provoking stimuli in a controlled environment and has been shown to be effective with situational triggers to anxiety (Abramowitz, Deacon, & Whiteside, 2011; Moscovitch, Antony, & Swinson, 2009).

Systematic desensitization is an exposure technique based on the behavioral therapy principle of classical conditioning. The counselor and client create an anxiety hierarchy based on gradual exposure to the fear producing stimulus. The client is exposed to the least fearful event and progressively works up to the most fearful event. In between these exposures, other techniques can be used, such as relaxation techniques or cognitive restructuring. Once the client feels they can cope with the feared stimulus, they can move up to the next one on the hierarchy.

During the exposure, the counselor employs interventions, such as breathing techniques or progressive relaxation, to lower symptoms of anxiety. For example, if a client is afraid of flying, the counselor may first show pictures of planes or use imagery to imagine being at the airport. Once the client is able to cope with these stimuli, the exposure might progress to going to the airport or even getting on a plane, a process referred to as *in vivo* exposure. Ultimately, the goal is for the client to be able to regulate their emotions and negative thoughts enough to be able to tolerate the anxiety provoking event. Once the client sees that they can get through the situation without the negative consequences they imagined, the associated anxiety begins to decrease.

Exposure therapy is particularly helpful for treating phobias. For example, in the case of Amy the counselor might begin working with Amy by constructing an anxiety hierarchy. Exposure to low-anxiety circumstances like a photo of a dog is followed by relaxation techniques, with the counselor and Amy working through the hierarchy until Amy can once again enjoy her own dog and get back to enjoying recess and playing outside with friends.

CBT interventions have numerous applications with different anxiety disorders. For example, psychoeducation can help panic disorder sufferers learn that their attacks are not heart attacks, or cognitive restructuring can help clients with social phobia learn to overcome their irrational belief that others are watching and judging them.

Motivational Interviewing

Client "buy in" to the therapeutic alliance, goals, and interventions is critical for positive counseling outcomes. Motivational interviewing (MI) is a method used to help clients increase their intrinsic desire for change, examine the costs and benefits of their thoughts and actions, and explore their ambivalence toward change (Aviram & Westra, 2011; Miller & Rollnick, 2002). MI only lasts a few sessions and is intended to get clients more involved and committed in subsequent counseling interventions.

MI is a well-established approach to health related issues (e.g., smoking), addictions, and eating disorders (Arkowitz, Westra, Miller, & Rollnick, 2007). More recently, it was used in conjunction with other treatment modalities for anxiety disorders. Several studies with clients suffering from Panic Disorder, GAD, and Social Phobia showed promising results (Westra & Dozois, 2006; Westra, Arkowitz, & Dozois, 2010). Clients who received MI prior to CBT exhibited better compliance with homework, greater symptom reduction, and experienced a more positive response to the counseling.

Mindfulness-Based Cognitive Therapy and Acceptance and Commitment Therapy

Mindfulness-Based Approaches are a relatively new group of intervention strategies which combine the underpinnings of CBT with the concepts of mindfulness and acceptance (Germer, Siegal, & Fulton, 2005; Herbert & Forman, 2011). These therapies have been termed the "third wave" of CBT; the first wave represented by the behavioral approaches of the 1960s, and the second wave defined by the cognitive approach championed by Beck and Ellis. Mindfulness refers to being present and conscious of the here and now in a purposeful way. In general, the goals of this type of approach are twofold. First, the client works on accepting unwanted thoughts and feelings instead of trying to control or avoid them. This takes away the power these thoughts hold over the person and shows the client they can withstand them without the negative consequences they imagined. The client then strives to live a more fulfilling life by becoming committed to meaningful endeavors.

A number of evidence-based treatments include some form of mindfulness: Acceptance and Commitment Therapy (ACT) (Hayes & Smith, 2005), Dialectical Behavioral Therapy (DBT) (Dimeff & Linehan, 2001), and Mindfulness-Based Cognitive Therapy (MBCT) (Germer, Siegal, & Fulton, 2005; Herbert & Forman, 2011). These approaches were found effective with anxiety disorders (Eifert & Forsyth, 2005), and with Generalized Anxiety Disorder (Roemer, Orsillo, & Salters-Pedneault, 2008) and Social Anxiety Disorder specifically (Gaydukevych, & Kocovski, 2012; Kocovski, Fleming, & Rector, 2009).

Other Treatment Considerations

When working with anxious children, research reveals that both individual and group approaches are effective. Involving the parents or other caregivers in treatment is particularly important, especially for children under twelve, since treatment outcomes are improved (Barrett, Duffy, & Dadds, 2001; Beidel & Alfano, 2011).

Medications

While counselors may not be the practitioners prescribing medication for anxiety disorders, it is important to keep abreast of current research and medication protocol, effectiveness, and side effects when working with clients who are prescribed medication for anxiety. Medications have been found to be effective in controlling feelings of anxiety. These medications are prescribed by a licensed physician, ideally a psychiatrist, who works in concert with the counseling professional implementing the other

components of treatment. Depending on the setting, the psychiatrist may choose to undertake the psychotherapy themselves; refer the counseling to another specialist; or work with a team of psychologists, counselors, social workers, and other mental health professionals. The primary medications used for anxiety disorders are antidepressants, antianxiety drugs, and beta-blockers which are further explained in Figure 6.3.

First let's look at the antidepressant class of medications. Although they were initially used for the treatment of depression, antidepressant drugs have been found to be effective with anxiety disorders as well.

The oldest group of antidepressant medications are the monoamine oxidase inhibitors (MAOIs), which are also used in treating panic disorder and social phobia. It is important to note that clients prescribed MAOIs cannot ingest certain types of foods, beverages, and medications, including some pain relievers and cold and allergy medications. These substances may cause a dangerous increase in blood pressure requiring medical attention.

Tricyclics are also used for anxiety, and seem to work as well as some of the newer medications for anxiety disorders other than OCD. Side effects include lethargy, dizziness, weight gain, and dry mouth.

The latest category of antidepressant medications used for anxiety is selective serotonin reuptake inhibitors (SSRIs). SSRIs have been shown to modify the levels of a neurotransmitter called serotonin in the brain, which helps brain cells interact with each other. Although these medications do not produce as many side effects as the older tricyclics, SSRIs can have side effects, including nausea, nervousness, and sexual dysfunction. These effects are usually mild and may fade with time, or the prescriber may try a different SSRI.

The next class of medications is antianxiety medications, including Benzodiazepines. These have few side effects other than sleepiness, but clients can build tolerance and need higher and higher doses for the medications to be effective. Thus, antianxiety medications are usually prescribed for shorter periods of time. Some downsides to these medications include withdrawal symptoms if a

Figure 6.3 Medications Used in the Treatment of Anxiety

Antidepressants	*Brand Medications*	*Typically Used to Treat These Conditions*
SSRIs	Prozac®, Zoloft®, Lexapro®, Paxil®, Celexa®	OCD, Panic Disorder, PTSD, Social Phobia
Tricyclics	Tofranil®, Anafranil®	Panic Disorder, GAD, OCD
MAOIs	Nardil®, Parnate®, Marplan®	Panic Disorders, Social Phobia
Anti-Anxiety Drugs	Klonopin®, Ativan®, Xanax®, Buspar®	Social Phobia, Panic Disorder, GAD
Beta-Blockers	Inderal®, Tenormin®	Social Phobia

client suddenly stops taking them, and the chance that anxiety can reoccur once the medication is stopped. Buspirone is a newer antianxiety drug typically used to treat GAD.

Another group of medications used to treat anxiety are the beta-blockers, which treat heart conditions like high blood pressure. Beta-blockers inhibit the physical symptoms of anxiety and are especially useful in social or performance situations, when a rapid heartbeat is often one of the primary symptoms. A beta-blocker can be taken prior to a predictable fearful event, such as flying or public speaking.

It is crucial that as you work with clients who have anxiety disorders, you work closely with a medical professional prescribing any medications. Counseling interventions have been shown to be quite effective for anxiety disorders, and may be able to replace medications as treatment progresses.

CASE CONCEPTUALIZATION FOR ANXIETY USING THE T/C MODEL

Clients who suffer from anxiety are often "triggered" by a situational context, physical sensation, belief, or thought. Many clients are unaware of these triggers, and often report that their anxiety "came out of nowhere." Even clients with specific phobias, while they are likely to recognize what triggers their current fear, may not remember accurately when or how the anxiety began. Thus, a crucial part of the case conceptualization with these clients is an exploration of the client's environment to identify these triggers.

The counselor may ask the client to keep a daily log so that client and counselor can together discover what preceded an episode of anxiety. What were the client's thoughts at that time? Where were they? What are the associations the client has for that situation? What are the client's beliefs about themselves and their ability to handle situations perceived as dangerous (self-efficacy beliefs)? Clients with anxiety disorders often have thoughts that revolve around overevaluation of the threat of danger and disastrous outcomes, as well as the undervaluation of their coping abilities. Common thoughts for both children and adults with anxiety are "I'm going to fail" or "Everyone will laugh at me" or "If I try this, I'll get hurt." Children are also likely to worry excessively that something bad will happen to their parents.

Sometimes even the physical signs of stress, like an elevated heart rate, coupled with hypervigilance, can trigger a full-blown panic attack. Clients who suffer from anxiety and panic may want to avoid caffeine and other stimulants that can create some of the physiological symptoms of panic.

Clients with anxiety disorders are often hypervigilant, always on the lookout for something that sets off their fear. This constant sense of imminent disaster creates a great deal of stress, and further increases the client's anxiety level. Clients with high levels of anxiety often have a sense of personal vulnerability, so it is important to gain a good understanding of their internal personality constructs. Their beliefs about having to stay vigilant against threats, coupled with beliefs that their internal/external resources are not enough to cope, can create feelings of foreboding for the future. Clearly, an assessment of the client's strengths and resources is crucial, which can be used to modify dysfunctional beliefs about being able to cope.

Clients often avoid or escape a situation, because of this tendency to over appraise the threat level of circumstances. Thus, the client never gets a chance to see if they can be successful or learn positive coping skills. Paradoxically, this heightened state of vigilance may be reinforced when the disaster does not happen, since the client may believe that their efforts were rewarded. The cycle of fear and avoidance that is created for many people with anxiety disorders creates a reinforcement schedule that unfortunately increases anxiety symptoms.

It is important to use the T/C Model to thoroughly investigate environmental factors contributing to the anxiety disorder. Experiencing multiple stressful life events can reduce feelings of safety and make the world seem like a dangerous and threatening place. This sets the stage for the hypervigilance and avoidance behaviors that put an individual at risk for an anxiety disorder.

There also can be a learned component to the anxiety so that it may be worthwhile to explore the origination of the anxiety. Clients may have learned their responses from others (anxious parents, teachers, caregivers, or peers), so some exploration of past experiences may lead to greater understanding and client insight. There may also be some genetic predisposition to generally higher levels of anxiety or difficulty with mood regulation, which can be explored in the client's history.

With these general considerations in mind, what follows is a case conceptualization using the T/C Model with a client named Jim.

The Case of Jim

Jim is a 24-year-old man who has recently decided to go back to college. He is married with two small children. He and his wife, Jen, both work full time. Jim works as a software support technician and Jen as an elementary school teacher. Jim has recently sought counseling for what he describes as his uncontrollable anxiety and feelings of impending doom. The event that finally triggered him to seek help was his first week of beginning college classes, during which he experienced several panic attacks. In his first few sessions with the counselor, Jim describes his panic attacks in detail and his everyday struggles with work, family life, and school.

Jim says that he has always struggled with anxiety and performance situations, especially when he feels like he is being evaluated. Jim went to a very competitive private school and describes his high school years as difficult and demanding. He was always under a great deal of stress to perform well academically and in extracurricular sports. His parents are both medical doctors and Jim describes them as strict and demanding, and has difficulty remembering times that they showed any warmth. Jim was always afraid in *class that teachers would call on him and that he would be unable to answer the questions correctly. Although he got high grades (A's and B's), he attributes this to hours of preparation and worry, and not to any internal positive characteristics. Jim decided because of his debilitating anxiety and to the great dismay of his parents, to postpone college even though he got into several good schools. He finally enrolled in night classes with the intention of getting a college degree.*

Jim chose his current profession because he felt he would have limited contact with people and would not experience the feeling of being evaluated or looked down on by his coworkers and supervisors. He has little face-to-face contact with his coworkers and works independently. Although he does a good job, he is limited in his upward mobility by his anxiety attacks and his lack of a college degree. His wife has been pushing him to get at least an associate's degree so that they can increase their family income, and Jim finally enrolled in classes at the local community college.

Since his last panic attack a week ago, Jim is unable to stay in his night classes for the whole time. He has to leave for extended periods of time, sits close to the exit, and has trouble concentrating on class material because of his intrusive thoughts about being called on and being unable to answer correctly.

THE CASE OF JIM

Example of T/C Case Conceptualization Model Outline

(* Areas that require more information)

Presenting Problem: Anxiety attacks that are impairing Jim's ability to function in school and work

Internal Personality Constructs and Behavior:

Self-efficacy: low, dismisses past history of academic success in the midst of challenge; details of academic history*

Self-esteem: low, feels like anxiety is destroying his life

Attitudes/Values/Beliefs: Others are judgmental and harsh; what other people think has important and long lasting consequences; I cannot cope with any kind of failure

Attachment Style: *

Biology/Physiology/Heredity: 24-year-old young adult; male; medical history*; family history of anxiety and substance use*

Affect: depressed, anxious, fearful

Cognition: Worries that people judge and look at him; believes his wife thinks he's a failure

Hot Thoughts: "I hope the teacher does not call on me", "I am not smart enough to stack-up", "People are looking at me", "I am going to pass out or do something stupid", "I have to get out of here before something really embarrassing happens"

Behavior: details of alcohol use*, avoidant behaviors, unable to fully function at work and school, calls in sick frequently

Symptomology: difficulty sleeping, lack of appetite, panic attacks (heart racing, sweating)

Coping Skills and Strengths: insight into issues, past academic achievement, stable relationship

Readiness for Change: action stage—aware of need for change and motivated toward treatment, sought counseling

Life Roles: father, husband, software support technician, student (recently went back to college)

Environment:

Relationships: married with 2 children, wife very supportive until recent panic attacks, conflict with father/mother; past relationship history*; relationship with children described as good and close

Culture: family background*; upper class upbringing, parents both MDs, specific cultural information*

Family Norms and Values: high parental expectations; academic and work success highly valued; gender roles and beliefs*; client feels like he needs to support family better; religious or spiritual beliefs*

Societal Influences:

Timeline:

Past Influences: Parental pressures for achievement, experiences of anxiety in K–12

Present Influences: panic attacks, recent conflict with wife, job-related issues, school-related issues

Future Goals: job security and upward mobility, associate's degree, ability to support family, diminished anxiety

Question: What else would you want to ask, to complete this case conceptualization?

COUNSELING KEYSTONES

- Anxiety is part of the human condition and can be useful when it helps us anticipate and respond to danger.
- People with generalized anxiety disorder suffer from extreme amounts of worry accompanied by physical distress and behavioral disturbances.
- Panic disorder's primary feature is recurring severe panic attacks that come out of nowhere—sudden and repeated bouts of fear that usually last for several minutes, but can last longer.
- Specific phobias, previously called simple phobias, refer to enduring irrational fear and anxiety caused by a specific object or situation that has little or no associated danger—even everyday social situations cause extreme feelings of anxiety, humiliation, and shame.
- Agoraphobia can be defined as fear of being outside, in public, or in a place where escape is difficult or embarrassing.

- Those suffering from a particular anxiety disorder are likely to fit the diagnostic criteria for one or more of the other anxiety disorders discussed in this chapter in addition.
- Both gender and culture are linked to prevalence and symptom variation of anxiety disorders.
- Studies suggest that anxiety disorders can be caused by biological, genetic, and environmental factors.
- Anxiety disorders can be effectively treated with specific types of counseling interventions, medications, or a combination of both.

EXERCISES

EXERCISE 6.1 Fight or Flight?

First, remember an incident in your life when you felt really panicked. For example, your alarm did not go off and you missed school. How did you feel? What thoughts went through your head? What were your physical experiences?

CLASS EXERCISE: Individual work followed by large group discussion.

EXERCISE 6.2 The Difference between Eustress and Distress

Think of times in which someone is under a tremendous amount of stress, but is still able to perform. For example, a professional athlete or a student who got a perfect score on the Graduate Record Examination (GRE).

CLASS EXERCISE: Small group discussion followed by large group feedback.

Question 1: What kind of thoughts do you think went through their heads?

Question 2: How do you think they dealt with the physical symptoms of their anxiety? Does anxiety sometimes bring out the best in people?

EXERCISE 6.3 Reactions to Anxiety

We all experience stress and anxiety in different ways. Take a few minutes and inventory the physical responses and thoughts you typically have in a stressful situation.

CLASS EXERCISE: Students work individually followed by small or large group discussion.

EXERCISE 6.4 Case Conceptualization Practice

Now that you listened in on several counselors working with clients with various types of anxiety disorders, it's time to see what you can do. How would you conceptualize the following case in order to most effectively develop a diagnosis and collaborate on a treatment plan?

CLASS EXERCISE: Small group discussion followed by large group discussion

Question 1: What is your case conceptualization of this case?

Question 2: What else would you want to know?

Question 3: What would be three possible goals for Jared in counseling?

Question 4: What interventions might you employ given the answers to your first two questions?

The Case of Jared

Jared is a 19-year-old college sophomore who is having a difficult time falling asleep and staying asleep. He often lies awake worrying about what he has to do the next day, and even when he falls asleep, he wakes up at 4 or 5 am and has difficulty falling asleep again. Jared says he has always been a worrier, especially at night, but it has never been this bad. He is also having problems in his classes, especially when he has to get up in front of the class and give a presentation. One of his courses this semester has a class presentation as the major final assignment, and although it's only October, Jared is already extremely anxious and anticipating failure.

When Jared does have to speak in front of people, he often stammers or has trouble finding the right words, and is sure that "I sound like an idiot." The problem is even worse when he tries to talk to women he's interested in—he stutters, blushes, and usually gives up before "I embarrass myself even more." Jared would like to date someone, but he has never been successful at asking anyone out.

Jared comes from a family of high achievers. His father is a successful state senator and his mother was a college basketball star who now owns a small business. The family motto is "If you don't at first succeed, try harder." Jared's older brother, Dean, followed in both parents' footsteps by playing basketball himself and then majoring in political science and going on to law school. Jared has tried to live up to the family's emphasis on competition, but it has come at the expense of social relationships. Jared studied hard all through high school, but had few friends.

His freshman semester, Jared lived with a roommate, but the two didn't get along. He begged his parents to intercede with the school and allow him to have a single room for his sophomore year, and they reluctantly agreed. Now that Jared has a room to himself, he rarely comes out of it. He's starting to miss classes, and his grades are starting to slip. He eats in his room and studies in his room and watches television alone. His resident assistant (RA) is worried about him, and has knocked on his door several times, but Jared keeps saying he's okay.

GO FURTHER

Mind Over Mood: Change How You Feel by Changing the Way You Think by Dennis Greenberger and Christine Padesky (1995) Guilford Press

The Expanded Dialectical Behavior Therapy Skills Training Manual: Practical DBT for Self-Help, and Individual & Group Treatment Settings by Lane Pederson (2012) Premiere Publishing and Media

The Mindfulness and Acceptance Workbook for Anxiety: A Guide to Breaking Free from Anxiety, Phobias, and Worry Using Acceptance and Commitment Therapy by John P. Forsyth and Georg H. Eifert (2007) New Harbinger

The Anxiety and Worry Workbook: The Cognitive Behavioral Solution by David A. Clark and Aaron T. Beck, MD (2012) Guilford Press

The Anxious Brain: The Neurobiological Basis of Anxiety Disorders and How to Effectively Treat Them by Steven M. Prinz and Margaret Wehrenberg (2007) W.W. Norton

The Dialectical Behavior Therapy Skills Workbook: Practical DBT Exercises for Learning Mindfulness, Interpersonal Effectiveness, Emotion Regulation & Distress Tolerance by Matthew McKay and Jeffrey C. Wood (2007) New Harbinger

7

OBSESSIVE COMPULSIVE AND RELATED DISORDERS

The Case of Sandy

Sandy is a 38-year-old stay-at-home mother of two small children. She came to counseling for help with her out-of-control obsession with the safety of her children. Sandy says this all started after the birth of her first child, Amanda. Sandy started having intrusive images of something terrible happening to the baby, like drowning in the tub, or being mauled by the neighbor's dog. She described the images as uncontrollable, nonsensical, and almost constant. She started to become very anxious and upset, which just seemed to fuel her out of control thoughts. The more she tried to push them aside, the more they seemed to intrude.

Sandy's thoughts and behaviors progressively got worse with her second child. Sandy then started to perform ritualized behaviors in an attempt to control her images of imminent disaster. At first, her behaviors seemed to make sense to her. If she saw her children in pink clothes in her images, she would dress them only in blue or green for the week. These behaviors developed into elaborate routines that Sandy needs to perform before she can cook a meal, take the kids to day care, or go to sleep for the night. She needs to turn the lights off and on five times before she leaves a room, and recently began to feel that something bad is going to happen to the kids if she doesn't tuck them into bed five times as well.

Sandy's husband is losing patience with her behavior, and Sandy has decided to seek counseling at his urging and on the advice of her family doctor.

Sandy was an only child and describes her childhood as normal except for her father, who she describes as "overbearing" and "downright mean." Both Sandy and her mother were terrified of her dad, who was constantly criticizing both of them, and says they

(Continued)

(Continued)

"always walked on eggshells whenever he was home." Sandy admits that she has struggled with anxiety for as long as she can remember, but felt that she could manage it until her intrusive thoughts became, in her words, "terribly out of control." She describes her husband as supportive but frazzled and says he does not understand why she can't "just stop thinking like that."

Sandy never went to college and was an administrative assistant before she had her first child. She describes herself as weak, fragile, and always worried about what others think of her.

INTRODUCTION

Most of us have experienced some sense of foreboding as we leave the house to head for work. Did I turn off the stove? Did I leave the iron plugged in and turned on? Several of us probably went back and checked occasionally before going on our way and forgetting our moment of apprehension. As with most disorders, obsessive-compulsive and related disorders are similar to the developmentally normal preoccupations and rituals all of us experience. However, as we can see from the case of Sandy, these disorders diverge from normal apprehensions. This divergence can be determined by assessing the time the client spends on the obsessions and compulsions, the client's level of distress, and his or her global level of functioning.

Obsessive-compulsive and related disorders include obsessive-compulsive disorder (OCD), hoarding disorder (HD), body dysmorphic disorder (BDD), trichotillomania (hair pulling), and excoriation disorder (skin-picking). This is a new grouping of disorders introduced in the fifth edition of the *Diagnostic and Statistical Manual of Mental Disorders* (APA, 2013) and reflects a belief in their relatedness and high degree of comorbidity. Although all of these disorders have a comparatively low prevalence, this chapter covers those disorders most often seen by counselors: Obsessive-compulsive disorder, body dysmorphic disorder, and hoarding disorder.

OBSESSIVE COMPULSIVE DISORDER (OCD)

The case of Sandy that began this chapter illustrates the dilemma of an individual with obsessive-compulsive disorder (OCD). People with OCD have obsessive thoughts and compulsive behaviors that can severely impact their ability to function normally in everyday situations (Eisena et al., 2006). The specific symptoms of OCD revolve around these intrusive thoughts (obsessions) and repetitive behaviors (compulsions). OCD has a lifetime prevalence of around 1 to 2% of the U.S. population, with the average age of 19 at onset (Kessler, Berglund, Demler, Jin, & Walters, 2005; Kessler, Chiu, Demler, & Walters, 2005).

Obsessions are defined as persistent and recurring thoughts, urges, or images that are intrusive and cause anxiety or distress (APA, 2013). Obsessive thoughts can be ruminating ideas, nonsensical phrases, or lists that pop into a person's head and become hard to dislodge. Some typical examples are the fear of being contaminated by germs and getting sick; horrific events happening in the near future; loved ones being unsafe; or images of destruction (APA, 2013). These thoughts create excessive apprehension and anxiety, which is why OCD at one time was classified as an anxiety disorder (APA, 2000). Together, these intrusive thoughts and negative emotions lead to hard to control behaviors, which are called compulsions. Compulsions are characterized by repeated rituals or patterns of behavior that the client feels compelled to perform in an attempt to control the anxieties (Abramowitz, Franklin, Schwartz, & Furr, 2003). Typical compulsions include putting things in a specific order, repeated object or item checking, hand washing, hoarding, and ritualized activities, such as silent repeating or praying.

In order to have a diagnosis of OCD, these symptoms need to be time consuming and need to severely impact daily functioning. It is important to note that obsessive thoughts and compulsions are not pleasurable or wanted. The repeated thoughts or behaviors are always felt as unpleasant and are often resisted by the person. At the same time, the fear that something bad will happen can be overwhelming—and acting on that fear can unfortunately be reinforcing, reducing the anxiety in the short term. Clients with OCD may appear to have lost touch with reality or seem paranoid when engaged in a compulsion,

but usually recognize their thoughts and behaviors as irrational. Paradoxically, this may actually increase their levels of anxiety and frustration as they are caught in a cycle of fear and avoidance. Over time, the individual may find it difficult to resist these thoughts and behaviors, which in turn can severely impact their day-to-day life (Abramowitz et al., 2003).

BODY DYSMORPHIC DISORDER (BDD)

Most of us tend to exaggerate or imagine our own physical flaws, but for most of us that doesn't get in the way of our daily lives or keep us up at night. However, clients with body dysmorphic disorder (BDD) believe that their body or face is fundamentally flawed and continually obsess over how they look. As we see from Christina's case, it is very hard for individuals with BDD to stop thinking about these perceived imperfections, which

---

The Case of Christina

Christina is a 15-year-old sophomore in high school. She was referred to counseling after a visit to the emergency room for an apparent suicide attempt. She ingested a large amount of pills she grabbed from her parents' medicine cabinet, after which she immediately went downstairs and told her parents what she had done. Christina has a history of depression, anxiety, school absence, and recently declining grades. She says that she has only a few friends and does not enjoy going to school or socializing. In fact, she mostly stays home with her parents and younger brothers if she is not at school.

Her mother says that although Christina has always been shy, these new issues came to light when Christina hit puberty. Her mother describes Christina as loving and caring, but obsessed with looks. She is always asking for makeup, skin treatments, acne medicine, and lately has asked for Botox and cosmetic surgery for her 16th birthday. What distresses Christina's mom the most is that she thinks Christina is tall and beautiful and cannot understand how she sees herself so differently.

Christina describes what led up to her suicide attempt when she meets with the counselor.

Christina: *"I just can't stand myself anymore. I'm so ugly, I don't want anyone to look at me. I don't even want to look at myself!"*

Counselor: *"Can you tell me what you see when you look at yourself?"*

(Continued)

(Continued)

Christina: "I see a disgusting person—I'm too tall, disproportionate . . ."

Counselor: "Disproportionate?"

Christina: "I look like a witch with a big nose and huge ears."

Counselor: "Is that why you wear your hair over your face?"

Christina: (glancing up at the counselor through her hair, which falls halfway over her face) "Yeah. I'm trying to grow it as long as I can so it can just cover me up. Or at least some of me. My ears are so big they stick out anyway."

Counselor: "How are your feelings about your appearance affecting your life?"

Christina: "I don't have a life. I don't go out anymore, I don't wanna see anyone. Why bother going to school when no one is ever gonna want to hire me anyway. Not as long as I look like this! I've begged my parents to let me get plastic surgery—I've even found photos of the perfect nose."

Counselor: "How did you decide on what that would look like?"

Christina: "I kept searching—went through hundreds of magazines and cut out photos and held them up to my face until I found the perfect one. But, my parents won't let me. It's hopeless. I can't stand looking this way anymore, I just can't."

causes a great deal of anxiety and discomfort (Phillips, 2009). The prevalence of BDD is about 2.4% of the adult U.S. population, though some experts believe that the number could be even greater (Phillips, 2004, 2009).

BDD almost always causes some impaired functioning, especially with interpersonal relationships (Phillips, 2005). Individuals with BDD avoid dating, have few friends, and engage in few hobbies or leisure activities. BDD can impact academic and occupational functioning as well. The disorder is a serious one. Studies of clients with BDD have found that over 60% of sufferers had suicidal thoughts, 50% had been hospitalized, almost 30% had been completely housebound for at least one week, and nearly 30% had attempted suicide (Phillips et al., 2005; Veale et al., 1996).

Much like OCD, symptoms of BDD fall into two general categories: obsessions (thoughts) and compulsions (behaviors). Typical obsessions include preoccupation with appearance, extreme self-consciousness, and the belief that an abnormality or defect makes the person unattractive. In public, they think that people are taking notice of their appearance in a negative way or talking about them behind their backs. Typical compulsions include repeatedly examining oneself in the mirror or avoiding mirrors altogether, habitually asking people for reassurance on their appearance, and avoidance of social situations (APA, 2013). Individuals with BDD are especially fearful of circumstances where they might be judged on their appearance, such as picture taking or posting photos online.

BDD can lead to extreme behaviors in an attempt to remedy the perceived inadequacy. Clients often undergo numerous plastic surgeries, dermatologic or cosmetic procedures, and/ or engage in excessive exercise. They are almost always dissatisfied with the outcomes of these actions. Some may take the other extreme and become housebound, not wanting to be seen or to have any contact with others.

People who suffer with BDD can obsess over any physical feature, but there are specific body parts that are more commonly the focus. These features include the face (especially nose, complexion), hair (balding), skin, general physical tone, breasts, and genitals (size, shape). Specific symptoms are associated with particular body part obsessions, including hair plucking, trying to conceal perceived flaws with makeup, growing a beard or wearing hair long, and excessive exercise targeted to reshaping the area of concern.

Hoarding Disorder (HD)

Hoarding has become a more visible issue thanks to the unlikely focus of reality television, but individuals who have this disorder have their lives seriously disrupted, as we can see from the case of Stan. Clients with hoarding disorder (HD) have a severe obsession with collecting or saving items, or in some cases, animals. Over time, this collecting leads to an inordinate level of disarray in their living and/or work place (APA, 2013). This hoarding activity takes up greater and greater amounts of time and hinders functionality in other areas of life. The hoarder has extreme anxiety and may exhibit aggressive behavior if asked to discard any of their items, which they perceive as necessary and valuable.

The hoarded items are usually viewed as worthless by other people, but not by the hoarder. Many times clients feel the need to increase hoarding activities in order to achieve the same level of emotional satisfaction and sense of safety. They attribute value to the items by the conviction that they will need it in the future, or because they feel insecure without them. It is believed that roughly 2 to 5% of the general U.S. population fit this diagnosis, most of these are older adults (i.e., ages 55 to 94) (APA, 2013). People with hoarding disorder may have tried to stop their hoarding several times, often with the help of a significant other or loved one. On the other hand, they may have tried to hide their hoarding, eventually to the point of not letting anyone in their residence.

The Case of Stan

Stan is a 59-year-old man who has never married, and has one child, David, now 41. Stan lives alone in a duplex he bought 32 years ago. He is a retired garbage man and describes himself as an "avid collector." As a garbage man, he would bring home his "finds" and display or store them in his house. Stan was referred to counseling after an altercation with his neighbor regarding the clutter in his backyard. Stan's son is also concerned about his father and says that the issues with Stan's overflowing home are becoming progressively worse.

Lately, Stan has not let anyone in his house other than his son, and when his son recently visited, he had trouble navigating the hallway or getting up the stairs because of the mounds of papers, magazines, and other items Stan has hoarded over the years. He could not even enter the basement, and describes the house as a "smelly fire trap."

Stan comes to counseling willingly, but does not see that there is a problem.

Stan: *"I know my son thinks I have a problem, but really, I don't. I'm just a little behind in getting my collections organized. I'm working on it, though."*

Counselor: *"Is there anything in your collections that you don't want to keep?"*

(Continued)

(Continued)

Stan: *"Not really. It's not like it's not worth something—it all has value."*

Counselor: *"So your collections have monetary value then?"*

Stan: *"A lot of it does, sure. And what doesn't has sentimental value to me. That's important too."*

Counselor: *"I can see that it is important to you. Are there any downsides to having your house so full of collectibles?"*

Stan: *"Look, I know my son is worried that I don't go out or spend time with friends. But frankly, I've always been a loner. I never did well in school and I hated it. I only ever really liked being a garbage collector."*

Counselor: *"You must miss it."*

Stan: *(looking wistful) "I do."*

Counselor: *"Can you tell me about your childhood?"*

Stan: *(shrugs) "It was ordinary, I guess. I was sort of shy and always worried about stuff. My mom was like that too. I stayed home a lot, didn't play sports or anything."*

Counselor: *"Did either of your parents collect things the way you do?"*

Stan: *"My mom did, yeah. My dad used to say she never threw anything away. She used to say, 'You never know when you'll need one of these.' Sometimes they'd fight about it, and my Dad would throw stuff out while my mom wasn't around."*

Previously, hoarding was included as a symptom or a subtype of obsessive compulsive disorder (OCD). When differentiating between the two, it is important to note that an OCD diagnosis should be given if the hoarding is driven by a fear of contamination or superstitious thoughts, the hoarding is anxiety provoking and unwanted, and the client shows no interest in the hoarded items except within the given obsession.

COMORBIDITY

It is important to perform a thorough intake interview with clients with these disorders because a majority of them will have an associated anxiety or depressive disorder (APA, 2013). For example, clients with OCD have a 76% chance of a co-occurring anxiety disorder, and a 63% chance of having a comorbid depressive or bipolar disorder. Clients with a hoarding disorder have about a 75% chance of a comorbid mood or anxiety disorder, most commonly major depressive disorder. Major depression is also the most common comorbid diagnosis for clients with BDD. The reasons for this large overlap are not clear, but are believed to be due to a combination of genetics, environment, and the negative impact of the disorders' symptoms (Phillips, 2009).

CULTURAL CONSIDERATIONS AND POPULATION FACTORS

OCD, BDD, and hoarding disorder (HD) occur throughout the world with substantial similarities in age of onset, gender distribution, and functional consequences. Cultural values and social preferences, however, may have an impact on how symptoms are expressed (APA, 2013). There are also some gender differences with regard to these disorders. Men with OCD have an earlier age of onset and are much more likely to have a co-occurring tic disorder. Men with BDD are more likely to obsess over the appearance of their genitalia, while females are more likely to have an eating disorder. Symptom clusters can also be somewhat gender related. For example, females may have more cleaning or shopping related obsessions (which may be culturally bound as well) while men have more forbidden thought obsessions (APA, 2013).

ETIOLOGY AND RISK FACTORS

Although specific causes are not known, OCD and BDD are thought to be impacted by a combination of genetic, biological, and environmental factors that all seem to contribute in some way (Cath, van Grootheest, Willemsen, van Oppen, & Boomsma, 2008; Fornaro et al., 2009). Research on the biological factors of OCD focus on the areas of the brain called the orbitofrontal cortex, striatum, and the basal ganglia, which play a role in the regulation of behaviors like aggression. The theory is that OCD results from problems in communication between the front part of the brain and deeper structures, which creates a feedback loop which does not shut off (Taylor, Asmundson, & Jang, 2011). An imbalance in the neurotransmitter serotonin may also be involved. Hoarding disorder has also been found to have specific biological underpinnings (Steketee & Frost, 2003).

Environmental theories on the causes of OCD and BDD focus on learned dysfunctional beliefs that give rise to obsessive thoughts—core beliefs learned during childhood and adolescence that eventually lead to the development of OCD. These include intolerance, perfectionism, and the need for control, in addition to an overreactive stress response. People susceptible to these disorders believe that their thoughts are overly important and that they need to be controlled or bad things will happen. The main

mechanism for acquiring these beliefs is through some kind of learning through exposure. For example, a worrying parent may teach a child to be overly fearful or vigilant.

Reinforcement may also be a contributing factor. For example, compulsive checking may begin when a parent asks a child before going to bed at night to check all the lights, lock all the doors, and then double check. The child receives praise for these behaviors and also feels a reduction in their anxiety about safety. This reduction in anxiety feels good and in turn reinforces the checking. Because of this reinforcement, every time the child experiences the obsessive worry (such as safety), they carry out the compulsion (checking locks and lights) to reduce their anxiety (Taylor, Asmundson, & Jang, 2011).

Environmental influences that may contribute to the onset of BDD include critical parenting, low self-esteem, and the experience of a traumatic event during childhood. Peer pressure and societal messages regarding attractiveness and its value may also play a part in the development of BDD (Phillips, 2004, 2009). In hoarding disorder, cognitive models focus on a pattern of maladaptive beliefs, impulsive and avoidant patterns of behavior, and cognitive impairments that start early in life (Frost & Hartl, 1996).

TREATMENT INTERVENTIONS

Both counseling interventions and medication treatment have been found to be effective in treating OCD and related disorders. Many of the interventions discussed in the anxiety disorders chapter are also used with obsessive compulsive and related disorders (Abramowitz, 1997).

Counseling Interventions

Cognitive behavior therapy has been found to be especially effective and, along with medications, is considered the first treatment option for OCD, BDD, and hoarding disorder (HD) (Abramowitz, 1997; Cherian, Math, Kandavel, & Reddy, 2014; Eddy, Dutra, Bradley, & Westen,

2004; Emmelkamp & Beens, 1991; Franklin, Abramowitz, Bux, Zoellner, & Feeny, 2002; Frost & Hartl, 1996; Olatunji, Davis, Powers, & Smits, 2013). Exposure and response prevention (ERP) is used with many clients for a variety of anxiety related disorders, and has been shown to be an effective cognitive behavioral therapy (CBT) treatment for the intrusive thoughts associated with OCD (Abramowitz, 2006; Huppert & Roth, 2003).

ERP involves the client confronting their fears while delaying and eventually stopping their compulsive behaviors (compulsions). First, a hierarchy of the client's worries and rituals is developed. The counselor then exposes the client to a lower-level scenario and asks the client to postpone their usual behavioral response (response prevention component). For example, a client who is afraid of germs may be asked to touch a door knob they believe to be contaminated. The counselor then asks the client to delay their typical response, such as using hand sanitizer, while employing other CBT interventions, such as cognitive restructuring or relaxation techniques. While ERP typically causes some short-term anxiety, it is effective in reducing obsessive and compulsive symptoms in the long run, breaking the reinforcement cycle which keeps the behavior in place (Ma et al., 2013). However, ERP can be challenging for some clients because it can trigger high levels of anxiety in the interim, which can lead to treatment refusal and dropout (Franklin & Foa, 1998).

Other alternative treatments have also been used for OCD, such as Acceptance and Commitment Therapy (ACT), and Mindfulness-Based Cognitive-Behavioral Therapy (Eifert & Forsyth, 2005; Fabricant, Abramowitz, Dehlin, & Twohig, 2013). Because of similar symptomology and presentation, the same CBT interventions used in treating OCD are commonly used with BDD and hoarding disorder. These include behavioral and cognitive components consisting mainly of exposure and response prevention to reduce avoidance and ritualistic behaviors. Using CBT with BDD resulted in consistently good

outcomes in studies of both group and individual treatment (Phillips, 2009; Wilhelm, Phillips & Steketee, 2012).

ERP was also shown to be effective in treating BDD, especially a technique called imaginal exposure. The client audiotapes short stories based on their obsessions, which are then used as exposure tools, allowing the client to experience fear-inducing situations that cannot be experienced through traditional ERP methods (Lovell & Bee, 2008). Cognitive restructuring and behavioral experiments also have been shown to be valuable interventions for BDD, where clients learn to challenge the rationality of their distorted body-related thoughts (Phillips, 2009).

Mindfulness-based CBT is another specific protocol that has been shown to be effective with BDD (Follette, Heffner, & Person, 2010). The primary goal of mindfulness-based CBT is to learn to accept uncomfortable thoughts and feelings without letting them escalate. The theory is that much of the client's anxiety and worry stem from trying to control and eliminate unwanted urges and thoughts. Specific to BDD, this client might carry out the behaviors they've been avoiding, such as looking in the mirror or going out in public, knowing that this produces unwanted thoughts, but that these thoughts need not develop the levels of discomfort that the client was allowing. One technique is for the client to view their experience like a movie, which allows them to experience the thoughts going through their minds while remaining a little detached from them, like watching a film of their own experience.

Treating clients with hoarding disorder is often difficult because they have trouble realizing the negative impact their hoarding is having on their lives and the lives of their loved ones (Tolin, 2011). This can be particularly true if the client's animals or hoarded possessions provide them comfort, which is often the case. CBT interventions are the most common forms of counseling used for this condition. Interventions typically include examining the feelings leading to hoarding, decision-making skills, visits to the home to de-clutter, relaxation techniques, and family or group sessions. A psychodynamic perspective can be helpful in examining elements of the client's past that are contributing to the hoarding behavior. Steketee and Tolin (2011) proposed a hoarding specific variation of CBT that focuses on the excessive acquiring behaviors that are characteristic of HD. This treatment incorporates skills training, motivational interviewing, sorting and discarding practice, and cognitive restructuring.

Medications

Clients with OCD, BDD, and Hoarding Disorder (HD) can be prescribed antidepressants to relieve the symptoms associated with their obsessive thoughts and compulsive behaviors (Eddy et al., 2004; Koran, Hanna, Hollander, Nestadt, & Simpson, 2007; Phillips, 2005; Phillips & Hollander, 2008; Saxena, 2011). These medications may also sometimes be effective in decreasing the thoughts themselves. With the use of SSRIs, it appears that increasing levels of serotonin in the brain can help normalize the communication between different parts of the brain. Antipsychotic medications are also sometimes used to treat OCD.

CASE CONCEPTUALIZATION FOR OCD AND RELATED DISORDERS USING THE T/C MODEL

As with the disorders already discussed, distorted cognitions are often a part of OCD, BDD, and HD. Once these cognitions are identified, they can be appropriate targets of challenge. Repetitive thoughts and compulsions are often fear-based, so the underlying fears are important to assess. The case conceptualization should assess not only the cognitive component of these disorders, but the behavioural manifestations as well.

Because there is sometimes a learned component to these disorders, the case conceptualization should also examine family and cultural attitudes and beliefs that might impact the client's symptoms. A thorough family history can bring to light beliefs that may have been passed on and reactions to stress which a client may have learned from parents. Is there a tradition of perfectionism, for example, or a strong emphasis on control?

Clients who suffer from hoarding disorder often find it difficult to change because of the perceived value to the client of the items hoarded. Sometimes this is due to a misperception of monetary value ("I can't throw this away, it's worth money"), which can be impacted by past experience of poverty or loss. For other clients, the value is psychological or emotional, because the item symbolizes something or someone lost ("I can't throw away this pizza box because my deceased wife and I had our first date at this restaurant" or "This was my dad's"). While there may be no clear value to the items hoarded to an outsider, when working with a client with hoarding disorder, the context which surrounds the symptoms is important to assess. If loneliness and social isolation are contributing factors, interventions can address these issues as well as the presenting symptoms. The prevalence of television shows and films about hoarding, obsessions, and obsessive compulsive disorder complicate the clinical picture by creating stereotypes for both clients and counselors that should be addressed.

It is important to consider the cultural and gender norms and values when working with a client diagnosed with BDD. For example, the norms for body size and type differ for males and females, for different cultural groups, and may differ for different sexual orientations as well. Assessment of suicidal ideation is, of course, always a critical part of case conceptualization; for clients with BDD in particular, there is a high risk of suicidal thoughts.

Now let's revisit the case of Sandy introduced at the beginning of this chapter, and develop a case conceptualization.

THE CASE OF SANDY

Example of T/C Case Conceptualization Model Outline

(*Areas that require more information)

Presenting Problem: Anxiety, obsessive thoughts about safety of children, compulsive behaviors

Internal Personality Constructs and Behavior:

Self-efficacy: low, feels like she cannot do anything right or take care of her kids or husband

Self-esteem: feels weak and fragile

Attitudes/Values/Beliefs: views the world as an unsafe place

Attachment Style: insecure attachment with father

Biology/Physiology/Heredity: female, 38, medical history*, family history of anxiety*

Affect: anxious, nervous, worried

Cognition: Belief that something bad will happen to her children if she does not perform certain behaviors, believing she is weak and fragile, worrying about what others think

Hot Thoughts: "Something bad will happen if I don't do this"; "Just stop thinking like that"

Behavior: compulsions, ritualized behaviors, difficulty performing daily routines

Symptomology: upset, crying, unfocused, sleeping*, eating*

Coping Skills and Readiness for Change: supportive but frazzled husband, other supports*, seems in action stage

Life Roles: Stay-at-home mom of two small children, job*

Environment:

Relationships: conflicted relationship with father*, current conflict with husband*

Culture: family background*

Family Norms and Values: females deferred to male in family of origin

Societal Influences:

Timeline:

Past Influences: father's possible abuse and criticism, mother's anxiety (modeling)

Present Influences: conflict with husband, raising two small children

Future Goals: able to carry out daily activities without anxiety, obsessive thoughts, and compulsive behavior, improved relationship with husband, greater self-efficacy at home and work

Question: What else would you want to ask, to complete this case conceptualization?

COUNSELING KEYSTONES

- Obsessive-compulsive and related disorders include obsessive-compulsive disorder (OCD), hoarding disorder (HD), body dysmorphic disorder (BDD), trichotillomania (hair pulling), and excoriation disorder (skin-picking); a new grouping of disorders introduced in DSM-5 and reflecting a belief in their relatedness and high degree of comorbidity.
- People with OCD have obsessive thoughts and compulsive behaviors that can severely impact their ability to function normally in everyday situations, with specific symptoms revolving around intrusive thoughts (obsessions) and repetitive behaviors (compulsions).
- Obsessions are defined as persistent and recurring thoughts, urges, or images that are intrusive and cause anxiety or distress.
- Compulsions are characterized by repeated rituals or patterns of behaviors the client feels compelled to perform in an attempt for control.
- Clients with body dysmorphic disorder (BDD) believe that their body or face is fundamentally flawed and continually obsess over how they look, becoming preoccupied with appearance and fearful that others are taking notice of their appearance in a negative way, or talking about them behind their backs.
- Clients with hoarding disorder have a severe obsession with collecting or saving items or in

some cases animals, which leads to an inordinate level of disarray in their living and/or workplace.

- Many clients with these disorders also have an associated anxiety or depressive disorder.
- OCD and BDD are thought to be impacted by a combination of genetic, biological, and environmental factors,
- Environmental theories on the causes of OCD and BDD focus on learned dysfunctional beliefs that give rise to obsessive thoughts—core beliefs learned during childhood and adolescence, such as intolerance, perfectionism, and the need for control, in addition to an over-reactive stress response, critical parenting, low self-esteem and the experience of a traumatic event during childhood.
- Both counseling interventions and medication treatment have been found to be effective in treating OCD and related disorders.
- Cognitive behavior therapy has been found to be especially effective and, along with medications, is considered the first treatment option for OCD, BDD, and hoarding disorder.
- Exposure and response prevention involves the client confronting their fears while delaying and eventually stopping their compulsive behaviors (compulsions).
- Clients with OCD, BDD, and Hoarding Disorder can be prescribed antidepressants to relieve the symptoms associated with their obsessive thoughts and compulsive behaviors.

EXERCISES

EXERCISE 7.1 Working with a Client with a Hoarding Disorder

Reality television shows such as *Hoarders* have created both stereotypes and misconceptions about clients with Hoarding Disorder. As counselors, it's important to be aware of our own biases, values, and preconceived notions about the issues facing our clients.

CLASS EXERCISE: Individual work followed by large group discussion.

Question 1: When you think of a client with Hoarding Disorder what images come to mind?

Question 2: Do you think a counselor needs to go to the client's house to be fully effective or can the talk therapy component in the counselor's office be equally effective?

Question 3: What would be the most difficult aspects of working with a client with Hoarding Disorder in their place of residence? (Consider the presence of animals, sanitation, or smell, and client's emotional state.)

EXERCISE 7.2
Counselor Self-Exploration: Working with Clients with BDD

Working with a client with body dysmorphic disorder can become difficult when you have to challenge their irrational beliefs about their image.

CLASS EXERCISE: Individual work followed by large group discussion.

Question 1: Identify three physical characteristics which a client might be obsessing about which would be uncomfortable for you to challenge.

Question 2: Would these challenges be more or less difficult working with a client whose gender is different than your own? Why?

EXERCISE 7.3 When Does OCD Cross the Line?

Doug is a sophomore in college who also holds down a full-time job at a local restaurant. He has sought counseling for what he describes as anxiety and feeling overwhelmed. He keeps extensive lists about what he needs to get done at school and work in an effort to "stay ahead of the game." He also worries frequently that he has forgotten to do an assignment at school or forgotten to turn the lights off at work when he leaves for the night. Sometimes he returns to check the lights once or twice before he finally gets in his car to drive home.

CLASS EXERCISE: Individual work followed by large group discussion.

The Case of Benny

Benny, a 14-year-old boy, comes to see you at a community agency where you're a counselor. His mother called to schedule the appointment, quite distraught. She says that Benny, who has always been a straight A student, has been late for school so many times in the past six months that he is in danger of not passing the year. Benny has always been an anxious child, and his mother says he has always been superstitious. When he was six, he refused to step on any cracks in the sidewalk or even on the lines between floor tiles, after he heard the children's rhyme "step on a crack, break your mother's back."

Benny's mother describes her son as a perfectionist, who flies into rages or despairs if he gets anything less than a perfect grade on a test. When he was young, he would tear up pictures that he had drawn or colored, insisting they "weren't good enough." Benny's mother describes her own mother as similar to her son, and acknowledges that she herself is a bit of a perfectionist. She has tried hard not to pass this on to her son, and is dismayed that he seems to be even more of a perfectionist than she.

Benny has developed elaborate and time-consuming rituals that he feels compelled to perform before he leaves the house. His compulsions include counting the number of times he brushes his teeth and combs his hair, as well as the steps he takes before leaving his room. If he doesn't count correctly, he must start over and go through the routine again, otherwise, Benny is convinced that something bad will happen to his mother, father, or younger sister.

Benny also is extremely concerned about germs, and uses hand sanitizer compulsively. He carries it with him at all times, and his hands are dry and cracking from overuse. He has been reluctant to go to friends' houses, since he fears there will be "too many germs there" and refuses to go to the bathroom at school or anywhere except home. The family wants to take a vacation over the holiday break, but Benny is already upset about having to travel and stay in a hotel.

His mother is not the only one upset. Benny has become increasingly depressed about his inability to "get anything done." He wants to stop the obsessive thoughts and compulsions, but feels helpless. Benny is also becoming very worried about his GPA, which has dropped as a result of his school tardies.

Question 1: Does Doug meet the criteria for OCD?

Question 2: What additional or greater magnitude of symptoms would Doug need to exhibit to meet the criteria for OCD?

Question 3: If you decide that Doug does not meet OCD criteria, would you still address these symptoms as part of the counseling treatment? If so, how?

EXERCISE 7.4 Case Conceptualization Practice

CLASS EXERCISE: Small group discussion followed by large group discussion.

Question 1: What is your case conceptualization of this case?

Question 2: What else would you want to know?

Question 3: What would be three possible goals for Benny in counseling?

Question 4: What counseling modalities might you want to employ to help Benny?

Go Further

The Hoarding Handbook: A Guide for Human Service Professionals by Gail Steketee, Christiana Bratiotis, and Cristina Sorrentino Schmalisch (2011) Oxford University Press

Treatment for Hoarding Disorder: Therapist Guide (Treatments That Work) by Gail Steketee and Randy O. Frost (2013) Oxford University Press

Exposure and Response (Ritual) Prevention for Obsessive-Compulsive Disorder: Therapist Guide (Treatments That Work) by Edna B. Foa, Elna Yadin, and Tracey K. Lichner (2013) Oxford University Press

The Mindfulness Workbook for OCD: A Guide to Overcoming Obsessions and Compulsions Using Mindfulness and Cognitive Behavioral Therapy by Jon Hershfield and Tom Corboy (2013) New Harbinger

What to Do When Your Brain Gets Stuck: A Kid's Guide to Overcoming OCD (What-to-Do Guides for Kids) by Dawn Huebner and Bonnie Matthews (Illustrator) (2007) Magination Press

The Broken Mirror: Understanding and Treating Body Dysmorphic Disorder by Katharine A. Phillips (2005) Oxford University Press

Cognitive-Behavioral Therapy for Body Dysmorphic Disorder: A Treatment Manual by Sabine Wilhelm, Katharine A. Phillips, and Gail Steketee (2012) Guilford Press

Body Dysmorphic Disorder: A Treatment Manual by David Veale and Fugen Neziroglu (2010) Wiley Publishing

8

TRAUMA AND STRESS-RELATED DISORDERS

Sora, a 21-year-old Korean American student, came to the university counseling center at the urging of her roommates. They are all concerned about her, since she's been missing classes. Previously, Sora was an excellent student, with a GPA of 3.88. This semester, however, she's in danger of failing two of her courses. She doesn't make eye contact when she sits down.

Counselor:	"It seems your friends are very worried about you. Can you tell me what's going on?"
Sora:	"I don't know if I can talk about it. I don't know if I should."
Counselor:	"Shall I go over confidentiality again?"
Sora:	(shaking her head) "No, no I understand that. I just mean, I don't want to think about it. It seems like I can't stop thinking about it, but I don't want to."
Counselor:	"'It'?"
Sora:	(looking down) "Something happened the first week of classes, and I just can't seem to get past it. I went out on a date with this new guy, and I, he, . . . he wouldn't take no for an answer."
Counselor:	"He sexually assaulted you?"
Sora:	(looking up) "I haven't said it out loud, but yes."
Counselor:	"I'm so sorry, no wonder you're having a hard time. Can you tell me how you've been feeling?"
Sora:	"I've been trying not to think about it, but it seems like the more I try, the more it doesn't work. I keep getting flashes of what happened, and it's like—it's like it's

(Continued)

(Continued)

> *happening all over again, right that second. I can see him, can hear the music that was playing at the party, can even smell the cologne he had on."*
>
> *(Sora is no longer making eye contact, her expression far away as though she's watching something else, looking terrified)*

Counselor: "Sora, are you with me? You're safe here, you're in my office, in the counseling center."

Sora: "Oh, I—I'm sorry."

Counselor: "Re-experiencing the traumatic event isn't uncommon, but it's very distressing."

Sora: "It keeps happening, I don't know how to stop it. I'm even dreaming about it—nothing seems safe anymore! I can't trust anyone, I don't even want to see anyone, and I'll never go on a date again—it's too dangerous."

Counselor: "Have you always felt that way, that the world was a dangerous place?"

Sora: "No, not really. My parents always told me that it was, but I guess I didn't believe them. I guess I've changed the way I look at a lot of things since this happened. Like, everything."

Counselor: "How have you been coping with these thoughts and feelings?"

Sora: "I don't want to be around people anymore. I stay in my room, I don't even want to go to class. Some of the people who were at the party will be there, and I just can't see them, I can't. I don't want to go to anyone else's room either, especially not the ones in the dorm where it happened."

Counselor: "So you're avoiding doing a lot of things you used to do."

Sora: "I guess I am. I feel so ashamed, like everyone is looking at me. And I keep jumping every time I see someone out of the corner of my eye. I must look like a freak."

Counselor: "Is there anyone helping you deal with these feelings, supporting you?"

Sora: "Not really. I can't even tell my parents what happened, they'll probably disown me. In my family—in my culture—it's just not okay to go off with a boy and drink. I'm not allowed to date at all; I was supposed to wait, my parents had a boy in mind for me when I was done college. This is all my fault . . . My parents are going to be so disappointed in me, school is everything to them. I'm going to be a doctor, that's what they've always wanted for me. Can you help me?"

INTRODUCTION

Everyone experiences stressful events in their lives, but we all react differently. In a similar circumstance, some individuals may react very strongly, some may react less, and others may not react much at all. The range of reactions may depend on the person's psychological makeup, including their level of resiliency, their history of stressful life experiences, and the resources and supports they have available in their life. A situation which is traumatic for one person may not be perceived as a trauma for another. But, when an event is experienced as traumatic, there can be intense physical, emotional, and psychological distress, as Sora described above.

Why do traumatic events carry such an impact? One of the reasons may be that these events are not processed in the same way as "normal" events; instead, they are encoded into memory in a preverbal form which makes them difficult to make sense of or to access. Instead of becoming integrated into the person's life story, these events remain frozen outside the timeline, unable to be revised, and largely remain unprocessed. Several counseling approaches, which we discuss later in this chapter, specifically address this dilemma, helping the person to understand the entirety of their life experience, including the trauma.

A person's sense of self is also impacted by trauma. Major traumatic experiences, such as natural disasters, war, accidents, abuse, assault, or serious injury can create a sense of "otherness" when the person has been through something that they didn't anticipate and couldn't control. Divorce, addiction, and poverty can have a similar impact. This sense of otherness can lead to shame, which discourages trauma survivors from sharing their feelings with others, and serves to intensify the isolation. Healing depends on the opportunity to express emotions and share the pain, and to make meaning from the experience (Herman, 1992).

It is not completely clear why some responses eventually turn into more severe mental health issues, such as acute stress disorder (ASD) or posttraumatic stress disorder (PTSD), but it is important to keep in mind that even severe reactions to traumatic events are normal and recovery can sometimes be slow or sporadic. The most common reactions are anxiety, fear, nightmares, amplified arousal response, and anger or irritability. These emotional reactions lead to behaviors, such as aggression, withdrawal, and avoidance. The traumatic events can sometimes be re-experienced through flashbacks, brief intrusive images, or nightmares. In many cases, people feel constantly on edge and have trouble concentrating or falling asleep. This continual state of arousal leads to fatigue and irritability, and can cause a domino effect into anxiety and depression.

There are also cognitive changes associated with experiencing trauma. A world once thought to be safe and secure is now perceived as dangerous and unpredictable, fundamental beliefs shaken by the real or perceived loss of safety and self-efficacy. Sora describes this change in her perception of her fellow students and the university campus after the sexual assault. A sweeping reevaluation of core values and beliefs may be triggered by what took place. Without the familiar belief system, trauma survivors may become confused as to what comes next in their lives and lose focus and direction, all of which makes them susceptible to anxiety and depression.

People respond to these emotional, behavioral, and cognitive changes in various ways. Some may try to repress unwanted emotions or thoughts, wishing (understandably) that things could go back to the way they were. Some respond by avoiding places or loved ones that remind them of the traumatic event, which can lead to an increasingly constricted and isolated life. For example, Sora's attempts to avoid triggers have kept her from going to class or going out with her friends. Many trauma survivors feel (again, understandably) angry at the world for the unfairness of the trauma occurrence.

Some people may self-medicate through alcohol or other substance use/abuse in an attempt to avoid the painful emotions and anxiety associated with remembering the trauma. They may not engage in activities they once found enjoyable, feeling too different from others to want to engage with them. Survivors of traumatic experiences, such as hurricanes, tornados, floods, or war, may wonder why they made it while others did not, feeling guilty about being able to "enjoy" life again. They may blame themselves, in part or in whole, for what took place or may blame others, feeling like they cannot trust anyone anymore. Close relationships can suffer if the traumatized person believes that no one can understand what they are going through. Some may even feel like they are going crazy or are losing touch with reality.

Grief and depressive episodes are normal reactions to traumatic events; however, the question is to determine when normal reactions to trauma become a mental health concern. Treatment may be needed if the person seems depressed, cannot reengage in life, and just can't seem to move on, even after a significant amount of time has passed. Other indicators include painful memories or images that do not seem to be fading over time, and an inability to regain a feeling of safety. The DSM-5 includes five disorders in the trauma and stressor related disorders section: reactive attachment disorder, disinhibited social engagement disorder, posttraumatic stress disorder (PTSD), acute stress disorder (ASD), and

adjustment disorder. In this chapter, we explore the stressor related disorders most often encountered by counselors: ASD and PTSD.

ACUTE STRESS DISORDER (ASD)

Acute stress disorder (ASD) was first included in the DSM-IV to describe severe stress reactions that take place soon after exposure to a traumatic event, but before the possibility of diagnosing

The Case of Stephanie

Stephanie is 32-year married mother of two, who was in a severe car accident three weeks ago. Her car hit a patch of black ice on her commute to work, skidded out of control, and rear-ended a truck. The police reported that she was trapped underneath the truck for 90 minutes before they were able to get her out using the Jaws of Life. She spent a week in the hospital with a mild concussion, a broken leg, and cracked ribs.

Stephanie does not remember any details of the car crash, but describes her mood as "extremely anxious" throughout the day. She cannot eat, sleep, or concentrate. She has trouble getting out of bed in the morning and was unable to go back to work this past week, causing her to seek counseling. She cannot even get into a car without having a strong reaction, which has severely impacted her ability to function normally.

She came to see a counselor eleven days after the accident.

Counselor: "Can you tell me how you've been feeling?"

Stephanie: "It's hard to describe, I just—I don't feel like myself. I don't feel normal. It's like sometimes I don't even feel real."

Counselor: "What's that like?"

Stephanie: "It's weird, it's like I'm watching myself from across the room, from another perspective almost. And time just sort of slows down, like nothing is real."

Counselor: "That's a common reaction to a traumatic event like the one that you've experienced."

Stephanie: "So I'm not going crazy? At first I thought it was because of the concussion, but the doc tells me that these sort of feelings aren't caused by that."

Counselor: "No, but it sounds like you're really struggling. How are you dealing with all these troubling feelings?"

Stephanie: "Mostly I'm just trying not to think about it—I don't want to remember it. I don't even want to think about driving or getting in a car, because it just stirs things up. I'm going to lose my job at this rate. Frankly, I just don't want to see anyone. I'm afraid something might remind me of what happened."

posttraumatic stress disorder (PTSD). It was intro-duced to cover those clients who did not fit the criteria for PTSD because 30 days had not passed since the traumatic event. The criteria for ASD are comparable to those for PTSD. However, the diagnosis of ASD can only be given in the first month after a traumatic event and the diagnostic criteria have a greater emphasis on dissociative symptoms. There is some discussion among experts as to whether the diagnostic criteria accu-rately reflect abnormal reactions to trauma and whether it is a predictor for a future PTSD diagno-sis (Bryant, Friedman, Spiegel, Ursano, & Strain, 2011; Marshall, Spitzer, & Liebowitz, 1999).

Research on survivors of various kinds of trauma show that a significant number, from 6% to 33%, ultimately fit criteria for ASD (Brewin, Andrews, Rose, & Kirk, 1999; Harvey & Bryant, 1998, 1999; Holeva, Tarrier, & Wells, 2001; Stabb, Grieger, Fullerton, & Ursano, 1996).

The first criteria for ASD is that the person needs to have been exposed to actual or perceived threatened death, serious injury, or sexual viola-tion. This exposure leads to emotional, cognitive, and behavioral symptoms that generally fall into five categories: intrusion symptoms, negative moods, dissociative symptoms, avoidance, and arousal symptoms. Intrusion symptoms include invasive and unwanted recollections of the trau-matic event. Dissociative symptoms are charac-terized by an altered sense of reality, including dissociation, and an inability to remember the traumatic event. Avoidance symptoms focus on behavioral and cognitive efforts to evade re-experiencing the traumatic event. Arousal symptoms involve the inability to end the flight or fight response and include sleep disturbance, irritability, problems with concentration, and hypervigilance (APA, 2013).

The symptoms must be present for a minimum of two days and a maximum of four weeks and must occur within four weeks of the traumatic event. In the case of Stephanie, she is obviously having a strong reaction to the car accident, but it is too early for her to be diagnosed with PTSD. However, she meets the criteria for ASD and can begin to get help in coping with her symptoms.

POSTTRAUMATIC STRESS DISORDER (PTSD)

Posttraumatic stress disorder (PTSD) is a serious disorder that can develop after exposure to a traumatic event that occurred sometime in the past. Examples of these events include: sexual assault, serious injury to self or loved one, natu-ral disaster, or severe and continuous threats of violence. When someone is in crisis or during an emergency, it is of course normal to experience anxiety and fear. This distress triggers a "flight or fight" response that is the body's normal reac-tion to attempt to cope with the crisis situation. After the crisis has passed, emotional reactions, such as shock, anger, and acute feelings of sor-row are expected. These reactions are also nor-mal, and for most people, as time goes on they decline and eventually subside.

The majority of people who experience a traumatic event do not develop PTSD (Breslau, Davis, Andreski, & Peterson, 1991; Galea, Nandi, & Vlahov, 2005). But for some individu-als, the emotional reactions to a trauma linger and even increase, eventually intensifying to a level that keeps them from functioning normally. The symptoms of PTSD are the long-term effects of traumatic experiences and can include intense fear, feelings of helplessness, and intense worry about such events reoccurring.

Most public attention related to PTSD sur-rounded veterans coming back from recent wars, but its prevalence is actually higher in women than in men. In one of the most comprehensive studies conducted to date, 5,877 people from communities across the United States were inter-viewed in order to determine how many had a diagnosis of PTSD at some point in their lifetime. Combining all respondents (regardless of age or sex), the study found that approximately 7.8% of the people interviewed had experienced PTSD at some point in their lifetime (Kessler, Sonnega, Bromet, Hughes, & Nelson, 1995).

Researchers and experts are unsure why trau-matic events cause PTSD in some people, but not in others. Genetics, biological predispositions, temperament, environment, and family situation may all play roles (APA, 2013). Unfortunately, a history of past traumatic events may increase the risk of developing PTSD. Researchers believe that after a trauma and a diagnosis of PTSD, the body's response to a stressful event is changed. Normally, after the stressful event the body recovers. The stress hormones and chemicals the body releases due to the stress return to normal levels. However, in an individual with PTSD, the body keeps releasing the stress hormones and chemicals, leading to a cycle of arousal.

For a diagnosis of PTSD, symptoms need to be linked to a past traumatic event, such as serious injury, threats of death or injury, and sexual violence. This includes witnessing the event, directly experiencing it, learning about it happening to a close friend or loved one, or repeated direct contact with such events (for example, first responders). In an era of social media and constant bombardment with traumatic events worldwide, the impact of this continuous exposure may be a contributing factor.

The symptoms of PTSD largely fall into four areas: hyperarousal, re-experiencing, avoidant behaviors, and mood and thought disturbances. Clients experiencing PTSD exhibit these symptoms for longer than one month and do not function as well as before the event(s) took place (APA, 2013). A state of hyperarousal is typical with PTSD clients and includes a combination of symptoms: exaggerated startle response, constant anxiety, muscle tension, irritability, insomnia, self-destructive behavior, and inability to concentrate or focus. The symptoms may also include hypervigilance, which is marked by a constant scanning of the environment for potential threats. Clients often express that these symptoms are constant, instead of being triggered by things that remind them of the traumatic event.

Re-experiencing symptoms include ruminating thoughts or memories about the traumatic event, dissociative symptoms, such as flashbacks and recurring bad dreams, and intense distress when something reminds them of the traumatic event. All of these symptoms are experienced as intrusive and unwanted by the client, but outside of their control.

Avoidance symptoms are the client's attempts to stop re-experiencing the trauma. These include not only staying away from environmental triggers, but trying not to even think about the traumatic events. The client may go to great lengths to not think about or be reminded of what took place. This may involve shunning the people, objects, and places that remind the client of their traumatic experience. Obviously, avoidance behavior can have negative consequences. For example, someone who has been in a bad car accident may find it difficult to get to work or accomplish daily activities that were commonplace before.

PTSD negatively impacts clients both cognitively and emotionally. These alterations include not being able to remember the traumatic event, lowered self-esteem, mood disturbance, lack of interest in significant activities, and feelings of guilt, shame, and anger. Clients often experience an inability to enjoy life or participate in social situations that once gave them pleasure. They feel detached from others and may start to isolate themselves, putting them at further risk for depression.

We saw many of these symptoms in the case of Sora at the beginning of this chapter. Because the assault occurred several months ago, Sora would qualify for a diagnosis of PTSD.

COMORBIDITY

Trauma-related disorders such as ASD and PTSD are linked to increased mood and anxiety disorders as well as substance abuse issues. Roughly 80% of those suffering from PTSD have a comorbid mental health disorder, many more than one (Kessler, Chiu, Demler, & Walters, 2005). Men who are diagnosed with PTSD are more likely to abuse alcohol than women (Kessler et al., 1995).

There are several theories about why comorbidity is so high with PTSD. One hypothesis is that these comorbid disorders also develop as a reaction to, or a result of, the traumatic event(s). The other line of thought is that there is a large overlap of symptoms, and the high comorbidity may be a byproduct of the symptoms used to diagnose both disorders (Brady, Killeen, Brewerton, & Lucerini, 2000). Whatever the explanation, it is important to assess for other issues when a client presents with a trauma-related disorder.

CULTURAL CONSIDERATIONS AND POPULATION FACTORS

For males, military combat and seeing someone badly injured or killed are the forms of trauma most regularly linked with a PTSD or ASD diagnosis. Sexual assault and molestation are the most common traumatic events associated with PTSD for females. Overall, women are more likely to experience more high impact trauma, and are also more likely to develop PTSD than men. Men and women differ in lifetime rates of PTSD, with women twice as likely as men to be diagnosed with PTSD at some point in their lives. However, it is important to keep in mind that cultural expectations for seeking treatment also vary by gender, with males more reticent to admit they need help and to look for assistance (APA, 2013).

Children are less likely to experience PTSD after trauma than adults, especially if they are under 10 years of age (Gabbay, Oatis, Silva, & Hirsch, 2004).

Rates of exposure to traumatic events, such as war, famine, and genocide, vary among cultures, along with the relative risk for PTSD. As with anxiety and mood disorders, symptom expression also varies between cultures, depending on cultural norms and gender norms for expression of emotions (APA, 2013).

ETIOLOGY AND RISK FACTORS

We know that most people will not develop symptoms severe enough to meet diagnostic criteria for ASD or PTSD after a traumatic event. The reasons why PTSD and ASD develop in some people, but not in others is not completely understood. It is known that the likelihood of developing PTSD depends on the severity, duration, and immediacy of the experienced trauma (Hidalgo & Davidson, 2000). Personal characteristics (risk factors) that present before the traumatic event, as well as resources (both internal and external) that present after the event, both play critical roles. These predispositions can be considered risk factors.

Risk factors before the traumatic event include a history of mental health issues, living through past traumatic events, and already having a high degree of stress. Risk factors associated with the traumatic event include seriousness of injury, severity of fear and anxiety, and level of trauma experienced (i.e., seeing someone get killed). Risk factors after the event include little or no support, effects of other stressors, such as loss of a loved one, injuries received, or loss of work, home, or relationships (Brewin, Andrews, & Valentine, 2000).

Certain characteristics also make an individual more resilient, and less likely to develop a trauma-related disorder. These include support from family, friends, and organizations; seeking help, such as counseling or support groups; self-esteem in the face of what happened; and having effective coping skills.

TREATMENT INTERVENTIONS

There are several treatments that have been found to be effective with ASD and PTSD, including medications and certain types of counseling. With many clients, medications are combined with counseling (Wampold et al., 2010).

Counseling Treatments for PTSD

Cognitive Behavioral Therapy (CBT)

There are several CBT interventions that have research support and that focus on exposure, reducing anxiety, and cognitive restructuring. Many of the same interventions used with anxiety disorders have been shown to be effective with PTSD as well (Ponniah & Hollon, 2009). Cognitive focused interventions help the client face, rethink, and manage their fears and anxiety; many professionals use some kind of exposure to the traumatic event in the relative safety of the counseling relationship. These include the use of the Socratic Method, imagery, writing, or exposure to the feared object or situation. The client's thoughts are then analyzed to reinterpret beliefs about the event in more realistic ways in order to reduce shame and guilt. Many clients inappropriately blame themselves or feel less worthwhile after trauma. Below are some specific evidence-based CBT interventions with prescribed protocols.

Cognitive Processing Therapy (CPT)

Cognitive Processing Therapy (CPT) is a form of CBT that focuses on the client first understanding and then modifying the meaning they attach to the traumatic event (Resick & Schnicke, 1993). This type of therapy is generally carried out in twelve sessions and has been effective with different populations, including use by the U.S. Department of Veteran's Affairs (Chard, 2005; Monson et al., 2006; Owens & Chard, 2001; Resick & Schnicke, 1993; Resick et al., 2008). CPT has four main components: psychoeducation, increased awareness of thoughts and behaviors, challenging maladaptive thoughts and feelings, and understanding the changes the traumatic events have caused.

CPT starts with the counselor gaining an understanding of the client's PTSD symptoms and educating the client about treatments that can improve their symptoms and increase their coping skills. One technique that is often used in the beginning sessions of CPT is something called an Impact Statement. The client is asked to describe their understanding of why the traumatic event took place and how it changed their beliefs about themselves, others, and the world. Through such techniques, the client becomes more aware of their thoughts, especially in relation to their self-image and the traumatic event(s). For example, Sora, the

client we met at the beginning of this chapter, may have thoughts like "I was asking for it by going to that party and drinking. It's my fault, I deserved it. I deserve whatever else happens, too." These types of thoughts are unearthed during this stage of CPT and the client is then asked to describe how the traumatic event is affecting them in the present. As the client becomes more aware of the impact the traumatic event has on their beliefs about themselves, the counselor gently challenges them to question the accuracy of their beliefs.

It is important for the counselor to uncover the client's beliefs about trust, safety, and interpersonal relationships. In Sora's case, her beliefs about others have also changed. Working from a CPT perspective, the counselor gently challenges those negative beliefs, which helps Sora to find ways to decide who to trust rather than withdrawing and trusting no one. The goal is to help the client think and feel differently about what took place and the impact it has on their life. This process of describing the events and their impact can be done through dialogue or by the client writing down their traumatic experiences and then reading them to the counselor. The counselor helps the client question their negative automatic thoughts about themselves, and come to a new understanding of their experience that is less debilitating. This part of the process has been shown to be helpful for many clients because it normalizes the experience and helps the client see that their reactions are not uncommon. They learn that others have had similar experiences after going through trauma.

Stress Inoculation Training

Stress Inoculation Training (SIT) was one of the first cognitive behavioral therapies used with PTSD and consists of teaching the client to manage their reactions to situations, triggers, and memories they normally fear and avoid (Meichenbaum, 1994). It has been found effective with PTSD and other stress-related disorders (Ponniah & Hollon, 2009). SIT teaches the client to self-monitor their reactions, then continues with psychoeducation, reconceptualizing the client's stress response, and finally reflecting on their reactions to stressors. SIT then focuses on skills acquisition and rehearsal of more appropriate and positive reactions to stressful events. For the physical manifestations of anxiety (heightened breathing and heart rate, hyperventilation, muscle tension), SIT teaches controlled breathing and progressive muscle relaxation. For intrusive thoughts and worrying, SIT teaches patients how to interrupt their thought patterns and think of positive imagery (Meichenbaum, 1994; Meichenbaum & Deffenbacher, 1988).

From this SIT perspective, a counselor working with Sora might focus on teaching her relaxation techniques which allows her to slowly resume some aspects of her normal life, such as going to classes or socializing with friends. These relaxation skills can also be helpful when Sora re-experiences the trauma, allowing her to anchor herself in the here and now instead of being lost in the traumatic memory, which is what happened in the session.

Prolonged Exposure Therapy (PET)

PET focuses on repeated exposures to memories or triggers to the traumatic event until the anxiety response decreases. Repeated exposure to thoughts, feelings, and situations combined with relaxation techniques eventually leads to a reduction in the flight-or-fight response (Foa, Hembree, & Rothbaum, 2007; Joseph, & Gray, 2008). Clients become better equipped to cope with reminders of the trauma and do not have to continually avoid them. Like CPT, PET has four components: education, relaxation training, talking about or imagining the trauma, and real life exposure (*in vivo*). For example, a counselor might have Sora return to the dorm where the assault took place, working with her to diminish her fear reactions using relaxation techniques.

PET lasts ten to twelve sessions and includes homework assignments which the client performs in the real world and reports back to the counselor. Through this process, clients learn to manage their reactions to stressful memories and present day triggers.

Eye Movement Desensitization and Reprocessing (EMDR)

EMDR was first developed by Francine Shapiro (2001) and involves the client following a back-and-forth moving object with their eyes while talking with the counselor about the traumatic event. There is some evidence, although limited, that shows its effectiveness (Ponniah & Hollon, 2009). The theory is that rapid eye movement augments the brain's ability to work through traumatic memories and associated emotions; included in the treatment are relaxation techniques and coping strategies.

EMDR has eight phases: history and treatment planning, preparation, assessment, desensitization, installation, body-scan, closure, and reevaluation. The first phases involve gathering client information, such as identification of target memories, images, and beliefs about the trauma. The core of the treatment is desensitization and reprocessing while the client recalls images during controlled eye movement. The client also focuses on tension or unwanted sensations in the body. Over time, EMDR can change how an individual reacts to memories of their trauma. A course of four to twelve sessions is common. The treatment has been controversial because of the risk of triggering a re-experiencing of the trauma (abreaction) and should not be practiced without the appropriate training.

Narrative Approaches to Counseling

One of the foundations of EMDR is the idea that trauma memories are not processed and stored in the same way as "normal" events; they exist outside the flow of time and are isolated from the rest of autobiographical memory. These memories may be encoded in a nonlinear form that makes them difficult to assimilate into the rest of the ongoing life story. Instead, they remain frozen and thus are unable to be revised or reevaluated.

Another way of accessing and reprocessing these memories is through expressive writing and narrative therapy, which helps clients create meaning of trauma (Stewart & Neimeyer, 2001).

According to Judith Herman in her 1992 seminal book *Trauma and Recovery*, recovery is

> the process of weaving the raw fragments of traumatic memory into a narrative that can then find a place in the lore—that is, the larger fabric of narratives—that constitutes the person's life experience and sense of identity. (p. 177)

Psychological distress is seen as a breakdown in the coherence of the life story and the human need to make meaning, and counseling is seen as a type of story repair that allows the reconstruction of a meaningful narrative.

Narrative therapy uses autobiographical stories that the counselor and client construct to create change, including the process of being heard as a crucial component of recovery. Clients are helped to uncover the trauma story that's defining and limiting their lives, to try out alternative narratives, and then to rewrite their own story in an empowered genuine way.

One of the most powerful methods of helping someone rework their own narrative is the technique of putting the client "in the director's chair," encouraging them to step outside their own experience and to view their life story (including the traumatic scenes) from a position of displacement. Using imaginal exposure and rescripting therapy, clients who experienced trauma as children imagine their adult selves entering the scene to rescue or comfort their child self. The clients "film" their own stories, narrating as they go, changing settings and characters and events as they see fit—at times to express the repressed emotions actually associated with an event, at other times to rewrite a scene with a more optimistic ending. The client's perceptions of themselves as powerless helpless victims are thus unfrozen and replaced with a sense of empowerment (Smucker & Niederee, 1995).

Counseling Treatments for Acute Stress Disorder

CBT interventions have been shown to be the most effective treatments directly following exposure to traumatic experiences (Bryant, 2011). The goals of such interventions are to reduce symptoms of acute stress responses and help prevent their development into PTSD. These interventions include techniques such as prolonged exposure, *in vivo* exposure, cognitive restructuring, and anxiety management, and have been found to be more effective than supportive counseling alone (Bryant et al., 2008; Bryant, Sackville, Dang, Moulds, & Guthrie, 1999).

Early intervention treatments called "psychological debriefing" were initially created to treat first responders and include psychoeducation and debriefing techniques. A review of the literature on debriefings, however, found little evidence of any effectiveness (Rose, Bisson, Churchill, & Wessely, 2002). It is possible that these interventions, if they were longer and more involved, might be effective, but to date there is no evidence to suggest that these types of interventions should be used.

Medications

Among the medications used to treat ASD and PTSD, SSRIs have received the most consideration. Some, like sertraline (Zoloft) and paroxetine (Paxil), have been approved by the U.S. Food and Drug Administration as indicated treatments for PTSD (Schnurr & Friedman, 2008). Several studies showed some effectiveness of these SSRIs (Brady et al., 2000; Davidson, Rothbaum, Van der Kolk, Sikes, & Farfel, 2001; Marshall, Beebe, Oldham, & Zaninelli, 2001; Martenyi, Brown, Zhang, Prakash, & Koke, 2002). However, there are some studies that question their effectiveness, especially with women (Martenyi, Brown, & Caldwell, 2007; Schnurr & Friedman 2008).

Counselors should also be aware that there are possible side effects of these SSRIs, including nausea, decreased interest in sex, drowsiness, tiredness, or oversleeping. The medications essentially treat the underlying symptoms of anxiety and depression, and thus are similar to the medications used for those disorders.

CASE CONCEPTUALIZATION FOR TRAUMA-RELATED DISORDERS USING THE T/C MODEL

When developing a case conceptualization for a client with ASD or PTSD, it's important to have a sense of the client's trauma history. Previous trauma tends to amplify the impact of subsequent trauma, so collecting data about past losses and traumas is critical. Conversely, the level of support that a client has after a trauma is a protective factor; therefore, the case conceptualization should include an understanding of the people and organizations in the client's life who can serve as resources and support. Similarly, self-esteem contributes to resilience, and should also be assessed.

Cognitive factors related to ASD and PTSD include distorted thoughts about the world as a dangerous place, viewing other people as not trustworthy, and a sense of shame or self-blame about the occurrence of the traumatic event. In addition, be certain to evaluate the client's sense of self-efficacy, as this will either help or hinder recovery and is often significantly impacted by the experience of trauma. The client's belief systems may have changed as a result of the traumatic event as well.

Physiological symptoms, such as difficulty sleeping, hypervigilance, rapid heart rate, muscle tension, and hyperventilation are common. Finally, some of the behavioral responses to trauma may be impacting the client's life, including avoidance, isolation, and possible substance abuse.

With these considerations in mind, let's revisit the case of Sora and see how a case conceptualization can be developed.

THE CASE OF SORA

Example of T/C Case Conceptualization Model Outline

(*Areas that require more information)

Presenting Problem: anxiety, isolation, nightmares, recent assault, intrusive thoughts, and flashbacks

Internal Personality Constructs and Behavior:

Self-efficacy: self-blame, feels helpless to keep herself safe

Self-esteem: low, questioning decision making

Attitudes/Values/Beliefs: sexual values and attitudes*

Attachment Style: possible insecure attachment/overprotection*

Biology/Physiology/Heredity: female, 20, medical history*, possible parental history of anxiety*

Affect: anxious, depressed, hopeless, ashamed

Cognition: Belief that the assault was her fault, belief that the world is an unsafe place, mistrust of others

Hot Thoughts: "I can't trust anyone", "I'll never go on a date again—it's too dangerous", "This is all my fault", "My parents are going to kill me."

Behavior: avoiding social situations, isolating, missing classes, eschewing friends

Symptomology: fatigue, nightmares, startling easily, re-experiencing

Coping Skills and Strengths: excellent student, supportive roommates

Readiness for Change: action stage

Life Roles: student, daughter, friend; anticipates being a physician

Environment:

Relationships: avoiding contact with parents and friends

Culture: Korean culture*

Family Norms and Values: Parents decide on dating behavior, underage drinking, female gender roles, parental influence on vocational choice, educational values*, family background*

Societal Influences: college environment

Timeline:

Past Influences: possible parental overprotection, past romantic relationships*, past friendships*

Present Influences: anxiety, flashbacks, relationship with mother*, relationship with father*

Future Goals: resume socializing, return to classes, comfortable with relationships

Question: What else would you want to ask, to complete this case conceptualization?

COUNSELING KEYSTONES

- The most common reactions to traumatic experiences are anxiety, fear, nightmares, amplified arousal response, anger or irritability, flashbacks and nightmares, which can lead to problematic behaviors, such as aggression, withdrawal, and avoidance.
- Cognitive changes associated with experiencing trauma include viewing the world as dangerous and unpredictable.
- Acute stress disorder (ASD) describes severe stress reactions that take place soon after exposure to a traumatic event (within 30 days), before the possibility of diagnosing posttraumatic stress disorder (PTSD).
- Posttraumatic stress disorder (PTSD) is a serious disorder that can develop after exposure to a traumatic event that occurred sometime in the past, including sexual assault, serious injury to self or loved one, natural disaster, or severe and continuous threats of violence.
- Researchers and experts are unsure why traumatic events cause PTSD in some people and not in others, but believe that genetics, biological predispositions, temperament, environment, exposure to past trauma, and family situation may all play roles.
- Re-experiencing symptoms include ruminating thoughts or memories about the traumatic event, dissociative symptoms, such as flashbacks and recurring bad dreams, and intense distress when something reminds them of the traumatic event.
- Avoidance symptoms are the client's attempts to stop re-experiencing the trauma, including attempts to stay away from environmental triggers and trying not to even think about the traumatic events.
- Roughly 80% of those suffering from PTSD have a comorbid mental health disorder, including anxiety and mood disorders and substance abuse.

- There are several CBT interventions for PTSD supported by research that focus on exposure, reducing anxiety, and cognitive restructuring.
- CBT interventions have been shown to be the most effective treatments directly following exposure to traumatic experiences (ASD).
- Among the medications used to treat ASD and PTSD, SSRIs are the most researched; however, counselors should be aware that these medications may have side effects.

EXERCISES

EXERCISE 8.1
Working with Victims of Trauma

Individuals who experienced trauma may have difficulty trusting and opening up to a counselor.

CLASS EXERCISE: Students work individually followed by large group discussion.

> **Question 1:** What are some techniques that you might use to build trust and rapport?

EXERCISE 8.2 Differentiating Between Trauma Reactions

Humans have a wide range of responses to trauma.

CLASS EXERCISE: Students work in small groups to brainstorm answers to questions.

> **Question 1:** Brainstorm five to ten typical reactions to a traumatic event.
> **Question 2:** Brainstorm five to ten atypical reactions to a traumatic event that may lead to a diagnosis of PTSD or a related disorder.
> **Question 3:** What distinguishes these two lists of symptoms (severity, duration, impact, etc.)?

EXERCISE 8.3 Counselor Self-Care: Vicarious Trauma

Hearing the client's stories of trauma can be challenging for counselors, especially over a period of time.

CLASS EXERCISE: Individual work followed by large group discussion.

> **Question 1:** What are some examples of trauma that might be personally difficult for you to hear about and work with?
>
> **Question 2:** What steps could you take to work effectively with clients who experienced these particular kinds of trauma?
>
> **Question 3:** What steps could you take to ensure that you are not overwhelmed or vicariously traumatized in this work?

EXERCISE 8.4 Case Conceptualization Practice

CLASS EXERCISE: Small group discussion followed by large group discussion.

> **Question 1:** What is your case conceptualization of this case?
>
> **Question 2:** What else would you want to know?
>
> **Question 3:** What would be three possible goals for Tony in counseling?

The Case of Tony

Tony is a 40-year-old Italian American man who comes to counseling for the first time. He reports being mugged at gunpoint on his way home from the grocery store three months ago. A personal trainer who is in excellent shape, Tony had walked to the store to get some exercise, and took a shortcut home, which took him off the main road and onto a side street. Two men with pistols jumped him soon after he turned the corner, taking his wallet, his watch, and his iPhone. Although Tony cooperated with his attackers, one of them struck him in the head with his pistol before they ran off, leaving Tony with a superficial head wound.

When the counselor asks what happened, Tony says he doesn't remember. He knows that he was mugged and filed a police report, but the details are hazy.

Tony:	*(angrily)* "One minute I was fine, you know? Just fine! Minding my own business! And out of nowhere these thugs came after me. Why me? I'm telling you, if I find them, they're dead."
Counselor:	"Of course it was wrong what they did, unfair. How has this been affecting you?"
Tony:	"I've been fighting with my wife—I just know she thinks this is my fault, because I cut through the alley. And at the gym too, I've been snapping at my clients, especially the men. Some of them just remind me of those guys, you know?"
Counselor:	"Are they doing something to set you off?"
Tony:	"That's the thing, they're not really. I just get into these rages, I don't even know why. It comes out of nowhere. The other day, I threw a five-pound weight right across the room."
Counselor:	"How long has this been happening?"
Tony:	"Since that night. I never had that bad a temper before, but now I just keep wanting to fight."

(Continued)

(Continued)

Counselor:	*"What else has been happening?"*
Tony:	*"I'm not sleeping very well, I keep waking up, and having these weird dreams . . ."*
Counselor:	*"Nightmares?"*
Tony:	*"I guess so. I never used to have them. I don't know what's wrong with me."*
Counselor:	*"Nightmares are pretty common after a trauma."*
Tony:	*"Is that what this is? I keep thinking I shouldn't be such a wuss; I should get over it. They didn't hurt me. I should have fought back—if my papa were alive, he'd whup me for being such a wuss. A man fights back, he doesn't let people take things from him."*
Counselor:	*"How are you coping with all these feelings?"*
Tony:	*"I'm drinking more, I guess. We drink a lot in my family anyway, but now . . . I guess it's more. I don't want to think about it anymore, and sometimes the thoughts just sneak in when I don't expect it. I hate this."*

GO FURTHER

Principles of Trauma Therapy: A Guide to Symptoms, Evaluation, and Treatment: DSM-5 Update **(2nd ed.)** by John N. Briere and Catherine Scott (2014) SAGE

Cognitive-Behavioral Therapy for PTSD: A Case Formulation Approach by Claudia Zayfert and Carolyn Black Becker (2008) Guilford Press

Trauma and Recovery by Judith Herman (1992) Basic Books

Trauma-Focused CBT for Children and Adolescents: Treatment Applications by Judith A. Cohen, Anthony P. Mannarino, and Esther Deblinger (2012) Guilford Press

Treating Complex Traumatic Stress Disorders (Adults): Scientific Foundations and Therapeutic Models by Christine A. Courtois and Julian D. Ford (2013) Guilford Press

A Terrible Thing Happened by Margaret M. Holmes (Author) and Cary Pillo (Illustrator) (2000) Magination Press

Eye Movement Desensitization and Reprocessing (EMDR): Basic Principles, Protocols, and Procedures **(2nd ed.)** by Francine Shapiro (2001) Guilford Press

Treating PTSD in Military Personnel: A Clinical Handbook by Bret A. Moore and Walter E. Penk (2011) Guilford Press

9

FEEDING AND EATING DISORDERS

Case Example: Northwest High School cafeteria at lunch

Tenth graders Katy, Jessica, and Haley are sitting at the lunch table. Katy and Jessica are both strikingly thin. Haley is average weight. Katy picks at a salad, while Jessica eats half a sandwich and throws the other half away. Haley finishes her bowl of soup and a bag of Doritos and then gets up.

Haley:	*"Be right back."*
	Katy and Jessica watch her head to the restroom.
Jessica:	*"You know she's going in there to puke, right?"*
Katy:	*"I'm sure she's fine—it's not like she's skinny or something."*
Jessica:	*"True. God, I wish I was skinny. I'm so fat—I think I'm getting fatter every day. I shouldn't have eaten that sandwich. Maybe I should take some lessons from Haley and get rid of it."*
Katy:	*"I know what you mean. I hate looking in the mirror. I took the mirror in my room down so I wouldn't have to look at myself anymore. I just put up a Cosmo spread of Kate Moss instead so that I'll remember not to eat and get on the treadmill."*
Jessica:	*"Hey, did you check out that website? They have lots of good suggestions for how to lose weight. Some of them are disgusting though—laxatives? I don't think so."*
Katy:	*"Well, if it makes you thin . . ."*

INTRODUCTION

At some time, almost everyone worries about staying in shape, eating healthier, or losing weight. For people suffering from an eating disorder, however, these thoughts and actions become excessive, extreme, and almost constant. Feeding and eating disorders are characterized by abnormal behaviors, emotions, and cognitions involving food and diet. These behaviors significantly impact the person's ability to either take in or absorb food and necessary nutrients. Consequently, the person's physical health is impacted in a substantial and negative way. These behaviors and physical consequences go hand in hand with a great deal of concern about body weight, shape, or physical appearance. Feeding and eating disorders commonly start with a preoccupation with counting calories, exercise, or weight, and eventually lead to thoughts and behaviors that are out of the norm and appear out of control.

In general, the symptoms of most eating disorders center on an unhealthy relationship with food, exercise, body image, and body weight. Typical thoughts and beliefs include low self-esteem, fear of gaining weight or being perceived as overweight, and feeling guilty about one's actions. Common behaviors include being secretive about food or eating, social withdrawal (especially when eating is involved), frequent weighing, trying to go as long as possible without eating, skipping meals, or constantly trying "fad diets" to lose weight. Typical emotional aspects include difficulty with emotional regulation, anxiety, depression, and in social situations, a relatively emotionless or flat affect.

People who struggle with an eating disorder often have unrealistic self-critical thoughts about body image, and engage in habits that disrupt normal body functions and affect daily activities. However, eating disorders are not just about food and weight. Clients may be using food as a coping mechanism to manage distress or uncomfortable emotions, or to feel more in control when events seem overwhelming.

Having an eating disorder often leads to severe physical, psychological, and emotional impairment which greatly impact the person's ability to function on a day-to-day basis. Eating disorders are often complex in presentation and can be devastating to not only the client, but their family and loved ones as well.

According to research conducted in 2011 (Wade, Keski-Rahkonen, & Hudson, 2011),

roughly 30 million people in the United States fit the criteria for a diagnosable eating disorder sometime during their lifetime. Additionally, experts believe that there are many cases that are not reported, but still cause significant impairment even though their symptoms may be subclinical. The lifetime prevalence for an eating disorder (defined by researchers as fitting the diagnosis for anorexia nervosa, bulimia nervosa, or binge-eating disorder) for adolescents (ages 13 to 17) is estimated at 2.7% (Merikangas et al., 2010). For young females in the United States, the 12-month prevalence for anorexia nervosa is .4%, and between 1% and 1.5% for bulimia nervosa (APA, 2013). For these two disorders the prevalence for males is significantly less, roughly 10:1. The 12-month prevalence for binge-eating disorder for adults in the United States (over age 18) is 1.6% for females and .8% for males (APA, 2013).

There are severe health issues that result from having an eating disorder for a prolonged period of time. With anorexia nervosa, the lack of nutrition can lead to low blood pressure and heart rate, low bone density, muscle weakness, internal organ issues, and overall weakness and fatigue. The mortality rate among people with anorexia has been estimated at 0.56% per year, or approximately 5.6% per decade, which is about 12 times higher than the annual death rate due to all causes of death among females ages 15 to 24 in the general population. The recurring cycle of bingeing and purging that is the main characteristic of bulimia nervosa can lead to electrolyte and chemical imbalances that can adversely affect the heart and other major organs in the body. Other issues can include tooth decay, inflammation of the esophagus, and bowel and stomach disorders. A binge-eating disorder often has similar health related issues as chronic obesity, and can include high cholesterol and blood pressure, elevated triglyceride levels, and a higher chance of developing Type II diabetes (Arcelus, Mitchell, Wales, & Nielsen, 2011; Sullivan, 1995).

The fifth edition of the *Diagnostic and Statistical Manual of Mental Disorders* (DSM-5) includes seven feeding and eating disorder diagnoses: pica, rumination disorder, avoidant/restrictive food intake disorder, anorexia nervosa, bulimia nervosa, binge-eating disorder, and other specified feeding and eating disorders. This chapter discusses three diagnoses that counselors commonly see—anorexia nervosa, bulimia nervosa, and binge-eating disorder.

ANOREXIA NERVOSA (AN)

Individuals with an anorexia nervosa (AN) diagnosis possess irrational fears of being fat, becoming fat, or gaining weight. In order to address these worries, they engage in abnormal behaviors, such as restricting caloric intake, fasting, or only eating certain kinds of foods. To fit the DSM-5 diagnosis the individual needs to fit all of the following three criteria. First, they restrict their caloric intake leading to weight loss or the inability to gain weight. This results in a "significantly low body weight" with age, gender, body type, and height taken into consideration. Second, they have recurring thoughts and high levels of associated anxiety involving being fat or gaining weight. Lastly, they have an inaccurate and irrational view of their behaviors, condition, body image, and self-image. For example, they may believe they are gaining weight when they are in fact losing it, or they may "feel" overweight when in fact they are significantly below what is deemed healthy. Because the disordered eating is a coping strategy, clients may be well defended in their beliefs and may distort reality or remain in denial in order to hang onto their distorted beliefs.

The DSM-5 diagnosis for anorexia nervosa also includes two distinct subcategories: restrictive type, or binge-eating/purging type. Restrictive type is reserved for those people who do not regularly engage in binge or purge behaviors. As discussed below, the binge-eating/purging type is differentiated from bulimia nervosa which does not include specific diagnostic criteria for weight loss. The DSM-5 also allows for the diagnosis to include specifiers, such as current severity (based on BMI—body mass index), or partial or full remission (APA, 2013).

The most apparent symptom of anorexia nervosa is weight loss. This weight loss can be rapid or severe, but does not have to be. Other physical symptoms may include feeling cold, fainting, dizziness or low blood pressure, amenorrhea (cessation of menstrual periods), heart problems, abnormal blood tests, constipation, and dehydration. Behaviors that may be noticed by family members or loved ones include not eating when attending family meals or parties where there is food, fad dieting, fasting or odd food rituals, compulsively exercising, wearing baggy clothes to hide weight loss, using diuretics or laxatives, and expressing a distorted body image.

Emotionally, clients may exhibit signs of anxiety, depression, or mood swings. They may display a perfectionistic attitude with an overreliance on others' judgments. Individuals struggling with eating disorders may be socially isolated or may avoid intimate relationships.

BULIMIA NERVOSA (BN)

Similar to anorexia nervosa, individuals suffering from bulimia nervosa (BN) are most likely extremely afraid of gaining weight or being fat. The main diagnostic criteria for bulimia nervosa is taking in a significant amount of food in a relatively short period of time (bingeing) and then getting rid of that food by self-inducing vomiting (purging). Other ways of purging include diuretics, diet pills, or laxatives. To fit the criteria for diagnosis, these behaviors need to happen at least once a week for a period of at least 3 months. Again, there are specifiers for severity and remission status.

Unlike anorexia nervosa, weight loss is not necessary for this diagnosis. The person may be over, under, or normal weight. Some signs family members and loved ones may notice include: constant sore throat, dizziness or light-headedness, fatigue, dental issues, heart palpitations, bowel difficulties, and electrolyte imbalances. The individual may avoid family or holiday meals, restaurants, and eating in places where they cannot easily get to a bathroom. Many people suffering from this disorder describe a feeling of being out of control or not able to control their emotions or behaviors.

Comparable to those suffering from anorexia nervosa, clients with BN may undergo mood swings, anxiety, and depression. Their self-efficacy and self-esteem are often quite low and individuals may have a need for approval or affirmations. People tend to feel a great deal of guilt and anxiety after an episode of bingeing and purging.

BINGE-EATING DISORDER

Binge-Eating Disorder is increasing in prevalence in both men and women of all cultures and ethnic groups. In recognition of this increase, the disorder is a new addition in the DSM-5, characterized by binge-eating episodes. Individuals with this disorder eat extremely large amounts of food in a comparatively small time frame until they feel sick or uncomfortable. These binges occur frequently and during an episode, the person feels unable to control or stop their eating. Unlike bulimia nervosa, with binge-eating disorder there is no occurrence of purging.

Some individuals binge to cope with negative emotions, such as sadness, inadequacy, and feelings of loss and isolation. Others try to deal with a desire to be thinner with strict dieting that can lead to episodes of binge eating. This sets up a destructive cycle of dieting, starvation, and binge eating, which then leads to shame and an even more negative self-image, which sets the stage for more dieting.

Indicators that someone may have binge-eating disorder include: eating when full, eating alone, eating small amounts of food in public and then bingeing in private, and "yo-yo" dieting. Associated moods swings, anxiety, depression, guilt, and shame may all be present. Individuals with binge-eating disorder may feel out of control, disgusted with their actions, and have low self-esteem and self-efficacy.

COMORBIDITY

Depressive and anxiety disorders commonly co-occur with eating disorders (APA, 2013) and individuals, especially adolescents, often present with a comorbid disorder, such as a mood or personality disorder (Swanson, Crow, Le Grange, Swendsen, & Merikangas, 2011). Depressive disorders often accompany a diagnosis of an eating disorder, and in many cases depression is the presenting problem, which leads the person to initially seek treatment (Grubb, Sellers, & Waligroski, 1993; Zerbe, 1995). Bipolar disorder also has a high comorbidity with binge-eating disorder, especially in reference to night bingeing (Kruger, Shugar, & Cooke, 1996).

Obsessional personality traits and symptoms are commonly reported with individuals diagnosed with AN, especially the restrictive type. Some experts believe that the similarities between obsessive compulsive disorder (OCD) and certain eating disorders may suggest that the OCD symptoms predate the onset of the eating disorder (Altman & Shankman, 2009; Thornton & Russell, 1997). Thornton and Russell (1997) discovered that roughly 37% of individuals with anorexia nervosa had co-occurring OCD. Individuals with bulimia nervosa, however, had a much lower co-occurring rate of 3%.

Yaryura-Tobias, Neziroglu, and Kaplan (1995) encourage counselors who are treating individuals diagnosed with an eating disorder, or with OCD and an eating disorder, to be attentive to the likelihood of self-mutilation behaviors. Additionally, those counseling individuals with self-mutilating behaviors should assess for symptoms of OCD and eating disorders.

CULTURAL CONSIDERATIONS AND POPULATION FACTORS

Eating disorders occur across cultures and with diverse populations, although research suggests that they are most prevalent in industrialized countries (Crago, Shisslak, Estes, 1996; Wildes, Emery, &

Simons, 2001). Although recent meta-analysis research has found that eating disorders are evident with all backgrounds and socioeconomic levels, Caucasians and those in higher socioeconomic levels may seek treatment more and express their symptoms in more clinical terms, thus they may be more readily diagnosed by medical professionals (Wildes, Emery, & Simons, 2001). There has been some recent research suggesting that lesbian, gay, bisexual, and transgender (LGBT) adolescents may be more susceptible to body image issues as well as eating disorders (Austin, Nelson, Birkett, Calzo, & Everett, 2013).

The prevailing wisdom used to be that eating disorders primarily impacted young women. However, it is now clear that eating disorders cut across gender, age, socioeconomic, racial, and cultural lines. The website for NEDA (National Eating Disorders Association) estimates that one-third of the 30 million Americans who develop an eating disorder will be men, and indicates that 43% of men are dissatisfied with their bodies. A 2012 study in the *International Journal of Eating Disorders* reported that 13% of women over fifty had some disordered eating characteristics (Shallcross, 2013).

Counselors should be careful to not develop expectations based on outdated stereotypes about which clients might have an eating disorder. Male clients may focus less on thinness and more on "bulking up" or wanting to be "ripped," attempting to adhere to unrealistic cultural standards for male bodies. Excessive exercise and use of performance enhancing drugs may be a danger sign for men instead of restricting eating. An additional challenge in working with male clients with disordered eating is the significant shame associated with this issue for males, adding to the critical need for a thorough assessment (Birli, Zhang, & McCoy, 2012).

Because the stereotype for eating disorders has been a young woman, disordered eating among older women is also often overlooked. Women in mid-life also face significant stressors, including physiological changes due to menopause and environmental transitions, such as children leaving home, the stress of caring for aging parents, or losses due to death or divorce. Eating disorders can be especially dangerous for older women because their health may be more fragile than younger clients.

Another stereotype that was perpetuated until recently is that eating disorders largely afflict white women, not women of color. However, research shows that the rates do not differ, though minority clients may be underdiagnosed (Shallcross, 2013). When working with minority clients, the impact of prejudice, racism, acculturation, and body concerns specific to each cultural group should be considered, as these may have an effect on body and self-image.

The importance of a thorough intake assessment and case conceptualization cannot be overstated when it comes to eating disorders. Clients often are ashamed about their disordered eating, and thus may come to counseling with presenting problems that focus on other issues. Counselors should ask about eating, weight concerns, and body image as part of the intake process.

ETIOLOGY AND RISK FACTORS

Disordered eating is a complex multifaceted problem that most experts believe has multiple causes and influences (APA, 2013). Certainly adhering to an ideal of unrealistic thinness is a risk factor. When clients subscribe to a thin ideal and judge their value in accordance with an impossible standard, the failure to live up to that standard creates a vulnerability for depression and negative self-image. Unfortunately, even by 6 years old, children can start to express worry about their weight or body shape. Pressure to conform to an ideal of thinness starts early; researchers found that 40% to 60% of girls ages 6 to 12 show concern about their weight or about becoming overweight (Cash & Smolak, 2011; Gustafson-Larson & Terry, 1992).

Originally, it was thought that eating disorders were triggered mainly by environmental stressors and pressures related to body image and physical appearance, which created an abnormal drive for weight loss and restrictive behaviors. More recently, genetics and biology are understood to play a larger role, and today most experts believe it is an interaction between environmental, cognitive, and biological factors that create a complex and multifaceted etiological landscape (Collier & Treasure, 2004). Eating disorders cannot be traced back to a single causal factor, but rather develop when internal and external environmental influences combine, including genetic vulnerabilities, family standards, cultural pressures, and stressful life events. Losses, such as experiencing the death of loved ones or the separation of divorce, and traumatic events can lead individuals to attempt to regain control through restricted eating. Transitions, such as puberty, leaving home, or having children leave home, are also risk factors for development of an eating disorder.

Assessment of risk factors for eating disorders should include both environmental and interpersonal factors, including information about the client's family of origin. It is within the family that most of us learn what is valued and internalize standards for appearance and behavior. Clients who are perfectionistic and are overly focused on gaining approval from others or who have obsessive personality traits may be at greater risk for developing an eating disorder. If in a client's family, belonging was contingent on being thin or "perfect," the client will try to conform, even if it means engaging in behaviors that are self-destructive.

TREATMENT INTERVENTIONS

It is important to have a multidisciplinary approach and involve other healthcare professionals to create a "treatment team." Research suggests that effective treatment includes longer term counseling or inpatient treatment combined with nutrition and medical interventions (Grilo & Mitchell, 2010).

Specific interventions, however, vary depending on the course, severity, and physical impact of the disorder, and should be tailored to the individual.

Depending on the level of severity, outpatient counseling (whether individual, group, or family), coupled with treatment from the client's primary medical care provider is usually the first level of intervention. Other first-level interventions include peer support groups, dietary and nutritional counseling, and some medications. Hospitalization, partial hospitalization, and other inpatient care models are considered second-level treatment options and are used when there are major medical concerns, severe behavioral issues, or when other treatment modalities have failed. Inpatient stays typically require a period of outpatient follow-up and aftercare to address underlying issues in the individual's eating disorder.

Generally, interventions should focus on the dynamics that support and maintain the disorder, including medical and nutritional issues, behaviors (eating and exercise habits, nutritional restrictions), cognitions and basic beliefs (body image, self-efficacy), and environmental factors (family dynamics, sociocultural influences). Evidence appears to indicate that early intervention for anorexia nervosa, especially during the initial treatment and the weight-gaining stage, should focus on providing empathic understanding, psychoeducation, praise for behavior modification, coaching, support, encouragement, and other positive behavioral reinforcement (National Institute for Clinical Excellence, 2004). For younger clients still living with parents or guardians, evidence suggests that family-based interventions are most effective (Lock & Le Grange, 2012; National Institute for Clinical Excellence, 2004). After a client gains some weight and medical concerns are diminished, counseling intervention should shift to focusing on the client's experience of their illness, cognitive reconstruction, body image issues, and how environmental cues impacted the disorder. Issues to explore include emotional regulation, how to deal with setbacks and relapse risks, coping skills, and increasing self-efficacy. Counselors should have a holistic approach, keeping in mind appropriate developmental and other important life issues (Lock & Le Grange, 2012).

Whatever the treatment modality, the main goals are addressing caloric intake and nutrition, dealing with maladaptive and destructive behaviors, and exploring cognitive themes, such as identity, self-esteem, and self-image.

The Case of Marjorie

Marjorie, a 52-year-old African American woman, came to see a counselor. She says she is feeling "down" recently and isn't sure why. Marjorie wears an oversize shirt and leggings, although it is a very hot day. While most of her body is hidden, the visible portion of her arms and legs appear quite thin.

Counselor: *"Have you lost weight recently?"*

Marjorie: *"I don't know . . . maybe. That's a good thing, right?"*

Counselor: *"Have you been trying to lose weight—on a diet?"*

Marjorie: *She laughs, but it seems forced. "I've been on a diet all my life."*

Counselor: *"Do you have strict standards for what is okay for you to eat and what is not?"*

Marjorie: *"I'm not sure what you mean. I guess so."*

Counselor: *"We all learn rules about how we should look and what's okay to eat from our families. Can you give me some examples of the rules you go by?"*

Marjorie: *"Well, I don't eat sugar. And you know, there's sugar in almost everything. I don't eat carbs, they're terrible for you. I don't eat meat, because hormones and all. And I don't eat between meals, not ever. And not after 6 pm. Is that what you mean?"*

Counselor: *"Exactly, yes. That sounds pretty strict. Can you tell me a little about your family? What did you learn from your family about appearances and weight?"*

Marjorie: *She laughs again, without humor. "That's an easy one. I learned that I had to keep up appearances at all costs. Don't ever be caught without your makeup on. Always be well dressed. And never, ever be fat!"*

The counselor normalizes the way we all internalize these messages from our families, and how difficult it can be to feel that you don't quite measure up. Marjorie becomes tearful.

Counselor: *"Can you tell me what's been going on in your life recently? What's it like to be 52, what sort of transitions are you dealing with?"*

Marjorie: *"I guess you don't know about menopause. Or what it's like to have your kids grow up and move out—and take jobs halfway across the country!"*

Counselor: *"That sounds like a lot to deal with—I'd like to hear more about it."*

Counseling Interventions

The most common counseling interventions for anorexia nervosa try to explore and address the core psychological and emotional issues that trigger the associated behaviors, as we can see from the counselor working with Marjorie. Issues related to body image, self-efficacy, and self-esteem usually manifest in early childhood experiences. A key goal of most counseling interventions is to have the individual gain insight into how their beliefs and values are affecting their behavior and condition. Many interventions try to challenge the individual's irrational beliefs, in an attempt to mitigate what triggers their restrictive and controlling behaviors. The belief is that if the individual can change the way they see themselves, then the motivation for these behaviors will diminish.

As stated previously, some form of counseling is the usual treatment for anorexia nervosa. Since eating disorders are often comorbid with mood or personality disorders, counseling interventions often have to be tailored to each individual's presenting issues and concerns. In fact, many in the field would argue that eating disorders are complicated and need a multidisciplinary approach for these reasons (Costin, 2006). This complexity makes researching effective treatments difficult.

Cognitive-Behavioral Based Interventions

CBT interventions are commonly used to treat eating disorders, and focus on the client's irrational beliefs, negative self-image and worldview, and associated maladaptive behaviors (Murphy, Straebler, Cooper, & Fairburn, 2010; Waller et al., 2007). Although more research has been done with CBT treatment for binge eating and BN, research shows that CBT holds promise for clients with anorexia nervosa as well (Bowers & Ansher, 2008). Behaviorally based programs that provide reinforcement for weight gain also have been shown to be effective, at least in the short term (Hsu, 1990).

Some specific treatment models of CBT, such as Enhanced Cognitive Behavioral Therapy

(CBT-E) or Transdiagnostic CBT for Eating Disorders have been shown to be effective for both AN and BN (Fursland et al., 2012; Poulsen et al., 2014). CBT-E was first proposed by Christopher Fairburn (2008) and specifically developed for clients with eating disorders. Fairburn believed that since most clients did not fit neatly into a diagnosis of either AN or BN, it was important to develop a CBT model especially geared toward the typical cognitive and behavioral underpinnings that counselors were seeing in their clients.

CBT-E includes valuation and collaboration with the client in an attempt to gain greater understanding of the cognitions and behaviors associated with the disordered eating, exploring the overvaluation of weight control and appearance, and eventually the modification of beliefs and behaviors with regard to food, body image, body checking, avoidance, and coping (Fairburn, 2008). The first stage of treatment attempts to normalize eating behaviors, ensuring that the client eats three meals a day and several snacks. This can interrupt the restrict-starve-binge-shame cycle that characterizes much of disordered eating. In the second phase, the client and counselor work together using a cognitive therapy model, identifying dysfunctional and irrational beliefs about body image, weight, and perfectionism. Finally, alternate coping strategies are developed to deal with negative emotions and stressful life events.

Family-Based Interventions

Family therapy interventions are often used for treatment of AN, especially for adolescents or young adults who are still living at home. This method of counseling emphasizes the family system and the role the client plays within that system. Therapeutic discussions focus on family dynamics and the role the client's disorder maintains in the family, as well as identifying the specific role the client has taken. Interventions are usually done in a group format, with a few sessions held with the client alone. This is done to help the family recognize the roles they are playing in sustaining the client's problem behaviors, and allows the counselor to recommend more supportive ways of interacting with the client (Lock & Le Grange, 2012). A recent meta-analysis looking at the effectiveness of psychological treatments of eating disorders found evidence for the effectiveness of family-based treatment of adolescents diagnosed with AN (Hay, 2013).

The "Maudsley Method" is a family-based intervention model in which family members are directly involved with the client's eating, in an attempt to support more positive eating behaviors and to help with weight gain. This method is composed of three phases: weight restoration, returning the control of eating behaviors to the client, and establishing a healthy self-image and identity (Treasure, Schmidt, & Macdonald, 2009). In the first phase, the parents temporarily take control of the client's eating behavior until a healthy weight is reached. Then, gradually they return control to the client. Some research suggests that such behaviorally based family interventions can sometimes be an effective treatment intervention (Eisler et al., 2000; Lock, Couturier, & Agras, 2006), although improvement may be difficult to sustain when the client is no longer living at home.

Psychodynamic Interventions

From a psychodynamic perspective, internal psychological conflict and problematic family dynamics are the underlying cause of eating disorders like anorexia. That is, the client attempts to cope with these conflicts through disordered eating. The intrapsychic conflicts are expressed through the problematic eating behavior symptoms, in the most adaptive way the individual can find. Thus, if the client's internal struggles are uncovered and processed, the need for the symptom is reduced and the disordered eating behaviors lessen (Gilbert, 2013).

As with all psychodynamic approaches, treatment focuses on taking a thorough history and helping the client come to an understanding of the impact of past experience on present symptoms, and how their disordered eating functions as a coping mechanism. There is some research evidence that psychodynamic counseling can be effective in treating eating disorders (Haase et al., 2008; Leichsenring & Klein, 2014).

Recent research on eating disorders and attachment suggests a relationship between attachment insecurity and emotion regulation that contributes to the development of an eating disorder (Tasca & Balfour, 2014; Thompson-Brenner, 2014). The rate of insecure attachment among individuals diagnosed with eating disorders is estimated at 70% to 100% (O'Shaughnessy & Dallos, 2009) and females with insecure attachment were found to have disordered responses to weight gain in puberty (Milan & Acker, 2014). A psychodynamic approach to eating disorders suggests that a discussion of family history and current family dynamics, as well as attachment style, is an important part of the case conceptualization process.

Interpersonal Therapies

Working from an Interpersonal Therapy (IPT) perspective, counselor and client work together to improve the client's interpersonal relationships, instead of focusing directly on weight and eating behaviors. When the client's relationships grow stronger, the client is able to get their emotional needs met through relationships, and thus requires less need for disordered eating behaviors.

Motivational Interviewing

A more recently used intervention is Motivational Interviewing (MI). Some experts believe that MI approaches show promise with clients diagnosed with anorexia because they often present for treatment in the early stages of Prochaska's model, and are thus ambivalent about change (as described in Chapter 3). The suggestion is to use MI interventions during the first stage of treatment, when commitment to change is the weakest. Interventions include affirming, empathizing, rolling with resistance, and asking for permission (Treasure & Schmidt, 2008). The research to support such interventions with AN is progressively increasing (Price-Evans & Treasure, 2011).

Feminist Approaches

In contrast to cognitive models of AN, feminist models emphasize a systemic basis for eating disorders, not an individual one. Feminist counselors view eating disorders as resistance to a culture which does not support female development, a symbolic way of denying attributes which are central to female identity and maturity (Steiner-Adair, 1991). Within the family context, when young women feel unheard and unrecognized, an eating disorder may be a way of being heard and noticed (Wastell, 1996).

Residential Treatment

Treatment of eating disorders is a specialized area of practice. Counselors who receive specific training tend to be more effective, resulting in a better outcome for clients. However, there are many instances when referral to a specialist is not practical or possible, so all counselors should be informed and capable of assessing and working with clients with eating disorders. At the same time, treatment in an inpatient or residential facility should be considered if the client is medically at risk.

Residential treatment facilities offer a complete array of treatment services in one place, and focus on the treatment of all the different types of eating disorders. Such facilities usually include a wide range of specialists—psychologists, medical doctors, nutritionists, meditation and relaxation professionals, and fitness experts.

In cases where a person with anorexia is severely ill and has a relapse from baseline weight, or is below 15% of appropriate body weight, or the individual has other serious medical problems, inpatient hospitalization may be necessary. During such hospitalizations, people with anorexia are encouraged to eat regular meals with liquid supplements, but those who refuse feedings are given feedings through a nasogastric tube (i.e., a plastic tube passed through the nose, down the esophagus, and into the stomach). Group and individual counseling supplements dietary and medical therapies.

At one time, inpatient treatment lasted many weeks, if not months, but in today's insurance climate the goals of hospitalization are weight gain and medical stabilization. The client is moved to outpatient therapy as soon as it is considered safe.

Individuals who are significantly underweight or overweight should be evaluated by a medical professional before outpatient treatment is undertaken, and continually monitored throughout treatment. Counselors have an ethical responsibility to work with clients diagnosed with eating disorders as part of a multidisciplinary team when possible, including a medical professional, and ideally a nutritionist.

Specific Counseling Interventions for Bulimia Nervosa and Binge-Eating Disorder

Much like AN, counseling interventions for BN and binge-eating disorder use different approaches, with counseling-based interventions mainly focusing on cognitive behavioral interventions and nutritional counseling.

Cognitive Behavioral Approaches

A recent meta-analysis by Hay (2013) found substantial evidence for the effectiveness of CBT as a first-line treatment for BN, in both individual and group formats of delivery. CBT interventions focus on the client's disordered and irrational thoughts, especially right before and right after the binging event. Like all CBT-based interventions, they stress the importance of both cognitive and behavioral factors in the onset and maintenance of the bingeing behaviors (Wilson, 1997; Wilson, Grilo, & Vitousek, 2007).

Along with mitigating negative thoughts, these interventions also try to help the client tolerate negative emotions and to change the ways they think about stress, food, and coping. Meeting behavioral goals eventually becomes a main focus of the treatment as well as rewarding the client for accomplishing these goals (Murphy, Straebler, Cooper, & Fairburn, 2010).

Counseling interventions used in treating binge-eating disorders are similar to those used to treat bulimia nervosa. CBT-E is used with all eating disorder diagnoses (Fairburn, 2008), and CBT in both individual and group form is shown effective for binge-eating disorder and to help with associated symptoms of low self-esteem and depression (Abilés et al., 2013).

Mindfulness-Based Interventions

More recently, mindfulness-based interventions have shown some efficacy in treating obesity-related eating behaviors like binge eating. Mindfulness training encourages clients to pay attention to their body's physiological cues, such as hunger and satiety, without judgment. Clients are also encouraged to focus attention on what they eat, and to regain a sense of pleasure in eating. Mindfulness-based counseling also can include behaviors to help clients accept and appreciate their bodies, such as dance, movement, or yoga. Mindfulness can also be combined with CBT approaches (O'Reilly, Cook, Spruijt-Metz, & Black, 2014) and psychoeducation about eating behavior and body image.

Medications

Unlike many of the other disorders discussed in this book, there are no specifically researched medications to treat AN. With some clients, especially those with comorbid mood disorders, antidepressants and antianxiety medications may be prescribed. Since there is some risk of bone density loss in severe cases, medications like estrogen may also be prescribed. For BN, Fluoxetine (Prozac) is the only medication approved by the U.S. Food and Drug Administration (FDA). Antidepressants like Fluoxetine can reduce episodes of binge eating and comorbid depression (Arnold et al., 2002).

CASE CONCEPTUALIZATION FOR EATING DISORDERS USING THE T/C MODEL

As previously discussed, eating disorders have a complex etiology influenced by a variety of factors. This makes thorough assessment and comprehensive case conceptualization critical. The T/C Model's emphasis on both internal and external influences makes it useful for working with clients dealing with disordered eating.

Assessment should include environmental factors, such as recent losses, trauma, and stressful life events. Family relationships and conflict are also important to understand. Many approaches to treating eating disorders emphasize the need to understand the client's family history, including attachment status and beliefs about self-worth and belonging.

In addition, cultural messages about appearance and weight absorbed from the society as well as the family should be explored. Keep in mind that developmental transitions, such as puberty or menopause, beginning college or leaving home, job change, or mid-life changes can be risk factors for developing an eating disorder.

Since most approaches consider eating disorder behaviors a coping strategy for dealing with overwhelming emotion or loss of control, assessment should also include the client's ability for emotion regulation and stress management. A thorough understanding of the behaviors surrounding the client's eating disorder is also necessary. Is there binge eating? Is there purging, and if so, how (e.g., vomiting, diuretics, laxatives, excessive exercise, etc.)?

Cognitive factors include perfectionism, low self-esteem and self-efficacy, obsessive thoughts, and distorted beliefs and perceptions. In addition, there may be a strong sense of shame.

Keep in mind that eating disorders can have serious physical consequences. A thorough case conceptualization also includes findings from a medical exam, current physiological symptoms, and weight.

With these general considerations in mind, let's examine the case of a client named Rebecca.

The Case of Rebecca

Rebecca is a sophomore in college who sought therapy in her college's counseling center after her disordered eating patterns transformed from binge eating to bulimia. She reported having started binge eating in high school, around the time of her parents' divorce and a breakup with her boyfriend. Rebecca, who through therapy was able to acknowledge her perfectionistic tendencies, is highly achievement oriented, has experienced a large degree of success in most endeavors she has attempted, and continues to experience academic success in college. However, she struggles with anxiety and depression.

Rebecca came from a single sex, private school, where she was known for her athletic talent, leadership skills, community service, intelligence, and beauty. What she was hiding then, and has continued to hide in college is the extreme sense of shame and embarrassment that accompanied her parents' alcohol instigated screaming fights, some of which spilled out onto the lawn of her otherwise pristine neighborhood. While she was relieved by the eventual divorce, the shame associated with her parents' public arguments and disorderly conduct remained. Her externally perfect image was somewhat of a defense against this shame. Additionally, she became a surrogate parent (was parentified) to her younger sister, whom she tried to protect from her parents' rages. When sober, both parents were warm and loving, which was difficult for Rebecca to reconcile with the people they became. Furthermore, while the parents were warm and loving to their children, there was an undercurrent of anger and rage toward each other. Rebecca was aware of this underlying anger, and became hypervigilant for feelings of anger in herself or others.

Rebecca started binge eating after her high school boyfriend broke up with her to date another girl, right around the time of her parents' divorce. She was both troubled by the divorce and anxious about her younger sister's emotional well-being. She felt her boyfriend saw more of her "true self" and "it was too much for him." Rebecca's binge eating became a way of managing her emotions, since emotion regulation was not modeled by her parents. Furthermore, she saw her eating as an addiction, similar to her parents' abuse of alcohol. Seeking therapy was difficult for her and, at times, her therapist was challenged by Rebecca's attempts to be the "perfect patient." Additionally, it took a long time for Rebecca to trust that she could reveal negative emotions to her therapist, whatever their manifestation, for fear that she would overwhelm the therapist, let her down, or otherwise lead to some abandonment, as happened with her ex-boyfriend.

Rebecca's high school athleticism and extracurricular activities kept her out of the house enough to keep the binge eating to a minimum, thus not impacting her weight. However, when she arrived at college, she experienced difficulty tolerating the degree of free time that comes with the change in schedule and structure, coupled with less obligations. Her binge eating increased, as did her weight. This was sufficiently concerning to Rebecca who despite her binge eating in high school had remained thin. Challenging her outwardly perfect image and falling further away from the sociocultural ideal of slimness, Rebecca began to purge after her binges. Having some understanding of the health ramifications involved in purging, this became scary to her, and as a result, Rebecca sought treatment.

In treatment, Rebecca often focused on feeling overwhelmed by the hyperfunctioning obligations she created for herself, caretaking for her friends, or the relationships with male students she sought to establish as a means of gaining intimacy and masking her sorrow. However, as the relationship became more serious, intimacy issues arose which Rebecca had difficulty tolerating. Rebecca responded well to the behavioral strategies discussed in treatment to avoid purging, which she was sufficiently motivated to stop. However, her binge-eating behaviors took significantly longer to overcome, as she did not have an arsenal of other coping strategies to regulate emotion and provide herself with comfort. She also had difficulty processing the issues associated with her family dynamics, as her parents could be responsive and caring at times. Thus, she had difficulty reconciling the anger she had toward them with her sense of dependency on them. Decisions about classes, summer jobs, and professional aspirations were determined in part by staying close to her younger sister, following her most recent relationship, and following what she considered she "should" do (as defined by others rather than herself). Identity development was a central theme throughout therapy.

THE CASE OF REBECCA

Example of T/C Case Conceptualization Model Outline

(*Areas that require more information)

Presenting Problem: disordered eating, anxiety, depression, issues with relationships

Internal Personality Constructs and Behavior:

Self-efficacy: low because of perfectionistic tendencies

Self-esteem: mixed, has experienced much success, but negatively impacted because of her inability to control behaviors

Attitudes/Values/Beliefs: achievement oriented, driven to achieve, what other people think matters

Attachment Style: possible insecure attachment due to parental inconsistency*

Biology/Physiology/Heredity: college-age female, medical issues*, parents alcohol abuse, history of family mental health issues*

Affect: anxiety, depression, inability to regulate emotions

Cognition: perfectionistic thinking, believes she easily overwhelms others, needs to protect younger sister, don't show people your true self

Hot Thoughts: "can't show anyone a negative side of me", "can't trust anyone", "show guys your real self and they will leave you", "I have to do everything right", "If people truly knew who I was, they wouldn't love me"

Behavior: binge and restrictive eating, hypervigilance, perfectionistic actions

Symptomology: restrictive eating, binge eating, weight gain, emotional deregulation

Coping Skills and Strengths: academic and athletic talent, friends*

Readiness for Change: just into action stage, seems motivated toward change, but unsure what changes to make

Life Roles: student, daughter, older sister, athlete*

Environment:

Relationships: parents*, younger sister*

Culture: *

Family Norms and Values: educational values, family values*

Societal Influences: went to single-sex private school, high SES

Timeline:

Past Influences: parents' divorce, parents' arguments, breakup with boyfriend, high school experiences

Present Influences: college, present relationship with sister, parents

Future Goals: healthier eating habits, significant decrease in anxiety and depression, romantic relationship*

Question: What else would you want to ask, to complete this case conceptualization?

COUNSELING KEYSTONES

- Feeding and eating disorders are characterized by abnormal behaviors, emotions, and cognitions involving food and diet that significantly impact the person's ability to either take in or absorb food and needed nutrients.
- Clients with eating disorders display a great deal of concern about body weight, shape, or physical appearance.
- Feeding and eating disorders commonly start with a preoccupation with counting calories, exercise, or weight and eventually lead to thoughts and behaviors that are out of the norm and appear out of control.
- Roughly 30 million people in the United States fit the criteria for a diagnosable eating disorder sometime during their lifetime.
- The DSM-5 includes seven feeding and eating disorder diagnoses: pica, rumination disorder, avoidant/restrictive food intake disorder, anorexia nervosa, bulimia nervosa, binge-eating disorder, and other specified feeding and eating disorders.
- Anorexia nervosa, bulimia nervosa and binge-eating disorder all can result in serious medical complications and often require a team approach to treatment.
- Individuals with an Anorexia Nervosa (AN) diagnosis possess irrational fears of being fat,

becoming fat, or gaining weight, and restrict their calorie intake, leading to significantly low body weight.
- Clients with AN have recurring thoughts and high levels of associated anxiety involving being fat or gaining weight, and an inaccurate and irrational view of their behaviors, condition, body image, and self-image.
- Clients with Bulimia Nervosa (BN) also have a fear of gaining weight or being fat. Bulimia Nervosa is characterized by taking in a significant amount of food in a relatively short period of time (bingeing) and then getting rid of that food by self-inducing vomiting, diuretics, diet pills, or laxatives (purging).
- Individuals with binge-eating disorder eat extremely large amounts of food in a comparatively small time frame until they feel sick or uncomfortable, and feel unable to control or stop their eating.
- Depressive and anxiety disorders commonly co-occur with eating disorders.
- Eating disorders cut across gender, age, socioeconomic, racial, and cultural lines.
- Treatment interventions focus on the dynamics that support and maintain the disorder, including medical and nutritional issues; behaviors (eating and exercise habits, nutritional restrictions); cognitions and basic beliefs (body image, self-efficacy); and environmental factors (family dynamics, sociocultural influences).

EXERCISES

EXERCISE 9.1
Ethics and Self-Awareness

Counselors are, of course, subject to the same cultural messages as our clients. Working with clients with eating disorders and body image issues can bring up our own doubts and vulnerabilities. Ethically, we are required to be aware of these issues so that they do not interfere with our effective counseling of clients. Take a moment and consider your own history and values.

CLASS EXERCISE: Individual work, followed by large group discussion.

Question 1: What norms and values about body size, weight, and eating did you internalize from your family of origin?

Question 2: What cultural messages have you absorbed from media?

Question 3: Have there been times when you were dissatisfied with your own body/weight? If so, how did you cope with these concerns?

EXERCISE 9.2 The Impact of Social Media

Social media has made it possible for individuals struggling with an eating disorder to connect with others who are also dealing with disordered eating. In some cases, clients can find support groups that help with their recovery. In other cases, clients may find groups which offer helpful "hints" about methods of restricting and purging, making recovery more difficult. Do an online search for both types of groups and see what you find.

CLASS EXERCISE: Discuss findings in small groups, followed by large group discussion.

EXERCISE 9.3 Case Conceptualization Practice

Now that you have listened in on several counselors working with clients who have various types of eating disorders, it's time to see what you can do. How would you conceptualize the following case, in order to most effectively develop a diagnosis and collaborate on a treatment plan?

The Case of Joe

Joe, a 21-year-old college junior, came to the counseling center because his partner, Jacob, is worried about him. Joe is short in stature and slender. He wears a tee shirt and jeans, and appears to be quite fit.

Counselor:	*"I understand that your partner is worried about you."*
Joe:	*"I don't know why. I've been hitting the gym a lot, yeah. Eating healthier too. So what? He doesn't want me to look good?"*
Counselor:	*"Is that what concerns you most, looking good?"*
Joe:	*"Damn right. I've never felt like I looked okay. I'm a shrimp, and I hate that. And until this year, I was fat too. It's hard to live like that, feeling so ugly. No wonder I could never hang onto a guy."*
Counselor:	*"Tell me more about that, feeling that way."*
Joe:	*"I've felt that way all my life. Not good enough. My dad wanted me to play basketball like he did, but obviously I couldn't do that. My dad did some modeling when he was young too—I know he's always wanted me to look good. Better. My mom and my older brother are the same—they're like perfect. I'm the one that got stuck with the bad genes."*
Counselor:	*"So, you got the message from your family that you had to be perfect physically in order to 'fit in'?"*

(Continued)

(Continued)

Joe: *"Exactly. I've always felt that pressure."*

Counselor: *"What sort of things are you doing to get yourself in this kind of shape?"*

Joe: *"I guess I'm controlling my eating. It's pretty much just protein and this special supplement I'm taking. And I'm working out. A lot, I guess."*

Counselor: *"You've started missing classes?"*

Joe: *"I guess. I just can't think about anything other than this—it's too important!"*

Counselor: *"Has there ever been a time when you ate something and then felt you had to do something to compensate for what you ate?"*

Joe: (breaks eye contact) *"Yeah. That's been happening a lot recently. I have to hit the treadmill after I eat or it makes me nuts. I can just feel the fat rolls coming back. I guess sometimes I overdo it. I passed out once or twice, and I guess that scared Jacob."*

Counselor: *"That sounds pretty scary. Would you be willing to see the physician over at the health center to make sure you're okay?"*

CLASS EXERCISE: Small group discussion followed by large group discussion

Question 1: What is your case conceptualization of this case?

Question 2: What else would you want to know?

Question 3: What would be three possible goals for Joe in counseling?

Question 4: Given the answers to your first two questions, what interventions would you employ?

GO FURTHER

Cognitive Behavior Therapy and Eating Disorders by Christopher Fairburn (2008) Guilford Press

Overcoming Binge Eating, Second Edition: The Proven Program to Learn Why You Binge and How You Can Stop by Christopher Fairburn (2013) Guilford Press

Beyond a Shadow of a Diet: The Comprehensive Guide to Treating Binge Eating Disorder, Compulsive Eating, and Emotional Overeating by Judith Matz and Ellen Frankel (2014) Routledge Press

Integrated Treatment of Eating Disorders: Beyond the Body Betrayed by Kathryn Zerbe (2008) W. W. Norton

The Body Image Workbook: An Eight-Step Program for Learning to Like Your Looks by Thomas Cash (2008) New Harbinger

The Treatment of Eating Disorders: A Clinical Handbook by Carlos Grilo and James Mitchell (2011) Guilford Press

10

SUBSTANCE-RELATED AND ADDICTIVE DISORDERS

The Case of Amy

Amy is a 48-year-old mother of two teenage girls. She has been married to her husband for 25 years and lives and works in a small town outside of Atlanta. Amy is a self-described worrier. She is often short-tempered at work and with her children. She has trouble sleeping at night and often takes over the counter sleep-aid medications. Her anxiety is mostly rooted in feelings of inadequacy and a belief that she cannot manage day-to-day tasks. She thinks that her husband will eventually leave her, her children hate her, and she will soon be fired from her job for incompetence. She has taken many different kinds of medication in the past and recently started to abuse the sedatives that her primary doctor prescribed for anxiety and sleep. Over the past month, she has seen several different doctors and received more than ten different prescriptions for sedatives. She comes to you feeling overwhelmed and at the end of her rope.

INTRODUCTION

Psychoactive substance use is pervasive in our society. A recent national survey estimated that roughly 9% of Americans over the age of twelve (approximately 22 million people) used illicit drug(s) in just the last month (Substance Abuse and Mental Health Services Administration (SAMHSA), 2012). A similar survey found that roughly 54% of Americans over the age of twelve had consumed alcohol, and 24% reported binge drinking in the past month (defined as four or more drinks for a woman and five or more for a man in one sitting) (SAMHSA, 2011). The illegal (in most states) drug of choice by far was marijuana, with 7% of Americans over twelve having used in the last month.

Why is substance use so pervasive? Research suggests that people generally take drugs to either feel good or feel better. Some substance use is about sensation seeking, as people experiment with drug use to feel high or different. Others are looking for symptom relief and are using substances to cope with anxiety, depression, trauma, or environmental stressors. Whatever the reason, it is important for the counselor to acknowledge that, at least at first, the client has some positive effects associated with substance use. Commonly used substances largely affect the motivation and pleasure pathways of the brain and mimic neurochemical effects, such as the feelings we have during normal pleasurable experiences like eating something that tastes good or falling in love.

For some individuals, this substance use eventually leads to abuse and addiction. The 12-month prevalence of alcohol use disorder in the U.S. population is estimated to be 4.6% with 12 to 17 year olds and 8.5% with those over the age of 18. For cannabis use disorder, the percentages are 3.4% for 12 to 17 year olds and 1.5% for those over 18 (APA, 2013). Keep in mind that even though alcohol and cannabis are two of the substances which are often abused, nearly any substance that results in a "high" can be abused.

Abuse and addiction cause serious health, interpersonal, work, and legal issues. It is estimated that substance abuse costs in the United States alone add up to more than $484 billion dollars per year in lost work, health issues, treatment, and other related costs (Office of National Drug Control Policy (ONDCP), 2001, 2004). Substance abuse can be devastating to not only the individual, but the entire family system. Unfortunately, these disorders frequently go untreated. The Substance Abuse and Mental Health Services Administration (SAMHSA) (2012) found that over 20 million people aged 12 or older needed treatment for a substance use disorder in 2011. Of these, only about 2 million reported seeking help from a treatment facility or mental health professional. This means that over 18 million people who could meet the criteria for addiction did not seek professional help.

Most of us have consumed alcohol or been prescribed a drug for medical purposes. How does use turn into addiction and why is it then considered a mental health disorder? Both physiological and psychological effects contribute to a cycle which can be difficult to break. Severe substance use alters the brain in vital ways, and brain chemistry becomes dysfunctional and unbalanced. Essentially, addicted users do not feel "normal" when not using. Their set point for "normal" is altered, and anything other than the new set point is uncomfortable and aversive. The priority becomes getting and using more of the substance, replacing typical needs and desires. This change leads to the behavioral symptoms that are not only characteristic of substance use disorders, but of other mental health disorders as well.

SUBSTANCE USE DISORDERS

Substance use disorder in the fifth edition of the *Diagnostic and Statistical Manual of Mental Disorders* (APA, 2013) took the place of both substance abuse and substance dependence diagnoses found in the fourth edition of the manual (DSM-IV). Professionals continue to debate the distinction between substance abuse and substance dependence, but, in general, established definitions describe dependence in terms of physiological and behavioral symptoms, while substance ab\use is defined in terms of social and interpersonal consequences. Some mental health professionals also make a distinction between physical addiction, a biologically based need for the substance to feel and function normally, and psychological addiction. Psychological addiction can be seen in terms of continued and increased use of the substance despite significant and consistent negative consequences.

Specific substances are given separate diagnostic codes in the DSM-5, but all are based on the same basic symptom criteria. The DSM-5 categories are alcohol, caffeine, cannabis, hallucinogens, inhalants, opioids, sedatives/hypnotics, stimulants, tobacco, and gambling (the only non-substance category). Keep in mind that with a majority of substance abusers, multiple substances are used.

The symptoms of substance disorders center around the continued use of a substance despite significant negative impact and problems related to that use. These problems include detrimental thoughts, destructive actions, and physiological symptoms, which eventually lead to considerable impairment. The eleven different criteria used are presented in Table 10.1. The DSM-5 allows the diagnosis to specify severity depending on how many symptoms are present. Two or three symptoms suggest mild, four or five symptoms suggest moderate, while six or more indicate a severe substance use disorder. Significant and continued abuse also leads to physical dependence and biological changes in the brain and body.

COMORBIDITY

The National Comorbidity Survey (Kessler, Chiu, Demler, Merikangas, & Walters, 2005) found that over 70% of individuals with a drug use disorder and over 40% of individuals with an alcohol use disorder had a least one additional mental health disorder. These co-occurring disorders can have a significant impact on the course of the substance use disorder, treatment planning, and client prognosis. Mood disorders, such as generalized anxiety disorder (GAD) and major depression, are among the most common disorders seen in individuals with substance use disorders (APA, 2013; Kushner, Krueger, Frye, & Peterson, 2008; Quello, Brady, & Sonne, 2005).

CULTURAL CONSIDERATIONS AND POPULATION FACTORS

Society and culture play a role in the type of substances used, access to substances, and attitude toward use and abuse of a substance. Individuals are influenced by availability, the attitudes and patterns of use among family and friends, social media, and cultural norms and values. Even though these cultural differences exist, alcohol and marijuana are the most widely used and abused drugs worldwide by a fairly wide margin (APA, 2013; Smart & Ogburne, 2000). Males have a higher rate of drinking and related disorders than women, but females who drink heavily

Table 10.1   General Description of DSM Substance Use Disorder Symptoms

1. Using a substance in larger amounts or over a longer period than intended

2. Indicating a desire to cut down or stop using the substance, but unable to

3. Spending a great deal of time getting, using, or recovering from using the substance

4. Experiencing strong cravings or urges to use the substance

5. Not fulfilling work, home, or school obligations because of substance use

6. Continuing use, despite it causing or exacerbating social or interpersonal problems

7. Giving up important social, career, or recreational activities because of substance use

8. Continuing use of substance in physically hazardous situations

9. Continuing use despite physical or psychological problem that can be caused or made worse by the substance

10. Needing more of the substance to get the same effect (tolerance)

11. Experiencing withdrawal symptoms, which can be relieved by taking more of the substance

may be more susceptible to physical consequences like liver disease. Socioeconomic level may also play a role in the type of drug used or usage patterns.

Some studies indicated that there are higher rates of alcohol and drug use among gay adolescents in urban areas (Rotherman-Borus, Hunter, & Rosario, 1994), but other studies show comparable rates to adolescents in general (Herdt & Boxer, 1993). In a 1997 multiethnic study of lesbian, gay, bisexual (LGB) adolescents, 93% of females and 90% of males self-reported substance use, with alcohol and marijuana use listed as the most popular (Rosario, Hunter & Gwadz, 1997). While LGB adolescents engage in substance use for the same normative reasons that many adolescents do (experimenting, asserting independence, or as a "social lubricant"), LGB young people may experience more social isolation, prejudice, and discrimination. Alcohol and drug use may be a way to deal with stigma and shame, to repress same-sex attractions, or to deal with bullying or violence (Zubernis, Synder, & McCoy, 2011).

The DSM-5 contains several changes regarding diagnosis. Specifically, drug cravings have been added to the list of symptoms, while problems with law enforcement have been eliminated because of cultural considerations that make the criteria difficult to apply globally (APA, 2013).

ETIOLOGY AND RISK FACTORS

Activation of the brain's reward system is the key to development of a substance use disorder; the rewarding feeling that people experience as a result of taking drugs may be so profound that they neglect other normal activities in favor of taking the substance. While the chemical mechanism for each class of drug may be somewhat different, the activation of the reward system is similar across substances in producing feelings of pleasure or euphoria, which is often referred to as a "high" (APA, 2013). With addictive disorders, it can be difficult to distinguish between causal and risk factors. How and why some users

develop severe addiction can be viewed from a physiological perspective (sometimes called the medical or disease model) or from a psychosocial perspective. Risk factors, on the other hand, might best be understood from a developmental approach. First, we'll consider some popular causal models of addiction, followed by a discussion of risk factors.

The medical or disease model focuses on the chemical changes that take place with substance use, and holds that addiction results mainly from biologic, genetic, and to a lesser extent, psychological mechanisms. Addictive substances contain psychoactive chemicals that disturb the normal processes of the brain and nervous system. These act by mimicking chemical messengers already present in the brain or by overloading the brain's pleasure center. For example, marijuana and heroin have analogous chemical structures to neurotransmitters naturally produced by the brain. These drugs mislead the body into activating nerve cells that would not have been activated otherwise. Cocaine and amphetamines trigger the brain to release abnormally large amounts of neurotransmitters like dopamine, or prevent neurotransmitter breakdown (Brick & Erickson, 2012). Over time, the brain adjusts to these large increases in dopamine by producing less dopamine or by reducing the number of dopamine receptors. This results in the crash many addicts describe when they are "coming down" from a high. The addict then needs more and more of the substance to achieve a "high" or to even achieve a feeling of normalcy (Brick & Erickson, 2012).

Psychosocial explanations of addiction focus more on interpersonal and intrapersonal and environmental variables. Some researchers like Thomas Szasz (2010) argue that addiction cannot be a "disease" because drug taking is a choice and a conscious decision. This theory is called the "free will" model and posits that physiology alone cannot determine whether someone will take a substance or eventually be addicted to a substance. Another view, called the "pleasure principle" model, theorized that substance use is a learned response aimed at increasing pleasure and avoiding discomfort (Bejerot, 1972).

The belief is that this striving for pleasure is an innate human characteristic and substance use is a learned behavioral expression of this natural drive.

The experimental model (Peele & Brodsky, 1992) focuses on environmental factors, such as peer influence, availability, perceived importance, and social outcomes. This model defines an addiction as more temporal and contextual than the disease model.

Experts in the field of addictions also recognize that cultural beliefs may have a large influence on certain addictions. For example, in many Middle Eastern countries the prevalence of alcohol addiction is almost nonexistent—alcohol is illegal and looked down on culturally.

The most controversial of these psychosocial models of addiction is the "moral model," which holds that addiction stems from some personal flaw or character defect. It posits that addiction can be linked to personality flaws or personal weaknesses, and is not due to biological causes or a genetic predisposition. The moral model is not commonly applied in mental health settings, but it is important for counselors to be aware that some people, including their client's family members, may hold these views.

When counselors are exploring client history or presentation for risk factors, psychological or physiological dependence can be viewed as a developmental process. As stated previously, drugs are taken for specific reasons, and at first the outcome(s) of this use are generally positive, which is reinforcing. This experimentation may lead to regular use, then heavy use, and finally lead to dependence. There may be different risk factors associated with the reason behind the initial drug use. Individuals looking for relief from symptoms may have higher rates of anxiety, depression, and environmental stressors. Those looking for a "high" may have risk factors more associated with personality, family values, societal norms, and previous risk taking behaviors.

There are also risk factors that exist depending on where the person falls along this developmental continuum. Factors, such as availability, family and societal values, risk taking behaviors,

and stress level may be stronger in the experimentation stage, while genetic and neurobiological variables may play a larger role with regard to dependence (Erickson, 2007). Although one can argue that all abuse and addiction begin with a conscious choice to use a substance, at some point, brain changes transpire to turn use into a chronic, debilitating illness.

Genetics may play a large part in how this change happens (Erickson, 2007), with some clients rapidly progressing to full-blown addiction and dependence. It is an important component of the case conceptualization process to understand the history and progression of use, as well as family and medical background. When gathering information during the initial stages of counseling, it may be important to discuss these different factors to gain a full understanding of how the substance use started and progressed to its present state. Also, keep in mind that not all people follow the same path toward dependence; some may have a long history with many different substances, while others may have become quickly dependent on one "drug of choice."

It is imperative for counselors, especially as it pertains to case conceptualization, to explore their own views on the root cause and factors that lead to addiction. Although every case is different, it is an important step in addictions treatment to help the client gain understanding into the "hows" and "whys" of their disorder.

TREATMENT INTERVENTIONS

Substance use disorders can be difficult to treat because they are multidimensional, pervasive, and have high comorbidity rates. Effective treatments usually include several components, each focused on a specific aspect or phase of the disorder or its consequences. Depending on severity, most clients require longer term, more intense, or repeated treatments to attain lasting results. No single treatment works for everyone, and a holistic approach is most effective. With that in mind, specific evidence-based practices are recommended.

For clients who are addicted, detoxification is the usual first stage of treatment. However, detoxification alone will not lead to positive long-term outcomes. Typical interventions after detox include medication, motivational interviewing, individual and group counseling, and other behavioral interventions. These are usually followed up with relapse prevention and peer support groups. Each component is important and builds on the work done in the earlier phase(s). Relapse is common with substance use disorders, so clients may require a return to prior treatment components.

The most effective treatment plans address multiple aspects of the client's life, including medical conditions, comorbid mental health disorders, career, and family issues. Continued support in the form of community or family-based support groups is a critical component of relapse prevention. The reasons for the initial substance use need to be addressed and the client has to learn new coping strategies, or the client may turn to substance use again as a coping tool.

SAMHSA established a National Registry of Evidence-Based Programs and Practices (SAMHSA, 2009) that is a tremendous resource for addictions counselors. This online database contains interventions that have been researched and reviewed. Some listed interventions are suggested for certain populations, while others are more general. The general approaches that are particularly applicable to the settings where mental health counselors work are Motivational Interviewing, Motivational Enhancement Therapy, Relapse Prevention Therapy, Twelve-Step Facilitation, and Skill Training. Inpatient therapeutic communities, family-based interventions, twelve-step based treatments, risk management, and medications are also discussed. We summarize some of these approaches in the next section.

Counseling Interventions

Cognitive-behavioral and behavioural approaches have been found by multiple sources to be effective as a stand-alone individual or group therapy, or as a component of a multidimensional approach (Carroll & Onken, 2005; McHugh, Hearon, & Otto, 2010; Miller, 2009). These include motivational, contingency management, and relapse prevention interventions.

Motivational Interventions

As described in some depth in previous chapters, motivational interventions (MI) are based on addressing ambivalence toward change. MI is a person-centered form of counseling that takes a cooperative approach to elicit and strengthen the client's motivation toward change (Miller & Rollnick, 1992). Counselors using this approach are careful to avoid arguments and conflict that can lead to client defensiveness and resistance.

The Case of David

David is a 24-year-old college senior who sought counseling because of his over-reliance on substances, especially marijuana. He is a self-described abuser who takes whatever is available to feel a certain way. He smokes marijuana to "de-stress from a hard day of schoolwork" or in his words "to unplug from it all." David has trouble getting his coursework done; consequently, he steals his roommate's ADHD medication or buys it illegally in order to stay focused on schoolwork. Several times in the past month, his roommate has confronted him about the theft, but David keeps denying it. On the weekends, David often drinks heavily with his friends and frequently experiences blackouts. He has experimented with other drugs as well, usually "whatever someone has to offer."

MI techniques are usually employed in the initial stages of counseling, and help the counselor gain an understanding of the client's own view of the problem(s), gauge the client's desire for change, instil hope, and expand the client's perceptions for the possibilities of positive change.

MI helps counselors tap into clients' intrinsic motivations by exploring and resolving their ambivalence toward stopping their substance use. A rationale for change is created when clients recognize discrepancies between current behavior and what they want out of life. They may have first seen their drug use as a positive or a way to enhance their life, but now they see the damage it has caused and the toll it has taken on their lives.

Some specific motivational interviewing tactics include: avoiding argumentative stance, expressing empathy through reflective listening, pointing out discrepancies between current and desired behaviors, boosting the client's belief that they possess the ability to change, and showing respect and acceptance of others and their feelings. Counselors usually explore discrepancies between what clients say they want and what they are actually doing. Counselors may also engage clients in a cost-benefit analysis of their usage, hoping that clients start to recognize that the scales have shifted sharply to the cost side. Once clients realize that they want to change, MI strategies switch toward exploring strengths, increasing self-efficacy, and client expectancies.

Contingency Management

Contingency Management (CM), sometimes called systematic use of reinforcement, stems from operant learning theory and involves the use of reinforcement following encouragement of abstaining behaviors (Petry, 2011). These reinforcements help supplement the primary gains of abstinence until the positive effects of abstinence can take hold. The hope is that the positive gains of abstinence eventually outweigh the perceived costs. These reinforcements can take many different forms, such as verbal praise, public recognition, the removal of something the client does not want (i.e. removal of probation), or some type of prize.

Examples of some CM interventions in hospital or inpatient systems include behavioral techniques, such as token economies, voucher systems, and level privilege systems. An example of a voucher system could be free movie tickets after a negative drug screening test. CM procedures may use variable, stable, or escalating reinforcement schedules to extinguish unwanted behaviors and increase desired ones. Unfortunately, CM interventions may be limited by financial resources in most clinical settings.

Relapse Prevention

Relapse Prevention (RP) strategies are cognitive-behavioral approaches that focus on the client's internal and external cues for substance use/abuse. The goals of RP are to prevent the occurrence of initial lapses after a commitment to change has been made and to prevent any lapses that do occur from escalating into a full-blown relapse. RP interventions are usually employed in the maintenance phase of treatment (Gorski & Grinstead, 2010).

The counselor's role is to assist clients in recognizing relapse triggers and developing alternative behavioral and cognitive responses. RP focuses on the recognition and prevention of high-risk situations that could trigger substance use (i.e. going to a neighborhood bar; Friday nights; a best friend who still uses) and internal construct triggers (i.e. "I am worthless," "my situation is hopeless"). Common techniques include challenging clients' perceived positive effects of use and providing psychoeducation to help them make a more informed choice in high-risk environments (Carroll et al., 2006).

Residential Treatments

Inpatient residential treatment programs or therapeutic communities can be very effective interventions, particularly for those engaging in treatment for the first time, clients with co-occurring disorders, or clients with high levels of severity. Residential treatment usually refers to highly systematized programs where patients remain "in residence" for periods from 28 days to as much as 12 months. Therapeutic communities rely heavily on group-based interventions and the use of others in recovery as key components to treatment. Clients who are further along in treatment become catalysts for change by influencing other clients' attitudes, perceptions, and behaviors regarding drug use.

Family-Based Therapeutic Interventions

As discussed previously, the client's family system and environment are factors impacting the etiology of substance abuse, but also need to be considered in the treatment of these disorders. Research suggests the effectiveness of family-based interventions, such as behavioral parent training, family skills training, in-home family support, brief family therapy, and family education (Kumpfer, Alvarado, & Whiteside, 2003). There is also evidence that suggests that treatment plans in general are more effective when family-based interventions are included (Kumpfer, Alvarado, & Whiteside, 2003).

One of many examples of such approaches is Family Behavior Therapy (FBT). FBT is a behaviorally based counseling intervention focused on reducing substance use and abuse in adults and youth while at the same time addressing comorbid issues, such as family discord, depression, school and work performance, and behavioral problems. Clients attend therapy sessions with at least one significant other; with adolescents, this is typically a parent or guardian (Donohue et al., 2009).

Twelve-Step Based Interventions

The twelve-step model, initially developed by Alcoholics Anonymous in 1939 and first published in *Alcoholics Anonymous: The Story of How More Than One Hundred Men Have Recovered from Alcoholism* (Wilson & Smith, 2001), defines a course for recovery from addiction, compulsion, or other uncontrolled behaviors. It includes a strong spiritual component and is based on a set of principles, including admitting that addictive behaviors can't be controlled,

---

Table 10.2   The Twelve Steps of Alcoholics Anonymous

1. We admitted we were powerless over alcohol—that our lives had become unmanageable

2. Came to believe that a Power greater than ourselves could restore us to sanity

3. Made a decision to turn our will and our lives over to the care of God as we understood Him

4. Made a searching and fearless moral inventory of ourselves

5. Admitted to God, to ourselves and to another human being the exact nature of our wrongs

6. Were entirely ready to have God remove all these defects of character

7. Humbly asked Him to remove our shortcomings

8. Made a list of all persons we had harmed, and became willing to make amends to them all

9. Made direct amends to such people wherever possible, except when to do so would injure them or others

10. Continued to take personal inventory and when we were wrong promptly admitted it

11. Sought through prayer and meditation to improve our conscious contact with God as we understood Him, praying only for knowledge of His will for us and the power to carry that out

12. Having had a spiritual awakening as the result of these steps, we tried to carry this message to alcoholics and to practice these principles in all our affairs

acknowledging a higher power that is a source of support, examining past behaviors with the help of a sponsor, and making amends for past deeds. Table 10.2 shows all twelve steps that are supposed to be undertaken sequentially (Wilson & Smith, 2001). Once someone has remained sober for a period of time, the expectation is that they will help others who suffer from addictions and joined a twelve-step program.

Although counselors may not be using twelve-step based interventions, it is important to be aware of how these programs function and what each step constitutes. Clients may have been exposed to the twelve-step program during inpatient treatment or may be using it to supplement their treatment and support their recovery.

Risk Management Approaches

Risk management approaches include several treatment modalities that focus on harm reduction and decreasing the impact that drug use has on the individual, family, or the community at large. These programs, often called harm reduction approaches, are used in residential treatment, outpatient treatment, and community-based facilities. The main focus of harm reduction is to reduce the negative impact of substance use, abuse, or dependence in clients' lives. This type of approach can be controversial because the focus is not necessarily on ending the substance use. An example of such an approach would be to provide new clean needles to heroin users to decrease the likelihood of contracting a communicable disease like HIV.

Another example of this approach is Harm Reduction Therapy (HRT). HRT takes into consideration the multifaceted relationship that clients develop with the substances they are using, with a focus on environmental context and impact. HRT treats substance use disorders from not only a personal level, but also from a social and occupational level. What is often controversial in harm reduction approaches is that the goals of interventions can range from continued abstinence to controlled or safer use. Proponents of HRT argue that it is important to acknowledge

that a client's desired treatment goals are based on their motivation to improve their health, relationships, and global level of functioning.

Medications

Medications used in the withdrawal process help lessen physical symptoms during detoxification. Once detoxification takes place, other medications may be prescribed to help reestablish normal brain functioning and help reduce physical cravings. Presently, there are medications which help with cessation of tobacco, opioids, and alcohol use, and emerging ones for stimulants and cannabis. An example of this type of medication is methadone prescribed for heroin addiction. These medications can help clients extinguish drug-seeking behaviors and related criminal behavior and become more receptive to counseling-based interventions. Medications are also prescribed for underlying symptoms of anxiety and depression as discussed in prior chapters.

CASE CONCEPTUALIZATION FOR SUBSTANCE-RELATED DISORDERS USING THE T/C MODEL

Case conceptualization with clients who have substance-related disorders should include a thorough understanding of the client's history of use and the progression of use over time. In addition, family history of substance abuse is relevant, as well as family and cultural beliefs about substance use. Both past and current stressors should also be assessed.

An understanding of why the client began using the substance is critical, including the positive gains of using so that these can later be contrasted with the costs. With regard to Internal Personality Constructs, take into account difficulties with emotional regulation and problems with anxiety and depression which can impact substance use. The client's self-efficacy and readiness for change are also crucial factors to consider. With regard to the client's environment, peer influence and interpersonal relationships are important to assess.

Support systems and resources are vital to the recovery process and to prevent relapse, including family relationships, peers, and spirituality, which is a traditional component of twelve-step approaches to treatment.

Because relapse is a significant concern with any substance related disorder, assessment should also include triggers and environmental cues for use and an understanding of the client's coping skills which can be carried forward.

With these considerations in mind, let's consider another client who enters counseling with symptoms that might be consistent with a Substance-Related Disorder.

The Case of J.J.

J.J. is a 15-year-old male who was born in a large northeastern town, where he still lives with his mother, stepfather, and two younger half-brothers. His father was an alcoholic who was sometimes abusive to J.J. and his mother. J.J.'s father abandoned the family when J.J. was seven. His stepfather, who has two kids from a previous marriage, is a sales rep and is on the road much of the time. His mother brings J.J. in because the school has required counseling—J.J. was caught stealing, was found in possession of marijuana twice, and most recently was caught selling prescription medications to another student. The school counselor refers J.J. to you for more intensive treatment than the school can offer.

Counselor: "Can you tell me what happened and why the school counselor feels you need some help?"

J.J.:   "You mean selling the Ritalin? When I was 9, I was getting in trouble a lot, so my mom took me to the doctor. She said I was out of control. The doctor said I had attention deficit disorder and gave me Ritalin. It helped a little, I guess. I don't know much about it. Now I tell my mom I take it, but really I sell it to other kids at school."

Counselor: "Can you tell me more about the reason you stopped taking it?"

J.J.:   "I stopped because I need the money. My stepdad doesn't give me anything, he wants it all for himself. What else am I gonna do to get money, to keep up with everyone else?"

Counselor: "That sounds pretty difficult. You mentioned using alcohol and smoking weed too. Can you tell me more about that?"

J.J.:   "I started drinking and smoking when I was 12, in 7th grade. I hated 7th grade and going to the junior high, not that my elementary school was any better. All the kids were talking about joining sports or clubs, and I was just trying to steal cigarettes and joints from my mom and stepdad. Now I smoke about a half pack a day, plus a couple of joints too. I have a cup of coffee in the morning before school and that's it. At night, I'll drink 3 or 4 beers. On the weekends is when I really like to get away from it all. I've played around with lots of stuff. You know, trying to see what's out there. I've tried pot, coke, speed, ecstasy, mushrooms. I even shot up heroin once at a party. It's no big deal. When I'm out I like to mix it up, depending on what's going on and who's *around. If I drink too much I black out, I've even OD'd a few times and had to go to the ER. But, hey, it wasn't any big deal or nothing, I lived. I do like speed though. If any drug is my favorite, aside from cigarettes and coffee, it'd be speed."*

Counselor: *"Tell me more about your stepdad and your mom. You said you sometimes get cigarettes and joints from them?"*

J.J.: *"When my stepdad's home he just drinks, smokes weed, and watches TV. It sucks, it always has. When he gets high, he screams at me and my mom and throws stuff around. He drinks all the time, but lately he is out of control, especially when he has his other kids over on the weekends. Mom also drinks and smokes cigarettes like a chimney. We've had the neighbors call the police on our house many times. Watch out when they both get 'tanked.' Boy, the curses really fly. I just get out of the house and go to my girlfriend's when it gets really bad. I hate my house, but I hate leaving my brothers there too. They're just kids, you know?"*

THE CASE OF J.J.

Example of T/C Case Conceptualization Model Outline

(*Areas that require more information)

Presenting Problem: alcohol and multiple substance use, academic problems, legal problems, family conflict, attention deficit disorder diagnosis

Internal Personality Constructs and Behavior:

Self-efficacy: helplessness, dependence on substances to cope

Self-esteem:*

Attitudes/Values/Beliefs:*

Attachment Style: possible insecure attachment due to parental substance use

Biology/Physiology/Heredity: 15-year-old male, mother's alcoholism, father's alcoholism, abusive behavior, difficult temperament, ADD diagnosis, use of multiple substances over a significant period of time, possible dependence

Affect: angry, possibly depressed

Cognition: "some family members do not care for me"; "life is unmanageable"; "I am not like other kids . . . something is wrong with me"; does not like school or feel capable as a student; substance use/abuse not a big deal

Hot Thoughts: desire to "get away from it all," "Parents don't care about me," "I hate my house"

Behavior: alcohol use, multiple substance use, conflict with stepfather, academic challenges

Symptomology: depression, anxiety, substance abuse

Coping Skills and Strengths:*

Readiness for Change: precontemplation stage

Life Roles: role in family system*, older brother, boyfriend, struggling student

Environment:

Relationships: conflict with mother and stepfather, attachment to younger siblings, relationship with girlfriend

Culture: *

Family Norms and Values: substance abuse in household

Societal Influences: influence of friends who are also substance abusers

Timeline:

Past Influences: mother's history of alcohol use, father's abandonment and abuse, diagnosis of ADD

Present Influences: conflict with stepfather and mother, academic difficulties, legal problems

Future Goals: *

Question: What else would you want to ask, to complete this case conceptualization?

COUNSELING KEYSTONES

- Psychoactive substance use is pervasive in many cultures, including the United States. A recent national survey estimated that roughly 9% of Americans over the age of 12 (22 million) used illicit drug(s) in just the last month (SAMHSA, 2012). Researchers find that people generally take drugs to either feel good or feel better.
- Commonly used substances largely affect the motivation and pleasure pathways of the brain and mimic the effects of the brain's neuro-chemicals, including the feelings we have during normal pleasurable experiences, such as eating something that tastes good or falling in love.
- Substance use turns into abuse and addiction in part because severe substance use alters the brain in vital ways and brain chemistry becomes dysfunctional and unbalanced. Essentially, addicted users do not feel "normal" when they are not using.
- Substance use disorder in the DSM-5 takes the place of both substance abuse and substance dependence diagnoses in the DSM-IV.
- Professionals continue to debate the distinction between substance abuse and substance dependence, but in general established definitions describe dependence in terms of physiological and behavioral symptoms, while substance abuse is defined in terms of social and interpersonal consequences.
- The National Comorbidity Survey (Kessler, Chiu, Demler, Merikangas, & Walters, 2005) found that over 70% of individuals with a drug use disorder and over 40% of individuals with an alcohol use disorder had a least one additional mental health disorder.
- Societal and cultural factors play a role in the type, access, and attitude toward use and abuse of a substance. Individuals are influenced by availability, family, friends, social media, and cultural norms and values.
- While the chemical mechanism for each class of drug may be somewhat different, the activation of the reward system is similar across substances by producing feelings of pleasure or euphoria, which is often referred to as a "high."
- The medical or disease model focuses on the chemical changes that take place and holds that addiction results mainly from biologic, genetic, and to a lesser extent, psychological mechanisms.
- Psychosocial explanations of addiction focus more on interpersonal, intrapersonal, and environmental variables.
- It is imperative for counselors, especially as it relates to case conceptualization, to explore their own views on the root cause and factors that lead to addiction. Although every case is different, it is an important step in addictions treatment to help the client gain understanding into the "hows" and "whys" of their disorder.
- SAMHSA established a National Registry of Evidence-Based Programs and Practices (SAMHSA, 2009) that is a tremendous resource for addictions counselors. This online database contains researched and reviewed interventions (see the "Go Further" section below).
- Effective research-based approaches useful in mental health counseling settings include Motivational Interviewing, Motivational Enhancement Therapy, Relapse Prevention Therapy, Twelve-Step Facilitation, and Skill Training.

EXERCISES

EXERCISE 10.1 Drinking and Drugs: Exploring Preconceptions

Everyone has grown up with examples of what it means to be an alcoholic or an addict, forming our ideas with input from media as well as through our experiences with friends and family members.

CLASS EXERCISE: Students spend ten minutes writing down two to three answers to each of the above questions, followed by small group discussion.

Question 1: What messages have you absorbed about the reasons why people become addicted to drugs or alcohol?

Question 2: What are your beliefs about how and why people stop (or don't stop) using?

The Case of Kira

Kira is a 19-year-old university student who was just transported by ambulance to the chemical dependency unit at the local hospital. You are asked to do an assessment on her to see if she needs to be admitted for a drug problem or sent to the psychiatric unit for further observation. You meet with Kira and notice that she is barefoot, wearing vintage-style clothing and jewelry, and her eyes are very dilated. Kira has no previous history of mental health problems and she has no police record.

Kira admits that she does have a long history of drug use. Kira started smoking "pot" daily at age 13. Her weekends were spent doing many different types of hallucinogens, including LSD, ecstasy (XTC), mescaline and "shrooms." She tells you the following story in a rapid pressured pattern of speech.

Kira:	*"My dad was career military. It sucked—we moved like every two years and it made it impossible to make friends, you know?"*
Counselor:	*"Sounds pretty tough."*
Kira:	*"Yeah, and pretty lonely. Then my mom and dad divorced when I was about ten, and that was hard too. I started taking drugs because it made me more interesting, like other people wanted to be around me more."*
Counselor:	*"Did it help with the loneliness too?"*
Kira:	*"It did, I guess. And the boredom. It made both seem better. And I did okay, I got through high school, but I didn't know what I wanted to do next. Then my mom decided to get married again, and told me it was better if I got out and went to college. Like, away to college."*
Counselor:	*"That had to be hard to hear."*
Kira:	*(shrugs) "Whatever. Anyway, a few hours ago I was at the Metallica concert and got to thinking that James—he's the lead singer—it felt like he was talking to me in my head. He told me not to leave the stadium, so I didn't. Everyone else left, my ride left, but I just couldn't."*
Counselor:	*"What happened then?"*
Kira:	*"I don't know. Then I got here somehow. I remember thinking I wouldn't get through and would really lose my mind, especially when my cell phone just started melting in my hand. I felt I had to talk really fast before it melted. I really don't remember much of the concert or anything from this morning. I do remember that I had trouble getting to my feet to walk up the stairs to my seat. I remember we all passed around something and the next thing I knew, I started feeling really restless. I just couldn't sit still."*
Counselor:	*"Can you describe how it felt?"*
Kira:	*"At first, I was high and really got into the people and the whole scene. The scenery was fantastic and I could actually see the sounds—there were waves and triangles dancing in front of my eyes to the music. Then it got scary. I started feeling jumpy, nervous, and sick to my stomach. My heart was racing and I was sweating, even though it wasn't very warm out. Things got blurry and faces started looking mean and ugly. That's when I started hearing James in my head telling me not to leave the stadium. Then I was all alone and everyone was gone and I started calling for help."*

EXERCISE 10.2 Case Conceptualization Practice

CLASS EXERCISE: Small group discussion followed by large group discussion.

Question 1: What is your case conceptualization of this case?

Question 2: What else would you want to know?

Question 3: What would be three possible goals for Kira in counseling?

Question 4: What interventions might you employ given the answers to your first two questions?

Go FURTHER

National Registry of Evidence-Based Programs and Practices by SAMHSA (2009) Government Printing Office. Retrieved from www.nrepp.samhsa.gov/

Principles of drug addiction treatment: A research-based guide (3rd ed.) [NIH Pub Number: 12-4180]. Washington, DC: National Institutes of Health, U.S. Department of Health and Human Services

Evidence-Based Treatments for Alcohol and Drug Abuse: A Practitioner's Guide to Theory, Methods, and Practice by Paul M. G. Emmelkamp and Ellen Vedel (2006) Routledge

Motivational Interviewing: Helping People Change **(3rd ed.)** by William R. Miller and Stephen Rollnick (2012) Guilford Press

The Mindfulness Workbook for Addiction: A Guide to Coping with the Grief, Stress and Anger that Trigger Addictive Behaviors by Rebecca E. Williams and Julie S. Kraft (2012) New Harbinger

Cognitive Therapy of Substance Abuse by Aaron T. Beck, Fred D. Wright, Cory F. Newman, and Bruce S. Liese (2001) Guilford Press

Addiction and Change: How Addictions Develop and Addicted People Recover by Carlo C. DiClemente (2006) Guilford Press

11

PERSONALITY DISORDERS

INTRODUCTION

Personality can be defined as the unique mixture of values, thoughts, feelings, and actions that make up a person's state of being. It shapes the way we view, understand, and relate to the outside world. But, what happens when an individual's understanding of the world diverges from the way that most of us see things? The consequences can be difficult for the person, and troubling for others. When a person's worldview is divergent enough, they may be diagnosed with a personality disorder.

As previously mentioned, what constitutes normal is defined by societal and cultural contexts. This is an important idea to keep in mind when working with clients whose difficulties are personality-based. What is considered functional in some cultures or contexts is defined as pathology in another.

Clinicians and researchers differ in the ways that they understand and treat personality disorders. Some view personality through the lens of trait theory—that personality is pervasive, unchanging, and largely untreatable. A traits-based treatment approach focuses on helping the client develop effective ways to cope with a personality trait which is unlikely to change, and on treating specific symptoms rather than a "personality disorder." Others emphasize the demonstrated effectiveness of empirically supported treatments for certain personality disorders, such as dialectical behavior therapy for the treatment of borderline personality disorder. The interventions included in this chapter assume that some degree of change is indeed possible.

Until the publication of the fifth edition of the *Diagnostic and Statistical Manual of Mental Disorders* (DSM-5), personality disorders were coded in the fourth edition of the manual under the classification Axis II, and listed as separate from the disorders we've discussed so far, which were all coded as Axis I disorders. The fifth edition of the manual discontinued the Axis system and instead, grouped the personality disorders into clusters, with disorders within a cluster sharing some symptoms. Personality disorders are characterized by a chronic inability to accurately perceive reality and relate to others. Individuals with personality disorders have harmful and inflexible ways of thinking and acting, especially in social situations. This rigidity of thinking and acting makes it difficult to deal with the stresses and problems of everyday life. People with personality disorders often have turbulent and destructive relationships with others, leading to chaos in their daily lives.

Estimates vary, but research suggests that about 9 to 14% of the adult U.S. population fit the diagnostic criteria for personality disorders (Grant et al., 2004; Lenzenweger, Lane, Loranger, & Kessler, 2007). The most predominant personality disorders are obsessive compulsive, paranoid, and antisocial. The features of these disorders usually become apparent in adolescence or early adulthood (Lenzenweger, 2008). Certain personality disorder types seem to remit some with age, while others do not (APA, 2013).

Personality disorders can substantially limit a person's ability to have significant and fulfilling relationships, a successful career, or even to feel satisfied in any aspect of life. However, many individuals with personality disorders do not seek treatment, since they often perceive their thoughts and actions as "normal" or resulting from the negative influence of others or environmental forces outside of their control. When they do seek treatment, it is usually because of problems with relationships and work.

There are actually 10 distinct personality disorders documented in the DSM-5, but these are clustered into three groups based on similar characteristics. The symptoms of each cluster and each personality disorder are somewhat different, but there are common themes that run across all of them. People with personality disorders exhibit atypical patterns of thinking, acting, and inner experience that markedly deviate from those accepted by the individual's culture (APA, 2013). These need to be demonstrated in many different situations and settings. These symptoms include frequent mood swings, poor impulse control, mistrust of others, and the need for instant gratification.

Unfortunately, such symptoms lead to difficulty making friends, troubled relationships, and social isolation. In addition, people with a personality disorder often engage in risky or destructive behaviors related to alcohol and other drug abuse, gambling, and sexual activity. People with one identified personality disorder may also have symptoms of at least one additional personality disorder.

Cluster A

Cluster A personality disorders include paranoid, schizoid, and schizotypal. These disorders are typified by odd or eccentric ways of thinking

The Case of Jerry—Paranoid Personality Disorder

Jerry is a 58-year-old man who lives alone in a neighborhood on the outskirts of a large city. He recently lost his job at a local grocery store because of altercations with his direct boss and management. He sought out counseling and other services at his local community health agency, as he's worried about finding another job. Jerry also reports having bad headaches and some difficulty sleeping due to anxiety.

Jerry believes that "the grocery store owners are out to get me" and believes that "rich businessmen" are the root of all ills in this country. He asserts that he lost his job because the "management" did not like his personal views and that they were afraid that he was going to unionize the grocery store and bring about "significant change." He accused his produce manager of hiring his coworkers to spy on him and filing false accusations against him in order for him to lose his job. He says that they altered the camera in the store to only tape him during his shifts and believes that his coworkers have recording devices and are trying to get Jerry to say something negative about the grocery store chain. He states that this has happened at his other jobs as well and believes he can no longer get a job because "the word is out to all the corporations not to hire me." He believes he is on a special "blacklist" that stops him from getting a job.

Jerry depicts himself as a martyr who does not deserve the lot he received in life. He feels that he has always been unjustly accused of some wrongdoing and says that he was labeled as a troublemaker a long time ago in high school. Jerry used to confide in his older brother, John, but has recently become convinced that his brother is trying to influence their parents to change their wills to leave all their money to John. Jerry's parents check on him from time to time, but he worries that they prefer John and he doesn't always believe them when they express concern about him.

Jerry was married in his early twenties, but divorced after five years. He describes his past marriage as dismal and is sure his ex-wife cheated on him numerous times, although she repeatedly insisted that she had not. He believes that he can never trust another woman again and feels isolated and alone.

and acting. Paranoid personality disorder symptoms focus on a pervasive distrust and suspicion of others. The individual believes that others want to do them physical or psychological harm. People diagnosed with paranoid personality disorder have thoughts of extreme suspicion and mistrust of others, perceive hidden meaning in common events or conversation where there is none, and frequently feel like someone is attacking their character or reputation. These thoughts lead to behaviors, such as holding grudges, accusing spouses or significant others of infidelity, and a reluctance to confide in others.

The next personality disorder in Cluster A is schizoid. This diagnosis is characterized by a persistent and pervasive pattern of social isolation and detachment from others, and a pervasive lack of social relationships. Individuals with schizoid personality disorder appear to have an absence of emotion and seem to lack any desire for a close personal relationship. They seem to neither enjoy nor desire social or physical contact with others, and may seem cold and detached from the world. People with schizoid personality disorder seem not to care what others think or say about them and choose instead to lead solitary lives.

The last in this cluster is schizotypal. Its main features include a lack of social relationships and an inability to understand normal social cues. Symptoms can include an absence of emotional expression, odd or magical thinking, and ideas of reference (the belief that everyday events, and people's conversations are referring to oneself when, in fact, they are not). People suffering from this personality disorder appear eccentric and odd and have few if any friends, although they may have some desire for relationships.

Cluster B

Cluster B personality disorders are distinguished by striking and intense cognitions and behaviors that are associated with overly dramatic expressions of emotion. The first of this cluster of disorders is antisocial, which was previously called sociopathic personality disorder. The essential feature of antisocial personality disorder is a persistent disregard for others (APA, 2013). Symptoms include a failure to abide by social norms or legal limits, aggressive and impulsive behaviors, and a lack of remorse over the person's actions. For this diagnosis, the client has to be over the age of 18; younger clients may fit the criteria for conduct disorder. Clients suffering from this disorder often steal, cheat, lie, con others out of money or personal possessions, or use false names. They tend to be irresponsible and have trouble holding down a job or honoring financial or familial obligations. They also have a lack for a concern for their own safety or the safety of others, and thus engage in risky behavior, such as driving fast or dealing drugs.

The Case of Tammy—Borderline Personality Disorder (BPD)

Tammy is a 17-year-old high school senior who was recently released from two weeks of inpatient care following an emergency visit to the hospital. Her parents are seeking outpatient counseling for her. She was admitted to the local emergency room for suicidal ideation and some fairly severe cutting on her arms and legs. Her parents took action after discovering some Instagram pictures Tammy posted of her cuts with captions alluding to suicide. Tammy's boyfriend recently broke up with her, which they believe triggered the suicidal thoughts and behavior. Until the breakup, Tammy had insisted that Paul was "perfect" and that they were "meant to be," even though her parents were worried that he was a bad influence on Tammy.

Tammy's parents report that Tammy is intelligent and was a good student, but recently stopped caring about school or doing homework. They describe Tammy as always having problems with emotional regulation and boundaries, but not to this recent degree. She was always very artistic and expressive and involved in many extracurricular activities. However, when Tammy started high school, she started engaging in increasingly risky behaviors, including experimenting with alcohol and other drugs. Tammy frequently stays out all night or does not come home from school. Her parents describe incidents in the middle of the night when Tammy calls asking them to pick her up miles away in the city or hours away at the beach. If they refuse or tell her it will take some time, she becomes "hysterical," screaming that her parents do not care about or love her and that they never have. Tammy's parents are tired, distressed, and unsure of how to help their daughter. She has been arrested for underage drinking, public nudity, and shoplifting over the past six months.

Tammy's parents also let the counselor know that Tammy was abused by a babysitter when she was quite young. The family does not discuss "the incident" and the parents say they are not sure that she even remembers it. Tammy has a younger brother, Ross, who was diagnosed with Attention Deficit Disorder two years ago. Tammy's parents are taking him to specialists fairly often, as Ross is having serious difficulty in school and socially.

When she meets with the counselor, Tammy explains that she wanted everyone to realize how devastated she was by her boyfriend's recent breakup with her. She says that he is her soulmate and that if she cannot be with him then she does not want to be alive. She tells you that no one understands her and that her friends are just overly concerned. She had a previous therapist who also did not understand her and cannot wait until she can just "do what I want without everyone getting all over me."

The next personality disorder in Cluster B is borderline (BPD). As we see from the case of Tammy, this disorder is evidenced by a pervasive pattern of unstable interpersonal relationships and emotional instability. Clients with BPD have relationships that fluctuate between idealization and devaluation and continually make desperate efforts to avoid real or imagined abandonment (APA, 2013). They also tend to engage in potentially risky behaviors in attempts at emotional regulation, such as substance abuse, disordered eating, sexual activity, and illegal activities like shoplifting.

Suicidal or self-mutilating behaviors are also common, and are often described as an effort to control their emotions, as a way of securing caregiving, or having people not abandon them. They have a very unstable self-image that seems to be predicated on what they perceive others think of them. Clients with borderline personality disorder often have angry outbursts that they have little control over. These outbursts usually stem from their fear of abandonment and a chronic feeling of emptiness.

The next type, Histrionic Personality Disorder (HPD), is characterized by excessive attention seeking behaviors and emotionality. Clients with HPD are upset and uncomfortable when they are not the center of attention or are not admired by others. Their behaviors may come across as sexually provocative, theatrical, dramatic, or inappropriate. They are overly concerned with physical appearance, spending excessive amounts of time and money on how they look, and may do things to stand out, such as vibrant hair color or outlandish dress.

The last in this cluster is Narcissistic Personality Disorder (NPD). Its main features include an inflated sense of self and a need for others' admirations and praise. Individuals with NPD consider themselves superior to and have a diminished regard for other people, often failing to recognize others' feelings. They regularly search for or fantasize about power, success, and desirability, and often exaggerate their accomplishments or talents. Behind this façade of self-importance, however, typically lies self-doubt and a need for adoration.

Cluster C

Cluster C personality disorders are characterized by anxiety, fearfulness, and avoidant behaviors. The first in Cluster C is avoidant personality disorder (AvPD). AvPD is marked by pervasive feelings of shyness, inadequacy, and sensitivity to rejection. People with AvPD are very timid and nervous in social situations and are hypersensitive to criticism. They have tremendously low self-esteem and self-efficacy, and even a minor negative comment is taken in a severely negative way.

Constructive criticism is difficult for someone with avoidant personality disorder to absorb, and often people with this disorder do not engage in activities where they could be judged are evaluated.

Dependent personality disorder (DPD) is an excessive dependence on others for care, safety, and personal needs. Like Linda in the case that follows, people with DPD see others as more able to complete tasks, to accomplish goals, and to deal with the stressors of life than they can. This dependence leads to becoming meek and subordinate to others and, in some cases, to a tolerance for abuse and poor treatment in close relationships. People with DPD also have an extreme need to start another relationship as quickly as possible if the one that they were enmeshed in ends.

Obsessive-compulsive personality disorder (OCPD) is characterized by perfectionism, preoccupation with rules, inflexibility of thought, and a fixation on control. OCPD has many of the same symptoms as obsessive-compulsive disorder (OCD). Clients with OCD, however, describe their intrusive thoughts and compulsions as unwanted, while clients with OCPD do not see their thoughts or behaviors as abnormal. Like individuals with OCD, they may have specific routines and rituals that cause great amounts of anxiety if they are not accomplished or are derailed by normal life intrusions. Clients with OCPD can be high achievers, but their perfectionistic tendencies may also impede their ability to accomplish tasks. They may not be able to engage in situations where they do not have complete control. All of these symptoms can hinder their ability to hold down a job or form close personal relationships. Other symptoms may include an inflexible value system, fanaticism, obsession with trivial details, and an inability to throw things away.

Individuals who are diagnosed with OCPD often have a lack of understanding of how they come across to others and become frustrated if their directions about how to do something are not followed precisely. They do not want other people doing things because they believe it will not get done the right way. They are preoccupied with work or school and "doing well" to the exclusion of leisure time or a personal life.

The Case of Linda—Dependent Personality Disorder

Linda sought counseling following the recent dissolution of her marriage of 24 years. She has been separated from her husband, Jerry, since the holidays and she holds little hope of them reconciling. The breakup devastated Linda. She was so anxious after her husband left that she was unable to sleep or eat, and eventually had to move in with her adult daughter for help. She is very excited to start counseling to get advice from an expert, and pleads with the counselor to "tell me what to do." She has not held a job for two decades and can't imagine a job she would be good at.

Linda describes her husband as "old school and not in a good way." Jerry was verbally abusive at times, but appreciated her ability to "keep a house." She was not allowed to have access to their bank account and has not driven a car in many years. The only times that she was allowed to drive were when Jerry had too much to drink at a party or he needed to be picked up from one of the local bars. Linda rarely left the house during their marriage, unless she needed to go shopping or take the children somewhere. Both of their two children are now adults with children of their own.

Reluctantly, Linda admits that she has started to date one of her daughter's neighbors. Her daughter is not in favor of this, since her neighbor is known to drink too much and is only recently separated himself. When pressed about the relationship, Linda insists that she is no good on her own and just can't manage life by herself.

COMORBIDITY

Personality disorders often occur with or underlie other mental health issues. For example, about 80% of people with borderline personality disorder also meet the diagnostic criteria for another mental illness (Kessler, Chiu, Demler, & Walters, 2005). These comorbid disorders can make it difficult to identify and treat the personality disorder, especially if the symptoms of the disorder overlap. Females are more inclined to have co-occurring depression, anxiety, or eating disorders. Men are more likely to have a co-occurring substance abuse disorder.

CULTURAL CONSIDERATIONS AND POPULATION FACTORS

What constitutes "normal" is of course defined by societal and cultural constructs. Environment plays a large part in how personality is developed.

What is viewed as normal in a specific family system may be viewed as dysfunctional by another or by society at large. Culture and upbringing also play a role in the definition, expectations, and expressions of the self (Alarcon, Foulks, & Vakkur, 1998). Therefore, upbringing, environment, and culture need to be taken into consideration when using these diagnoses.

ETIOLOGY AND RISK FACTORS

Although the exact cause of personality disorders is not fully understood, genetics and childhood experiences seem to play major roles. Researchers believe that there are genetic vulnerabilities to developing a personality disorder. These inherited characteristics are the "nature" component of the "nature versus nurture" discussion. The "nurture" component refers to experiences and the family environment where an individual's personality developed.

The risk factors associated with personality disorders seem to support these theories and to fall into both "nature" and "nurture" categories. These include: experience of trauma, neglect, or extreme chaos in childhood; low socioeconomic status; and a family history of mental illness. The roots of personality disorders often begin in childhood and continue to develop in adolescence. Consequently, a diagnosis of childhood conduct disorder is also a risk factor for developing a subsequent personality disorder (Courtney-Seidler, Klein, & Miller, 2013).

TREATMENT INTERVENTIONS

Personality disorders have a reputation for being difficult to treat. The treatments chosen depend on the client's type and cluster of personality disorder, comorbid disorders, and general level of functioning. Clients may need longer and more substantial treatment than with mood disorders since personality disorders tend to be persistent and debilitating (Bateman & Tyrer, 2004). Because personality disorders tend to be chronic and can sometimes last much of adult life, in many cases a client may see several health professionals, including a psychiatrist, social worker, or marriage and family therapist. Several treatment modalities are used for personality disorders, including medication, counseling, and in some cases partial or inpatient hospitalization.

It is important to keep in mind that many clients seeking treatment do not initially do so for a personality disorder (Crits-Christoph & Barber, 2002). Because of the large number of clients who also have a mood or anxiety disorder, the initial reasons for seeking treatment are usually because of a mood or substance abuse issue (Kessler, Chiu, Demler, & Walters, 2005). Accurate diagnosis is important because research has shown that comorbidity of a personality disorder leads to more difficulty with treatment and less positive outcomes. The research on counseling-based interventions for personality disorders is limited with small sample sizes, complicated treatments, questionable assessment methods, limited focus on a single personality disorder, and confounding variables (Bateman, & Tyrer, 2004). There is, however, some evidence that Cognitive Behavioral Therapy (CBT) and psychodynamic interventions show the best promise (Matusiewicz, Hopwood, Banducci, & Lejuez, 2010).

Counseling Treatments

Counseling treatments for personality disorders usually begin with focusing on symptom relief. The related symptoms of depression and anxiety can be treated by the counseling interventions discussed in those chapters. Along with medication, some symptom relief can usually be achieved (Perry, Banon, & Ianni, 1999). These interventions, however, are not geared toward changing personality constructs. Personality is developed over the course of a person's life, and reconstructing it can take extended treatment and considerable insight and motivation to change. Research suggests that long-term intervention may be needed to treat these more ingrained disorders.

Clients with a personality disorder can be especially challenging to work with since they generally do not see their thinking or behavior to be maladaptive, abnormal, or the cause of their problems. Counselors need to continually tie the client's thoughts and behaviors to the negative consequences they are experiencing. Group and family interventions may also be helpful in confronting harmful behaviors and thought patterns.

Cognitive Behavioral Therapy (CBT)

Cognitive behavioral approaches have been used for years with personality disorders (Beck, Freeman, & Davis, 2004; Linehan, 1993). From a CBT perspective, these disorders develop from irrational thoughts and maladaptive beliefs about the world, self, and others. These thoughts lead to problematic behavior, an inability to regulate emotions, and a lack of coping skills. As we've discussed in previous chapters, the thoughts and behaviors are often reinforced by contextual and environmental factors (Bateman & Fonagy, 2000; Bateman, & Tyrer, 2004; Beck, Freeman, & Davis, 2004).

Researchers have studied the effectiveness of CBT protocols with personality disorders, including such techniques as cognitive restructuring, behavior modification, exposure, psychoeducation, and skills training. CBT for personality disorders also focuses on the role of the client-counselor relationship, which needs to be supportive, collaborative and have well-defined boundaries. CBT is especially suggested for clients with avoidant or dependent personality disorders, since clients with these disorders have irrational thoughts and maladaptive beliefs about their capabilities. More recently, Aaron Beck and his coworkers have successfully extended the cognitive therapy approach to a broader range of personality disorders (Beck & Freedman, 1990).

There are many specific CBT protocols that have been researched for treatment of personality disorders and their associated symptoms, especially self-injury, and parasuicidal behaviors. Some examples of evidence-based practices include Manual-Assisted Cognitive-behavioral Therapy (MACT), Cognitive Analytic Therapy, and Problem-Solving Therapy (PST). The goals of these protocols are to increase self-efficacy, provide training in rational problem solving, decrease impulsivity, and reduce avoidant behaviors (Evans et al., 1999; D'Zurilla & Nezu, 2010).

Dialectical Behavior Therapy (DBT)

DBT is a specific form of cognitive behavioral therapy which blends traditional CBT therapy with aspects of Eastern philosophies. The treatment was originally designed for individuals with borderline personality disorder, or for clients with suicidal and self-injurious behaviors. It has since been applied to a variety of disorders, including depression and substance abuse. One of the main components of DBT is the teaching of important life skills, such as mindfulness, emotion regulation, interpersonal effectiveness, and distress tolerance. Overall, DBT helps people who tend to think and act in extremes to approach their lives

in a more balanced way (Linehan, 2000). DBT also teaches coping skills to help clients tolerate stress, regulate emotions, and improve relationships (Scheel, 2000).

Psychodynamic Approaches

Psychodynamic approaches are less often utilized in treating personality disorders. A psychodynamic approach would focus on increasing the client's awareness of unconscious thoughts and behaviors, gaining understanding of what motivates the client, and the resolution of interpersonal conflicts. For those clients with maladaptive behaviors, expectations, and beliefs (such as narcissistic or obsessive-compulsive personality), psychoanalytic approaches have shown some success (Leichsenring & Leibing, 2003).

Feminist Approaches

Certain personality disorders, borderline personality disorder (BPD) in particular, are characterized by a variety of what can be seen as gender-specific behaviors and attributes, and women are diagnosed with BPD more often than men. Feminist counselors question the way that traditional theories explain BPD, which focus on the client's inability to develop the capacity for self-soothing and emotional regulation. Thus, treatment is based on helping the client develop ways to self-soothe and cope with rage episodes more effectively. However, from a feminist perspective BPD symptoms are viewed as a result of the social construction of what mental health should look like from a male normative perspective, with the symptoms a reaction against the devaluing of interconnectedness and the corresponding overvaluing of independence. A feminist counselor might work with a client with BPD to normalize her valuing of connectedness instead of pathologizing her fear of abandonment, and thus explore both the sociocultural expectations and the individual psychological needs (Wastell, 1996).

From a feminist perspective, Tammy's behavior (whose case we explored earlier in this chapter) might be seen as a defense against forming relationships that work out as a protection from being abused again, and her self-harm as an attempt to be seen and recognized by her overwhelmed parents.

Hospitalization and Residential Treatment Programs

The symptoms and maladaptive behaviors exhibited by clients with a personality disorder can become so severe that they require some form of hospitalization. Psychiatric hospitalization is usually a last resort, but is recommended when the client is in danger of hurting themselves or others, or is unable to care for themselves. Psychiatric hospitalization includes different levels of care—inpatient, partial or day hospitalization, or residential treatment. Day or partial day treatment programs have been found to be effective for personality disorders. This type of program offers intensive treatment, including individual therapy, group therapy, medication management, family-based approaches, and social and occupational therapy (Bateman & Fonagy, 1999).

The length of stay in such treatment facilities varies, but some can last several months and lead to stepped down levels of care, such as a halfway house or outpatient treatment program. Programs can vary in their treatment approaches, so it is important to investigate a specific program before referring a client (de Beaurepaire, Honig, & MacQueen, 2011).

Group Counseling

Group counseling is frequently useful for clients with distorted thoughts about social interactions or avoidant behaviors because it helps them develop social skills. This type of counseling has also been recommended for patients with histrionic and antisocial personality disorders. These clients can benefit from having other group members challenge their acting out behaviors. It is important to note, however, that too many clients with personality disorders can destabilize a group, making it difficult to establish universality and cohesion (Bateman & Tyrer, 2004; Blum et al., 2008).

Family Therapy

Family therapy may be recommended for clients whose symptoms have significantly disrupted their family system. Because there is a large environmental component to personality disorders, family interventions may also be recommended for clients with dysfunctional family symptoms (James & Vereker, 1996).

Medications

The Food and Drug Administration has not approved any medications for the specific treatment of personality disorders. However, several types of psychiatric medications may be helpful with the various associated symptoms. Antidepressants like SSRIs may be beneficial for clients suffering from depression, irritability, and hopelessness. Antianxiety medications can be used with clients suffering from anxiety, sleeplessness, and agitation. Mood stabilizers can aid in leveling out mood swings and reducing irritability. Antipsychotics may be prescribed if a client is having symptoms associated with losing touch with reality. The prescribing doctor will take the client's symptoms into account and consider the applicable cluster specific to their personality disorder when making medication recommendations (Paris, 2011).

CASE CONCEPTUALIZATION OF PERSONALITY DISORDERS USING THE T/C MODEL

When developing a case conceptualization that includes the diagnosis of a personality disorder, keep in mind that what constitutes "normal" is defined by societal and cultural constructs. Careful consideration of cultural and family norms for behavior should be part of the assessment, as environment plays a large part in how personality is developed. What is viewed as normal in a specific family system may be viewed as dysfunctional by another or by society at large.

Culture and upbringing also play a role in the development of identity and sense of self.

Feminist conceptualizations of personality disorders remind us that gender norms also vary, and can influence the definition of appropriate and inappropriate behavior.

In addition, many personality disorders have a cognitive component, with problematic beliefs and distorted thinking getting in the way of optimal functioning.

Let's revisit the case of Jerry, who we met earlier in this chapter.

THE CASE OF JERRY

Example of T/C Case Conceptualization Model Outline

(*Areas that require more information)

Presenting Problem: Job loss, isolation, paranoid thinking, sleep problems

Internal Personality Constructs and Behavior:

Self-efficacy: feels like a martyr, feels ganged up on and helpless to do anything about it

Self-esteem:*

Attitudes/Values/Beliefs: That he does not deserve his lot in life, "personal views" that he feels got him fired*, cannot trust women, parents, coworkers, and family members

Attachment Style: conflicted relationship with parents*

Biology/Physiology/Heredity: 58-year-old male, medical history*, family history*, temperament (negative affect)*, past marriage and divorce*

Affect: anger, anxiety

Cognition: Belief that people are out to get him, spying on him, and saying negative things about him, belief that people cannot be trusted, including his coworkers, ex-wife and family members, he does not deserve what is happening to him

Hot Thoughts: "The grocery store owners are out to get me"; "My coworkers have been spying on me

and filing false accusations against me"; "I can't get a job because word is out not to hire me"

Behavior: work conflict, family conflict, difficulty sleeping, headaches

Symptomology: headaches, difficulty sleeping

*Coping Skills and Strengths:**

Readiness for Change: contemplation stage— ambivalent about change, but willing to consider, hopeless

Life Roles: worker

Environment:

Relationships: conflicted relationship with parents, boss, coworkers, brother, ex-wife*

Culture: family background*

Family Norms and Values: *

Societal Influences: *

Timeline:

Past Influences: early marriage and divorce, history of job conflict and loss, "troublemaker" in high school

Present Influences: unemployment, conflict with parents and brother

Future Goals: job success, reduced conflict with family, reduced isolation

COUNSELING KEYSTONES

- Personality can be defined as the unique mixture of values, thoughts, feelings, and actions that makes up one's state of being. It shapes the way we view, understand, and relate to the outside world.
- Personality disorders are characterized by a chronic inability to accurately perceive reality and relate to others. Individuals with a personality disorder have harmful and inflexible ways of thinking and acting, especially in social situations.
- Personality disorders can substantially limit a person's ability to have significant and fulfilling relationships, a successful career, or feel satisfied in any aspect of life.

- There are ten distinct personality disorders in the DSM-5, but they are clustered into three groups based on similar characteristics.
- The symptoms of each cluster and each personality disorder are somewhat different, but there are common themes and symptoms, including mood swings, poor impulse control, mistrust of others, and the need for instant gratification.
- Cluster A personality disorders include paranoid, schizoid, and schizotypal and are typified by odd or eccentric ways of thinking and acting.
- Cluster B personality disorders include antisocial, histrionic, and borderline and are distinguished by striking and intense cognitions and behaviors that are associated with overly dramatic expressions of emotion.
- Cluster C personality disorders are characterized by anxiety, fearfulness, and avoidant behaviors and include avoidant, dependent, and obsessive-compulsive.
- Personality disorders often co-occur with or underlie other mental health issues.
- The risk factors associated with personality disorders include experience of trauma, neglect, or extreme chaos in childhood, low socioeconomic status, and a family history of mental illness.
- Clients with personality disorders may be difficult to treat and can take significant resources to treat. Clients may need longer and more substantial treatment than with mood disorders since personality disorders tend to be persistent and debilitating.
- It is important to keep in mind that many clients seeking treatment do not initially do so for a personality disorder.
- Counseling treatments for personality disorders usually begin with symptom relief, focusing on the related symptoms of depression and anxiety.

EXERCISES

EXERCISE 11.1
What Is Personality?

The idea of "personality" is integral to how we all see ourselves. But, what is personality?

CLASS EXERCISE: Students work individually, followed by large group discussion.

> **Question 1:** How would you define personality?

> **Question 2:** How does personality develop and what is the balance between nature and nurture influences?

> **Question 3:** How difficult are personality constructs to change?

EXERCISE 11.2
What if people really are trying to persecute your client?

Reality and perceptions of reality can sometimes be hard to distinguish. As counselors, we only have the information that our client gives us to determine what is real and what is not.

CLASS EXERCISE: Students work in small groups to discuss these questions, followed by large group discussion.

> **Question 1:** How would you go about determining whether the client's story is based on fact or caused by paranoid thoughts?

> **Question 2:** When is challenging a client's reality testing beneficial in counseling and when might it not be helpful?

EXERCISE 11.3 Case
Conceptualization Practice

See The Case of Christopher on the next page.

CLASS EXERCISE: Small group discussion followed by large group discussion.

> **Question 1:** What is your case conceptualization of this case?

> **Question 2:** What else would you want to know?

> **Question 3:** What would be three possible goals for Christopher in counseling?

> **Question 4:** What counseling modalities would you want to employ to help Christopher?

The Case of Christopher

Christopher is receiving mandated counseling for a recent DUI charge. He says that he will be an easy client because he really was not drunk and it was all a big misunderstanding. He describes the night of the incident, going into great detail about the five-star restaurants he went to, the model he took on the date, and the BMW 5-series he was driving when he was pulled over, without giving many details about his own drinking.

Christopher is a small business owner/operator and relies on his sales ability and charisma for his livelihood. He went to a private boarding school for high school and a small prestigious liberal arts college for a degree in marketing. He tried to make a career as a stockbroker, but the recent crash, he explains, forced "many a good man out of that business." His parents bankrolled his business franchises, which Christopher describes as complex and demanding.

Christopher: "I just can't find good workers, what can I say? I'm constantly having to fire people and then it's hard to find qualified applicants to replace them."

Counselor: "Can you tell me more about the DUI. The report says that you were over the legal limit."

Christopher: (scoffing) "Look, I'm a great driver—I've driven race cars even. Frankly, I'm a much better driver drunk than most people are sober."

Counselor: "Why do you think the officer pulled you over?"

Christopher: "He was probably just jealous of my car or under his quota for the month. Listen, Mr.—Jones, is it?—I wonder if you could ask the judge to cut the number of mandated sessions back, like maybe in half. I'm sure I could complete them in half the time it takes other people, just like when I went to college."

Counselor: "I'm afraid that's not something I have control over."

Christopher: (frowning) "I really don't see the point of counseling; it's for weak-minded people." (pauses) "Though I have to say, I probably could have used you a long time ago, back in high school . . ."

GO FURTHER

CBT for Personality Disorders by Henck van Bilsen and Brian Thomson (2013) SAGE

Personality Disorders: Toward the DSM-V by William T. O'Donohue, Katherine Alexa Fowler, and Scott O. Lilienfeld (2007) SAGE

Skills Training Manual for Treating Borderline Personality Disorder by Marsha M. Linehan (1993) Guilford Press

The Personality Disorders Treatment Planner by Neil R. Bockian and Arthur E. Jongsma, Jr. (2001) Wiley

Doing Dialectical Behavior Therapy: A Practical Guide (Guides to Individualized Evidence-Based Treatment) by Kelly Koerner (2011) Guilford Press

Treating Personality Disorders in Children and Adolescents: A Relational Approach by Efrain Bleiberg (2004) Guilford Press

12

DISORDERS WITH TYPICAL CHILDHOOD ONSET

INTRODUCTION

You may have an idea of the population you most want to work with as a counselor. Perhaps you're fascinated by adolescents, with their mix of cognitive complexity and emotional volatility. Perhaps you'd rather change professions all together than work with middle schoolers. Some of us are motivated to work with the elderly, a population which is rapidly growing across cultures and in need of experienced counselors to help navigate the changes and challenges of aging; others want to work with children.

In reality, none of us really knows where we will end up, or what population will be our specialized focus. This text is intended to prepare you for working with a wide range of clients, of varying ages, developmental stages, cultures, and presenting problems. In this chapter, we focus on several of the most common disorders occurring in childhood. But, before we begin, ask yourself what might be different when working with this specific population.

Mental health issues commonly diagnosed in childhood or adolescence are divided into two main categories: childhood onset disorders and learning disorders. These disorders are usually first diagnosed in infancy, childhood, or adolescence, and are described in the fifth edition of the *Diagnostic and Statistical Manual of Mental Disorders* (APA, 2013) in several different sections. Here we focus on the disorders that counselors will see and treat most often. This is by no means a suggestion about which issues are more severe; as in other sections of this book, we focused our attention on the presenting problems most likely encountered in counseling settings. These include autism spectrum disorder and attention deficit/hyperactivity disorder, which are found in the Neurodevelopmental Disorders chapter, as well as Oppositional Defiant Disorder and Conduct Disorder, which are found in the Disruptive, Impulse-Control, and Conduct Disorders chapter of the DSM-5.

AUTISM SPECTRUM DISORDER (ASD)

Autism Spectrum Disorder, generally referred to as Autism, encompasses a group of complex and varying neurodevelopmental disorders which can severely impact a child's ability to understand and interact with others and their environment. The use of the term "spectrum" speaks to the wide range of severity and symptoms included under this umbrella term. Prior to the DSM-5, autistic disorder, childhood disintegrative disorder, pervasive developmental disorder-not otherwise specified (PDD-NOS), and Asperger's Syndrome were all distinct diagnostic categories with specified criteria.

The revisions in the DSM-5 reflect current research that identifies social/communication deficits and repetitive/restrictive behaviors as the core features of ASD. Researchers believe that the new diagnostic criteria will result in fewer children being misdiagnosed with autism (Ozonoff, 2012). The DSM-5 also added a new diagnosis of Social (pragmatic) Communication Disorder (SCD). Some clients who do not qualify for an ASD diagnosis may qualify for SCD, which is defined as an impairment of pragmatics. Individuals with SCD have difficulty with the appropriate social use of verbal and nonverbal communication in real-life contexts. For example, there may be impaired ability to change communication styles to match a changed context, difficulty making inferences, or following the rules of conversation. Social relationships and ability to understand social conversation are adversely impacted. A diagnosis of ASD must be ruled out before the diagnosis of SCD is applied.

The new category of ASD in DSM-5 is intended to include DSM-IV diagnoses of Autism, Asperger's Syndrome, and Pervasive Developmental Disorder-Not Otherwise Specified. Although Asperger's syndrome is no longer in the DSM as a diagnosis, some may continue to use the term to refer to those on the mild end of autism spectrum disorder. There is some concern among practitioners that discontinuing the separate diagnosis of Asperger's Syndrome will impact the ability of those individuals at the high functioning end of the spectrum to have access to appropriate services. Other changes in the DSM-5 include the removal of language delay as a criterion for ASD.

In addition, there is a more inclusive age-of-onset criterion so that while symptoms must be present since early childhood, it is recognized that they may not fully manifest until later in life when social demands exceed the capacity of the individual to cope (Lai, Lombardo, Chakabarti, & Baron-Cohen, 2013). Rather than requiring a diagnosis in early childhood, DSM-5 facilitates adult diagnosis by acknowledging that some symptoms may not become apparent until adolescence or adulthood, when social demands increase. There must be symptoms in the early developmental period, but these may not be evident until later when situational demands overtax coping skills. Developmental history, delays, and regression are also taken into account by the DSM-5 criteria.

ASD is characterized by deficits in communication skills and reciprocal communication, repetitive patterns of behavior, and neurological and developmental delays. Although every diagnosis of ASD presents somewhat differently, children suffering from this disorder typically show little interest in making or retaining friendships or initiating social interaction, and can become engrossed with a single object or idea to the exclusion of whatever is going on around them. ASD can also be associated with intellectual disabilities, motor coordination issues, and other health issues (i.e., sleep and gastrointestinal disturbances). On the other hand, some with ASD can excel in such areas as visual skills, music, math, or art.

The number of cases of ASD has increased drastically over the past few decades, with the most current studies reporting that approximately one child in every 88 could potentially fit the diagnosis (Volkmar, Paul, Rogers, & Pelphrey, 2014). More conservative estimates are that prevalence is approaching 1% of the population, both children and adults (American Psychiatric Association, 2013), which makes ASD one of the most common developmental disabilities. It is unclear if the recent rise in reported cases is due to increased awareness, lower thresholds for diagnosis, or a true increase in prevalence. The disorder usually appears quite early, between 12 and 24 months of age (APA, 2013). Depending on the severity, ASD can be a devastating diagnosis for a child and family.

DSM-5 groups the diagnostic criteria for ASD in two general categories: persistent deficits in communication and interaction across multiple contexts, and restrictive and repetitive patterns of behavior.

Deficits in social communication and interaction must not be accounted for by general developmental delays, and are manifested by problems with social-emotional reciprocity; for example, difficulty having a normal back and forth conversation, or in developing or maintaining friendships. This may look like a reduced sharing of interests or emotions, or a failure to initiate social interaction at all. The individual also must have deficits in nonverbal communication, such as abnormal eye contact, facial expressions, or body language. There is also a distinctly abnormal approach to social interaction and difficulty developing and maintaining relationships. The child may display little or no affect, have difficulty engaging in pretend play, or display little interest in interpersonal communication. Unfortunately, these shortfalls result in difficulty making friends, understanding verbal and nonverbal cues, and adjusting behaviors to fit various social situations.

The second diagnostic criteria centers on restrictive, repetitive patterns, interests, behaviors, or activities. Typical behaviors might include repetitive speech, use of objects, or motor movements. Examples include such things as lining up toys by size or repeating a teacher's instructions numerous times. The child may be highly restrictive, rigid, and inflexible, and very resistant to change. Children may insist on having the same thing for lunch every day, or having a specific bathroom or bedtime ritual. Some children may be interested in studying only one subject, or one topic. In addition, individuals with ASD may be either hypersensitive or hyposensitive to sensory input. For example, children may seem indifferent to pain, or have a severe reaction to loud noises or vibrant colors. Alternatively, children may show an unusually strong interest in sensory aspects of their environment that can result in excessive smelling or touching of certain objects or a fascination with objects that are lit or spin.

In the DSM-5, severity and specifiers are also important concepts to keep in mind when considering an ASD diagnosis. The severity scale is designed to be more descriptive of the impact that ASD has on everyday functioning, and refers to the level of care or support the individual is likely to need. Practitioners are hopeful that the

severity scale will help substantiate the need for workplace accommodations and a more supportive workplace environment for individuals diagnosed with ASD.

There are three severity levels: requiring support, requiring substantial support, and requiring very substantial support. An example of level one severity may be a child who is able to communicate in complete sentences, but has trouble engaging in peer communication and back and forth conversation, and has trouble engaging socially with peers. The child may also have rituals and repetitive behaviors that are difficult to interrupt.

Level two is typified by marked deficits in both verbal and nonverbal social communication skills. The child may speak only in simple sentences, have limited and stunted social interaction, and exhibit marked repetitive behaviors that are noticeable to casual observers and interfere with functioning.

Level three is marked by severe communication deficits in verbal and nonverbal communication. The child rarely initiates interaction with peers, and needs substantial help with day-to-day activities. There is marked distress if there is any interference with repetitive behaviors and rituals. Specifiers include: with or without accompanying intellectual impairment; with or without accompanying language impairment; and associated with a known medical or genetic condition or environmental factor.

Social Communication Disorder, in contrast, involves impairment of pragmatics and low communication abilities and social participation, but not the restricted, repetitive patterns of behavior and interests that would result in an ASD diagnosis.

COMORBIDITY

ASD frequently co-occurs with intellectual impairment and language difficulties. A majority of those with ASD will also have another mental health diagnosis (van Steensel, Bögels, & de Bruin, 2013; Volkmar, Paul, Rogers, & Pelphrey, 2014). Specific learning disabilities, eating and sleeping issues, and developmental coordination disorder are common co-occurring disorders (APA, 2013).

There are some overlapping symptoms with ADHD, such as hyperactivity, inattention, and distractibility. A diagnosis of ADHD would be made if those symptoms are above and beyond what you would expect to see with ASD and for that developmental stage. An individual can be diagnosed with both, but only if he or she meets the criteria for both disorders.

Cultural Considerations and Population Factors

Although there may be differences in communication styles and early childhood developmental expectations from culture to culture, those with ASD would be considered out of the norm in any context. The DSM-5 takes into account varying norms for social interaction, and requires that the individual's behavior and communication patterns be out of the norm for that social cultural group. Recognition and diagnosis may be delayed for specific populations, especially those of lower socioeconomic status and those with limited access to adequate health care. This is an important consideration, since early intervention is thought to be a key to treatment.

ASD is four to five times more likely in boys than girls. Again, there is no specific causal link for this discrepancy, although some experts believe that this is due in part to underdiagnosis in females (Volkmar, Paul, Rogers, Pelphrey, 2014). DSM-5 uses identical diagnostic criteria for ASD for males and females, but some researchers believe that gender-specific criteria would be more accurate, and might shed light on potential underdiagnosis of females. Some researchers speculate that the higher incidence in males may be related to fetal testosterone levels and sex differences in brain structure (Baron-Cohen et al., 2011)

An alternative explanation that has been proposed for the male bias is that females, especially those with milder symptoms, may be misdiagnosed with other conditions that also involve the exercise of excessive attempts to control the environment or others, such as Borderline Personality Disorder or Anorexia. Females could also be underdiagnosed if they are more motivated to learn to conform socially (Baron-Cohen et al., 2011).

Etiology and Risk Factors

Although ASD has no identified cause, there are many theories regarding what risk factors are associated with the diagnosis, including low birth rate or premature birth, advanced age of parents, and fetal exposure to carcinogens. Although once popular in mainstream media, the belief that the use of vaccines has a link to ASD has been disproven by many research and meta-analysis studies (Volkmar, Paul, Rogers, & Pelphrey, 2014). Given the wide variance in symptoms and severity, there is most likely a complex etiology that includes genetics, brain development, and environmental factors. Studies are focusing on issues, such as viral infections, complications during pregnancy, and pollutants to see if any of these are contributing factors.

Some children may have a genetic vulnerability that environmental variables can compound. There appear to be several different genes associated with ASD, which may influence brain chemistry and development, throwing off the brain's delicate balance and ability to develop normally. These genes may be inherited or disrupted by trauma or other factors. Many studies have found autistic syndromes, symptoms, or traits in the close relatives of children diagnosed with ASD, including individuals whose personality traits are similar to autistic symptoms (Pickles et al., 2000). A recent study reported that for the 85% of cases of ASD where specific multigenic influences could not be identified, it was found that in approximately one quarter of families affected by autism, multiple family members had either clinical or subclinical autistic traits (Constantino, Zhang, Frazier, Abbachhi, & Law, 2010; Virkud, Todd, Abbacchi, Zhang, & Constantino, 2009).

TREATMENT INTERVENTIONS

Research shows that early intervention is key. This usually involves several educational, compensatory (helping the child use areas of strength to address areas of need), and behavioral interventions (Handleman & Harris, 2000; National Research Council, 2001). These services typically include help with communication, gross and fine motor skills, and social interaction. Children diagnosed with or at high risk for developing ASD may be eligible for services through the Individuals with Disabilities Education Act (IDEA), so it is important to coordinate intervention efforts with other professionals and to help the family look for resources within their community.

Treatment most often focuses on symptom reduction and supporting developmental and communication skills (Sicile-Kira, 2014). Educational interventions concentrate on improving academic and cognitive skills and are intended to be administered in school-based settings. Allied health interventions include therapies typically provided by speech and language, occupational, and physical therapists, and may include auditory and sensory integration, music therapy, and language therapies.

Behavioral interventions focus on minimizing behaviors that interfere with daily functions, such as self-injury or repetitive movements. Counselors are more likely to be involved in teaching children how to act in social situations, developing social skills, and helping the family develop structured environments and coping strategies. Most of these interventions use principles of applied behavioral analysis (ABA), but may vary in specific methods or environmental setting. One example of a studied ABA intervention is Pivotal Response Treatment (PRT). PRT is a play-based intervention that concentrates on "pivotal" areas of childhood development, including self-management, emotional regulation, motivation, and behavioral cues in social interaction. PRT highlights naturally occurring reinforcement and motivational strategies. The belief is that by targeting these important developmental hurdles, the effects of PRT would generalize to other environmental settings (Koegel & Koegel, 2005, 2012). PRT strategies are a core component of an early intervention approach called the Early Start Denver Model, which we discuss below.

The UCLA/Lovaas and the Early Start Denver Model (ESDM) are specific manualized sets of interventions that have gained some popularity and have research supporting their effectiveness (Rogers & Dawson, 2009a,b,c; Rogers, Dawson, & Vismara, 2012). Specific interventions emphasize social skills and include such interventions as social stories, imitation, joint attention training, peer training, and play therapy.

Interventions tend to be intense, comprehensive, and involve many different helping professionals. Some may be delivered in specialized programs or centers, while others are home, agency, or school-based.

ATTENTION DEFICIT/ HYPERACTIVITY DISORDER (ADHD)

Most children will have times when they fidget, have trouble paying attention, or just can't seem to sit still and focus on a task. For children suffering from ADHD, these behaviors can seem constant and out of control. Inattentiveness and hyperactivity interfere with their day-to-day functioning and can have a severe impact on the child's ability to function and thrive in a school environment.

As part of the diagnostic criteria, ADHD begins in childhood. The disorder is most often diagnosed during the early years of schooling, but in some cases is not diagnosed until adolescence or adulthood even though, in retrospect, symptoms began much earlier. It is important to note that research shows that between 30 and 70% of children with ADHD continue to have symptoms of the disorder when they become adults (Kessler et al., 2006). Counselors may have adult clients who have been struggling with ADHD for much of their lives, and may not have received any treatment until adulthood; often the lifelong struggle has a negative effect on self-esteem as individuals may be repeatedly told that they are "stupid" or "lazy."

The Case of Gabby

Gabby is an 8-year-old third grader who is struggling at school. Although she seemed to do fine in school until now, third grade is turning out to be a struggle for her. She misplaces her homework or forgets to complete it at home. She frequently fails to complete her tasks fully or read all of her reading assignments. Gabby's teacher has noticed her inability to focus, difficulty with working in a group, and lack of attention to details. Although she can sometimes work on her own and in small time frames, Gabby gets easily distracted when working with peers; she tends to ramble when she talks and often will go off on tangents when asked a question.

Gabby's teacher reached out to her parents to express her concern over Gabby's behaviors and lack of attention. Her parents first noticed there was an issue in first grade. She seemed disorganized and wasn't able to tell them her homework assignments. They felt as if they had to repeat instructions to her and many times she did not seem to be listening. She never seemed to finish reading any of her books, always moving on to something else before she even got halfway through. Gabby has two older brothers and one younger sister. One of the older brothers has a diagnosis of ADHD.

Gabby says that she likes school and tries very hard, but just can't seem to follow directions or "get it." She likes more active classes, such as gym, art, and music, but struggles with math and English. She has several close friends and loves to talk and play games. She loves dance and is on a traveling soccer team.

ADHD is usually diagnosed before the age of 12 and surveys suggest it affects roughly 5% of children (APA, 2013). Many parents or caregivers first observe the hyperactivity, although it may be hard to distinguish this from normative behaviors of children at a young age. The DSM-5 diagnostic criteria are split into two main areas: the first criterion is marked by persistent patterns of inattentiveness, and the second focuses on hyperactivity and impulsivity.

Inattentiveness and distractibility can manifest in many ways. The child may often make careless mistakes, or may have difficulty readily organizing or accomplishing even simple tasks. Children may have trouble following directions and may not seem to be listening, even when they are spoken to directly. They are often forgetful, lack the ability to follow through on things, such as daily chores and homework, and lose or misplace things easily. All of these issues can combine to make the child reluctant to engage in school fully, especially when asked to perform complicated or time-consuming tasks (which become more prevalent as the child moves up in grades).

The other set of criteria focuses on impulsive behaviors and hyperactivity. Children may often fidget or seem unable to control their bodily movement, sometimes finding things to drum on or making other repetitive movements that may be loud and distracting to other students in the classroom. They tend to interrupt the teacher or other students, and have great difficulty waiting for their turn. They may leave their seat or place in line for no apparent reason, or climb or run in situations where that behavior is not appropriate. Many children with ADHD talk inappropriately in class, again because they are unable to control their impulsivity. Teachers or parents may describe them as "always on the go," "high energy," or "out of control."

COMORBIDITY

Roughly 60% of children diagnosed with ADHD fit the criteria for another mental health disorder (Pliszka, 2011). The most common comorbid diagnoses are mood disorders, such as anxiety and depression, conduct disorder, and language and communication disorders. It is important to note that differential diagnosis is key with ADHD, as its symptoms can present as similar to certain anxiety and mood disorders, such as Generalized Anxiety Disorder (GAD) or Bipolar disorder. Prior to the DSM-5, the diagnosis of ADHD was not made for individuals diagnosed with a disorder on the autistic spectrum. DSM-5 now allows for both disorders to be diagnosed if criteria for both are met.

CULTURAL CONSIDERATIONS AND POPULATION FACTORS

A greater percentage of children from higher socioeconomic levels appear to receive a diagnosis of ADHD. Research found that parents of minority children were less likely to seek treatment and felt that there were substantial issues that prevented their children from being properly diagnosed or receiving effective treatment (Livingston, 1999; Taylor & Leitman, 2003). These barriers included fear of labeling, lack of knowledge regarding mental health issues, fear of misdiagnosis, and language issues (Hervey-Jumper, Douyo, Falcone, & Franco, 2008).

There are also many theories as to why there is a significant discrepancy in diagnosis levels with regard to gender. Girls with ADHD frequently do not exhibit the observable behavior problems that boys do, such as violent outbursts or aggressive behaviors. Instead, girls often exhibit symptoms associated with inattentiveness, and busy teachers may easily miss these more subtle cues (Hinshaw, 2002).

ETIOLOGY AND RISK FACTORS

As with all of the disorders in this chapter, the specific causes of ADHD are not fully known. However, it is clear that there is a strong genetic component and that ADHD appears to be highly heritable; studies show that parents with ADHD have a greater than 50% chance of having a child with the same diagnosis (APA, 2013). Studies also show that children and adults with ADHD tend to have abnormal levels of certain neurotransmitters like dopamine as well as irregular nerve pathways that regulate behavior (APA, 2013). Neurotransmitter levels have been linked to issues, such as attention, learning, movement, sleep, and mood. In many cases, however, there is no hereditary linkage.

There also appear to be common environmental factors that contribute to the likelihood of an ADHD diagnosis. These include smoking, taking drugs, or drinking during pregnancy, premature birth or low birth weight, and birth or early brain injury related medical issues. Additionally, there is some evidence that environmental toxins, such as lead or PCBs, may also be linked to higher risk of developing ADHD.

TREATMENT INTERVENTIONS

Counseling interventions employed for ADHD typically include behavioral, cognitive behavioral, family-based, and relaxation techniques (National Institute of Health, 2008). Most research suggests that medications like stimulants are most effective in treating the primary symptoms of ADHD. Although behavioral techniques when used alone seem to have limited impact on symptomology, they can decrease disruptive behaviors and improve social skills and parent-child relationships (Brown et al.,

2005). Those interventions that include multiple approaches, such as medication, family, school-based, and behavioral techniques appear to have a greater impact than any one intervention alone (Brown et al., 2005). It is important to note that CBT interventions are more often used with adult populations, and appear to be less effective with younger populations (Roman, 2010).

Behavioral Therapy

Behaviorally based treatments focus on training parents, teachers, or other caregivers to implement contingency management programs and reinforcement schedules. Parents generally attend parent training programs where they are given assigned readings and instruction in standard behavioral techniques. Some research shows behavioral interventions to be effective in the treatment of ADHD (Fabiano et al., 2009; Daley et al., 2014). Interventions typically include creating everyday routines, organizational interventions, and behavioral reinforcement. Environmental interventions can include limiting choices, reducing distractions, chunking of assignments, and changing parent and teacher interactional strategies. Typical behavioral interventions revolve around goals and reinforcements, as well as discipline when necessary.

Counselors and school counselors often work with teachers in a consultation model to teach behavioral strategies for application in the classroom. The use of a daily report card system where the child receives tokens or points for certain target behaviors in the classroom is a popular example of a behavioral program for children with ADHD.

Cognitive-Behavioral Interventions

CBT interventions focus on emotional regulation, self-talk and self-instruction, self-monitoring, and problem-solving strategies. As with CBT interventions discussed in previous chapters, the goal of these interventions revolves around teaching self-control, decatastrophizing, and self-reinforcement. Counselors typically try to accomplish these goals through modeling, role playing, and practicing cognitive strategies (cognitive restructuring, thought stopping and thought replacement, scaling, and contingency management) (Szigethy, Weisz, & Findling, 2012). For example, a child may be taught to stop a thought of "I am out of control and everyone is looking at me" and replace it with a more effective emotion-regulating thought like "I can get back on track and I only missed a little of what the teacher said."

The premise is that individuals with ADHD tend to lack internal cues that keep then on task or the ability to take in cues from the environment. It is important to note that cognitive behavioral interventions were prevalent in the 1980s and 1990s for ADHD, but the use of CBT with younger populations has waned in the absence of strong research to support its efficacy.

Medication

For those individuals with ADHD, stimulant medications such as Adderall or Ritalin are the best known and most widely used treatments (Greenhill & Ford, 2002). Typically, these stimulant medications are paired with behavioral or cognitive behavioral interventions. Contrary to popular belief, it is important to note that not all children with this diagnosis are given a prescription for stimulants; however, between 70% to 80% of children with ADHD respond positively to these medications, which may help with concentration. But, there is mixed evidence of significant long-term effects on school achievement or behavioral management (Prasad et al., 2013).

OPPOSITIONAL DEFIANT DISORDER (ODD)

Every child can have a bad day, a day where they totally lose control or throw a tantrum in a supermarket because their mom would not buy them their favorite sugary cereal. For some, however, an irritable mood and frequent outbursts are more the rule than the exception. Oppositional defiant disorder (ODD) is characterized by irritability

The Case of Drew

Drew, a 7-year-old first grader, has been sent to the school counselor and principal on numerous occasions. The most recent incident involved an incident of elopement. Drew walked away from the playground and refused to come in after recess was over. After the incident, while in the school counselor's office, Drew refused to talk or even acknowledge that the counselor was present. Drew's teachers have expressed high levels of frustration and feel as though the interventions they have tried so far have had little impact. Drew refuses to be placed in "time-out," and when disciplined makes comments like "I don't care if I can't eat lunch with my friends, I don't like them anyway." His teachers believe that his outbursts and disruptive behaviors are negatively impacting the other children's ability to learn.

Drew argues almost constantly with peers, and is obsessed with catching other students who are not following the rules. He talks almost nonstop while in school, and in less structured environments, such as the bus or recess, his talking increases. He repeatedly ignores the rules his teachers set and the directions they give in class. He does not accept responsibility for anything, and often accuses other students of doing the same thing that earned him a reprimand from the teacher.

Drew's parents were divorced when he was four, and he now lives with his mother and two older brothers. Drew's mom describes him as "out of control" with "no respect for me or his father." When she tries to punish or reprimand him at home, Drew says he does not care about losing TV or computer privileges. His mother says that he is always going into his older brothers' rooms and taking things from them without asking. He hardly ever comes when called and sometimes "runs away" for hours at a time to other houses in the neighbourhood or to the neighborhood playground. He also tries to play one parent against the other with comments like "Dad lets me stay up till nine when I'm at his house, that's why I like him more."

When Drew finally opens up to his school counselor, he quickly becomes loud and overemotional. He says that no one understands him and he does not care about school or getting good grades. He describes his older brothers as bullies and his mother as overbearing and domineering. He says that none of the trouble he gets into at school is his fault, and no one likes him. When asked if there is anything he would like to do differently or change, he replies "Why should I change, it's not my fault!"

and negativity in almost every setting and evidenced by frequent outbursts and verbal tirades. Often, these outbursts are directed at those individuals in authority, such as teachers, caregivers, and parents. At other times, behaviors may be purposeful attempts to annoy peers. Children with ODD are easily offended and described by peers as jealous, vengeful, blaming, unstable, and difficult to be around (Essau, 2014).

It is clear from the above list of symptoms that these children can cause significant distress to family, friends, and school systems. Consequently, children with ODD have difficulty making friends or functioning successfully in a school system, resulting in significant distress for the child as well.

ODD is a comparatively common childhood disorder with prevalence estimated in the

National Comorbidity Survey Replication at between 6% to 10% (APA, 2013; Nock, Kazdin, Hiripi, & Kessler, 2007). ODD is diagnosed more often in boys than in girls, and diagnosed more often in younger children, perhaps to avoid mislabeling what is thought to be normative teenage behavior (Essau, 2014).

To fit the DSM-5 diagnosis for ODD, the child must regularly exhibit four of the following behaviors: arguing with adults, losing temper, actively defying or refusing to comply with rules or requests from authority figures, intentionally behaving in a way that annoys another person, being angry or resentful, being easily annoyed by others, being vengeful or spiteful, and blaming others for their own misbehavior or mistakes. Negativity and defiance are often expressed through obstinacy, resistance to direction, and unwillingness to share or compromise. Examples of defiance may also include constant testing of limits and boundaries, arguing, ignoring, and failing to accept blame or consequences.

The aggression may manifest itself in verbal or physical hostility, though this is usually without the more severe aggression and physicality seen in Conduct Disorder, which is described in the next section. These behaviors need to last at least six months to fit the diagnosis and symptoms must cause significant impairment in social, academic, and occupational functioning. Keep in mind that in almost all cases, the child does not see themselves as out of control or in the wrong, but views their behaviors as appropriate in response to the unreasonable demands that the authority figures put on them.

COMORBIDITY

Studies suggest that roughly 15 to 20% of those diagnosed with ODD also fit the criteria for ADHD. Anxiety (14%) and depressive disorders (9%) are also highly correlated with ODD (Angold, Costello, & Erkanli, 1999). Most children with Conduct Disorder (CD) begin with ODD-like behaviors. Studies indicate that the majority of children with ODD do not develop

CD, but ODD is usually present as a forerunner to childhood-onset CD (APA, 2013).

CULTURAL CONSIDERATIONS AND POPULATION FACTORS

Although present at all economic levels, ODD appears to be overrepresented in lower socioeconomic groups (Loeber, Burke, Lahey, Winters, & Zera, 2000). This may be due to limited access to medical and psychiatric services in younger years, as well as an increased exposure to the risk factors examined below.

In addition, research suggests that children from minority populations who have anxiety or depressive disorders may be misdiagnosed with ODD or CD instead, in part because of stereotypes and biased attributions for behavior. For example, children with affective and anxiety disorders may also exhibit irritability and may refuse to take part in situations perceived as dangerous; as a result, this may be misinterpreted as oppositional behavior (Lau et al., 2004).

ETIOLOGY AND RISK FACTORS

Like most of the disorders discussed in this chapter, research has not found any specific environmental trigger or underlying cause of ODD. Most experts believe that there are many contributing environmental and biological risk factors, including the child's temperament, developmental delays in cognition or communication, lack of or inconsistent parental support and supervision, previous abuse or neglect, and possible brain chemical imbalances. Environmental stressors affecting a child's sense of consistency and security may also play a role in increasing disruptive behaviors. Examples include parental divorce, financial issues, frequent moves or school changes, and child care changes.

ODD may be best understood in the context of a biopsychosocial model, which considers biological risk factors and harmful aspects of the child's environment. Some experts believe that children with ODD seem to lack the cognitive or emotional skills required for executive functions (i.e., problem solving, working memory, task completion) to comply with the requests from authority figures. These deficits undercut the child's capacity to regulate emotion; thus, the child loses his or her temper as well as the ability to cope or problem solve (McKinney & Renk, 2007).

TREATMENT INTERVENTIONS

Counseling treatment usually involves behavioral, cognitive behavioral, or family approaches. Individual counseling interventions usually focus on emotional regulation, healthy expression of feelings, and cognitive restructuring, which helps the child to look at events more realistically.

Behavioral-based intervention emphasizes extinguishing inappropriate behaviors and learning more appropriate and adaptive behaviors. Caregivers and parents are taught reinforcement techniques, and when appropriate, punishment techniques. The hope is that appropriate behaviors eventually become habitual and naturally reinforced by the child's everyday environment.

Family-based interventions focus on parent training, communication, family roles, and behavioral interventions. Parents are taught to implement behavioral contracts, as well as methods for extinguishing unwanted behaviors and reinforcing positive ones. Counselors stress to caregivers the need to be consistent in the use of secondary gain (appropriate rewards) and the importance of the child eventually getting primary gains (naturally occurring rewards from the environment). Again, the hope is that these new appropriate behaviors become more habitual as they get reinforced. For example, if a child is able to stay on task longer in class they may answer a teacher's question correctly. The teacher then gives verbal praise which increases the likelihood of that appropriate behavior continuing.

One specific family intervention, parent-child interaction therapy (PCIT) focuses on parent-child interaction patterns and on improving the parent-child relationship. PCIT is divided into two stages: parent-child relationship development and discipline training. The goals of the first stage are to develop a loving and nurturing parent-child bond through interactive play. The goals of the second stage mainly focus on skill development and behavioral reinforcement. Sessions consist of the therapist coaching parents in behavioral techniques, usually with the help of a one-way mirror and a headset audio device (Bodiford McNeil, Hembree-Kigin, & Anhalt, 2011).

Although medications are not normally used in the treatment of ODD, children with co-occurring disorders, such as ADHD or Generalized Anxiety Disorder (GAD), may be taking some form of medication.

CONDUCT DISORDER (CD)

Any counseling professional will tell you that it is not uncommon for adolescents to test boundaries, break rules, and get in trouble. However, there are some children and adolescents who show consistent patterns of violating others' rights and displaying behaviors that fly in the face of established social norms and the law. Conduct disorder is exemplified by prolonged periods of antisocial behaviors, the breaking of established rules and social norms, and violations of the law. Most often, professionals view conduct disorder as similar, but much more serious than ODD and a possible precursor to antisocial personality disorder (Murphy, Cowan, & Sederer, 2001).

Because of the behaviors associated with this diagnosis, individuals with CD are frequently viewed by peers, adults, and agencies as delinquent, "bad," or "the criminal type." Symptoms vary depending on the severity of the disorder and the age of the child, but fall into four distinct behavioral clusters: destructive, deceitful, aggressive, and violating established rules. Examples of destructive behaviors include arson and vandalism. Aggressive behaviors include bullying, cruelty to animals, physical altercations, and forcing sexual activity. Deceitful behaviors involve lying, cheating, shoplifting, and other criminal activity.

The Case of Ryan

Ryan is a 15-year-old sophomore in high school who has had many "run-ins with the law." The most recent incident involved stealing his mother's credit cards and going on a shopping spree with his friends. His mother called the police and Ryan spent six months in a juvenile detention center and currently has a parole officer. His presenting problems in counseling include issues with probationary restrictions, violent outbursts, alcohol and other drug use/abuse, and feelings of overall anxiety and depression.

As a child, Ryan moved from town to town and school to school. Ryan has four siblings and two stepsiblings. His parents divorced when he was six, and he lives with his mother and three of his siblings. Ryan states that his father is an "angry drunk" and used to hit him when he was younger. His mother was also an alcoholic and drug addict, but seems to be abstaining at this point. Ryan's mom has also been diagnosed with Bipolar Disorder and is taking medication. He was very close to his paternal grandfather, who was killed in a car accident when Ryan was twelve.

Ryan has been suspended from school several times and removed from his most recent school for bullying, marijuana possession, and several fights with fellow classmates. His school record indicates that he has a history of skipping school, failing classes, and having altercations with teachers. He has been arrested on several occasions, once for arson, and twice for disorderly conduct.

Ryan's mom reports that he continually lies about where he is going or what he is doing. After this most recent incident, she no longer wants Ryan living with her and his other siblings. She says that Ryan "has always gotten into things he shouldn't have way earlier then he should have." He started smoking and drinking at a very early age. Mom remembers the first time he got in trouble with the law was when he was ten and stole candy and playing cards from the local grocery store.

Rule breaking examples include skipping school, running away, or engaging in activities not suitable for that age group.

Children with CD have more difficulty in terms of academic struggles, interpersonal relationships, and drug and alcohol use. The legal system is more often involved as well, putting youth at risk for a downward spiral if intervention does not happen (Boesky, 2002).

The lifetime prevalence of CD is estimated to be around 10%. Similar to ODD, more males than females receive the diagnosis (12.0% among males and 7.1% among females). Based on specific research, it is interesting to note, however, that there is a great deal of variance in the presence of specific behavioral criteria from 33% reporting repeatedly staying out at night without parental permission to 0.3% reporting that they forced some kind of sexual activity (Nock, Kazdin, Hiripi, & Kessler, 2006).

COMORBIDITY

Those diagnosed with CD are at a significantly higher risk of meeting the criteria for at least one other disorder, especially substance abuse and impulse control disorders (APA, 2013). Some research suggests that the correlation with ADHD may be as high as 50% (Nock, Kazdin, Hiripi, &

Kessler, 2006). Approximately 30 to 40% of those persons diagnosed with CD will have a co-occurring mood disorder. Most will have academic issues and co-occurring learning disabilities. Because at least 60% will have an additional mental health or learning disability, it is important to have a multidisciplinary approach to treatment, including incorporating medical, educational, community, and mental health services (Essau, 2014).

CULTURAL CONSIDERATIONS AND POPULATION FACTORS

CD is more commonly diagnosed in neighborhoods characterized by social disorganization and high crime rates (Loeber et. al., 2000). The symptoms of the disorder revolve around breaking rules, violating others' rights, and violating social norms. This leaves open the question of who decides which norms and rules are appropriate, how to judge when these norms and rules have been broken, as well as the impact that the environment and poverty play.

As with ODD, children from minority cultures who have anxiety or depressive disorders may be misdiagnosed with CD if their behavior is misattributed to oppositional reasons (Lau et al., 2004).

ETIOLOGY AND RISK FACTORS

Conduct disorder involves an interaction of genetic/biological, environmental, and social influences; there is no single cause of CD. Research suggests genetic and biological influences, since behavioral disorders tend to cluster in families. Some research found that individuals with CD may inherit a lower baseline autonomic nervous system, and may need greater levels of stimulation to feel normal or "alive." This genetic predisposition may account for the higher level of sensation seeking activity associated with this disorder (Davidge et al., 2004; Lahey, Hart, Pliszka, Applegate, & McBurnett, 1993). Children

with CD have a low resting heart rate (Mawson, 2009); this underarousal may result in sensation seeking and engaging in disruptive behaviors in order to get to an optimal arousal state, or it may reduce a sense of guilt or anxiety that inhibits such behaviors in other children (van Goozen, Snoek, Matthys, Rossum, & Engeland, 2004).

Environmental factors include parental mental health issues and substance abuse, chaotic family situations, and childhood abuse and neglect (APA, 2013). Another risk factor appears to be inconsistent parenting styles where the child does not learn the relationship between behaviors and consequences, or is reinforced for tantrums and noncompliance by overwhelmed or uninformed parents. Early childhood temperament patterns, such as irritability and inconsolability, are risk factors as well. Finally, social risk factors include lack of structure, community violence, lack of parental supervision, and dysfunctional family environments.

TREATMENT INTERVENTIONS

Treatment of children with conduct disorder is complex and challenging; depending on the severity of the behaviors, treatment can be provided in a variety of different settings. Adding to the challenge of treatment are the child's uncooperative attitude, and sometimes fear and distrust on the part of the adults. In developing a comprehensive treatment plan, a child and adolescent psychiatrist may use information from the child, family, teachers, community (including the legal system), and other medical specialties to understand the causes of the disorder.

As we've emphasized throughout this book, every client and every situation is different. Individualized treatment plans should be developed to address the particular problems and severity of each child and family situation.

Counseling Interventions

Behavior interventions and counseling are frequently employed to assist the child in appropriately expressing and controlling anger and aggression. Parents are often trained in behavioral management and educational programs as well as ways to cope with the chaos that this disorder can bring to the family structure. Because of the high comorbidity rates, interventions may also include medication as well as typical treatments for the co-occurring disorders. Because of the severity of the symptoms involved, the course of treatment is seldom brief and may include a multidisciplinary approach.

Eyberg, Nelson, and Boggs (2008) identified sixteen evidence-based treatments for disruptive behavior disorders that all include a focus on increasing reinforcement of more prosocial and compliant behaviors, utilizing appropriate punishment for disruptive behaviors, and training parents to be consistent and predictable in their application of reinforcement and punishment. Other factors which impacted the success of these interventions were the parents' willingness to make changes to their own behavior, such as discontinuing substance abuse.

Family-Based Interventions

One popular approach is Parent Management Training (PMT) (Feldman & Kazdin, 1995; Kazdin, 2005). In this highly researched and evidence-based approach, parents are trained in ways to assist their children in problem solving, emotional regulation, and impulse control. PMT interventions focus on maladaptive parent-child interactions mainly involving discipline practices, and rely heavily on principles of operant conditioning. The counselor starts by providing an overview of underlying concepts and instructional sessions that involve social learning principles and behavioral techniques, modeling behaviors for parents, and coaching in implementation of specific conditioning techniques.

Multisystemic Therapy (Henggeler & Lee, 2003) is another evidence-based, integrative, family-based treatment designed to improve psychosocial functioning for children and their families.

Behavioral Family Therapy is another evidence-based approach that has been used for many years with children diagnosed with ODD and CD (Eyberg, Nelson, & Boggs, 2008). Techniques in

Behavioral Family Therapy include shaping, reinforcement, behavioral contingencies, and behavioral contracts. The counseling process involves several steps, including establishing rapport, identifying problematic behaviors, developing goals, choosing rewards/punishments, and finally creating the behavioral contracts. In behavioral family therapy, the family environment, the child's temperament, unproductive behaviors, and negative reinforcement are all addressed in an attempt to modify the family system as well.

Other Treatment Approaches

Group assertiveness training has also been used effectively in school-based groups for middle schoolers (Huey & Rank, 1984).

When CD is severe and persistent, or when the family is unable or unwilling to commit to treatment, children may need an alternative placement to keep either the child or the family safe. As always, the least restrictive setting should be used for the briefest time possible. Therapeutic foster care or respite care may also be an option.

Studies show that multifocused psychosocial interventions that are delivered early in development to at-risk children show the most effectiveness. The importance of prevention and early intervention cannot be overstated (Connor et al., 2006).

The use of medication for CD and ODD has not been well studied, and current research suggests that medication should be used only when evidence-based psychosocial treatments have not worked, and that medication should not be the sole treatment for these disorders (Connor, 2002: Connor et al., 2006). On the other hand, medication may help treat comorbid disorders so that the child can benefit from the psychosocial interventions for CD/ODD.

CASE CONCEPTUALIZATION CONSIDERATIONS USING THE T/C MODEL

The disorders described in this chapter are diverse in terms of etiology and treatment. Keep in mind that environmental stressors may play a substantial role in the development of disruptive behavior disorders, such as parental conflict, divorce, poverty, and unsafe neighborhoods. Additionally, deficits in problem solving, emotion regulation, and coping skills may play a role. Temperament is also a factor; therefore, assessing both environmental, cognitive, and behavioral influences is critical.

Of course, whenever you work with children and adolescents, the role of the family is significant. A thorough assessment of family norms, values, discipline styles, and interaction patterns is a necessary component of the case conceptualization process.

Now that we examined the research and diagnostic categories for the various childhood onset disorders, let's turn to another case example and case conceptualization.

THE CASE OF PHILLIP

Example of T/C Case Conceptualization Model Outline

(*designates issues to further explore)

The Case of Phillip

Phillip is a 12-year-old boy who was recently diagnosed by his family physician with ADHD and prescribed medication. His mother and father came to you for help with Phillip's behaviors at home and school. Phillip's father discloses that he also has a diagnosis of ADHD, and reveals that he sees many of his traits in Phillip. Phillip is very messy and unorganized both at school and at home. Phillip's mom describes him as a "wild child" who does not follow directions. Phillip also has two younger siblings, and his mom describes them all as unable to listen or sit still for more than a few minutes. Mom describes the home environment as "chaotic, where one child just feeds off the other two. We can't sit down to a family meal or watch a movie or have quiet time to read." Dad describes Phillip as "spacy" and "in his own little world."

Phillip's teachers report that he often appears unaware of what is taking place around him. He consistently daydreams, and doesn't respond to peers or to the teachers. When the teacher asks what he is thinking about, he responds "I don't know." Phillip especially has trouble with self-motivation and written tasks. Phillip is extremely unorganized and spends a great deal of time looking for lost homework, pencils, or his lunch. He makes careless mistakes and seems not to be listening when given instructions. When asked to complete any activity that lasts longer than five minutes, he becomes distracted, often distracting others in the process.

Phillip frequently misplaces things, such as his coat or his lunchbox, and has trouble following even simple directions on where to go or what to do. He does not seem to have any close friends, and usually wanders around aimlessly or daydreams during recess or lunch breaks. He has trouble completing assignments on time or according to the directions, and often forgets to bring the right books to school. Phillip is resentful of the extra attention he gets and would like the teachers and aides to just leave him alone.

Phillip prefers to sit in the back of the classroom, and if allowed, would spend as much time as he could doodling in his notebook or staring out the window. While in the counselor's office, Phillip spends most of the initial session swiveling and rolling around in the office chair. The counselor habitually has to repeat questions several times, and mom and dad have to continually prompt Phillip to stay on task.

Presenting Problem: difficulty following directions, inattention, distraction, academic problems

Internal Personality Constructs and Behavior:

Self-Efficacy: low

Self-Esteem: low*

Attitudes/Values/Beliefs: low valuing of education

Attachment Style: Parents are involved and concerned*

Biology/Physiology/Heredity: male, 12 years old, siblings also have attention problems, father has ADHD as well, currently prescribed stimulant medication

Affect: distracted, irritable, possible depression

Cognition: Belief that he should be left alone

Hot Thoughts: "Just leave me alone."

Behavior: loses things, disorganized, "spacy," wanders around aimlessly, unable to sit still, isolated

Symptomology: irritable, distractible, social isolation

Coping Skills and Strengths: few coping skills, supportive parents

Readiness for Change: precontemplation

Life Roles: student, sibling, son

Environment:

Relationships: conflicted relationship with parents, few friends

Culture:

Family Norms and Values: family values organization and quiet

Societal Influences: school and societal value on organization, quiet

Timeline:

Past Influences: past school experience*

Present Influences: depressed mood, difficulty concentrating, conflicted relationship with parents, siblings*

Future Goals: increased concentration in school and at home, academic success, closer friendships, higher self-efficacy, improved relationships with family

COUNSELING KEYSTONES

- Autism spectrum disorder (ASD), generally referred to as autism, encompasses a group of complex and varying neurodevelopmental disorders that can severely impact a child's ability to understand and interact with others and their environment.
- ASD is characterized by deficits in communications skills and reciprocal communication, repetitive patterns of behavior, and neurological and developmental delays.
- The number of cases of ASD has increased drastically over the past few decades, with the most current studies reporting that approximately one child in every 88 could potentially fit the diagnosis.
- DSM-5 groups the diagnostic criteria for ASD in two general categories: persistent deficits in communication and interaction across multiple contexts, and restrictive and repetitive patterns of behavior.
- Although there may be differences in communication styles and early childhood developmental expectations from culture to culture, those with ASD would be considered out of the norm in any context.
- Given the wide variance in symptoms and severity of ASD, there is most likely a complex picture of etiology that includes genetics, brain development, and environmental factors.
- Research on ASD has shown that early intervention is key and usually involves several educational, compensatory (helping the child use areas of strength to address areas of need), and behavioral interventions.
- Attention deficit/hyperactivity disorder (ADHD) is usually diagnosed before the age of 12 and affects roughly 5% of children.
- Diagnostic criteria for ADHD are split into two main areas; the first set of criteria are marked by persistent patterns of inattentiveness,

and the second focuses on hyperactivity and impulsivity.

- Roughly 60% of children diagnosed with ADHD fit the criteria for another mental health disorder, including mood disorders, such as anxiety and depression, conduct disorder, and language and communication disorders.
- Research shows that there is a strong genetic component and that ADHD appears to be highly heritable.
- Counseling interventions employed for ADHD typically include behavioral, cognitive behavioral, family-based, and relaxation techniques.
- Oppositional defiant disorder (ODD) is characterized by irritability and negativity in almost every setting and evidenced by frequent outbursts and verbal tirades.
- To fit the DSM-5 diagnosis for ODD, the child must have regularly exhibited four of the following behaviors: arguing with adults, losing temper, actively defying or refusing to comply with rules or request from authority figures, intentionally behaving in a way that annoys another person, being angry or resentful, being easily annoyed by others, being vengeful or spiteful, and blaming others for their own misbehavior or mistakes.
- Studies suggest that roughly 15% to 20% of those diagnosed with ODD also fit the criteria for ADHD.
- Most experts believe that there are many contributing environmental and biological risk factors to an ODD diagnosis, including the child's temperament, developmental delays in cognition or communication, lack of or inconsistent parental support and supervision, previous abuse or neglect, and possible brain chemical imbalances.
- Conduct disorder (CD) is exemplified by prolonged periods of anti-social behaviors, the breaking of established rules and social norms, and violations of the law.
- Those diagnosed with CD are at a significantly higher risk of meeting the criteria for at least one other disorder, especially substance abuse and impulse-control disorders.
- Counseling interventions employed with ODD and CD are usually behaviorally based and focus on appropriately expressing and controlling anger and aggression.

EXERCISES

EXERCISE 12.1 Making Certain That Language and Communication Styles Are Developmentally Appropriate

CLASS EXERCISE: Small group work followed by large group discussion.

> **Question 1:** Would you change your counseling focus toward certain constructs (i.e. focus more on behavior) when working with children and adolescents? Why or why not?

> **Question 2:** Are there words or phrases that you would typically use with adults that you would not use while working with younger children? Which ones? (Identify 5 to 10)

> **Question 3:** Would you change your nonverbal communication style when working with children? Adolescents? If so, how?

EXERCISE 12.2 Working with Parents, Caregivers, and Home Environments

CLASS EXERCISE: Small group discussion followed by large group discussion.

> **Question 1:** How does working with children change your approach to your role as counselor?

> **Question 2:** How would you work with parents/caregivers? What could be the potential benefits? Potential drawbacks?

> **Question 3:** How is consultation with parents different/similar to the counseling process?

EXERCISE 12.3 Counseling Interventions with Children and Adolescents

CLASS EXERCISE: Individual work followed by large group discussion.

The Case of Bill

Sixteen-year-old Bill was brought to the office by his mother because of several incidents at school. The last incident was so severe that Bill is required to have a mental health evaluation and letter before he is able to return to school. Bill was suspended indefinitely for bringing a weapon to school. Bill has also been suspended in the past for marijuana possession, fighting with peers, assaulting a teacher, and misconduct in a bathroom. Mom reports that Bill leaves the apartment for days at a time, does not listen to anything she says or asks him to do, and has stolen money from her purse. She is "at her wits end," and does not know what to do with him.

Bill says that everything that he does is blown out of proportion. He leaves the house for days at a time after what he calls a "blow out" fight with his mother. Bill's father is incarcerated and he has no recollection of any significant relationship with him. Bill complains that his mother regularly works at night and on the weekends and leaves him in charge of his two younger siblings.

Question 1: In your opinion, what types of interventions might work better with younger children? With adolescents?

Question 2: Using the T/C Case Conceptualization Model, what constructs might you focus on more with children, and which might you emphasize with adolescents? Environment? Cognition? Behaviors? Why or why not?

Question 3: What areas of strength can you focus on when working with children?

EXERCISE 12.4
Case Conceptualization
Practice Using the T/C Model

See The Case of Bill, above.

CLASS EXERCISE: Small group discussion followed by large group discussion.

Question 1: What is your case conceptualization of this case?

Question 2: What else would you want to know?

Question 3: What would be three possible goals for Bill in counseling?

Go Further

Treatment of Autism Spectrum Disorders: Evidence-Based Intervention Strategies for Communication

and Social Interactions edited by Patricia Prelock and Rebecca McCauley (2012) Brookes

Autism Spectrum Disorders: From Theory to Practice by Laura Hall (2012) Pearson

The SAGE Handbook of Emotional and Behavioral Difficulties edited by Philip Garner, James Kauffman, and Julian Elliot (2014) SAGE

Driven to Distraction: Recognizing and Coping with Attention Deficit Disorder by Edward M. Hallowell and John J. Ratey (2011) Anchor

The ADHD Workbook for Kids: Helping Children Gain Self-Confidence, Social Skills, and Self-Control by Lawrence Shapiro (2010) Instant Help

Parenting Children with ADHD: 10 Lessons That Medicine Cannot Teach (APA Lifetools) by Vincent J. Monastra (2005) American Psychological Association

Mastering Your Adult ADHD: A Cognitive-Behavioral Treatment Program Therapist Guide (Treatments That Work) by Steven Safren, Carol Perlman, Susan Sprich, and Michael Otto (2005) Oxford University Press

Oppositional Defiant Disorder and Conduct Disorder in Children by Walter Matthys and John Lochman (2011) Wiley

Conduct and Oppositional Defiant Disorders: Epidemiology, Risk Factors, and Treatment edited by Cecilia A. Essau (2014) Routledge

PART III

CASE CONCEPTUALIZATION AND TREATMENT IN PRACTICE

13

CASE CONCEPTUALIZATION IN PRACTICE

CASE CONCEPTUALIZATION AND THE T/C MODEL

By the time you reach the end of this text, you should possess a thorough understanding of the process of case conceptualization and how to utilize the T/C Model to effectively diagnose and treat the clients who come to you for help. An important component of your professional identity as a counselor is how you conceptualize cases and discern your role in the helping process. The background you gained in understanding the history of the profession and the ways in which the various helping professions are both unique and integrated provides the foundation for a well-defined professional identity as you find your place as a counselor.

As you can see, counseling is both an art and a science. Diagnosis does not lead directly into treatment—it is the case conceptualization process which reminds counselors to consider context. As the T/C Model makes clear, context refers not only to what is getting in the way of a client's optimal development, but also to the strengths and supports that every individual brings to the table. The plan and course of treatment are influenced not only by the symptoms set out in the *Diagnostic and Statistical Manual of Mental Disorders* (DSM), but also by client variables,

such as coping skills, personality characteristics, life experience, and readiness for change. Rather than using the DSM alone, the T/C Model helps shape the questions that you ask and your understanding of the client answers, which results in a more nuanced and sensitive method of assessment; this text and the T/C Model provide the tools you need to gather information, generate hypotheses, and plan treatment strategies that make you an effective counselor.

Accrediting bodies like the Council for Accreditation of Counseling and Related Educational Programs (CACREP) emphasize the need for evidence-based treatment; consequently, this text includes a discussion of recommended treatment methods for the most commonly encountered mental health disorders. Additionally, an understanding of evidence-based treatments is necessary to work effectively with insurance companies, managed care environments, and other regulatory agencies where counselors often work.

GOING FORWARD: THE T/C MODEL IN PRACTICE

Case conceptualization and assessment do not end after the initial sessions and diagnosis; the

T/C Model is also valuable during the treatment phase and beyond, by enabling continuous assessment and evaluation of the effectiveness of interventions. The initial case conceptualization is also very useful when employed as a yardstick once interventions have been implemented, in order to gauge their effectiveness. Although this text does not describe specific assessments, your ability to conceptualize cases gives you an understanding of *what* to assess, and there are effective structured assessments that can also be used for that purpose.

The application of the T/C Model helps you become more intentional in the way you approach case conceptualization and in how to manage case conceptualization so that it flows naturally into intervention strategies and assessment. In addition, the breadth of the model and its structured questions encourage your development as a reflective counselor.

Of course, challenging is an important component of effective counseling, and the T/C Model facilitates this process as well. The clear articulation of the case conceptualization using the T/C Model helps the counselor to see clearly and then to challenge possible distortions in the client's thinking. For example, the T/C Model's use of articulated domains can produce a focus of challenge when the internal personal constructs do not match the environmental data.

Finally, the T/C Model does more than help counselors become more intentional—the model can also serve as a tool for collaboration. The act of sharing the case conceptualization with the client and constructing it collaboratively helps the client to be more intentional in making changes; thus sharing the T/C Model's conceptualization can serve as a mirror for the client, allowing greater insight and facilitating those "aha" moments that move the counseling process forward. Articulating the case conceptualization also provides a way of checking the counselor's understanding, and allows the client to correct the conceptualization, if necessary.

The profession of counselor is both challenging and rewarding. We, as counselors, are privileged to be able to help others become the best that they can be. We are also charged with the ethical responsibility to do our best as we assist our clients, using the most current data and effective tools possible. The T/C Model provides a powerful tool to help you help your clients. The model shapes the questions you ask, serves as a bridge to goals, and allows you and your client to go beyond DSM diagnosis to evaluate strengths and coping strategies. The T/C Model can be a means of collaborating with your client to help them create a holistic and comprehensive understanding of experience and to weave a more integrated self-narrative. Because the model is atheoretical, it provides a consistent vehicle to look at different diagnoses, instead of applying a different case conceptualization model for each. Finally, using the T/C Model encourages you to be a more intentional and reflective counselor, and provides a structured framework for continuous assessment and evaluation.

As you go forward in your career as a counselor, this text and the T/C Model gives you a framework to integrate all of your coursework and field experience into a meaningful counseling approach for diverse populations and settings, and a variety of mental health issues. Based on your training and education as a counselor, and on current theory, practice, and research, your use of the T/C Model distinguishes you as a professional counselor and separates you from the ways that other helping professionals conceptualize cases. We wish you the best as you complete your journey to establishing a practice as a professional counselor.

EXERCISES

EXERCISE 13.1
Working with Clients

CLASS EXERCISE: Individual work followed by large group discussion.

> **Question 1:** As a counselor in training, what blind spots might you have with regard to developing a comprehensive case conceptualization? Are there issues that you may be unwilling to ask about or address?

EXERCISE 13.2
When Clients Are Evasive

Clients may find many ways to evade your questions, either because trust and rapport have not been established or because of the client's defenses.

CLASS EXERCISE: Small group brainstorming, followed by individual discussion.

Question 1: Brainstorm some of the ways that clients might evade answering questions.

Question 2: What are some strategies you could employ to move beyond these roadblocks to gather the information you need to develop an accurate picture of the client's world?

EXERCISE 13.3 Case Conceptualization and Interventions

CLASS EXERCISE: Individual work followed by large group discussion.

Question 1: In the treatment intervention phase, are there specific area of the T/C Model that you would focus on? Why?

Question 2: How do you help the client decide what is in their ability to change and what is outside of their ability to change?

EXERCISE 13.4 Case Conceptualization and Supervision

Many times supervision involves discussing case conceptualization and evaluating treatment outcomes.

CLASS EXERCISE: Large group discussion.

Question 1: How would you use the T/C Model in this process?

EXERCISE 13.5 Going Further

This text is just the start of your professional development. Take some time now to consider the developmental pathway you plan to take as you move forward.

CLASS EXERCISE: Individual work followed by large group discussion.

Question 1: Are there specific populations or settings where you would like to work?

Question 2: What draws you to working with those populations or in those settings?

Question 3: What do you believe you need to do to become more prepared to work with those populations?

EXERCISE 13.5 Final Thoughts

Think back to when you began this course.

CLASS EXERCISE: Individual work followed by large group discussion.

Question 1: What was your understanding of "case conceptualization"?

Question 2: How has your understanding changed after reading this book?

REFERENCES

Abilés, V. V., Rodríguez-Ruiz, S. S., Abilés, J. J., Obispo, A. A., Gandara, N. N., Luna, V. V., & Fernández-Santaella, M. C. (2013). Effectiveness of cognitive-behavioral therapy in morbidity obese candidates for bariatric surgery with and without binge eating disorder. *Nutricion Hospitalaria, 28*(5), 1523–1529.

Abramowitz, J. (1997). Effectiveness of psychological and pharmacological treatments for obsessive-compulsive disorder: A quantitative review. *Journal of Consulting and Clinical Psychology, 65,* 44–52.

Abramowitz, J. (2006). The psychological treatment of obsessive-compulsive disorder. *Canadian Journal of Psychiatry, 51*(7), 407–416.

Abramowitz, J., Deacon, B., & Whiteside, S. (2011). *Exposure therapy for anxiety: Principles and practice.* New York, NY: Guilford Press.

Abramowitz, J., Franklin, M., Schwartz, S., & Furr, J. (2003). Symptom presentation and outcome of cognitive-behavioral therapy for obsessive-compulsive disorder. *Journal of Consulting and Clinical Psychology, 71*(6), 1049–1057.

Alarcon, R., Foulks, E., & Vakkur, M. (1998). *Personality disorders and culture: Clinical and conceptual interactions.* New York, NY: John Wiley.

Alexopoulos, G. S., Raue, P., Kiosses, D. N., Mackin, R. S., Kanellopoulos, D., McCulloch, C., & Areán, P. S. (2011). Problem solving therapy and supportive therapy in older adults with major depression and executive dysfunction: Effect on disability. *Archives of General Psychiatry, 68*(1), 33–41.

Alloy, L. B., Abramson, L. Y., Walshaw, P. D., Gerstein, R. K., Keyser, J. D., Whitehouse, W. G., & Harmon-Jones, E. (2008). Behavioral approach system (BAS)—relevant cognitive styles and bipolar spectrum disorders: Concurrent and prospective associations. *Journal of Abnormal Psychology, 118*(3), 459–471.

Altman, S. E., & Shankman, S. A. (2009). What is the association between obsessive-compulsive disorder and eating disorders? *Clinical Psychology Review, 29,* 638–646.

Altschuler, I. L., Kupka, R.W., Hellemann, G., Frye, M. A., Sugar, C. A., McElroy, S. L., & Suppes, T. (2010). Gender and depressive symptoms in 711 patients with bipolar disorder evaluated prospectively in the Stanley Foundation Bipolar Treatment Outcome Network. *American Journal of Psychiatry, 167*(6), 708–715.

American Counseling Association. (2009). *20/20 statement of principles advances the profession.* Retrieved from http://www.counseling.org

American Counseling Association. (2010). *20/20: A vision for the future of counseling: Background.* Retrieved from http://www.counseling.org

American Counseling Association. (2014). *Code of ethics and standards of practice.* Alexandria, VA: Author.

American Mental Health Counselors Association. (2010). *Code of ethics of the American Health Counselors Association* (2010 rev.). Alexandria, VA: Author.

American Psychiatric Association (APA). (2000). *Diagnostic and statistical manual of mental disorders* (4th ed., text rev.). Washington, DC: Author.

American Psychiatric Association (APA). (2002). *Practice guidelines for the treatment of patients with bipolar disorder* (2nd ed.). Washington, DC: Author, Steering Committee on Practice Guidelines.

American Psychiatric Association. (2013). *Diagnostic and statistical manual of mental disorders* (5th ed.). Arlington, VA: Author.

American Psychological Association. (2013). *Division 12, Society of Clinical Psychology*. Retrieved from http://www.div12.org

Anand, A., Verhoeff, P., Seneca, N., Zoghbi, S. S., Seibyl, J. P., Charney, D. S., & Innis, R. B. (2000). Brain SPECT imaging of amphetamine-induced dopamine release in euthymic bipolar disorder patients. *American Journal of Psychiatry, 157,* 1109–1114.

Anderson, H. (1997). *Conversations, language, and possibilities*. New York, NY: Basic Books.

Angold, A., Costello, E., & Erkanli, A. (1999). Comorbidity. *Journal of Child Psychology & Psychiatry, 40,* 57–87.

Antony, M. (2011). Recent advances in the treatment of anxiety disorders. *Canadian Psychology, 52,* 1–9.

Antony, M., & Stein, M. (Eds.). (2009). *Oxford handbook of anxiety and related disorders*. New York, NY: Oxford University Press.

Arcelus, J., Mitchell, A. J., Wales, J., & Nielsen, S. (2011). Mortality rates in patients with anorexia nervosa and other eating disorders. *Archives of General Psychiatry, 68*(7), 724–731.

Areán, P. A., Raue, P., Mackin, R. S., Kanellopoulos, D., McCulloch, C., & Alexopoulos, G. S. (2010). Problem-solving therapy and supportive therapy in older adults with major depression and executive dysfunction. *American Journal of Psychiatry, 167*(11), 1391–1398.

Arkowitz, H., Westra, H., Miller, W., & Rollnick, S. (2007). *Motivational interviewing and the treatment of psychological problems*. New York, NY: Guilford Press.

Arnold, L. M., McElroy, S. L., Hudson, J. I., Wegele, J. A., Bennet, A. J., & Kreck, P. E. (2002). A placebo-controlled randomized trial of fluoxetine in the treatment of binge-eating disorder. *Journal of Clinical Psychiatry, 63,* 1028–1033.

Arnow, B. A., & Constantino, M. J. (2003). Effectiveness of psychotherapy and combination treatment for chronic depression. *Journal of Clinical Psychology, 59*(8), 893–905.

Arredondo, P., & Perez, P. (2003). Expanding multicultural competence through social justice leadership. *The Counseling Psychologist, 31,* 282–289.

Arredondo, P., & Toporek, R. (2004). Multicultural counseling competencies = ethical practice. *Journal of Mental Health Counseling, 26*(1), 44–55.

Arts, B., Jabben, N., Krabbendam, L., & Van, O. J. (2011). A 2-year naturalistic study on cognitive functioning in bipolar disorder. *Acta Psychiatrica Scandinavica, 123*(3), 190–205.

Aubrey, R. F. (1977). Historical development of guidance and counseling and implications for the future. *Personnel and Guidance Journal, 55,* 288–295.

Austin, S., Nelson, L., Birkett, M., Calzo, J., & Everett, B. (2013). Eating disorder symptoms and obesity at the intersections of gender, ethnicity, and sexual orientation in U.S. high school students. *American Journal of Public Health, 103*(2), 16–22.

Aviram, A., & Westra, H. (2011). The impact of motivational interviewing on resistance in cognitive behavioural therapy for generalized anxiety disorder. *Psychotherapy Research. 21*(6), 698–708.

Baldwin, S. A., Berkeljon, A., Atkins, D. C., Olsen, J. A., & Nielsen, S. L. (2009). Rates of change in naturalistic psychotherapy: Contrasting dose-effect and good-enough level models of change. *Journal of Consulting and Clinical Psychology, 77*(2), 203–211.

Barker, R. (2003). *The social work dictionary* (5th ed.). Washington, DC: NASW Press.

Baron-Cohen, S., Lombardo, M.V., Auyeung, B., Ashwin, E., Chakrabarti, B., & Knickmeyer, R. (2011). Why are autism spectrum conditions more prevalent in males? *PLOS Biology, 9*(6).

Barrett, P., Duffy, A., & Dadds, M. (2001). Cognitive-behavioral treatment of anxiety disorders in children: Long-term (6-year) follow-up. *Journal of Consulting and Clinical Psychology, 69,* 135–141.

Bateman, A., & Fonagy, P. (1999). Effectiveness of partial hospitalization in the treatment of borderline personality disorder: A randomized controlled trial. *American Journal of Psychiatry, 156,* 1563–1569.

Bateman, A., & Fonagy, P. (2000). Effectiveness of psychotherapeutic treatment of personality disorder. *British Journal of Psychiatry, 177,* 138–143.

Bateman, A., & Tyrer, P. (2004). Psychological treatment for personality disorders. *Advances in Psychiatric Treatment, 10,* 378–388.

Bauer, M. S., McBride, L., Williford, W. O., Glick, H., Kinosian, B., Altshuler, L., . . . Sajatovic, M. (2006a). Collaborative care for bipolar disorder: Part I Intervention and implementation in a randomized effectiveness trial. *Psychiatric Services, 57*(7), 927–936.

Bauer, M. S., McBride, L., Williford, W. O., Glick, H., Kinosian, B., Altshuler, L., . . . Sajatovic, M. (2006b). Collaborative care for bipolar disorder: Part II Impact on clinical outcome, function, and costs. *Psychiatric Services, 57,* 937–945.

Beck, A.T. (1976). *Cognitive therapy and the emotional disorders.* New York, NY: International Universities Press.

Beck, A.T., & Freedman, A. (1990). *Cognitive therapy of personality disorders.* New York, NY: Guilford Press.

Beck, A. T., Freeman, A., & Davis, D. (2004). *Cognitive therapy of personality disorders.* New York, NY: Guilford Press.

Beck, A. T., Rush, A. J., Shaw, B. F., & Emery, G. (1979). *Cognitive therapy of depression.* New York, NY: Guilford Press.

Beck, J. (1995). *Cognitive therapy: Basics and beyond.* New York, NY: Guilford Press.

Beck, J. (2011). *Cognitive therapy: Basics and beyond.* New York, NY: Guilford Press.

Beers, C. W. (1908). *A mind that found itself: An autobiography* (2nd ed.). (Original work published 1906). New York, NY: Project Gutenberg.

Beesdo, K., Knappe, S., & Pine, D. (2009). Anxiety and anxiety disorders in children and adolescents: Developmental issues and implications for DSM-V. *Psychiatric Clinics of North America, 32*(3), 483–524.

Beidel D., & Alfano, C. (2011). *Child anxiety disorders: A guide to research and treatment.* (2nd ed.). New York, NY: Routledge Taylor & Frances.

Bejerot, N. (1972). *Addiction: An artificially induced drive.* Springfield, IL: Charles C. Thomas.

Betan, E., & Binder, J. (2010). Clinical expertise in psychotherapy: How expert therapists use theory in generating conceptualizations and interventions. *Journal of Contemporary Psychotherapy, 40,* 141–152.

Birli, J., Zhang, N., & McCoy, V. (2012). Eating disorders among male college students. *VISTAS Online, 4*(101), 1–15. Retrieved from http://www.counseling.org/knowledge-center/vistas

Blum, N., St. John, D., Pfohl, B., Stuart, S., McCormick, B., Allen, J., . . . Black, D. (2008). Systems training for emotional predictability and problem solving (STEPPS) for outpatients with borderline personality disorder: A randomized controlled trial and 1-year follow-up. *American Journal of Psychiatry, 165,* 468–478.

Bodiford McNeil, C., Hembree-Kigin, T., & Anhalt, K. (2011). *Parent-child interaction therapy.* New York, NY: Springer.

Boesky, L. M. (2002). *Juvenile offenders with mental health disorders: Who are they and what do we do with them?* Lanham, MD: American Correctional Association.

Bohlmeijer, E., Smit, F., & Cuijpers, P. (2003). Effects of reminiscence and life-review on late-life depression: A meta-analysis. *International Journal of Geriatric Psychiatry, 18*(12), 1088–1094.

Bolton, J. M., Robinson, J., & Sareen, J. (2009). Self-medication of mood disorders with alcohol and drugs in the National Epidemiologic Survey on Alcohol and Related Conditions. *Journal of Affective Disorders, 115*(3), 365–375.

Bottlender, R., Rudolf, D., Strauss, A., & Moller, H. (2001). Mood-stabilizers reduce the risk of developing antidepressant-induced maniform states in acute treatment of bipolar I depressed patients. *Journal of Affective Disorders, 63*(1-3), 79–83.

Bowden, C. L., Grunze, H., Mullen, J., Brecher, M., Paulsson, B., Jones, . . . Svensson, K. (2005). A randomized, double-blind, placebo-controlled efficacy and safety study of quetiapine or lithium as monotherapy for mania in bipolar disorder. *Journal of Clinical Psychiatry, 66*(1), 111–121.

Bowen, M. (1978). *Family therapy in clinical practice.* Northvale, NJ: Jason Aronson.

Bowers, W., & Ansher, L. (2008). The effectiveness of cognitive behavioral therapy on changing eating disorder symptoms and psychopathy of 32 anorexia nervosa patients at hospital discharge and one year follow-up. *Annals of Clinical Psychiatry, 20,* 79–86.

Bozikas, V. P., Tonia, T., Fokas, K., Karavatos, A., & Kosmidis, M. H. (2006). Impaired emotion processing in remitted patients with bipolar disorder. *Journal of Affective Disorders, 91*(1), 53–56.

Brady, K., Killeen, T., Brewerton, T., & Lucerini, S. (2000). Comorbidity of psychiatric disorders and posttraumatic stress disorder. *Journal of Clinical Psychiatry, 61*(7), 22–32.

Brady, K., Pearlstein, T., Asnis, G., Baker, D., Rothbaum, B., & Sikes, C. (2000). Efficacy and safety of sertraline treatment of posttraumatic stress disorder: A randomized controlled trial. *Journal of the American Medical Association, 283,* 1837–1844.

Breslau, N., Davis, G., Andreski, P., & Peterson, E. (1991). Traumatic events and posttraumatic stress disorder in an urban population of young adults. *Archive of General Psychiatry, 48,* 216–222.

Brewin, C. R., Andrews, B., Rose, S., & Kirk, M. (1999). Acute stress disorder and posttraumatic stress disorder in victims of violent crime. *American Journal of Psychiatry, 156,* 360–366.

Brewin, C. R., Andrews, B., & Valentine, J. (2000). Meta-analysis of risk factors for posttraumatic stress disorder in trauma-exposed adults. *Journal of Consulting Clinical Psychology, 68(5),* 748–766.

Brick, J., & Erickson, C. (2012). *Drugs, the brain, and behavior: The pharmacology of drug use disorders.* New York, NY: Routledge Press.

Brickman, P., Rabinowitz, V., Karuza, J., Coates, D., Cohen, E., & Kidder, L. (1982). Models of helping and coping. *American Psychology, 37,* 368–384.

Bridge, J.A., Iyengar, S., Salary, C.B., Barbe, R.P., Birmaher, B., Pincus, H.A., Ren, L., & Brent, D.A. (2007). Clinical response and risk for reported suicidal ideation and suicide attempts in pediatric antidepressant treatment, a meta-analysis of randomized controlled trials. *Journal of the American Medical Association, 297*(15), 1683–1696.

Briggs-Gowan, M., Carter, A., Clark, R., Augustyn, M., McCarthy, K., & Ford, J. (2010). Exposure to potentially traumatic events in early childhood: Differential links to emergent psychopathology. *Journal of Child Psychology and Psychiatry, 51*(10), 1132–1140.

Bronfenbrenner, U. (1979). *The ecology of human development: Experiments by nature and design.* Cambridge, MA: Harvard University Press.

Brott, P. E., & Myers, J. E. (1999). Development of professional school counselor identity: A grounded theory. *Professional School Counseling, 2,* 339–349.

Brown, R., Amler, R., Freeman, W., Perrin, J., Stein, M., & Feldman, H. (2005). Treatment of attention-deficit/hyperactivity disorder: Overview of the evidence. *Pediatrics, 115,* 749–757.

Brown, T., & Barlow, D. (1992). Comorbidity among anxiety disorders: Implications for treatment and DSM-IV. *Journal of Consulting and Clinical Psychology, 60*(6), 835–844.

Brown, T., Campbell, L., Lehman, C., Grisham, J., & Mancill, R. (2001). Current and lifetime comorbidity of the DSM-IV anxiety disorders in a large clinical sample. *Journal of Abnormal Psychology, 110*(4), 585–599.

Bryant, R. (2011). Acute stress disorder as a predictor of posttraumatic stress disorder: A systematic review. *Journal of Clinical Psychiatry, 72*(2), 233–239.

Bryant, R., Friedman, M., Spiegel, D., Ursano, R., & Strain J. (2011). A review of acute stress disorder in DSM-5. *Depression and Anxiety, 28*(9), 802–817.

Bryant R., Mastrodomenico, J., Felmingham, K., Hopwood, S., Kenny, L., Kandris, E., . . . Creamer, M. (2008). Treatment of acute stress disorder: A randomized controlled trial. *Archives of General Psychiatry, 65*(6), 659–667.

Bryant, R., Sackville, T., Dang, S., Moulds, M., & Guthrie, R. (1999). Treating acute stress disorder: An evaluation of cognitive behavior therapy and supportive counseling techniques. *American Journal of Psychiatry, 156*(11), 1780–1786.

Budd, R., & Hughes, I. (2009). The dodo bird verdict: Controversial, inevitable and important: A commentary on 30 years of meta-analyses. *Clinical Psychology and Psychotherapy, 16,* 510–522.

Buhrke, R. A., & Douce, L. A. (1991). Training issues for counseling psychologists in working with lesbian women and gay men. *The Counseling Psychologist, 19,* 216–234.

Bureau of Labor Statistics. (2013). *Occupational outlook handbook: Mental health counselors and marriage and family therapists* (2012–2013 ed.). Washington, DC: U.S. Department of Labor. Retrieved from http://www.bls.gov/ooh/community-and-social-service/mental-health-counselors-and-marriage-and-family-therapists.htm

Bystritsky, A., Khalsa, S., Cameron, M., & Schiffman, J. (2013). Current diagnosis and treatment of anxiety disorders, pharmacy and therapeutics. *Journal of Pharmacy and Therapeutics, 38*(1), 30–38.

Calabrese, J. R., Hirschfeld, R. M., Frye, M. A., & Reed, M. L. (2004). Impact of depressive symptoms compared with manic symptoms in bipolar disorder: Results of a U.S. community-based sample. *Journal of Clinical Psychiatry, 65*(11), 1499–1504.

Cape, J., Whittington, C., Buszewicz, M., Wallace, P., & Underwood, L. (2010). Brief psychological therapies for anxiety and depression in primary care: Meta-analysis and meta-regression. *BMC Medicine, 8*(38).

Carkhuff, R. R., & Anthony, W. A. (1979). *The skills of helping: An introduction to counseling.* Amherst, MA: Human Resource Development Press.

Carlfred, B., & Broderick, C. B. (1993). *Understanding family process: Basics of family systems theory.* Thousand Oaks, CA: SAGE.

Carroll, K. M., Easton, C. J., Nich, C., Hunkele, K. A., Neavins, T. M., Sinha, R., . . . Rounsaville, B. J. (2006). The use of contingency management and motivational/skills-building therapy to treat young adults with marijuana dependence. *Journal of Consulting and Clinical Psychology, 74,* 955–966.

Carroll, K., & Onken, L. (2005). Behavioral therapies for drug abuse. *The American Journal of Psychiatry, 168*(8), 1452–1460.

Carthy, T., Horesh, N., Apter, A., & Gross, J. (2009). Patterns of emotional reactivity and regulation in children with anxiety disorders. *Journal of Psychopathological Behavior Assessment, 32,* 23–36.

Cash, T., & Smolak, L. (2011). *Body image: A handbook of science, practice and prevention.* New York, NY: Guilford Press.

Cass, V. C. (1979). Homosexual identity formation: A theoretical model. *Journal of Homosexuality, 4,* 219–235.

Cassano, P., & Fava, M. (2002). Depression and public health, an overview. *Journal of Psychosomatic Research, 53,* 849–857.

Castonguay, L. G., & Beutler, L. E. (2006). *Principles of therapeutic change that work.* New York, NY: Oxford University Press.

Castonguay, L. G., Constantino, M. J., McAleavey, A. A., & Goldfried, M. R. (2010). The therapeutic alliance in cognitive-behavioral therapy. In J. C. Muran & J. P. Barber (Eds.), *The therapeutic alliance: An evidence-based approach to practice and training* (pp. 150–171). New York, NY: Guilford Press.

Cath, D., van Grootheest, D., Willemsen, G., van Oppen, P., & Boomsma, D. (2008). Environmental factors in obsessive-compulsive behavior: Evidence from discordant and concordant monozygotic twins. *Behavioral Genetics, 38*(2), 108–120.

Centore, A. J., & Milacci, F. (2008). A study of mental health counselors' use of and perspectives on distance counseling. *Journal of Mental Health Counseling, 30*(3), 267–282.

Chard, K. M. (2005). An evaluation of cognitive processing therapy for the treatment of posttraumatic stress disorder related to childhood sexual abuse. *Journal of Consulting and Clinical Psychology, 73,* 965–971.

Charney, D. (2003). Neuroanatomical circuits modulating fear and anxiety behaviors. *Acta Psychiatrica Scandinavica, 417,* 38–50.

Cherian, A., Math, S., Kandavel, T., & Reddy, Y. (2014). A 5-year prospective follow-up study of patients with obsessive-compulsive disorder treated with serotonin reuptake inhibitors. *Journal of Affective Disorders,* 152–154; 387–394.

Chickering, A., & Reisser, L. (1969). *Education and identity.* San Francisco, CA: Jossey-Bass.

Churchill, R., Hunot, V., Corney, R., Knapp, M., McGuire, H., Tylee, A., & Wessely, S. (2001). A systematic review of controlled trials of the effectiveness and cost-effectiveness of brief psychological treatments for depression. *Health Technology Assessment, 5*(35), 1–173.

Clark, D. M., Fairburn, C. G., & Wessley, S. (2007). Psychological treatment outcomes in routine NHS services: A commentary on Stiles et al. (2007). *Psychological Medicine, 38,* 629–634.

Clarkin, J. F., Glick, I. D., Haas, G. L., Spencer, J. H., Lewis, A. B., Peyser, J., . . . Lestelle, V. (1990). A randomized clinical trial of inpatient family intervention V. results for affective disorders. *Journal of Affective Disorders, 18*(1), 17–28.

Cochran S. V., & Rabinowitz, F. E. (1998). *Men and depression: Clinical and empirical perspectives.* San Diego, CA: Academic Press.

Colangelo, J. L. (2009). The American mental health counselors association: Reflection on 30 historic years. *Journal of Counseling & Development, 87,* 234–240.

Coleman, H. L. K. (1998). General and multicultural counseling competency: Apples and oranges? *Journal of Multicultural Counseling and Development, 26*(3), 147–156.

Collier, D., & Treasure, J. (2004). The aetiology of eating disorders. *The British Journal of Psychiatry, 185*(5), 363–365.

Colom, F., Vieta, E., Martinez-Aran, A., Reinares, M., Goikolea, J. M., Benabarre, A., . . . Corominas, J. (2003). A randomized trial on the efficacy of group psychoeducation in the prophylaxis of recurrences in bipolar patients whose disease is in remission. *Archives of General Psychiatry, 60*(4), 402–407.

Colombo, C., Benedetti, F., Barbini, B., Campori, E., & Smeraldi, E. (1999). Rate of switch from depression into mania after therapeutic sleep deprivation in bipolar depression. *Psychiatry Research, 86,* 267–270.

Comas-Diaz, L. (2006). Cultural variation in the therapeutic relationship. In C. D. Goodheart, A. E. Kazdin, & R. J. Sternberg (Eds.), *Evidence-based psychotherapy: Where practice and research meet* (pp. 81–105). Washington, DC: American Psychological Association.

Connor, D. (2002). *Aggression and antisocial behavior in children and adolescents: Research and treatment.* New York, NY: Guilford Press.

Connor, D., Carlson, G., Chang, K., Daniolos, P., Ferziger, R., Findling, R., . . . Steiner, H. (2006). Juvenile maladaptive aggression: A review of prevention, treatment, and service configuration and a proposed research agenda. *Journal of Clinical Psychiatry, 67*(5), 808–820.

Consoli, A., Bouzamondo, A., Guile, J. M., Lechat, P., & Cohen, D. (2007). Comorbidity with ADHD decreases response to pharmacotherapy in children and adolescents with acute mania: Evidence from a meta-analysis. *Canadian Journal of Psychiatry, 52,* 323–328.

Constantino, J. N., Zhang, Y., Frazier, T., Abbacchi, A. M., & Law, P. (2010). Sibling recurrence and the genetic epidemiology of autism. *American Journal of Psychiatry, 167,* 1349–1356.

Conway, K. P., Compton, W., Stinson, F. S., & Grant, B. F. (2006). Lifetime comorbidity of DSM-IV mood and anxiety disorders and specific drug use disorders: Results from the national epidemiologic survey on alcohol and related conditions. *Journal of Clinical Psychiatry, 67*(2), 247–257.

Corey, G. (2009). *Theory and practice of counseling and psychotherapy.* Belmont, CA: Brooks/Cole.

Cormier, S., & Cormier, B. (1998). *Interviewing strategies for helpers: Fundamental skills and behavioral interventions* (4th ed.). Pacific Grove, CA: Brooks/Cole.

Cosgrove, V. E., Roybal, D., & Chang, K. D. (2013). Bipolar depression in pediatric populations. *Paediatric Drugs, 15*(2), 83–91.

Costin, C. (2006). *Eating disorders sourcebook: A comprehensive guide to the causes, treatments, and prevention of eating disorders.* New York, NY: McGraw Hill.

Council for Accreditation of Counseling and Related Educational Programs (CACREP). (2009). *2009 standards for accreditation.* Alexandria, VA: Author.

Courtney-Seidler, E., Klein, D., & Miller, A. (2013). Borderline personality disorder in adolescents. *Clinical Psychology: Science & Practice, 20*(4), 425–444.

Crago, M., Shisslak, C. M., & Estes, L. S. (1996). Eating disturbances among American minority groups: A review. *International Journal of Eating Disorders, 19,* 239–248.

Crethar, H. C., Torres Rivera, E., & Nash, S. (2008). In search of common threads: Linking multicultural, feminist, and social justice counseling paradigms. *Journal of Counseling and Development, 86,* 269–278.

Crits-Christoph, P., & Barber, J. P. (2002). Psychological treatments for personality disorders. In P. E. Nathan & J. M. Gorman (Eds.), *A guide to treatments that work.* New York, NY: Oxford University Press.

Crits-Christoph, P., Gallop, R., Temes, C. M., Woody, G., Ball, S. A., Martino, S., & Carroll, K. M. (2009). The alliance in motivational enhancement therapy and counseling as usual for substance use problems. *Journal of Consulting and Clinical Psychology, 77,* 1125–1135.

Cuijpers, P., Berking, M., Andersson, G., Quigley, L., Kleiboer, A., & Dobson, K. (2013). A meta-analysis of cognitive behavioural therapy for adult depression, alone and in comparison with other treatments. *Canadian Journal of Psychiatry, 58*(7), 376–385.

Cuijpers, P., Brannmark, J. G., & Van Straten, A. (2008). Psychological treatment of postpartum depression: A meta-analysis. *Journal of Clinical Psychology, 64*(1), 103–118.

Cuijpers, P., Dekker, J., Hollon, S.D., & Andersson, G. (2009). Adding psychotherapy to pharmacotherapy in the treatment of depressive disorders in adults: A meta-analysis. *Journal of Clinical Psychiatry, 70,* 1219–1229.

Cuijpers, P., Driessen, E., Hollon, S. D., van Oppen, P., Barth, J., & Andersson, G. (2012). The efficacy of non-directive supportive psychotherapy for adult depression: A meta-analysis. *Clinical Psychology Review, 32,* 280–291.

Cuijpers, P., van Straten, A., & Smit, F. (2006). Psychological treatment of late-life depression: A meta-analysis of randomized controlled trials. *International Journal of Geriatric Psychiatry, 21,* 1139–1149.

Cuijpers, P., van Straten, A., Warmerdam, L., & Smits, N. (2008). Characteristics of effective psychological treatments of depression: A metaregression analysis. *Psychotherapy Research, 18*(2), 225–236.

Culver, J. L., Arnow, B. A., & Ketter, T. A. (2007). Bipolar disorder: Improving diagnosis and optimizing integrated care. *Journal of Clinical Psychology, 63*(1), 73–92.

Cummings, N. A. (1990). The credentialing of professional psychologists and its implication for the other mental health disciplines. *Journal of Counseling and Development, 87,* 234–240.

Cyranowski, J. M., Frank, E., Young, E., & Shear, M. K. (2000). Adolescent onset of the gender difference in lifetime rates of major depression. *Archives of General Psychiatry, 57,* 21–27.

Daley, A. (2008). Exercise and depression: A review of reviews. *Journal of Clinical Psychology in Medical Settings, 15,* 140–147.

Daley, D., van der Oord, S., Ferrin, M., Danckaerts, M., Doepfner, M., Cortese, S., & Sonuga-Barke, E. (2014). Behavioral interventions in attention-deficit/hyperactivity disorder: A meta-analysis of randomized controlled trials across multiple outcome domains. *Journal of the American Academy of Child & Adolescent Psychiatry, 53*(8), 835–847.

Daniels, L. G. (2002). The relationship between counselor licensure and aspects of empowerment. *Journal of Mental Health Counseling, 24,* 213–223.

Dattilo, F., & Norcross, J. (2006). Psychotherapy integration and the emergence of instinctual territoriality. *Archive of Psychiatry and Psychotherapy, 8*(1), 5–6.

Davidge, K., Atkinson, L., Douglas, L., Lee, V., Shapiro, S., Kennedy, L., & Beitchman, J. (2004). Association of the serotonin transporter and 5HT1D genes with extreme, persistent, and pervasive aggressive behavior in children. *Psychiatric Genetics, 14,* 143–146.

Davidson, J., Rothbaum, B., Van der Kolk, B., Sikes, C., & Farfel, G. (2001). Multicenter double-blind comparison of sertraline and placebo in the treatment of posttraumatic stress disorder. *Archives of General Psychiatry, 58,* 485–492.

Davies, D., Matthews, G., Stammers, R., & Westerman, S. (2013). *Human performance: Cognition, stress and individual differences.* New York, NY: Psychology Press, Taylor and Francis.

Dawis, R. V. (1992). The individual differences tradition in counseling psychology. *Journal of Counseling Psychology, 39,* 7–19.

de Beaurepaire, R., Honig, A., & MacQueen, G. (2011). Effectiveness of outpatient, day hospital, and inpatient psychotherapeutic treatment for patients with cluster B personality disorders. *Current Medical Literature: Psychiatry, 22*(2), 74–75.

de Graaf, R., Bijl, R. V., Ravelli, A., Smit, F., & Vollenbergh, W. (2002). Predictors of first incidence of DSM-III-R psychiatric disorders in the general population: Findings from the Netherlands Mental Health Survey and Incidence Study. *Acta Psychiatrica Scandinavica, 106,* 303–313.

Dell'Osso, B., Buoli, M., Baldwin, D., & Altamura, A., (2010). Serotonin norepinephrine reuptake inhibitors (SNRIs) in anxiety disorders: A comprehensive review of the clinical efficacy. *Human Psychopharmacology, 25,* 17–29.

Delong, P., & Berg, I. K. (2008). *Interviewing for solutions* (3rd ed.). Belmont, CA: Thompson Brooks/Cole.

Demant, K. M., Almer, G. M., Vinberg, M., Kessing, L. V., & Miskowiak, K. W. (2013). Effects of cognitive remediation on cognitive dysfunction in partially or fully remitted patients with bipolar disorder: Study protocol for a randomized controlled trial. *Trials, 14,* 378.

deShazer, S. (1991). *Putting difference to work.* New York, NY: Norton.

deShazer, S., & Dolan, Y. (2007). *More than miracles: The state of the art of solution focused brief therapy.* New York, NY: Haworth Press.

Devane, C. L., Chiao, E., Franklin, M., & Kruep, E. J. (2005). Anxiety disorders in the 21st century: Status, challenges, opportunities, and comorbidity with depression. *American Journal of Managed Care, 12,* S344–353.

Dimeff, L., & Linehan, M. (2001). Dielectical behavior therapy in a nutshell. *The California Psychologist, 34,* 10–14.

Dobson, K. S. (1989). A meta-analysis of the efficacy of cognitive therapy of depression. *Journal of Consulting and Clinical Psychology, 57,* 414–419.

Dobson, K. S., Hollon, S. D., Dimidjian, S., Schmaling, K. B., Kohlenberg, R. J., Gallop, R. J. . . . Jacobson, N. S. (2008). Randomized trial of behavioral activation, cognitive therapy, and antidepressant medication in the prevention of relapse and recurrence in major depression. *Journal of Consulting and Clinical Psychology, 76,* 468–477.

Donohue, B., Azrin, N., Allen, D., Romero, V., Hill, H., Tracy, K., . . . Van Hasselt, V. (2009). Family behavior therapy for substance abuse: A review of its intervention components and applicability. *Behavior Modification, 33,* 495–519.

Duncan, B., Miller, S. D., Hubble, M., & Wampold, B. E. (Eds.). (2010). *The heart and soul of change: Delivering what works* (2nd ed.). Washington, DC: American Psychological Association.

Duncan, B. L., Miller, S. D., & Sparks, J. A. (2004). *The heroic client: A revolutionary way to improve effectiveness through client-directed, outcome-informed therapy.* San Francisco, CA: Jossey-Bass.

Duran, E., Firehammer, J., & Gonzalez, J. (2008). Liberation psychology as the path toward healing cultural soul wounds. *Journal of Counseling and Development, 86,* 288–295.

Dworkin, S. H. (2001). Individual therapy with lesbian, gay and bisexual clients. In R. M. Perez, K. A. DeBord, & K. J. Bieschke (Eds.), *Handbook of counseling and psychotherapy with lesbian, gay and bisexual clients* (pp. 157–182). Washington, DC: American Psychological Association.

D'Zurilla, T., & Nezu, A. (2010). Problem-solving therapy. In K. S. Dobson (Ed.), *Handbook of cognitive-behavioral therapies* (3rd ed., pp. 197–225). New York, NY: Guilford Press.

Eddy, K., Dutra, L., Bradley, R., & Westen, D. (2004). A multidimensional meta-analysis of psychotherapy and pharmacotherapy for obsessive-compulsive disorder. *Clinical Psychology Review, 24,* 1011–1030.

Egan, G. (1970). *Encounter: Group processes for interpersonal growth.* Pacific Grove, CA: Thomson Brooks/Cole.

Egan, G. (1975). *The skilled helper: A model for systematic helping and interpersonal relating.* Monterey, CA: Thomson-Brooks/Cole.

Egan, G. (2007). *The skilled helper* (8th ed.). Belmont, CA: Thomson-Brooks/Cole.

Ehlers, A., Bisson, J., Clark, D. M., Creamer, M., Pilling, S., Richards, A., . . . Yule, W. (2010). Do all psychological treatments really work the same in posttraumatic stress disorder? *Clinical Psychology Review, 30,* 269–276.

Eifert, G., & Forsyth, J. (2005). *Acceptance and commitment therapy for anxiety disorders: A practitioner's treatment guide to using mindfulness, acceptance, and values-based behavior change.* Oakland, CA: New Harbinger.

Eisena, J., Manceboa, M., Pintoa, A., Colesb, M., Paganoa, M., Stouta, R., & Rasmussena, S. (2006). Impact of obsessive-compulsive disorder on quality of life. *Comprehensive Psychiatry, 47*(4), 270–275.

Eisler, I., Dare, C., Hodes, M., Russell, G., Dodge, E., & Le Grange, D. (2000). Family therapy for adolescent anorexia nervosa: The results of a controlled comparison of two family interventions. *Journal of Child Psychology and Psychiatry, and Allied Disciplines, 41*(6), 727–736.

Elkin, I., Shea, M. T., Watkins, J. T., Imber, S. D., Sotsky, S. M., Collins, J. F. . . . Parloff, M. B. (1989). National institute of mental health treatment of depression collaborative research program: General effectiveness of treatments. *Archives of General Psychiatry, 46,* 971–982.

Elliott, R., Bohart, A. C., Watson, J. C., & Greenberg, L. S. (2011). Empathy. *Psychotherapy, 48,* 43–49.

Ellis, A. (1961). *A guide to rational living.* Englewood Cliffs, NJ: Prentice-Hall.

Elvins, R., & Green, J. (2008). The conceptualization and measurement of therapeutic alliance: An empirical review. *Clinical Psychology Review, 28,* 1167–1187.

Emmelkamp, P., & Beens, H. (1991). Cognitive therapy with obsessive-compulsive disorder: A comparative evaluation. *Behaviour Research and Therapy, 29*(3), 293–300.

Erford, B. T. (2011). *Transforming the school counseling profession.* Columbus, OH: Pearson Merrill Prentice Hall.

Erickson, C. (2007). *The science of addiction: From neurobiology to treatment.* New York, NY: W. W. Norton.

Eriksen, K., & Kress, V. E. (2006). The DSM and the professional counseling identity: Bridging the gap. *Journal of Mental Health Counseling, 28*(3), 202–217.

Erikson, E. (1994). *Identity and the life cycle.* New York, NY: W.W. Norton.

Essau, C. (2014). *Conduct and oppositional defiant disorders: Epidemiology, risk factors, and treatment.* New York, NY: Routledge Press.

Evans, K., Tyrer, P., Catalan, J., Schmidt, U., Davidson, K., Dent, J., . . . Thompson, S. (1999). Manual-assisted cognitive-behaviour therapy (MACT): A randomized controlled trial of a brief intervention with bibliotherapy in the treatment of recurrent deliberate self-harm. *Psychological Medicine, 29*(1), 19–25.

Eyberg, S., Nelson, M., & Boggs, S. (2008). Evidence-based psychosocial treatments for children and adolescents with disruptive behavior. *Journal of Clinical Child & Adolescent Psychology, 37,* 215–237.

Fabiano, G., Pelham, W. E., Coles, R., Gnagy, E., Chronis, A., & O'Connor, B. (2009). A meta-analysis of behavioral treatments for attention-deficit/hyperactivity disorder. *Clinical Psychology Review, 29,* 129–140.

Fabricant, L. E., Abramowitz, J. S., Dehlin, J. P., & Twohig, M. P. (2013). A comparison of two brief interventions for obsessional thoughts: Exposure and acceptance. *Journal of Cognitive Psychotherapy, 27*(3), 195–209.

Fairburn, C. (2008). *Cognitive behavior therapy and eating disorders.* New York, NY: Guilford Press.

Fancher, R. T. (1995). *Cultures of healing: Correcting the image of American mental health care.* New York, NY: W. H. Freeman.

Farber, B. A., & Doolin, E. M. (2011). Positive regard and affirmation. *Psychotherapy, 48,* 58–64.

Farber, B. A., & Lane, J. S. (2002). Positive regard. In J. C. Norcross (Ed.), *Psychotherapy relationships that work: Therapist contributions and responsiveness to patients* (4th ed., pp. 175–194). New York, NY: Oxford University Press.

Feldman, J., & Kazdin, A. E. (1995). Parent management training for oppositional and conduct problem children. *The Clinical Psychologist, 48*(4), 3–5.

Field, T., Hernandez-Reif, M., & Diego, M. (2006). Intrusive and withdrawn depressed mothers and their infants. *Developmental Review, 26,* 15–30.

Findling, R. L., Correll, C. U., Nyilas, M., Forbes, R. A., McQuade, R. D., Jin, N., . . . Carlson, G. A. (2013). Aripiprazole for the treatment of pediatric bipolar I disorder: A 30-week, randomized, placebo-controlled study, *Bipolar Disorders, 15,* 138–149.

Foa, E., Hembree, E., & Rothbaum, B. (2007). *Prolonged exposure therapy for PTSD: Emotional processing of traumatic experiences therapist guide.* New York, NY: Oxford University Press.

Follette, V., Heffner, M., & Person, A. (2010). *Acceptance and commitment therapy for body image dissatisfaction: A practitioner's guide to using mind-*

fulness, acceptance & values-based behavioral change strategies. Oakland, CA: New Harbinger.

Fong, M. L., & Cox, B. G. (1983). Trust as an underlying dynamic in the counseling process: How clients test trust. *Personnel and Guidance Journal, 62,* 163–166.

Food and Drug Administration (FDA). (2008). *Information for health care professionals: Suicidality and antiepileptic drugs.* Washington, DC: Government Printing Office. Available from http://www.fda.gov

Fornaro, M., Filippo, G., Albano, C., Fornaro, S., Rizzato, S., Mattei, C., . . . Fornaro, P. (2009). Obsessive-compulsive disorder and related disorders: A comprehensive survey. *Annals of General Psychiatry, 8*(13).

Fox, R. C. (2000). Bisexuality in perspective: A review of theory and research. In B. Greene & G. L. Croom (Eds.), *Education, research and practice in lesbian, gay, bisexual and transgendered psychology* (pp. 161–206). Thousand Oaks, CA: SAGE.

Frank, E., Kupfer, D. J., Thase, M. E., Mallinger A. G., Swartz, H. A., Fagiolini, A. M., . . . Monk, T. (2005). Two-year outcomes for interpersonal and social rhythm therapy in individuals with bipolar I disorder. *Archives of General Psychiatry, 62*(9), 996–1004.

Franklin, M., Abramowitz, J., Bux, D., Jr., Zoellner, L., & Feeny, N. (2002). Cognitive-behavioral therapy with and without medication in the treatment of obsessive-compulsive disorder. *Professional Psychology: Research & Practice, 33*(2), 162.

Franklin, M., & Foa, E. (1998). Cognitive-behavioral treatment of obsessive compulsive disorder. In P. Nathan & J. Gorman (Eds.), *A guide to treatments that work* (pp. 339–357). Oxford, England: Oxford University Press.

Friedlander, M. L., Escudero, V., Heatherington, L., & Diamond, G. M. (2011). Alliance in couple and family therapy. *Psychotherapy, 48,* 25–33.

Friedman, M. A., Detweiler-Bedell, J. B., Leventhal, H. E., Horne, R., Keitner, G. I., & Miller, I. W. (2004). Combined psychotherapy and pharmacotherapy for the treatment of major depressive disorder. *Clinical Psychology: Science and Practice, 11,* 47–68.

Frost, R., & Hartl, T. (1996). A cognitive-behavioral model of compulsive hoarding. *Behavioral Research Therapy Journal, 34*(4), 341–350.

Fursland, A., Byrne, S., Watson, H., La Puma, M., Allen, K., & Byrne, S. (2012). Enhanced cognitive behavior therapy: A single treatment for all eating disorders. *Journal of Counseling & Development, 90*(3), 319–329.

Gabbay, V., Oatis, M. D., Silva, R. R., & Hirsch, G. (2004). Epidemiological aspects of PTSD in children and adolescents. In R. R. Silva (Ed.), *Posttraumatic stress disorder in children and adolescents: Handbook.* New York, NY: Norton.

Galea, S., Nandi, A., & Vlahov, D. (2005). The epidemiology of post-traumatic stress disorder after disasters. *Epidemiological Review, 27,* 78–91.

Garnets, L., Hancock, K. A., Cochran, S. D., Goodchilds, J., & Peplau, I. A. (1991). Issues in psychotherapy with lesbians and gay men. *American Psychologist, 46,* 964–972.

Gaydukevych, D., & Kocovski, N. L. (2012). Effect of self-focused attention on post-event processing in social anxiety. *Behaviour Research and Therapy, 50,* 47–55.

Geddes, J. R., Burgess, S., Hawton, K., Jamison, K., & Goodwin, G. M. (2004). Long-term lithium therapy for bipolar disorder systematic review and meta-analysis of randomized controlled trials. *American Journal of Psychiatry, 161*(2), 217–222.

Gelso, C. J., & Hayes, J. A. (2002). The management of countertransference. In J. C. Norcross (Ed.), *Psychotherapy relationships that work: Therapist contributions and responsiveness to patients* (pp. 267–284). New York, NY: Oxford University Press.

Germer, K., Siegal, R., & Fulton, P. (Eds.). (2005). *Mindfulness and psychotherapy.* New York, NY: Guilford Press.

Gilbert, N. (1977). The search for professional identity. *Social Work, 22,* 401–406.

Gilbert, S. (2013). *Therapy for eating disorders: Theory, research and practice.* Thousand Oaks, CA: SAGE.

Gilligan, C. (1982). *In a different voice: Psychological theory and women's development.* Cambridge, MA: Harvard University Press.

Gladding, S. T. (1997). *Community and agency counseling.* Upper Saddle River, NJ: Merrill Prentice Hall.

Gladding, S. T. (2008). *Group work: A counseling specialty* (5th ed.). Upper Saddle River, NJ: Merrill/Prentice Hall.

Gladding, S. (2009). *Counseling, a comprehensive profession.* Upper Saddle River, NJ: Pearson.

Gladding, S. T., & Newsome, D. W. (2010). *Clinical mental health counseling in community and agency settings.* Upper Saddle River, NJ: Pearson.

Glickman, N. S. (2009). Adapting best practices in CBT for deaf and hearing persons with language and learning challenges. *Journal of Psychotherapy Integration, 19,* 354–384.

Gloaguen, V., Cottraux, J., Cucherat, M., & Blackburn, I. M. (1998). A meta-analysis of the effects of cognitive therapy in depressed patients. *Journal of Affective Disorders, 49,* 59–72.

Godart, N., Flament, M., Perdereau, F., & Jeammet, P. (2002). Comorbidity between eating disorders and anxiety disorders: A review. *International Journal of Eating Disorders. 32,* 253–270.

Goldberg, J. F., & Chengappa, K. N. (2009). Identifying and treating cognitive impairment in bipolar disorder. *Bipolar Disorder, 11,* 123–137.

Goldberg, J. F., & Harrow, M. (2011). A 15-year prospective follow-up of bipolar affective disorders: Comparisons with unipolar nonpsychotic depression. *Bipolar Disorder, 13,* 155–163.

Goldfried, M. R., Pachankis, J. E., & Bell, A. C. (2005). A history of psychotherapy integration. In J. C. Norcross & M. R. Goldfried (Eds.), *Handbook of psychotherapy integration* (2nd ed., pp. 24–60). New York, NY: Oxford University Press.

Goldstein, A. P., & Higginbotham, H. N. (1991). Relationship-enhancement methods. In F. H. Kanfer & A. P. Goldstein (Eds.), *Helping people change* (4th ed., pp. 20–69). New York, NY: Pergamon.

Goodwin, F., & Jamison, K. (2007). *Manic-depressive illness: Bipolar disorders and recurrent depression* (2nd ed.). Cambridge, England: Oxford University Press.

Goodyear, R. K. (2000). An unwarranted escalation of counselor-counseling psychologist professional conflict: Comments on Weinrach, Lustig, Chan, and Thomas (1998). *Journal of Counseling and Development, 66,* 402–405.

Gorski, T., & Grinstead, S. (2010). *Relapse prevention therapy workbook* (Rev. ed.). Independence, MO: Herald.

Grant, B. F., Hasin, D., Stinson, F., Dawson, D., Chou, S., Ruan, W., & Pickering. R. (2004). Prevalence, correlates, and disability of personality disorders in the United States: Results from the national epidemiologic survey on alcohol and related conditions. *Journal of Clinical Psychiatry, 65*(7), 948–958.

Greenberg, D., Stravynski, A., & Bilu, Y. (2004). Social phobia in ultra-orthodox Jewish males: Culture-bound syndrome or virtue? *Mental Health, Religion and Culture, 7,* 289–305.

Greenburg, D., & Padesky, C. (1995). *Mind over mood: Change how you feel by changing the way you think.* New York, NY: Guilford Press.

Greenhill, L., & Ford, R. (2002). Childhood attention-deficit/hyperactivity disorder: Pharmacological treatments. In P. E. Nathan & J. M. Gorman (Eds.), *A guide to treatments that work* (2nd ed., pp. 25–55). New York, NY: Oxford University Press.

Grilo, C., & Mitchell, J. (2010). *The treating of eating disorders: A clinical handbook.* New York, NY: Guilford Press.

Grubb, H., Sellers, M., & Waligroski, K. (1993). Factors related to depression and eating disorders: Self-esteem, body image, and attractiveness. *Psychological Reports, 72,* 1003–1010.

Guerney, B. G., Jr. (1977). *Relationship enhancement: Skill-training programs for therapy, problem prevention, and enrichment.* San Francisco, CA: Jossey-Bass.

Guindon, M. H. (2011). *A counseling primer: An introduction to the profession.* New York, NY: Routledge.

Gustafson-Larson, A. M., & Terry, R. D. (1992). Weight-related behaviors and concerns of fourth-grade children. *Journal of American Dietetic Association, 92*(7), 818–822.

Haase, M., Frommer, J., Franke, G., Hoffman, T., Schulze-Muetzel, J., Jager, S., & Schmitz, N. (2008). From symptom relief to interpersonal change: Treatment outcome and effectiveness in inpatient psychotherapy. *Psychotherapy Research, 18*(5), 615–624.

Hamacheck, D. E. (1988). Evaluating self-concept and ego development within Erikson's psychosocial framework: A formulation. *Journal of Counseling and Development, 66,* 354–360.

Handleman, J., & Harris, S. (Eds.). (2000). *Preschool education programs for children with autism* (2nd ed.). Austin, TX: Pro-Ed.

Hanrahan, F., Field, A., Jones, F., & Davey, G. (2013). A meta-analysis of cognitive therapy for worry and generalized anxiety disorder. *Clinical Psychology Review, 33,* 120–132.

Hansen, J. T. (2000). Psychoanalysis and humanism: A review and critical examination of integrationist efforts with some proposed resolutions. *Journal of Counseling & Development, 78,* 21–28.

Hansen, J. T. (2003). Including diagnostic training in counseling curricula: Implications for professional identity development. *Counselor Education & Supervision, 43,* 96–107.

Harmon, C., Hawkins, E. J., Lambert, M. J., Slade, K., & Whipple, J. L. (2005). Improving outcomes for poorly responding clients: The use of clinical support tools and feedback to clients. *Journal of Clinical Psychology/InSession, 61,* 175–185.

Harrow, M., Goldberg, J. F., Grossman, L. S., & Meltzer, H. Y. (1990). Outcome in manic disorders: A naturalistic follow-up study. *Archives of General Psychiatry, 47,* 665–671.

Harvey, A. G., & Bryant, R. A. (1998). The relationship between acute stress disorder and posttraumatic stress disorder: A prospective evaluation of motor vehicle accident survivors. *Journal of Consulting and Clinical Psychology, 66,* 507–512.

Harvey, A. G., & Bryant, R. A. (1999). Acute stress disorder across trauma populations. *Journal of Nervous and Mental Disease, 187,* 443–446.

Hay, P. (2013). A systematic review of evidence for psychological treatments in eating disorders: 2005–2012. *International Journal of Eating Disorders, 46*(5), 462–469.

Hayes, S., & Smith, S. (2005). *Get out of your mind and into your life: The new acceptance and commitment therapy.* Oakland, CA: New Harbinger.

Haynes, D. T., & White, B. W. (1999). Will the "real" social work please stand up? A call to stand for professional unity. *Social Work, 44,* 385–392.

Helms, J., & Cook, D. (1999). *Using race and culture in counseling and psychotherapy.* Boston, MA: Allyn & Bacon.

Henggeler, S., & Lee, T. (Ed.). (2003). *Evidence-based psychotherapies for children and adolescents.* New York, NY: Guilford Press.

Herbert, J. D., & Forman, E. M. (Eds.). (2011). *Acceptance and mindfulness in cognitive behavior therapy: Understanding and applying the new therapies.* Hoboken, NJ: Wiley.

Herdt, G., & Boxer, A. (1993). *Children of horizons: How gay and lesbian teens are leading a new way out of the closet.* Boston, MA: Beacon Press.

Herman, J. (1992). *Trauma and recovery.* New York, NY: Basic Books.

Herr, E. L. (1985). AACD: An association committed to unity through diversity. *Journal of Counseling and Development, 63,* 395–404.

Hershenson, D. B., & Berger, G. P. (2001). The state of community counseling: A survey of directors of CACREP-accredited programs. *Journal of Counseling and Development, 79,* 188–193.

Hershenson, D. B., Power, P. W., & Waldo, M. (1996). *Community counseling: Contemporary theory and practice.* Needham Heights, MA: Allyn & Bacon.

Hervey-Jumper, H., Douyo, K., Falcone, T., & Franco, K. N. (2008). Identifying, evaluating, diagnosing, and treating ADHD in minority youth. *Journal of Attention Disorders, 11*(5), 522–528.

Hettema, J., Neale, M., & Kendler, K. (2001). A review and meta-analysis of the genetic epidemiology of anxiety disorders. *American Journal of Psychiatry, 158*(10), 1568–1578.

Hian, L. B., Chuan, S. L., Trevor, T. M., & Detenber, B. H. (2004). Getting to know you: Exploring the development of relational intimacy in computer-mediated communication. *Journal of Computer Mediated Communication, 9,* 1–24.

Hibbeln, J. R., Nieminen, L. R. G., Blasbalg, T. L., Riggs, J. A., & Lands, W. E. M. (2006). Healthy intakes of n-3 and n-6 fatty acids: Estimations considering worldwide diversity. *Journal of Clinical Nutrition, 83,* 14835–14935.

Hidalgo, R., & Davidson, J. (2000). Posttraumatic stress disorder: Epidemiology and health-related considerations. *Journal of Clinical Psychiatry, 61,* 5–13.

Hinshaw, S. (2002). Preadolescent girls with attention-deficit/hyperactivity disorder: I. Background characteristics, comorbidity, cognitive and social functioning, and parenting practices. *Journal of Consulting and Clinical Psychology, 70*(5), 1086–1098.

Hirshfeld-Becker, D., Masek, B., Henin, A., Blakely, L., Rettew, D., Dufton, L., & Biederman, J. (2008). Cognitive-behavioral intervention with young anxious children. *Harvard Review of Psychiatry, 16*(2), 113–125.

Hoffman, D. L., Dukes, E. M., & Wittchen, H. (2008). Human and economic burden of generalized anxiety disorder. *Depression & Anxiety, 25*(1), 72–90.

Hoffmann, S., Asnaani, A., & Hinton, D. E. (2010). Cultural aspects in social anxiety and social anxiety disorder. *Depression & Anxiety, 27*(12), 1117–1127.

Hoffmann, S., & Smits, J. (2008). Cognitive-behavioral therapy for adult anxiety disorders: A meta-analysis of randomized placebo-controlled trials. *Journal of Clinical Psychiatry, 69,* 621–632.

Holeva, V., Tarrier, N., & Wells, A. (2001). Prevalence and predictors of acute stress disorder and PTSD following road traffic accidents: Thought control strategies and social support. *Behavior Therapy, 32,* 65–83.

Horvath, A. O., & Bedi, R. P. (2002). The alliance. In J. C. Norcross (Ed.), *Psychotherapy relationships that work: Therapist contributions and responsiveness to patients* (pp. 37–70). New York, NY: Oxford University Press.

Horvath, A. O., Del Re, A. C., Fluckiger, C., & Symonds, D. (2011). Alliance in individual psychotherapy. *Psychotherapy, 48,* 9–16.

Hoshmand, L. (1991). Clinical inquiry as scientific training. *Counselling Psychologist, 19,* 431–453.

Houenou, J., Frommberger, J., Carde, S., Glasbrenner, M., Diener, C., Leboyer, M., & Wessa, M. (2011). Neuroimaging-based markers of bipolar disorder: Evidence from two meta-analyses. *Journal of Affective Disorders, 132*(3), 344–355.

Hsu, L. (1990). *Eating disorders*. New York, NY: Guilford Press.

Hubble, M. A., Duncan B. L., Miller, S. D., & Wampold, B. E. (2010). Introduction. In B. L. Duncan, S. D. Miller, B. E. Wampold, & M. A. Hubble (Eds.), *The heart and soul of change: Delivering what works in therapy* (2nd ed., pp. 23–46). Washington, DC: American Psychological Association.

Huey, W., & Rank, R. (1984). Effects of counselor and peer-led group assertive training on black adolescent aggression. *Journal of Counseling Psychology, 31*(1), 95–98.

Huppert, J., & Roth, D. (2003). Treating obsessive-compulsive disorder with exposure and response prevention. *The Behavior Analyst Today, 4*(1), 66–70.

Hypericum Depression Trial Study Group. (2002). Effect of hypericum perforatum (St. John's wort) in major depressive disorder: A randomized controlled trial. *Journal of the American Medical Association, 287*(14), 1807–1814.

Imel, Z. E., Wampold, B. E., Miller, S. D., & Fleming, R. R. (2008). Distinctions without a difference: Direct comparisons of psychotherapies for alcohol use disorders. *Journal of Addictive Behaviors, 22*(4), 533–543.

Inskipp, F. (2006). 3.3 Generic Skills. In C. Feltham and I. Horton (Eds.), *Sage Handbook of Counseling and Psychotherapy* (2nd ed.). Thousand Oaks, CA: SAGE.

IsHak, W. W., Brown, K., Aye, S. S., Kahloom, M., Mobaraki, S., & Hanna, R. (2012). Health-related quality of life in bipolar disorder. *Bipolar Disorders, 14,* 6–18.

Ivey, A. E. (1971). *Microcounseling: Innovations in interviewing training*. Springfield, IL: Charles C Thomas.

Ivey, A. E., D'Andrea, M., Ivey, M. B., & Simek-Morgan, L. (2007). *Counseling and psychotherapy: A multicultural perspective* (6th ed.). Boston, MA: Allyn & Bacon.

Ivey, A. E., Gluckstern, N. B., & Ivey, M. B. (1993). *Basic attending skills* (3rd ed.). North Amherst, MA: Micotraining.

James, A., & Vereker, M. (1996). Family therapy for adolescents diagnosed as having borderline personality disorder. *Journal of Family Therapy, 18,* 269–283.

Jané-Llopis, E., & Matytsina, I. (2006). Mental health and alcohol, drugs and tobacco: A review of the comorbidity between mental health disorders and the use of alcohol, tobacco and illicit drugs. *Drug and Alcohol Review, 25,* 515–536.

Joesch, J., Golinelli, D., Sherbourne, C., Sullivan, G., Stein, M., Craske, M., & Roy-Byrne, P. (2013). Trajectories of change in anxiety severity and impairment during and after treatment with evidence-based treatment for multiple anxiety disorders in primary care. *Depression & Anxiety, 30*(11), 1099–1106.

Johnson, D. W. (2006). *Reaching out: Interpersonal effectiveness and self-actualization* (9th ed.). Boston, MA: Allyn & Bacon.

Johnson, S. L., Cuellar, A. K., Ruggero, C., Winett-Perlman, C., Goodnick, P., White, R., & Miller, I. (2008). Life events as predictors of mania and depression in bipolar I disorder. *Journal of Abnormal Psychology, 117*(2), 268–277.

Johnson, S. L., & Miller, I. (1997). Negative life events and time to recovery from episodes of bipolar disorder. *Journal of Abnormal Psychology 106,* 449–457.

Johnson, S. L., Sandrow, D., Meyer, B., Winters, R., Miller, I., Solomon, D., & Keitner, G. (2000). Increases in manic symptoms following life events involving goal-attainment. *Journal of Abnormal Psychology, 109,* 721–727.

Joseph, J., & Gray, M. J. (2008). Exposure therapy for posttraumatic stress disorder. *Journal of Behavior Analysis of Offender and Victim: Treatment and Prevention, 1*(4), 69–80.

Judd, L. L., Schettler, P. J., & Akiskal, H. S. (2002). The prevalence, clinical relevance and public health significance of subthreshold depressions. *Psychiatric Clinics of North America, 25,* 685–698.

Kahn, M. (1991). *Between therapist and client: The new relationship*. New York, NY: Freeman.

Kaplan, D. M. (2002). Celebrating 50 years of excellence! *Journal of Counseling and Development, 80,* 261–263.

Kaplan, D. M. (2014). An overview of the revised ACA Code of Ethics. *Counseling Today, 57*(1), 20–21.

Kaplan, D. M., & Gladding, S. T. (2011). A vision for the future of counseling: The 20/20 principles for unifying and strengthening the profession. *Journal of Counseling and Development, 89,* 367–372.

Karver, M. S., Handelsman, J. B., Fields, S., & Bickman, L. (2006). Meta-analysis of therapeutic relationship variables in youth and family therapy: The evidence for different relationship variables in the child and adolescent treatment outcome literature. *Clinical Psychology Review, 26,* 50–65.

Kaslow, N. J., Broth, M. R., Smith, C. O., & Collins, M. H. (2012). Family-based interventions for child and adolescent disorders. *Journal of Marital and Family Therapy, 38,* 82–100.

Kaye, W., Bulik, C., Thornton, L., Barbarich, N., & Masters, K. (2004). Comorbidity of anxiety disorders with anorexia and bulimia nervosa. *American Journal of Psychiatry, 161*(12), 2215–2221.

Kazdin, A. (2005). *Parent management training: Treatment for oppositional, aggressive, and antisocial behavior in children and adolescents.* New York, NY: Oxford University Press.

Kazdin, A. E. (2008). Evidence-based treatment and practice. *American Psychologist, 63,* 146–159.

Kazdin, A. E., Hoagwood, K., Weisz, J. R., Hood, K., Kratochwill, T. R., Vargas, L. A., & Banez, G. A. (2010). A meta-systems approach to evidence-based practice for children and adults. *American Psychologist, 65,* 85–97.

Kessler, R. C., Adler, L., Barkley, R., Biederman, J., Conners, C. K., Demler, O., . . . Zaslavsky, A. M. (2006). The prevalence and correlates of adult ADHD in the United States: Results from the National Comorbidity Survey Replication. *American Journal of Psychiatry, 163,* 716–723.

Kessler, R. C., Berglund, P., Demler, O., Jin, R., & Walters, E. (2005). Lifetime prevalence and age-of-onset distributions of DSM-IV disorders in the National Comorbidity Survey Replication (NCS-R). *Archives of General Psychiatry, 62*(6), 593–602.

Kessler R. C., Chiu, W., Demler, O., & Walters, E. (2005). Prevalence, severity, and comorbidity of twelve-month DSM-IV disorders in the National Comorbidity Survey Replication (NCS-R). *Archives of General Psychiatry, 62*(6), 617–627.

Kessler, R. C., Chiu, W. T., Jin, R., Ruscio, A. M., Shear, K., & Walters, E. E. (2006). The epidemiology of panic attacks, panic disorder, and agoraphobia in the National Comorbidity Survey Replication. *Archives of General Psychiatry, 63,* 415–424.

Kessler, R. C., Sonnega, A., Bromet, E., Hughes, M., & Nelson, C. B. (1995). Posttraumatic stress disorder in the National Comorbidity Survey. *Archives of General Psychiatry, 52,* 1048–1060.

Kieseppa, T., Partonen, T., Hauldea, J., Kaprio, J., & Lonnqvist, J. (2004). High concordance of bipolar I disorder in a nationwide sample of twins. *American Journal of Psychiatry, 161,* 1814–1821.

Kilbourne, A. M., Post, E. P., Nossek, A., Drill, L., Cooley, S., & Bauer, M. (2008). Improving general medical care for patients with bipolar disorder: A randomized controlled pilot study. *Psychiatric Services, 59,* 760–768.

Kirmayer, L. J. (2001). Cultural variations in the clinical presentation of depression and anxiety: Implications for diagnosis and treatment. *Journal of Clinical Psychiatry, 62*(Suppl. 13), 22–28.

Kocovski, N., Fleming, J., & Rector, N. (2009). Mindfulness and acceptance-based group therapy for social anxiety disorder: An open trial. *Cognitive and Behavioral Practice, 16,* 276–289.

Koegel, R., & Koegel, L. (2005). *Pivotal response treatments for autism: Communication, social, and academic development.* Baltimore, MD: Paul H. Brookes.

Koegel, R., & Koegel, L. (2012). *The PRT pocket guide: Pivotal response treatment for autism spectrum disorders.* Baltimore, MD: Paul H. Brookes.

Kohut, H. (1971). *The restoration of the self.* New York, NY: International Universities Press.

Kohut, H. (1984). *How does analysis cure?* Chicago, IL: University of Chicago Press.

Kolden, G. G., Klein, M. H., Wang, C. C., & Austin, S. B. (2011). Congruence/genuineness. *Psychotherapy, 48,* 65–71.

Koran, L., Hanna, G., Hollander, E., Nestadt, G., & Simpson, H. (2007). Practice guideline for the treatment of patients with obsessive-compulsive disorder. *The American Journal of Psychiatry, 164*(7), 5–53.

Kraft, D. P. (2011). One hundred years of college mental health. *Journal of American College Health, 59,* 477–481.

Kraus, R. (2004). Ethical and legal considerations for providers of mental health services online. In R. Kraus, J. Zack, & G. Strickler (Eds.), *Online counseling: A handbook for mental health professionals.* New York, NY: Elsevier.

Kruger, S., Shugar, G., & Cooke, R. (1996). Comorbidity of binge eating disorder and the partial binge eating syndrome with bipolar disorder. *International Journal of Eating Disorders, 19,* 45–52.

Krupnick, J. L., Sotsky, S. M., Simmens, S., Moyer, J., Elkin, I., Watkins, J., & Pilkonis, P. A. (1996). The role of the therapeutic alliance in psychotherapy and pharmacotherapy. *Journal of Consulting and Clinical Psychology, 64,* 532–539.

Kumpfer, K., Alvarado, R., & Whiteside, H. (2003). Family-based interventions for substance use and misuse prevention. *Substance Use and Misuse, 38*(11–13), 1759–1787.

Kupfer, D. J. (2005). The increasing medical burden in bipolar disorder. *Journal of the American Medical Association, 293,* 2528–2530.

Kupka, R. W., Altshuler, L. L., Nolen, W. A., Suppes, T., Luckenbaugh, D. A., Leverich, G. S., . . . Post, R. M. (2007). Three times more days depressed than manic or hypomanic in both bipolar I and bipolar II disorder. *Bipolar Disorder, 9,* 531–535.

Kushner, M., Krueger, R., Frye, B., & Peterson, J. (2008). Epidemiological perspectives on co-occurring anxiety disorder and substance use disorder. In S. H. Stewart & P. J. Conrod (Eds.), *Anxiety and substance use disorders: The vicious cycle of comorbidity* (pp. 3–17). New York, NY: Springer.

LaFleur, L. B. (2007). *Counselors' perceptions of identity and attitudinal differences between counselors and other mental health professionals* (Doctoral dissertation, Paper 554). New Orleans, LA: University of New Orleans Theses and Dissertations.

Lahey, B., Hart, E., Pliszka, S., Applegate, B., & McBurnett. K. (1993). Neurophysiological correlates of conduct disorder: A rationale and a review. *Journal of Clinical Child Psychology, 22,* 141–153.

Lai, M., Lombardo, M., Chakrabarti, B., & Baron-Cohen, S. (2013). Subgrouping the autism "spectrum": Reflections on DSM-5. *PLOSBiology, 11*(4), 1–7.

Lam, D. H., Hayward, P., Watkins, E. R., Wright, K., & Sham, P. (2005). Relapse prevention in patients with bipolar disorder: Cognitive therapy outcome after 2 years. *The American Journal of Psychiatry, 162,* 324–329.

Lam, D. H., Watkins, E. R., Hayward, P., Bright, J., Wright, K., Kerr, N., . . . Sham, P. (2003). A randomized controlled study of cognitive therapy of relapse prevention for bipolar affective disorder: Outcome of the first year. *Archives of General Psychiatry, 60,* 145–152.

Lambert, M. J. (1992). Psychotherapy outcome research: Implications for integrative and eclectic therapists. In J. C. Norcross & M. R. Goldfried (Eds.), *Handbook of psychotherapy integration,* (pp. 94–129). New York, NY: Basic.

Lambert, M. J. (2011). Psychotherapy research and its achievements. In J. C. Norcross, G. R. Vandenbos, & D. K. Freedheim (Eds.), *History of psychotherapy* (2nd ed., pp. 299–332). Washington, DC: American Psychological Association.

Lambert, M. J. (2013). Outcome in psychotherapy: The past and important advances. *Psychotherapy, 50*(1), 42–51.

Lambert, M. J., & Anderson, E. M. (1996). Assessment for the time-limited psychotherapies. *Annual Review of Psychiatry, 15,* 23–47.

Lambert, M. J., & Archer, A. (2006). Research findings on the effects of psychotherapy and their implications for practice. In C. D. Goodheart, A. E. Kazdin, & R. J. Sternberg (Eds.), *Evidence-based psychotherapy: Where practice and research meet* (pp. 111–130). Washington, DC: American Psychological Association.

Lambert, M. J., & Barley, D. E. (2002). Research summary on the therapeutic relationship and psychotherapy outcome. In J. C. Norcross (Ed.), *Psychotherapy relationships that work: Therapist contributions and responsiveness to patients* (pp. 17–32). Oxford, England: Oxford University Press.

Lambert, M. J., & Cattani-Thompson, K. (1996). Current findings regarding the effectiveness of counseling: Implications for practice. *Journal of Counseling & Development, 74,* 601–608.

Lambert, M. J., & Ogles, B. M. (2004). The efficacy and effectiveness of psychotherapy. In M. J. Lambert (Ed.), *Bergin and Garfield's handbook of psychotherapy and behavior change* (5th ed., pp. 139–193). New York, NY: Wiley.

Lau, A., Garland, A., Yeh, M., McCabe, K., Wood, P., & Hough, R. (2004). Race/ethnicity and interinformant agreement in assessing adolescent psychopathology. *Journal of Emotional and Behavioral Disorders, 12*(3), 145–156.

Lazarus, R. (1966). *Psychological stress and the coping process.* New York, NY: McGraw-Hill.

LeDoux, E. (2000). Emotion circuits in the brain. *Annual Review of Neuroscience, 23,*155–184.

Leibenluft, E. (1996). Women with bipolar illness: Clinical and research issues. *American Journal of Psychiatry, 153,* 163–173.

Leichsenring, F., & Klein, S. (2014). Evidence for psychodynamic psychotherapy in specific mental disorders: A systematic review. *Journal of Analytical Psychology, 59*(4), 596–599.

Leichsenring, F., & Leibing, E. (2003). The effectiveness of psychodynamic therapy and cognitive behavior therapy in the treatment of personality disorders: A meta-analysis. *American Journal of Psychiatry, 160*(7), 1223–1232.

Lenzenweger, M. (2008). Epidemiology of personality disorders. *Psychiatric Clinics of North America, 31*(3), 395–403.

Lenzenweger, M., Lane, M., Loranger, A., & Kessler, R. (2007). DSM-IV personality disorders in the National Comorbidity Survey Replication. *Biological Psychiatry, 62*(6), 553–564.

Leon, A., Portera L., & Weissman, M. (1995). The social costs of anxiety disorders. *British Journal of Psychiatry, 27,* 19–22.

Levav, I., & Rutz, W. (2002). The WHO world health report 2001: New understanding—New hope. *Israel Journal of Psychiatry & Related Sciences, 39,* 50–56.

Levitt, H., Butler, M., & Hill, T. (2006). What clients find helpful in psychotherapy: Developing principles for facilitating moment-to-moment change. *Journal of Counseling Psychology, 53,* 314–324.

Lewis, J., Beavers, W., Gossett, J., & Phillips, V. (1976). *No single thread: Psychological health in family systems.* Oxford, England: Brunner/Mazel.

Lewis-Fernandez, R., Hinton, D. E., Laria, A. J., Patterson, E. H., Hofmann, S. G., Craske, . . . Liao, B.

(2009). Culture and the anxiety disorders: Recommendations for DSM-V. *Depression and Anxiety, 0,* 1–18.

Linehan, M. (1993). *Cognitive-behavioral treatment of borderline personality disorder.* New York, NY: Guilford Press.

Linehan, M. (2000). The empirical basis of dialectical behavior therapy: Development of new treatments versus evaluation of existing treatments. *Clinical Psychology: Science and Practice, 1,* 113–119.

Lisanby, S. H. (2007). Electroconvulsive therapy for depression. *New England Journal of Medicine, 357,* 1939–1945.

Litrownik, A., Newton, R., Hunter, W., English, D., & Everson, M. (2003). Exposure to family violence in young at-risk children: A longitudinal look at the effects of victimization and witnessed physical and psychological aggression. *Journal of Family Violence, 18*(1), 59–73.

Livingston, R. (1999). Cultural issues in diagnosis and treatment of ADHD. *Journal of American Academy of Child and Adolescent Psychiatry, 38,* 1591–1594.

Livneh, H., & Sherwood, A. (2001). Application of personality theories and counseling strategies to clients with physical disabilities. *Journal of Counseling & Development, 69,* 528–538.

Lock, J., Couturier, J., & Agras, W. (2006). Comparison of long-term outcomes in adolescents with anorexia nervosa treated with family therapy. *Journal of the American Academy of Child and Adolescent Psychiatry 45*(6), 666–672.

Lock, J., & Le Grange, D. (2012). *Treatment manual for anorexia nervosa: A family-based approach* (2nd ed.). New York, NY: Guilford Press.

Loeber, R., Burke, J., Lahey, B., Winters, A., & Zera, M. (2000). Oppositional defiant and conduct disorder: A review of the past 10 years, part I. *Journal of the American Association of Child and Adolescent Psychiatry, 39*(12), 1468–1484.

Lolich, M., Vazquez, G. H., Alvarez, L. M., & Tamayo, J. M. (2012). Psychosocial interventions in bipolar disorder: A review. *Actas Espanola de Psiquiatria, 40*(2), 77–85.

Lovell, K., & Bee, P. (2008). Implementing the NICE OCD/BDD guidelines. *Psychology and Psychotherapy: Theory, Research, and Practice, 81,* 365–376.

Luborsky, L., Singer, B., & Luborsky, L. (1975). Comparative studies of psychotherapies: Is it true that "everybody has won and all must have prizes?" *Archives of General Psychiatry, 32,* 995–1008.

Lumley, J., Austin, M. P., & Mitchell, C. (2004). Intervening to reduce depression after birth: A systematic review of the randomized trials. *International Journal of Technology Assessment in Health Care, 20,* 128–144.

Luoma, J. B., Martin, C. E., & Pearson, J. L. (2002). Contact with mental health and primary care prior to suicide: A review of the evidence. *American Journal of Psychiatry, 159*(6), 909–916.

Lutz, W., Leon, S. C., Martinovich, Z., Lyons, J. S., & Stiles, W. B. (2007). Therapist effects in outpatient psychotherapy: A three level growth curve approach. *Journal of Counseling Psychology, 54,* 32–39.

Lynch, R. K., & Maki, D. (1981). Searching for structure: A trait-factor approach to vocational rehabilitation. *Vocational Guidance Quarterly, 30,* 61–68.

Lyseng-Williamson, K. A. (2013). Oral olanzapine: A guide to its use in adults with schizophrenia or bipolar I disorder. *Drugs & Therapy Perspectives, 29,* 291–296.

Ma, J., Wang, C., Li, H., Zhang, X., Zhang, Y., Hou, Y., & Hu, X. (2013). Cognitive-coping therapy for obsessive-compulsive disorder: A randomized controlled trial. *Journal of Psychiatric Research, 47*(11), 1785–1790.

MacCluskie, K. C., & Ingersoll, R. E. (2001). *Becoming a 21ˢᵗ century agency counselor: Personal and professional explorations.* Belmont, CA: Wadsworth.

Mackin, P., Targum, S. D., Kalali, A., Rom, D., & Young, A. H. (2006). Culture and assessment of manic symptoms. *British Journal of Psychiatry, 189,* 379–380.

Malkoff-Schwartz, S., Frank, E., Anderson, B. P., Hlastala, S. A., Luther, J. F., Sherrill, J. T., . . . Kupfer, D. J. (2000). Social rhythm disruption and stressful life events in the onset of bipolar and unipolar episodes. *Psychological Medicine, 30,* 1005–1016.

Manji, H. K., Chen, G., Shimon, H., Hsiao, J. K., Potter, W. Z., & Belmaker, R. H. (1995). Guanine nucleotide-binding proteins in bipolar affective disorder. Effects of long-term lithium treatment. *Archives of General Psychiatry, 52,* 135–144.

March, J., Silva, S., Petrycki, S., Curry, J., Wells, K., Fairbank, J., . . . Severe, J. (2004). Fluoxetine, cognitive-behavioral therapy, and their combination for adolescents with depression: Treatment for adolescents with depression study (TADS) randomized controlled trial. *Journal of the American Medical Association, 292*(7), 807–820.

Martin, D. J., Garske, J. P., & Davis, M. K. (2000). Relation of the therapeutic alliance with outcome and other variables: A meta-analytic review. *Journal of Consulting and Clinical Psychology, 68,* 438–450.

Marchand, W. R., & Yurgelun-Todd, D. (2010). Striatal structure and function in mood disorders: A comprehensive review. *Bipolar Disorders, 12*(8), 764–785.

Marshall, R., Beebe, K., Oldham, M., & Zaninelli, R. (2001). Efficacy and safety of paroxetine treatment for chronic PTSD: A fixed-dose, placebo-controlled study. *American Journal of Psychiatry, 158,* 1982–1988.

Marshall, R., Spitzer, R., & Liebowitz, M. (1999). Review and critique of the new DSM-IV diagnosis of acute stress disorder. *American Journal of Psychiatry, 156,* 1677–1685.

Martenyi, F., Brown, E., & Caldwell, C. (2007). Failed efficacy of fluoxetine in the treatment of posttraumatic stress disorder: Results of a fixed-dose, placebo-controlled study. *Journal of Clinical Psychopharmacology, 27,* 166–170.

Martenyi, F., Brown, E., Zhang, H., Prakash, A., & Koke, S. (2002). Fluoxetine versus placebo in posttraumatic stress disorder. *Journal of Clinical Psychiatry, 63,* 199–206.

Martin, D. J., Garske, J. P., & Davis, M. K. (2000). Relation of the therapeutic alliance with outcome and other variables: A meta-analytic review. *Journal of Consulting and Clinical Psychology, 68,* 438–450.

Matusiewicz, A., Hopwood, C., Banducci, A., & Lejuez, C. (2010). The effectiveness of cognitive behavioral therapy for personality disorders. *Psychiatric Clinics of North America, 33*(3), 657–685.

Mawson, A. (2009). On the association between low resting heart rate and chronic aggression: Retinoid toxicity hypothesis. *Progress in Neuropychopharmacology & Biological Psychiatry, 33*(2), 205–213.

McAuliffe, G. J., & Lovell, C. W. (2006). The influence of counselor epistemology on the helping interview: A qualitative study. *Journal of Counseling and Development, 8,* 308–317.

McCormack, P. L., & Wiseman, L. R. (2004). Olanzapine: A review of its use in the management of bipolar I disorder, *Drugs, 64*(23), 2709–2726.

McHugh, R. K., Hearon, B., & Otto, M. (2010). Cognitive behavioral therapy for substance use disorders. *Psychiatric Clinics of North America, 33,* 511–525.

McIntyre, R. S., Konarski, J. Z., Soczynska, J. K., Wilkins, K., Panjwani, G., Bouffard, B., . . . Kennedy, S. H. (2006). Medical comorbidity in bipolar disorder: Implications for functional outcomes and health service utilization. *Psychiatric Services, 57,* 1140–1144.

McIntyre, R. S., Soczynska, J. K., Beyer, J. L., Woldeyohannes, H. O., Law, C.W., & Miranda, A. (2007). Medical comorbidity in bipolar disorder: Re-prioritizing unmet needs. *Current Opinion, (20)*29, 406–416.

McKinney, C., & Renk, K. (2007). Emerging research and theory in the etiology of oppositional defiant disorder: Current concerns and future directions. *International Journal of Behavioral Consultation & Therapy, 3*(3), 349–371.

McNally, R. J. (1997). Atypical phobias. In G. C. L. Davey (Ed.), *Phobias: A handbook of theory, research and treatment* (pp. 183–199). Chichester, England: Wiley.

Meekums, B. (2005). Creative writing as a tool for assessment: Implications for embodied working. *The Arts in Psychotherapy, 32,* 95–105.

Meichenbaum, D. (1994). *A clinical handbook/practical therapist manual for assessing and treating adults with post-traumatic stress disorder.* Waterloo, Ontario: Institute Press.

Meichenbaum, D., & Deffenbacher, J. L. (1988). Stress inoculation training. *Counseling Psychologist, 16,* 69–90.

Merikangas, K. R., Akiskal, H. S., Angst, J., Greenberg, E. E., Hirschfeld, R. M. A., Petukhova, M., & Kessler, R. C. (2007). Lifetime and 12-month prevalence of bipolar spectrum disorder in the National Comorbidity Survey Replication. *Archives of General Psychiatry, 64,* 543–552.

Merikangas, K. R., He, J., Burstein, M., Swanson, S. A., Avenevoli, S., Cui, L., . . . Swendsen, J. (2010). Lifetime prevalence of mental disorders in U.S. adolescents: Results from the National Comorbidity Study-Adolescent Supplement (NCS-A). *Journal of the American Academy of Child and Adolescent Psychiatry, 49*(10), 980–989.

Merikangas, K. R., Jin, R., He, J. P. P., Kessler, R., Less, S., Sampson, N., & Zarkov, Z. (2011). Prevalence and correlates of bipolar spectrum disorder in the World Mental Health Survey Initiative. *Archives of General Psychiatry, 68*(3), 241–251.

Messer, S. B. (1992). A critical examination of belief structures in integrative and eclectic psychotherapy. In J. Norcross & M. R. Goldfried (Eds.), *Handbook of psychotherapy integration* (pp. 130–165). New York, NY: Basic Books.

Messer, S. B. (2007). Integration and eclecticism in counseling and psychotherapy: Cautionary notes.

British Journal of Guidance and Counselling, 17(3), 274–285.

Meyer, B., Johnson, S. I., & Winters, R. (2001). Responsiveness to threat and incentive in bipolar disorder: Relations of the BIS/BAS scales with symptoms. *Journal of Psychopathology and Behavioral Assessment, 23,* 133–143.

Miklowitz, D. J. (2008). Adjunctive psychotherapy for bipolar disorder: State of the evidence. *American Journal of Psychiatry, 165*(11), 1408–1419.

Miklowitz, D. J., George, E. L., Richards, J. A., Simoneau, T. L., & Suddath, R. L. (2003). A randomized study of family-focused psychoeducation and pharmacotherapy in the outpatient management of bipolar disorder. *Archives of General Psychiatry, 60*(9), 904–912.

Miklowitz, D. J., & Goldstein, M. J. (1990). Behavioral family treatment for patients with bipolar affective disorder. *Behavior Modification, 14*(4), 457–489.

Miklowitz, D. J., Otto, M. W., Frank, E., Reilly-Harrington, N. A., Kogan, J. N., Sachs, G. S., . . . Wisniewski, S. R. (2007). Intensive psychosocial intervention enhances functioning in patients with bipolar depression: Results from a 9-month randomized controlled trial. *American Journal of Psychiatry, 164*(9), 1340–1347.

Miklowitz, D. J., & Scott, J. (2009). Psychosocial treatments for bipolar disorder: Cost-effectiveness, mediating mechanisms, and future directions. *Bipolar Disorder, 11*(2), 110–122.

Milan, S., & Acker, J. C. (2014). Early attachment quality moderates eating disorder risk among adolescent girls. *Psychological Health, 29*(8), 896–914.

Miller, P. (Ed.). (2009). *Evidence-based addiction treatment.* Burlington, MA: Academic Press.

Miller, R. C., & Berman, J. S. (1983). The efficacy of cognitive behaviour therapies: A quantitative review of research evidence. *Psychological Bulletin, 94,* 39–53.

Miller, S. D., Duncan, B. L., Sorrell, R., & Brown, G. S. (2005). The partners for change outcome management system. *Journal of Clinical Psychology/InSession, 61,* 199–208.

Miller, W., & Rollnick, S. (1992). *Motivational interviewing: Preparing people to change addictive behavior.* New York, NY: Guilford Press.

Miller, W., & Rollnick, S. (2002). *Motivational interviewing: Helping people change.* New York, NY: Guilford Press.

Mohr, D. C. (1995). Negative outcome in psychotherapy: A critical review. *Clinical Psychology: Science and Practice, 2,* 1–27.

Monson, C. M., Schnurr, P. P., Resick, P. A., Friedman, M. J., Young-Xu, Y., & Stevens, S. P. (2006). Cognitive processing therapy for veterans with military-related posttraumatic stress disorder. *Journal of Consulting and Clinical Psychology, 74,* 898–907.

Moscovitch, D., Antony, M., & Swinson, R. (2009). Exposure-based treatments for anxiety disorders: Theory and process. In M. Antony & M. Stein (Eds.), *Oxford handbook of anxiety and related disorders* (pp. 461–475). New York, NY: Oxford University Press.

Murphy, M., Cowan, R., & Sederer, L. (2001). *Disorders of childhood and adolescence* [Blueprints in Psychiatry Series, 2nd ed.]. Malden, MA: Blackwell Science.

Murphy, R., Straebler, S., Cooper, Z., & Fairburn, C. (2010). Cognitive behavioral therapy for eating disorders. *Psychiatric Clinic of North America, 33*(3), 611–627.

Myers, J. E., Sweeney, T. J., & White, V. E. (2002). Advocacy for counseling and counselors: A professional imperative. *Journal of Counseling & Development, 80,* 394–402.

Namjoshi, M. A., Risser, R., Shi, L., Tohen, M., & Breier, A. (2004). Quality of life assessment in patients with bipolar disorder treated with olanzapine added to lithium or valproic acid. *Journal of Affective Disorders, 81*(3), 223–229.

National Institute for Clinical Excellence. (2004). *Eating disorders: Core interventions in the treatment and management of anorexia nervosa, bulimia nervosa and related eating disorders: Clinical guideline 9.* London, England: Author.

National Institute of Health. (2008). *Attention deficit hyperactivity disorder (ADHD)* [Publication No. 08–3572]. Washington, DC: U.S. Department of Health and Human Services.

National Institute of Health. (2009). *Anxiety disorders* [Publication No. 09–3879]. Washington, DC: Author.

National Institute of Health. (2010a). *Generalized anxiety disorder* [Publication No. 10-4677]. Washington, DC: Author.

National Institute of Health. (2010b). *Panic disorder: When fear overwhelms* [Publication No. 10-4679]. Washington, DC: Author.

National Research Council. (2001). *Educating children with autism.* Washington, DC: National Academy Press.

Neukrug, E., & Switzer, A. (2006). *Skills and tools for today's counselors and psychotherapists: From natural helping to professional helping.* Belmont, CA: Brooks/Cole.

Nichols, M. P. (2010). *Family therapy: Concepts and methods* (9th ed.). Boston, MA: Allyn & Bacon.

Nichols, M. P., & Schwartz, R. C. (2004). *Family therapy: Concepts and methods* (6th ed.). Boston, MA: Pearson.

Nock, M., Kazdin, A., Hiripi, E., & Kessler, R. (2006). Prevalence, subtypes, and correlates of DSM-IV conduct disorder in the National Comorbidity Survey Replication. *Psychological Medicine, 36,* 699–710.

Nock, M., Kazdin, A., Hiripi, E., & Kessler, R. (2007). Lifetime prevalence, correlates, and persistence of oppositional defiant disorder: Results from the National Comorbidity Survey Replication. *Journal of Child Psychology and Psychiatry, 48*(7), 703–713.

Norcross, J. C. (2002a). Empirically supported therapy relationships. In J. C. Norcross (Ed.), *Psychotherapy relationships that work: Therapist contributions and responsiveness to patients* (pp. 3–16). New York, NY: Oxford University Press.

Norcross, J. C. (Ed.). (2002b). *Psychotherapy relationships that work: Therapist contributions and responsiveness to patients.* New York, NY: Oxford University Press.

Norcross, J. C. (Ed.). (2011). *Psychotherapy relationships that work: Evidence-based responsiveness* (2nd ed.). New York, NY: Oxford University Press.

Norcross, J. C., & Beutler, L. E. (2011). Integrative psychotherapies. In R. J. Corsini & D. Wedding (Eds.), *Current psychotherapies* (9th ed., pp. 502–535). Belmont, CA: Brooks/Cole, Cengage Learning.

Norcross, J. C., & Lambert, M. J. (2011a). Evidence-based therapy relationships. In J. C. Norcross (Ed.), *Psychotherapy relationships that work: Evidence-based responsiveness* (2nd ed., pp. 3–21). New York, NY: Oxford University Press.

Norcross, J. C., & Lambert, M. J. (2011). Psychotherapy relationships that work II. *Psychotherapy, 48*(1), 4–8.

Norcross, J. C., & Wampold, B. E. (2011). Evidence-based therapy relationships: Research conclusions and clinical practices. In J. C. Norcross (Ed.), *Psychotherapy relationships that work: Evidence-based responsiveness* (2nd ed., pp. 423–430). New York, NY: Oxford University Press.

Office of National Drug Control Policy (ONDCP). (2001). *U.S. alcohol epidemiologic data reference manual: The economic costs of drug abuse in the United States 1992–1998* (Vol. 8, No. 2). Washington, DC: Government Printing Office.

Office of National Drug Control Policy. (2004). *The economic costs of drug abuse in the United States: 1992–2002* (Pub. No. 207303). Washington, DC: Executive Office of the President.

O'Hanlon, W., & Weiner-Davis, M. (1989). *In search of solutions: A new direction in psychotherapy.* New York, NY: Norton.

Ohlsen, M. M. (1983). *Introduction to counseling.* Itasca, IL: F. E. Peacock.

Okun, B., & Cantrowitz, R. (2008). *Effective helping: Interviewing and counseling techniques* (7th ed.). Belmont, CA: Thompson Brooks-Cole.

Olatunji, B., Davis, M., Powers, M., & Smits, J. (2013). Cognitive-behavioral therapy for obsessive-compulsive disorder: A meta-analysis of treatment outcome and moderators. *Journal of Psychiatric Research, 47*(1), 33–41.

O'Reilly, G. A., Cook, L. L., Spruijt-Metz, D. D., & Black, D. S. (2014). Mindfulness-based interventions for obesity-related eating behaviours: A literature review. *Obesity Reviews, 15*(6), 453–461.

Orlinsky, D. E., Rønnestad, M. H., & Willutzki, U. (2004). Fifty years of process-outcome research: Continuity and change. In M. J. Lambert (Ed.), *Bergin and Garfield's handbook of psychotherapy and behavior change* (5th ed., pp. 307–390). New York, NY: Wiley.

Ornstein, E. D., & Ganzer, C. (2005). Relational social work: A model for the future. *Families in Society, 86,* 565–572.

O'Shaughnessy, R., & Dallos, R. (2009). Attachment research and eating disorders: A review of the literature. *Clinical Child Psychology and Psychiatry, 14,* 559–574.

Owens, G. P., & Chard, K. M. (2001). Cognitive distortions among women reporting childhood sexual abuse. *Journal of Interpersonal Violence, 16,* 178–191.

Ozonoff, S. (2012). Editorial perspective: Autism spectrum disorders in DSM-5—an historical perspective and the need for change. *Journal of Child Psychology and Psychiatry, 53*(10), 1092–1094.

Pace, T. M., & Dixon, D. N. (1993). Changes in depressive self-schemata and depressive symptoms following cognitive therapy. *Journal of Counseling Psychology, 40,* 288–294.

Pampanolla, S., Bollini, P., Tibaldi, G., Kupelnick, B., & Munizza, C. (2004). Combined pharmacotherapy and psychological treatment for depression: A systematic review. *Archives of General Psychiatry, 61,* 714–719.

Parikh, S. V., Hawke, L. D., Zaretsky, A., Beaulieu, S., Patelis-Siotis, I., MacQueen, G., . . . Cervantes, P. (2013). Psychosocial interventions for bipolar disorder and coping style modification: Similar clinical outcomes, similar mechanisms. *Canadian Journal of Psychiatry, 58*(8), 482–486.

Paris, J. (2011). Pharmacological treatments for personality disorders. *International Review of Psychiatry, 23*(3), 303–309.

Parsons, R. D., & Zhang, N. (2014). *Becoming a skilled counselor.* Los Angeles, CA: SAGE.

Patterson, L., & Welfel, E. (2005). *The counseling process* (4th ed.). Pacific Grove, CA: Brooks/Cole.

Paul, G. L. (1967). Strategy of outcome research in psychotherapy. *Journal of Counseling Psychology, 31,* 109–118.

Paulson, B., Truscott, D., & Stuart, J. (1999). Clients' perceptions of helpful experiences in counseling. *Journal of Counseling Psychology, 46,* 317–324.

Peele, S., & Brodsky, A. (1992). *The truth about addiction and recovery.* New York, NY: Touchstone.

Pelaez, M., Field, T., Pickens, J., & Hart, S. (2008). Disengaged and authoritarian parenting behavior of depressed mothers with their toddlers. *Infant Behavior and Development, 31,* 145–148.

Perry, J. C., Banon, E., & Ianni, F. (1999). Effectiveness of psychotherapy for personality disorders. *American Journal of Psychiatry, 156,* 1312–1321.

Persons, J. (1989). *Cognitive therapy in practice: A case formulation approach.* New York, NY: W.W. Norton.

Persons, J. (2012). *The case formulation approach to cognitive-behavior therapy.* New York, NY: Guilford Press.

Peruzzolo, T. L., Tramontina, S., Rohde, L. A., & Zeni, C. P. (2013). Pharmacotherapy of bipolar disorder in children and adolescents: An update. *Revista Brasileira de Psiquiatria, 35,* 393–405.

Petry, N. (2011). *Contingency management for substance abuse treatment: A guide to implementing this evidence-based practice.* New York, NY: Routledge.

Phillips, K. A. (2004). Body dysmorphic disorder: Recognizing and treating imagined ugliness. *World Psychiatry, 3*(1), 12–17.

Phillips, K. A. (2005). *The broken mirror: Understanding and treating body dysmorphic disorder.* New York, NY: Oxford University Press.

Phillips, K. A. (2009). *Understanding body dysmorphic disorder: An essential guide.* New York, NY: Oxford University Press.

Phillips, K. A., Coles, M., Menard, W., Yen, S., Fay, C., & Weisberg, R. (2005). Suicidal ideation and suicide attempts in body dysmorphic disorder. *Journal of Clinical Psychiatry, 66,* 717–725.

Phillips, K. A., & Hollander, E. (2008). Treating body dysmorphic disorder with medication: Evidence, misconceptions, and a suggested approach. *Body Image, 5,* 13–27.

Phillips, L. J., Ladouceur, C. D., & Drevets, W. C. (2008). A neural model of voluntary and automatic emotion regulation. Implications for understanding the pathophysiology and neurodevelopment of bipolar disorder. *Molecular Psychiatry, 13,* 833–857.

Pickles, A., Starr, E., Kazak, S., Bolton, P., Papanikolaou, K., Bailey, A., . . . Rutter, M. (2000). Variable expression of the autism broader phenotype: Findings from extended pedigrees. *Journal of Child Psychology and Psychiatry, 41,* 491–502.

Pistole, M. C., & Roberts, A. (2002). Mental health counseling: Toward resolving identity confusions. *Journal of Mental Health Counseling, 24,* 1–19.

Pliszka, S. (2011). *Treating ADHD and comorbid disorders: Psychosocial and psychopharmacological interventions.* New York, NY: Guilford Press.

Ponniah, K., & Hollon, S. D. (2009). Empirically supported psychological treatments for adult acute stress disorder and posttraumatic stress disorder: A review. *Depression & Anxiety, 26*(12), 1086–1109.

Post, R. M., Baldassano, C. F., Perlis, R. H., & Ginsberg, D. L. (2003). Treatment of bipolar depression. *CNS Spectrums, 8*(12), 1–10.

Post, R. M., & Calabrese, J. R. (2004). Bipolar depression: The role of atypical antipsychotics. *Expert Review of Neurotherapeutics, 4*(6, Suppl. 2), S27–33.

Poulsen, S., Lunn, S., Daniel, S. I., Folke, S., Mathiesen, B. B., Katznelson, H., & Fairburn, C. G. (2014). A randomized controlled trial of psychoanalytic psychotherapy or cognitive-behavioral therapy for bulimia nervosa. *Journal of American Psychiatry, 171,* 109–116.

Powers, M. B., Halpern, J. M., Ferenschak, M. P., Gillihan, S. J., & Foa, E. B. (2010). A meta-analytic review of prolonged exposure for posttraumatic stress disorder. *Clinical Psychology Review, 30,* 635–641.

Prasad, V., Brogan, E., Mulvaney, C., Grainge, M., Stanton, W., & Sayal, K. (2013). How effective are drug treatments for children with ADHD at improving on-task behaviour and academic achievement in the school classroom? A systematic review and meta-analysis. *European Child & Adolescent Psychiatry, 22*(4), 203–216.

Price-Evans, K., & Treasure, J. (2011). The use of motivational interviewing in anorexia nervosa. *Child and Adolescent Mental Health, 16*(2), 65–70.

Prochaska, J., & DiClemente, C. (1986). Toward a comprehensive model of change. In W. Miller & N. Heather (Eds), *Treating addictive behaviours: Process of change.* New York, NY: Plenum Press.

Prochaska, J., DiClemente, C., & Norcross, J. (1992). In search of how people change: Applications to addictive behaviors. *American Psychologist, 47,* 1102–1114.

Prochaska, J. O., & Norcross, J. C. (2010). *Systems of psychotherapy: A transtheoretical analysis* (7th ed.). Belmont, CA: Brooks/Cole, Cengage Learning.

Quello, S., Brady, K., & Sonne, S. (2005). Mood disorders and substance use disorder: A complex comorbidity. *Science & Practice Perspectives, 3*(1), 13–21.

Radnitz, C. L. (Ed.). (2000). *Cognitive-behavioral interventions for persons with disabilities.* Northvale, NJ: Jason Aronson.

Rapee, R. M., & Melville, L. F. (1997). Recall of family factors in social phobia and panic disorder: Comparison of mother and offspring reports. *Depression and Anxiety, 5*(1), 7–11.

Rea, M. M., Tompson, M., Miklowitz, D. J., Goldstein, M. J., Hwang, S., & Mintz, J. (2003). Family focused treatment vs. individual treatment for bipolar disorder: Results of a randomized clinical trial. *Journal of Consulting and Clinical Psychology, 71*(3), 482–492.

Reilly-Harrington, N. A., Alloy, L. B., Fresco, D. M., & Whitehouse, W. G. (1999). Cognitive styles and life events interact to predict bipolar and unipolar symptomatology. *Journal of Abnormal Psychology, 108,* 567–578.

Reese, R., Conoley, C., & Brossart, D. (2002). Effectiveness of telephone counseling: A field-based investigation. *Journal of Counseling Psychology, 49,* 233–242.

Regier, D. A., Rae, D. S., Narrow, W. E., Kaebler, C. T., & Schatzberg, A. F. (1998). Prevalence of anxiety disorders and their comorbidity with mood and addictive disorders. *British Journal of Psychiatry, 173,* 24–28.

Reisetter, M., Korcuska, J. S., Yexley, M., Bonds, D., Nikels, H., & McHeniy, W. (2004). Counselor educators and qualitative research: Affirming a research identity. *Counselor Education and Supervision, 44,* 2–16.

Remer, P. (2008). Origins and evolution of feminist therapy. In J. Frew & M. D. Spiegler (Eds.), *Contemporary psychotherapies for a diverse world* (pp. 397–441). New York, NY: Lahaska Press.

Remley, T. P., & Herlihy, B. (2005). *Ethical, legal, and professional issues in counseling* (2nd ed.). Upper Saddle River, NJ: Person-Merrill/Prentice-Hall.

Remley, T. P., & Herlihy, B. (2010). *Ethical, legal, and professional issues in counseling* (3rd ed.). Upper Saddle River, NJ: Pearson Education.

Resick, P. A., Galovski, T. A., Uhlmansiek, M. O., Scher, C. D., Clum, G. A., & Young-Xu, Y. (2008). A randomized clinical trial to dismantle components of cognitive processing therapy for posttraumatic stress disorder in female victims of interpersonal violence. *Journal of Consulting and Clinical Psychology, 76,* 243–258.

Resick, P. A., & Schnicke, M. K. (1993). *Cognitive processing therapy for rape victims: A treatment manual.* Newbury Park, CA: SAGE.

Resnick, R. J. (1997). A brief history of practice—Expanded. *American Psychologist, 52,* 463–468.

Ridley, C. R., & Lingle, D. W. (1996). Cultural empathy in multicultural counseling: A multidimensional process model. In P. B. Pedersen & J. G. Draguns (Eds.), *Counseling across cultures* (4th ed., pp. 21–46). Thousand Oaks, CA: SAGE.

Robinson, L. A., Berman, J. S., & Neimeyer, R. A. (1990). Psychotherapy for the treatment of depression: A comprehensive review of controlled outcome research. *Psychological Bulletin, 108,* 30–49.

Roemer, L., Orsillo, S., & Salters-Pedneault, K. (2008). Efficacy of an acceptance-based behavior therapy for generalized anxiety disorder: Evaluation in a randomized controlled trial. *Journal of Consulting and Clinical Psychology, 76,* 1083–1089.

Rogers, C. (1942). *Counseling and psychotherapy.* Boston, MA: Houghton Mifflin.

Rogers, C. (1951). *Client-centered therapy.* Boston, MA: Houghton Mifflin.

Rogers, C. (1957). The necessary and sufficient conditions of therapeutic personality change. *Journal of Counseling Psychology, 21,* 95–103.

Rogers, C. (1961). *On becoming a person: A therapist's view of therapy.* Boston, MA: Houghton.

Rogers, C. (1995). *On becoming a person: A therapist's view of psychotherapy* (2nd ed.). New York, NY: Houghton Mifflin Harcourt.

Rogers, S., & Dawson, G. (2009a). *Play and engagement in early autism: The early start Denver model. Volume I: The treatment.* New York, NY: Guilford Press.

Rogers, S., & Dawson, G. (2009b). *Play and engagement in early autism: The early start Denver model. Volume II: The curriculum.* New York, NY: Guilford Press.

Rogers, S., & Dawson, G. (2009c). *Early start Denver model for young children with autism: Promoting language, learning, and engagement.* New York, NY: Guilford Press.

Rogers, S., Dawson, G., & Vismara, L. (2012). *An early start for your child with autism.* New York, NY: Guilford Press. Shallcross, L.

Roman, M. W. (2010). Treatments for childhood ADHD Part II: Non-pharmacological and novel treatments. *Issues in Mental Health Nursing, 31*(9), 616–618.

Ronnestad, M., & Skovholt, T. (1993). Supervision of beginning and advanced graduate students of counseling and psychotherapy. *Journal of Counseling and Development, 71,* 396–405.

Rosario, M., Hunter, J., & Gwadz, M. (1997). Exploration of substance abuse among lesbian, gay and bisexual youth: Prevalence and correlates. *Journal of Adolescent Research, 12,* 454–476.

Rose, S., Bisson, J., Churchill, R., & Wessely, S. (2002). Psychological debriefing for preventing posttraumatic stress disorder (PTSD). *Cochrane Database of Systematic Reviews, 2,* CD000560.

Rotherman-Borus, M., Hunter, J., & Rosario, M. (1994). Suicidal behaviour and gay-related stress among gay and bisexual male adolescents. *Journal of Adolescent Research, 9*(4), 498–508.

Rubinow, D. R., Schmidt, P. J., & Roca, C. A. (1998). Estrogen-serotonin interactions: Implications for affective regulation. *Biological Psychiatry, 44*(9), 839–850.

Sachs, G., Chengappa, K. N., Suppes, T., Mullen, J. A., Brecher, M., Devine, N. A., & Sweitzer, D. E. (2004). Quetiapine with lithium or divalproex for the treatment of bipolar mania: A randomized, double-blind, placebo-controlled study. *Bipolar Disorder 6*(3), 213–223.

Sachs, G., Sanchez, R., Marcus, R., Stock, E., McQuade, R., Carson, W., . . . Iwamoto, T. (2006). Aripiprazole study group: Aripiprazole in the treatment of acute manic or mixed episodes in patients with bipolar I disorder: a 3-week placebo-controlled study. *Journal of Psychopharmacology, 20,* 536–546.

Safran, J., & Muran, J. (2006). Has the concept of the therapeutic alliance outlived its usefulness? *Psychotherapy, 43,* 286–291.

Safran, J. D., Muran, J. C., Samstang, L. W., & Winston, A. (2005). Evaluating alliance-focused intervention for potential treatment failures: A feasibility and descriptive analysis. *Psychotherapy: Theory, Research, Practice, & Training, 42,* 512–531.

Safran, J., Muran, J., Wallner Samstag, L., & Stevens, C. (2002). Repairing alliance ruptures. In J. C. Norcross (Ed.), *Psychotherapy relationships that work: Therapist contributions and responsiveness to patients* (pp. 235–254). New York, NY: Oxford University Press.

Sajatovic, M., Blow, F. C., & Ignacio, R. V. (2006). Psychiatric comorbidity in older adults with bipolar disorder. *International Journal of Geriatric Psychiatry, 21,* 582–587.

Sajatovic, M., Davies, M., & Hrouda, D. R. (2004). Enhancement of treatment adherence among patients with bipolar disorder. *Psychiatric Services, 55*(3), 264–269.

Saxena, S. (2011). Pharmacotherapy of compulsive hoarding. *Journal of Clinical Psychology, Special Issue: Hoarding Disorder, 67*(5), 477–484.

Scheel, K. R. (2000). The empirical basis of dialectical behavior therapy: Summary, critique, and implications. *Clinical Psychology-Science & Practice, 7*(1), 68–86.

Scherk, H., Pajonk, F. G., & Leucht, S. (2007). Second-generation antipsychotic agents in the treatment of acute mania: A systematic review and meta-analysis of randomized controlled trials. *Archives of General Psychiatry, 64,* 442–455.

Schnurr, P., & Friedman, M. (2008).Treatments for PTSD: Understanding the evidence. *PTSD Research Quarterly, 19*(3), 965–971.

Scott, J., & Gutierrez, M. J. (2004). The current status of psychological treatments in bipolar disorders: A systematic review of relapse prevention. *Bipolar Disorder, 6*(6), 498–503.

Scott, J., Paykel, E., Morriss, R., Bentall, R., Kinderman, P., Johnson, T., . . . Hayhurst, H. (2006). Cognitive behaviour therapy for severe and recurrent bipolar disorders: A randomised controlled trial. *The British Journal of Psychiatry, 188,* 313–320.

Seligman, L. (1993). Teaching treatment planning. *Counselor Education and Supervision, 33,* 287–297.

Seligman, L. (1996). *Diagnosis and treatment planning* (2nd ed.). New York, NY: Plenum Press.

Seligman, L. (2004). *Diagnosis and treatment planning* (3rd ed.). New York, NY: Plenum Press.

Seligman, L., & Reichenberg, L. W. (2012). *Selecting effective treatments: A comprehensive, systematic guide to treating mental disorders* (4th ed.). San Francisco, CA: Jossey-Bass.

Seligman, M. E. P. (2002). *Authentic happiness.* New York, NY: Free Press.

Seligman, M. E. P. (2011). *Flourish: A visionary new understanding of happiness and well-being.* New York, NY: Free Press.

Shaffer, D., Gould, M. S., Fisher, P., Trautman, P., Moreau, D., Kleinman, M., & Flory, M. (1996). Psychiatric diagnosis in child and adolescent suicide. *Archives of General Psychiatry, 53*(4), 339–348.

Shalev, A.Y., Freedman, S., Perry, T., Brandes, D., Sahar, T., Orr, S. P., & Pitman, R. K. (1998). Prospective study of posttraumatic stress disorder and depression following trauma. *American Journal of Psychiatry, 155*(5), 630–637.

Shallcross, L. (2011). Seeing potential, not disability. *Counseling Today, 54*(2), 28–35.

Shallcross, L. (2013). Body language. *Counseling Today, 56*(1), 30–42.

Shapiro, F. (2001). *Eye movement desensitization and reprocessing: Basic principles, protocols, and procedures.* New York, NY: Guildford Press.

Shedler, J. (2010). The efficacy of psychodynamic psychotherapy. *American Psychologist, 65,* 98–109.

Shirk, S. R., & Karver, M. (2003). Prediction of treatment outcome from relationship variables in child and adolescent therapy: A meta-analytic review. *Journal of Consulting and Clinical Psychology, 71,* 452–464.

Sicile-Kira, C. (2014). *Autism spectrum disorder: The complete guide to understanding autism.* New York, NY: Perigee Trade Press.

Siegel, D. J. (2006). An interpersonal neurobiology approach to psychotherapy: Awareness, mirror neurons, and neural plasticity in the development of well-being. *Psychiatric Annals, 36,* 248–256.

Simoneau, T. L., Miklowitz, D. J., Richards, J. A., Saleem, R., & George, E. L. (1999). Bipolar disorder and family communication: Effects of a psychoeducational treatment program. *Journal of Abnormal Psychology, 108*(4), 588–597.

Smart, R. G., & Ogburne, A. C. (2000). Drug use and drinking among students in 36 countries. *Addictive Behaviors, 25,* 455–460.

Smith, H. L. (2012). The historical development of community and clinical mental health counseling in the United States. *Turkish Psychological Counseling and Guidance Journal, 37,* 1–10.

Smith, L. (2005). Psychotherapy, classicism, and the poor: Conspicuous by their absence. *American Psychologist, 60,* 687–696.

Smucker, M. R., & Niederee, J. (1995). Treating incest-related PTSD and pathogenic schemas through imaginal rescripting. *Cognitive and Behavioral Practice, 2,* 63–93.

Sobczak, S., Honig, A., Nicolson, N. A., & Riedel, W. J. (2002). Effects of acute tryptophan depletion on mood and cortisol release in first degree relatives of type I and type II bipolar patients and healthy matched controls. *Neuropsychopharmacology, 27,* 834–842.

Sperry, L. (2001). *Spirituality in clinical practice: Incorporating the spiritual dimension in psychotherapy and counseling.* New York, NY: Routledge.

Sperry, L. (2010). *Core competencies in counseling and psychotherapy: Becoming a highly competent and effective counselor.* New York, NY: Routledge.

Spijker, J., de Graaf, R., Bijl, R.V., Beekman, A.T., Ormel, J., & Norman, W. A. (2002). Duration of major depressive episodes in the general population: Results from the Netherlands mental health survey and incidence study (NEMESIS). *The British Journal of Psychiatry, 181,* 208–213.

Sprenkle, D., & Blow, A. J. (2004). Common factors and our sacred models. *Journal of Marital and Family Therapy, 30,* 113–129.

Spurgeon, S. L. (2012). Counselor identity—a national imperative. *Journal of Professional Counseling: Practice, Theory, and Research. 39,* 3–16.

Stabb, J. P., Grieger, T. A., Fullerton, C. S., & Ursano, R. J. (1996). Acute stress disorder, subsequent posttraumatic stress disorder and depression after a series of typhoons. *Anxiety, 2,* 219–225.

Steiner-Adair, C. (1991). When the body speaks: Girls, eating disorders and psychotherapy. In C. Gilligan, A. Rogers, & D. Tolman (Eds.), *Women, Girls, and Psychotherapy: Reframing Resistance.* New York, NY: Harrington Park Press.

Steketee, G., & Frost, R. (2003). Compulsive hoarding: Current status of the research. *Clinical Psychology Review, 23,* 905–927.

Steketee, G., & Tolin, D. F. (2011). Cognitive-behavioral therapy for hoarding in the context of contamination fears. *Journal of Clinical Psychology, 67*(5), 485–496.

Stevens, M. J., & Morris, S. J. (1995). A format for case conceptualization. *Counselor Education and Supervision, 35*(1), 82–94.

Stewart, A., & Neimeyer, R. (2001). Emplotting the traumatic self: Narrative revision and the construction of coherence. *The Humanistic Psychologist, 29,* 8–39.

Stiles, W. B. (2006). The client-therapist relationship. In C. Feltham, & I. Horton (Eds.), *Sage Handbook of Counseling and Psychotherapy* (2nd ed.). Thousand Oaks, CA: SAGE.

Stiles, W. B., Barkham, M., Connell, J., & Mellor-Clark, J. (2008). Responsive regulation of treatment duration in routine practice in United Kingdom primary care settings: Replication in a larger sample. *Journal of Consulting and Clinical Psychology, 76,* 298–305.

Stripling, R. O. (1978). ACES guidelines for doctoral preparation in counselor education. *Counselor Education and Supervision, 17,* 163–166.

Strong, E. K., Jr. (1943). *Vocational interests of men and women.* Stanford, CA: Stanford University Press.

Substance Abuse and Mental Health Services Administration (SAMHSA). (2009). *National Registry of Evidence-Based Programs and Practices.* Washington, DC: Government Printing Office. Retrieved from http://www.nrepp.samhsa.gov/

Substance Abuse and Mental Health Services Administration (SAMHSA). (2011). *Results from the 2010 National Survey on Drug Use and Health: Summary of National Findings* [NSDUH Series H-41, HHS Publication No. (SMA) 11-4658]. Rockville, MD: Author.

Substance Abuse and Mental Health Services Administration (SAMHSA). (2012). *Results from the 2011 National Survey on Drug Use and Health: Summary of National Findings* [NSDUH Series H-44, HHS Publication No. (SMA) 12-4713]. Rockville, MD: Author.

Sue, D. W., Arredondo, P., & McDavis, R. J. (1992). Multicultural competencies and standards: A call to the profession. *Journal of Counseling & Development, 70,* 477–486.

Sue, D. W., Bernier, J. E., Durran, A., Feinberg, L., Pedersen, P., Smith, E. J., & Vasquez-Nuttall, E. (1982). Cross cultural counseling competencies. *The Counseling Psychologist, 10,* 45–52.

Sue, D. W., Capodilupo, C. M., Torino, G. C., Bucceri, J. M., Holder, A. M. B., Nadal, K. L., & Esquilin, M. (2007). Racial microaggressions in everyday life: Implications for clinical practice. *American Psychologist, 62,* 271–286.

Sue, D. W., & Sue, D. (2003). *Counseling the culturally diverse* (4th ed.). New York, NY: Wiley.

Sue, S., & Lam, A. G. (2002). Cultural and demographic diversity. In J. C. Norcross (Ed.), *Psychotherapy relationships that work: Therapist contributions and responsiveness to patients* (pp. 401–421). New York, NY: Oxford University Press.

Sullivan, P. (1995). Mortality in anorexia nervosa. *American Journal of Psychiatry, 152*(7), 1073–1074.

Suveg, C., & Zeman, J. (2004). Emotion regulation in children with anxiety disorders. *Journal of Clinical Child and Adolescent Psychology, 33,* 750–759.

Swanson, S., Crow, S., Le Grange, D., Swendsen, J., & Merikangas, K. (2011). Prevalence and correlates of eating disorders in adolescents: Results from the national comorbidity survey replication adolescent supplement. *Archive of General Psychiatry, 68*(7), 714–723.

Szasz, T. (2010). *The myth of mental illness: Foundations of a theory of personal conduct.* New York, NY: Harper Perennial.

Szigethy, E., Weisz, J., & Findling, R. (2012). *Cognitive-behavior therapy for children and adolescents.* Arlington, VA: American Psychiatric.

Tasca, G. A., & Balfour, L. (2014). Eating disorders and attachment: A contemporary psychodynamic perspective. *Psychodynamic Psychiatry, 42*(2), 257–276.

Taylor, H., & Leitman, R. (Eds). (2003). Barriers to the diagnosis and treatment of attention deficit hyperactivity disorder (ADHD) among African American and Hispanic children. *Health Care News, 3,* 7.

Taylor, S., Asmundson, G. G., & Jang, K. L. (2011). Etiology of obsessive-compulsive symptoms and obsessive-compulsive personality traits: Common genes, mostly different environments. *Depression & Anxiety, 28*(10), 863–869.

Teyber, E. (2006). *Interpersonal process in psychotherapy* (5th ed.). Belmont, CA: Thomson-Brooks/Cole.

Thiruvengadam, A. R., & Chandrasekaran, K. (2007). Evaluating the validity of blood-based membrane potential changes for the identification of bipolar disorder I. *Journal of Affective Disorders, 100,* 75–82.

Thompson-Brenner, H. (2014). Discussion of eating disorders and attachment: A contemporary psychodynamic perspective: Does the attachment model of eating disorders indicate the need for psychodynamic treatment? *Psychodynamic Psychiatry, 42*(2), 277–284.

Thornton, C., & Russell, J. (1997). Obsessive compulsive comorbidity in the dieting disorders. *International Journal of Eating Disorders, 21*(1), 83–87.

Tohen, M., Chengappa, K. N., Suppes, T., Zarate, C. A. Jr., Calabrese, J. R., Bowden, C. L., . . . Breier, A. (2002). Efficacy of olanzapine in combination with valproate or lithium in the treatment of mania in patients partially nonresponsive to valproate or lithium monotherapy. *Archives of General Psychiatry, 59,* 62–69.

Tolin, D. F. (2011). Challenges and advances in treating hoarding. *Journal of Clinical Psychology, 67*(5), 451–455.

Tolin, D. F., & Foa, E. B. (2006). Sex differences in trauma and posttraumatic stress disorder: A quantitative review of 25 years of research. *Psychological Bulletin, 132,* 959–992.

Tondo, L., Vazquez, G., & Baldessarini, R. J. (2010). Mania associated with antidepressant treatment: Comprehensive meta-analytic review. *Acta Psychiatrica Scandinavica, 121*(6), 404–414.

Torrent, C., Martinez-Aran, A., del Mar, B. C., Reinares, M., Sole, C., Rosa, B., . . . Vieta, E. (2012). Long-term outcome of cognitive impairment in bipolar disorder. *Journal of Clinical Psychiatry, 73*(7), 899–905.

Tramontina, S., Schmitz, M., Polackzyk, G., & Rohde, L. A. (2003). Juvenile bipolar disorder in Brazil: Clinical and treatment findings. *Biological Psychiatry, 53,* 1043–1049.

Treasure, J., & Schmidt, U. (2008). Motivational interviewing in eating disorders. In H. Arkowitz, H. Westra, W. R. Miller, & S. Rollnick (Eds.), *Motivational interviewing and the promotion of mental health* (pp. 194–224). New York, NY: Guilford Press.

Treasure, J., Schmidt, U., & Macdonald, P. (2009). *The clinician's guide to collaborative caring in eating disorders: The new Maudsley method.* New York, NY: Routledge Press.

Tsuang, M. T., & Faraone, S. V. (1990). *The genetics of mood disorders.* Baltimore, MD: Johns Hopkins University Press.

Tursi, M., & Cochran, J. (2006). Cognitive-behavioral tasks accomplished in a person-centered framework. *Journal of Counseling and Development, 84,* 387–396.

van Brakel, A., Muris, P., Bogels, S., & Thomassen, C. (2006). A multifactorial model for the etiology of anxiety in non-clinical adolescents: Main and interactive effects of behavioral inhibition, attachment, and parental rearing. *Journal of Child and Family Studies, 15,* 569–579.

van Goozen, S., Snoek, H., Matthys, W., Rossum, I., & Engeland, H. (2004). Evidence of fearlessness in behaviourally disordered children: A study on startle reflex modulation. *Journal of Child Psychology and Psychiatry, 45,* 884–892.

Van Hesteren, F., & Ivey, A. E. (1990). Counseling and development: Toward a new identity for a profession in transition. *Journal of Counseling and Development, 68,* 524–528.

van Steensel, F., Bögels, S., & de Bruin, E. (2013). Psychiatric comorbidity in children with autism spectrum disorders: A comparison with children with ADHD. *Journal of Child Family Studies, 22*(3), 368–376.

Veale, D., Boocock, A., Gournay, K., Dryden, W., Shah, F., Willson. R., & Walburn, J. (1996). Body dysmorphic disorder: A survey of fifty cases. *British Journal of Psychiatry, 169,* 196–201.

Vieta, E., Martinez-De-Osaba, M. J., Colom, E. M., Martinez-Aran, A., Bernabarre, A., & Gasto, C. (1999). Enhanced corticotropin response to corticotropin-releasing hormone as a predictor of mania in euthymic bipolar patients. *Psychological Medicine, 29,* 971–978.

Vieta, E., & Valenti, M. (2013). Pharmacological management of bipolar depression: Acute treatment, maintenance, and prophylaxis. *CNS Drugs, 27,* 515–529.

Virkud, Y. V., Todd, R. D., Abbacchi, A. M., Zhang, Y., & Constantino, J. N. (2009). Familial aggregation of quantitative autistic traits in multiplex versus simplex autism. *American Journal of Medical Genetics Part B: Neuropsychiatric Genetics, 150B,* 328–334.

Vitiello, B. (2013). How effective are the current treatments for children diagnosed with manic/mixed bipolar disorder? *CNS Drugs, 27,* 331–333.

Vittengl, J. R., Clark, L. A., Dunn, T. W., & Jarrett, R. B. (2007). Reducing relapse and recurrence in unipolar depression: A comparative meta-analysis of cognitive-behavioral therapies effects. *Journal of Consulting Clinical Psychology, 75,* 475–488.

Volkmar, F., Paul, R., Rogers, S., & Pelphrey, K. (Eds.). (2014). *Handbook of autism and pervasive developmental disorders, diagnosis, development, and brain mechanisms.* Hoboken, NJ: Wiley Press.

Wade, T. D., Keski-Rahkonen A., & Hudson J. (2011). Epidemiology of eating disorders. In M. Tsuang & M. Tohen (Eds.), *Textbook in psychiatric epidemiology* (3rd ed., pp. 343–360). New York, NY: Wiley.

Wagner, E. H., Austin, B. T., & Von Korff, M. (1996). Organizing care for patients with chronic illness. *Milbank Q, 74,* 511–544.

Wagner, B. (1990). Major and daily stress and psychopathology: On the adequacy of the definitions and methods. *Stress Medicine, 6*(3), 217–226.

Walker, C. E., & Roberts, M. D. (Eds.). (2001). *Handbook of clinical child psychology* (3rd ed.). New York, NY: Wiley.

Waller, G., Cordery, H., Corstorphine, E., Hinrichsen, H., Lawson, R., Mountford, V., & Russell, K.

(2007). *Cognitive behavioral therapy for eating disorders: A comprehensive treatment guide.* Cambridge, UK: Cambridge University Press.

Wampold, B. E. (2001). *The great psychotherapy debate: Models, methods and findings.* Mahwah, NJ: Lawrence Erlbaum.

Wampold, B. E. (2006). What should be validated? The psychotherapist. In J. C. Norcross, L. E. Beutler, & R. P. Levant (Eds.), *Evidence-based practices in mental health: Debate and dialogue on the fundamental questions* (pp. 200–208). Washington, DC: American Psychological Association.

Wampold, B. E. (2007). Psychotherapy: The humanistic (and effective) treatment. *American Psychologist, 62,* 857–873.

Wampold, B. E. (2010). *The basics of psychotherapy: An introduction to theory and practice.* Washington, DC: American Psychological Association.

Wampold, B. E., & Brown, G. S. (2005). Estimating therapist variability: A naturalistic study of outcomes in managed care. *Journal of Consulting and Clinical Psychology, 73,* 914–923.

Wampold, B. E., Imel, Z. E., Laska, K. M., Benish, S., Miller, S. D., Fluckiger, C., . . . Budge, S. (2010). Determining what works in the treatment of PTSD. *Clinical Psychology Review, 30,* 923–933.

Wampold, B. E., Minami, T., Baskin, T. W., & Tierney, S. C. (2002). A meta-(re)analysis of the effects of cognitive therapy versus "other therapies" for depression. *Journal of Affective Disorders, 68,* 159–165.

Wastell, C. A. (1996). Feminist developmental theory: Implications for counseling. *Journal of Counseling and Development, 74,* 575–581.

Watson, S., Thompson, J. M., Ritchie, J. C., Ferrier, I. N., & Young, A. H. (2006). Neuropsychological impairment in bipolar disorder: The relationship with glucocorticoid receptor function. *Bipolar Disorders, 8,* 85–90.

Weems, C., Zakem, A., Costa, N., Cannon, M., & Watts, S. (2005). Physiological response and childhood anxiety; Association with symptoms of anxiety disorders and cognitive bias. *Journal of Clinical Child and Adolescent Psychology, 34,* 712–723.

Weissman, M. M., Wolk, S., Goldstein, R. B., Moreau, D., Adams, P., Greenwald, S., . . . Wichramaratne, P. (1999). Depressed adolescents grown up. *Journal of the American Medical Association, 281*(18), 1701–1713.

Weisz, J. R., McCarty, C. A., & Valeri, S. M. (2006). Effects of psychotherapy for depression in children and adolescents: A meta-analysis. *Psychological Bulletin, 132,* 132–149.

Welge, J. A., & DelBello, M. P. (2013). Treatment of youth with bipolar disorder: Long-term versus maintenance. *Bipolar Disorder, 15,* 150–152.

Westra, H., & Dozois, D. (2006). Preparing clients for cognitive behavioral therapy: A randomized pilot study of motivational interviewing for anxiety. *Cognitive Therapy and Research, 30,* 481–498.

Westra, H., Arkowitz, H., & Dozois, D. (2010). Adding a motivational interviewing pre-treatment to cognitive behavioural therapy for generalized anxiety disorder: A preliminary randomized control trial. *Journal of Anxiety Disorders, 23,* 1106–1117.

White, M. (2007). *Maps of narrative practice.* New York, NY: W. Norton.

White, M., & Epston, D. (1990). *Narrative means to therapeutic ends.* New York, NY: W. Norton.

Wilcox-Matthew, L., Ottens, A., & Minor, C. (1997). An analysis of significant events in counseling. *Journal of Counseling & Development, 75,* 282–291.

Wildes, J. E., Emery, R. E., & Simons, A. D. (2001). The roles of ethnicity and culture in the development of eating disturbance and body dissatisfaction: A meta-analytic review. *Clinical Psychology Review, 21,* 521–551.

Wilhelm, S., Phillips, K., & Steketee, G. (2012). *Cognitive-behavioral therapy for body dysmorphic disorder: A treatment manual.* New York, NY: Guilford Press.

Williamson, E. G., & Biggs, D. A. (1979). Trait-factor theory and individual differences. In H. M. Burks, Jr., & B. Stefflre (Eds.), *Theories of counseling* (3rd ed., pp. 91–131). New York, NY: McGraw-Hill.

Wilson, B., & Smith, B. (2001). *Alcoholics Anonymous* (4th ed.). New York, NY: Alcoholics Anonymous World Services.

Wilson, G. (1997). Cognitive behavioral treatment of bulimia nervosa. *The Clinical Psychologist, 50*(2), 10–12.

Wilson, G., Grilo, C., & Vitousek, K. (2007). Psychological treatment of eating disorders. *American Psychologist, 62*(3), 199–216.

Winnicott, D. W. (1958). *The maturational processes and the facilitating environment.* New York, NY: International Universities Press.

Witmer, J. M., & Granello, P. F. (2005). Wellness in counseling education and supervisions. In J. M. Witmer & P. F. Granello (Eds.), *Counseling for wellness: Theory, research, and practice* (pp. 261–271). Alexandria, VA: American Counseling Association.

Witmer, L. (1896). Practical work in psychology. *Pediatrics, 2,* 462–471.

Wittchen, H. (2002). Generalized anxiety disorder: Prevalence, burden, and cost to society. *Depression & Anxiety, 16,* 162–171.

Wittchen, H., & Fehm, L. (2001). Epidemiology, patterns of comorbidity, and associated disabilities of social phobia. *Psychiatric Clinics of North America Journal, 2024*(4), 617–641.

Worona, S. (2003). Privacy, security and anonymity: An evolving balance. *Education Review, 38,* 62–63.

Yalom, I. D. (1980). *Existential psychotherapy.* New York, NY: Basic Books.

Yan, I. J., Hammen, C., Cohen, A. N., Daley, R. M., & Henry, R. M. (2004). Expressed emotion versus relationship quality variable in the prediction of recurrence in bipolar patients. *Journal of Affective Disorders, 83,* 199–206.

Yaryura-Tobias, J., Neziroglu, F., & Kaplan S. (1995). Self-mutilation, anorexia and dysmenorrhea in obsessive compulsive disorder. *International Journal of Eating Disorders*, *17*(1), 33–38.

Yatham, L. N., Grossman, F., Augustyns, I., Vieta, E., & Ravindran, A. (2003). Mood stabilisers plus risperidone or placebo in the treatment of acute mania. International, double-blind, randomised controlled trial. *British Journal of Psychiatry, 182,* 141–147.

Yatham, L. N., Paulsson, B., Mullen, J., & Vagero, A. M. (2004). Quetiapine versus placebo in combination with lithium or divalproex for the treatment of bipolar mania. Erratum in: Journal of Clinical Psychopharmacology. *Journal of Clinical Psychopharmacology, 25*(2), 201.

Yonkers, K., Dyck, I., Warshaw, M., & Keller, M. (2000). Factors predicting the clinical course of generalized anxiety disorder. *British Journal of Psychiatry, 176,* 544–549.

Young, M. (2005). *Learning the art of helping: Building blocks and techniques.* Upper Saddle River, NJ: Prentice-Hall.

Young, R. C., & Klerman, G. L. (1992). Mania in late life: Focus on age at onset. *American Journal of Psychiatry, 149,* 867–876.

Zerbe, K. J. (1995). *The body betrayed.* Carlsbad, CA: Gurze Books.

Zubernis, L. S., Snyder, M., & McCoy, V. (2011). Counseling lesbian and gay college students through the lens of Cass's and Chickering's developmental models. *Journal of LGBT Issues in Counseling, 5,* 122–150.

INDEX

About the Authors

Lynn Zubernis, Ph.D., is a licensed clinical psychologist and an associate professor at West Chester University of Pennsylvania. She has over 20 years of counseling experience in a variety of settings, including serving as the assistant director of a university counseling center and working as a school psychologist. Her experience also encompasses clinical work at inpatient psychiatric hospitals, community mental health organizations, eating disorder clinics, and juvenile detention facilities, and serving as coordinator for the Council for the Accreditation of Counseling and Related Educational Programs (CACREP) for West Chester University's fully accredited counselor education program. Dr. Zubernis has published numerous articles and books, and presented at national conferences on various topics, including counseling diverse populations, motivational interviewing, psychological understanding, positive psychology, and the psychology of being a fan.

Matthew Snyder, Ph.D., is a licensed professional counselor, an associate professor, and department chair of Counselor Education at West Chester University of Pennsylvania. He has practiced in a number of diverse settings, such as working as a high school counselor, inpatient psychiatric specialist, university counselor, drug and alcohol counselor, university professor, and in private practice. He has over 20 years of clinical, teaching, and supervision experience. He has written several articles and presented at national conferences on motivational interviewing, treating adolescent depression, and counseling diverse populations.

Lightning Source UK Ltd.
Milton Keynes UK
UKHW032330040822
406858UK00006B/148

9 781483 340081